Department of Youth Services
Pelletier Assessment
Zara Cisco Brough Center
P.O. Box 784
Westborough, MA 01581

Betty

Life

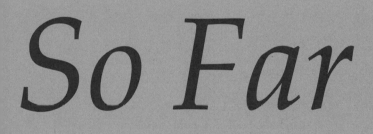

Friedan

So Far

SIMON & SCHUSTER PAPERBACKS

NEW YORK   LONDON   TORONTO   SYDNEY

SIMON & SCHUSTER PAPERBACKS
Rockefeller Center
1230 Avenue of the Americas
New York, NY 10020

First Simon & Schuster paperback edition 2006
SIMON & SCHUSTER PAPERBACKS and colophon are
registered trademarks of Simon & Schuster, Inc.
Designed by Edith Fowler
Picture research by Natalie Goldstein

For information about special discounts for bulk purchases,
please contact Simon & Schuster Special Sales:
1-800-456-6798 or business@simonandschuster.com

Manufactured in the United States of America

10   9   8   7   6   5   4   3   2   1

The Library of Congress has cataloged the hardcover
edition as follows:

Friedan, Betty.
  Life so far / Betty Friedan.
    p.   cm.
    1. Friedan, Betty.   2. Feminists—United States
—Biography.   3. Feminism—United States—
History.   I. Title.
HQ1413.F75 A3 2000
305.42'092—dc21
[B]   00-023920
ISBN-13: 978-0-684-80789-8
ISBN-10:   0-684-80789-0
ISBN-13: 978-0-7432-9986-2 (Pbk)
ISBN-10:   0-7432-9986-8 (Pbk)

*To my children and grandchildren
and my extended family
of friends*

Contents

Life So Far

Introduction

I never intended to write a memoir about my so-called life. First of all, a memoir usually signals the end of a person's career or profession, and I'm still going strong. Second, I think looking backward is boring. I'd rather spend my time looking forward. But my hand was forced, really, when my family, friends and colleagues, past and present, told me a few years ago that they were being contacted for interviews for books *other* people were writing about *my* life. Well, really.

I guess there was rekindled interest toward the end of the millennium in the revolutionary book I wrote in the sixties—*The Feminine Mystique*—and the subsequent women's movement I helped start that changed the face of American history. Over the years countless people have asked me "What made you do it?" And I never could answer that question. Because I never set out to start a women's revolution. I never planned it. It just *happened*, I would say, by some miracle of convergence of my life and history, serendipity, one thing leading to another.

What I am sure of, though, is that ideology has to come from personal truth, has to test against real life. Personal life, personal truth is not an abstract concept; the life it comes from and feeds back into is real. So what, in my personal truth, made me—and gave me the power to—help bring about that wonderful massive change in society? That's really the question, isn't it?

But I got really annoyed, even alarmed, when those self-appointed "biographers" started contacting me and asking me questions that were peripheral to my life and work and seemed to lead to conclusions that were biased or just plain wrong. I sensed then—and was proven right—that the unauthorized biographies they would publish about me would be in large or small part false, mistaken, sensational and trivializing. What I have done with my life is already history. I can't control what historians or sensationalists do with it. But I could—and did—decide, before it's too late, to put down my life the way I experienced it.

The book took me ages to write, as books always do. Writing is such hard work. I refreshed my NOW memories by reading "Feminist Chronicles—1953–1993," a valuable record of the organization I helped found compiled by several of my former colleagues, Toni Carabillo, Judith Meuli and June Bundy Csida. Margaret Peet, my long-suffering manuscript typist, faithfully translated my handwritten pages into the first chapters. Jack Langguth, a good friend and professor at the University of Southern California, read them and generously gave me his comments. I was helped as well by my assistants, Roseanne Miller in Sag Harbor and Hilde Carney in Washington.

But I took a long pause, halfway through the book. I was working on new projects as a Visiting Distinguished Professor at Cornell, with a $1 million grant from the Ford Foundation. Besides, reliving the triumphs of my life was exhilarating, but revisiting the pain and frustration—who needs it? Only the prodding of my editor, Alice Mayhew, the encouragement of my wonderful agent, Peter Ginsberg, and the editorial assistance of my longtime friend Linda Bird Francke brought the book to the finish line. Now, at least, boring or not, I've set the record straight.

Sag Harbor, 1999

ONE

My Mother, My Father and Peoria

My first conscious memory, I must have been three or so, I looked at myself in the mirror in my mother's bedroom, and I said, "How tall I am!" I looked in the mirror and saw a tall girl. But, of course, I wasn't tall really. I was, I am, quite short. What made me see myself as tall back then in Peoria in my mother's room?

Every night, before we went to bed, we had to say our prayers. The *Shema Yisrael,* then "Now I lay me down to sleep," then "God bless Mother and Daddy, and Amy and Harry, and Rex, our dog," who used to escort me to school every day and got killed crossing Main Street on the way home. And after "God bless" we could make a personal prayer, a wish to God. And I would wish two things: "A boy that likes me best" (that must have been when I was in fourth grade, maybe ten or so, when kissing games, post office behind the couch, and "Bobby likes Marian" teasing began; of course, I learned later, it was Daddy I really wanted to like me best).

My second prayer was: "When I grow up, I want a work to do," because I knew, I *knew,* that was what was wrong with my mother, why she made our life so miserable, my father, us kids, *me* especially, and why, inside, she was so miserable herself. She didn't have any work of her own to do. (And how I knew that, then, I don't know. Because women like my mother, then, didn't have jobs or careers. Nobody even asked women then, "What do you do?" Nobody asked little girls then, "What do you want to be when you grow up?")

My mother, Miriam, was beautiful. (Except when she was discontented, or angry at one of us, which was most of the time. Though, when she wasn't, she could be a lot of fun.) She loved shopping. Everything she did, she did perfectly—perfect grooming, her clothes perfectly tailored, meals cooked and served to perfection under her orders. I remember how she would tinkle the dinner bell, then, later, press the electric buzzer under the table for the maid. But she didn't *do* anything herself. On Thursday night when the maid was off, she insisted that we learn to cook. But she was so impatient that when it was my turn, I cut the potatoes wrong, or burned the butter. She swam, played bridge, mahjong, tennis, golf, though it was a constant sore that she couldn't play at the Peoria Country Club, which, of course, didn't take Jews. She was a superb driver, she always drove on our trips. She must have taken over the driving early on, though I remember my father driving us as a Sunday treat in our new Peerless, our first car. But I remember how nervous we were when he drove us to the hospital when my little brother was born. To this day I myself am a nervous, reluctant driver.

Our house was beautifully decorated, or so it seemed to me then, compared to my friends' houses in Peoria, the silver and china and the Louis whatever furniture. My mother's dresses and suits were tailored by her dressmaker to fit with elegant precision, and she even looked good in hats. (I refused to wear hats until last summer when, after my heart valve surgery, a young friend brought me one to hide unwashed hair.) But she never had anything that she thought was important to do. One year she would run the Sunday School, another year the women's division of the Community Chest. At one point she took up something called eurhythmics, and I have a hazy memory of her taking a writing class once, or was it art?

My mother was born in Peoria in 1898, Dr. Sandor Horwitz's daughter. My grandfather had been studying to be a rabbi when he left Hungary to escape the pogroms, somehow got to St. Louis, went to grade school, high school and college in one year (an apocryphal story), graduated in the first class of Washington University Medical School, was a lieutenant colonel in the army medical corps in World War I, and then came to Peoria and became Health Commissioner in charge of public health in all the outlying farm towns. Mother went to grade school and high school in Peoria, as I did, and then two years to the local college, Bradley. Ever since I can remember, she put it in my mind that I had to go away to college—in fact, to Smith, the best, largest women's college (women couldn't go to Harvard or Yale then) where the brightest of the girls at the Peoria Country Club seemed to go.

Actually, my mother did work after college for the Peoria newspaper (the *Journal,* or the *Star;* it's now the *Journal-Star).* She loved the job and became the women's page editor. She could not wait for me to get into junior high to put it into my mind to try for the school newspaper. But, of course, she had to quit her job when she married my father. Wives of businessmen did not work in towns like Peoria then, not even in the Depression, which clouded my childhood.

My mother, growing up in Peoria, did not enjoy being Jewish. But she married my father, Harry Goldstein, when she was not yet twenty, an older Jewish businessman with no formal American education and a heavy Jewish accent. My father's first wife had died years before, and he had been a bachelor for many years. I was born in 1921, a year and a half later. He was forty when I was born, and that was old then. My father had also come to Peoria by way of St. Louis to escape pogroms in Eastern Europe, the oldest of thirteen children. He started out with a street corner stand selling collar buttons, did well enough to send his youngest brother to Harvard Law School, built up a fancy jewelry store, a kind of midwestern Tiffany's, on South Adams Street, two blocks off Main, in downtown Peoria. The farmers and the farm machinery workers at Caterpillar and Keystone bought their wedding rings and china and silver and watches there. However, when depression hit the farm machinery business and the distilleries, people in Peoria didn't buy jewelry and fine china. My first vivid memory of my mother and father is fighting over money.

My mother got an allowance from my father, and when she would overspend it or charged the limit on her charge accounts at the local department stores, she would try to recoup at one of the gambling houses in the outskirts of Peoria. Or, even more daring then, play the stock market. And she would lose more money, the huge bills would come due, and my father would yell and scream. (Maybe I get my hot temper from him.) I would put my head under the pillow, not to hear them fighting over money in the middle of the night.

My sister, Amy, and I shared a room. She was eighteen months younger than me and to be honest, I don't have too many childhood memories of her. My brother, Harry Junior, was born in 1926, five years after me. My parents had wanted a boy, of course, and finally they had one. Harry was darling, but I remember being quite cruel to him and to my sister. I was the oldest and probably didn't want to share the attention, but that's now, looking back on it.

My mother, to all of us, was the most important person in the house. If she was in a good mood, everything was fine. If she was in a bad mood, which, unaccountably, she was most often, we all shrank from her, were miserable, and tried to keep out of her way. Everything she did, she did perfectly, and nothing we did was ever good enough. Once my father gave her a watch set in sapphires for Christmas. She pouted and raved because it wasn't a diamond and ruby watch. I felt so bad for my father. I thought he was handsome, I've seen pictures of him as a young man and he was handsome then. By the time I was born, he was a little stout and stooped, and his hair was getting gray. It surprised me, and I got quite angry, when one of our maids said he wasn't handsome at all. I knew my mother was ashamed of his accent and his big nose, and that made me feel very bad. (And, I suppose, I also felt ashamed, and didn't want to, back then in Peoria.)

My father used to tell me about the tenement in which he lived in St. Louis near Edna Ferber, or was it Fannie Hurst, or both. As soon as I started writing in school, he would save the papers I brought home and put them in his safe. If I wrote a poem, it was surely a masterpiece. Every morning, before he went to work, my father would take me and my sister for a little walk in Bradley Park, across Farmington Road, the street we lived on, with salt to put on a robin's tail. I can't remember what that salt was supposed to do, or if we ever got close enough to a robin to do that. Daddy would come home for dinner every night, except when he had to work late, and he sat at the foot of the table and my mother at the head, where she could press the buzzer with her foot for the maid to come in and clear the table. Before the Depression, we had a cook, sometimes a second maid, and a chauffeur, though I doubt my father then made more than $15,000 a year. At the dinner table, we each would tell what we had done that day, and my father would give us little lectures on important developments, like Lindy crossing the Atlantic. But, especially as the Depression worsened, my parents would get into arguments. Or I would say something, or do something, that got my mother mad, or, even worse, my father. And he would shout at me and I would cry. And he would shout even worse. He couldn't stand women crying, he would say. I would get sent upstairs to my room.

But it was Mother who ran our lives. As the Depression worsened, she created a kind of conspiracy with us, to keep it a secret from Daddy that she had bought something, a dress for one of us or for herself, something for the house. And I was part of that conspiracy, which made Daddy the enemy, and part of me felt bad about that, sad for him. Mostly my mother made me feel bad about myself. Nothing I did was ever right, ever satisfied her. She made me take swimming lessons, tennis, golf, piano lessons, dancing school. I wasn't good at any of it. I was a mess.

School was something else. At school I came alive. I learned to read very quickly. I think I learned early so that I could escape my miserable mother, and the uncertain anger of my father. I would go to the library and take out six books at a time (the maximum) until one day my father saw me walking up Main Street hill carrying those books. It wasn't ladylike, he scolded me, I must take out only three books at a time. For some reason I liked to read lying on my stomach on our living-room floor. The rest of the family would walk over me. If I was bad, my parents discovered that a spanking didn't have much effect on me. The only punishment that worked was forbidding me to read for a day. But when they shouted at me, or when my mother simply walked around the house, offended, miserable, as she so often did, or when they shouted at each other, I felt bad inside. A quite unbearable feeling, sometimes. During my second year in high school, or was it my third, I made a vow my parents would never make me cry again. And the next time they shouted, I went numb. A wall went up around me, and I didn't cry again. For many years, I couldn't cry.

School was my safe place, school was my relief, school I loved. I always knew the answer. I got all A's, of course. They skipped me, in fourth grade, I believe, and again later. I used big words that I only learned I mispronounced years later, because before Smith and New York I never heard them said out loud. I don't remember playing much with dolls, though I did like furnishing dollhouses. But the game I really liked was "dress up." My mother would put dresses, hats, shoes, coats she no longer wore in a big chest, and we would dress up and act out stories that I would make up. Me and my friends after school, or, if worse came to worst, my little brother and sister. I would make up the stories, scary stories, with evil witches to outwit, or later, outside in the park, after I started reading mystery stories, smugglers and criminal gangs to track down. I was very bossy, they would complain. Once I hit the boy next door over the head with a hoe. Or, I would organize a club and decorate a room in our basement behind the furnace as the clubhouse with old blankets and chairs covered with dressups. And we would give the club a name and adopt the bylaws, and then get bored and go on to something else.

One day in school, in the fourth grade, I believe, or was it third, I started a club called the "Baddy Baddy Club." Everyone who was not in the club was a "goody goody." The point of the club was to drive our substitute teacher out of her mind. We loved our real teacher, who I think was out having a baby. I don't remember why we hated the substitute. At a signal from me, all the "baddy baddies" would push our schoolbooks off the desks onto the floor. That did get the teacher a bit harassed in time. So I was summoned down to the principal's office. Mr. Murphy was his name. "Miss Goldstein," he said, "you have a great talent for leadership. You must use it for good, not evil."

I also remember, early on, my father telling me I had a "fine sense of justice." It was a question of dividing something—some fruit, oranges, bananas, or grapefruit?—and I objected loudly that the slices weren't equal. I don't think I was even the one getting gypped, but someone was.

The thing I loved best about birthdays and Christmas was getting books. The first time, I must have been six, I got all six Honey Bunch books. I think I read them all that day. I read *The Lit-*

tle Colonel and *The Little Princess,* the Bobbsey Twins and Tom
Swift—I don't know how I got hold of those books, they weren't
given to girls. But they actually weren't as interesting as Nancy
Drew or *Little Women.* And then my mother gave me something
like a Junior Literary Guild or Book-of-the-Month Club membership, and I read wonderful British children's books—*Swallows
and Amazons,* E. Nesbit's the "Bastable Children" and *Five Children and It,* adventurous naughty families of children who went
on sailing expeditions or time travels to magical kingdoms. And,
of course, *Alice in Wonderland* and Kipling. I loved *Stalky and Co.*
And then, from my parents' bookcase, Dreiser, Sinclair Lewis and
Agatha Christie.

Every evening after dinner my father read philosophy; his
favorite was Robert Ingersoll, the midwestern pragmatist. He
would insist on talking philosophy to me. His best friend Uncle
Charlie, a bachelor, owned the local theater, which housed one-
night stands of plays and vaudeville troupes before the movies
took over. My father showed him one of my stories and they decided I must write a play for him to produce. So Sundays, the only
day Daddy was home—men worked all day Saturday then—
after Sunday School and Sunday noon dinner, I was sent to my
room to work on my play. I would hear the other kids playing
outside, and that's where I wanted to be, not writing a play. I
don't remember how many weeks it took before I got the nerve to
show him blank pages and announce I couldn't, wouldn't write a
play. I was just a little girl, after all.

My biggest sorrow was that they wouldn't let me have a bicycle. The other kids went off on their bikes every afternoon. I
somehow learned to ride a bike when I could borrow one. When
my sister got old enough and demanded a bike too, they finally
relented. I loved riding my bicycle and exploring. I loved being a
Girl Scout, because we would take hikes and explore. I loved
camp and hikes and canoe trips, even though I was never any
good at tennis, or volleyball, or golf. I loved swimming underwa-
ter, but was terrified of the high dive.

But I took all those lessons, including piano lessons, and riding lessons, until one day I said no. I was never going to be any
good at piano, I was beginning to hate music because of those
piano lessons. In school I sang so badly that by the fifth grade the

teacher told me not to sing during music lesson, I was getting the whole class off key. I persuaded my mother to let me take "dramatics" instead of piano. The vaudeville and the one-night stands had stopped; we went to movies instead. But I discovered the Peoria Players, the amateur local theater company, which gave semi-professional sold-out performances successful enough that they built a theater building. Whenever there was a child part, I would try out and get it. I loved hanging around that theater.

By this time, I was in junior high school and did try out for the newspaper, as my mother made sure I would. From the beginning, I loved newspapers. In high school, I couldn't take journalism because I was on the strict college entrance track, with Latin, French, algebra, geometry. So I didn't get a chance to edit the newspaper. But I wrote a column, "Cabbages and Kings," with John Parkhurst, who later married my best friend Harriet and became a Republican state legislator.

When I was almost thirteen, getting ready for confirmation (as the *bas mitzvah* was called then in reform congregations), I went in to see the rabbi alone before class. "Rabbi," I said, "I have something to tell you. I've decided I don't believe there is a God." He was very smooth, that rabbi in Peoria. He didn't argue with me. He said, "All right. But keep it to yourself until after confirmation." I had been chosen to give the Floral Offering. In my white dress, clutching my bouquet of flowers, I soulfully raised my eyes to the heavens and spoke the prayer, good actress that I was, as if I was a candidate for Jewish sainthood.

About that time, I won an essay contest for Peoria schoolkids on "Why I Am Proud to Be an American." There was nothing hypocritical about pride in being American in my family. My grandfather was an avid member of the American Legion. That legionnaire's cap was as important to him as the shofar he blew on Rosh Hashanah and Yom Kippur services in the "temple," as we called the synagogue then. My father was a freethinker; he often boasted about attending the debate on evolution between Clarence Darrow and William Jennings Bryan. He must have inspired my essay, but I can't remember now ever really asking him, getting the real story from him, of how they left that town in Eastern Europe—I don't even know the name of the town, whether it is now Poland or Russia or the Ukraine. And how they got to St. Louis, and why he came to Peoria to put up his street corner stand. Or how my mother's father and mother got to St. Louis from Hungary, and why, and how my grandfather really got to medical school, and ended up in Peoria. I think now that it is a wonderful story of courage, gutsiness, adventurous spirit, risking the unknown, the immigrants' story—and not only my Jewish father and grandparents but all the immigrants who escaped poverty and persecution and the deadness of a closed, restricted, class- or race-bound society, Irish, Italian, Slav, Swedish, Russian, German, African, to make their own free way and fortune in America. I understood and shared my father's and grandfather's genuine patriotism about America. Because in this land they were free to move and aspire and make their lives as they would and could, make whatever of fortune, and give their children the education to be whatever they were able to be. And even though my father would sometimes say, bitterly, about the equality of opportunity and freedom from prejudice America promised, "only until six o'clock when the store closes"—for in social life in Peoria, Jews were not free and equal—the promise was real enough, for his children, surely his grandchildren.

They surely *qvelled*, on that Fourth of July in the Pekin Fairground outside Peoria, when, as a prize for that essay, "Why I Am Proud to Be an American," this particular thirteen-year-old was the one to read out loud the Declaration of Independence. And Everett Dirksen, our congressman, patted me on the head before he gave the main speech. Later, in the Senate, I admired his magnificent oratorical periods. But growing up in Peoria, I knew nothing about political issues, the developments leading up to the Depression and into the war. The world was bounded by Peoria, uptown, downtown, the shadowy slum below the Bluff where the poor people lived. I think I visualized Europe as a brown island on a map. The rest of the world I didn't visualize at all. I never saw a mountain or the ocean until after I went east to college, to Smith. We took our vacations at a fishing camp in Wisconsin, on Round Lake near Hayward, because fishing was the only sport my father ever tried. Mother would drive us up—we all fought over who would get to sit on the front seat with her—and Daddy would come two weeks later. He would only take two weeks off from the store, and sometimes he would call and say he couldn't get off until the next week. He worked all day Saturday and late on Thursday night when the store stayed open. It seemed as if my mother took up most of the parental space, but when Daddy didn't come for that vacation week, or had to work late and didn't come home for dinner, something was missing—texture, heart? I realized it after he died, the heart, the center was gone.

Until I was thirteen, school was heaven, escape from the screaming tortures of home, the continual assessing of my badness, my inadequacy. Of course, I got a bit uncomfortable when, as a result of all that skipping of grades, the other girls were getting breasts and periods and wearing brassieres and high heels, and I was still flat-chested, wearing white socks and patent leather Mary Janes and smocked loose dresses my mother sent for from Best's in New York.

Dancing school was sheer misery; Miss Coleman's, it was called. The one Jewish boy in my class was told by his mother to dance with me, which he did until he had practiced enough to go after Marian Sweeney, the prettiest, most popular girl in our class. Entering high school, the other girls and boys who lived on the West Bluff, which was the nice part of town then, were rushed for sororities and fraternities. No Jewish kids were ever invited to join those sororities or fraternities, which ran high school social life in Peoria.

But my mother didn't want me to even think of myself as Jewish, she didn't send me to Jewish camp, something was wrong with *me* that I didn't get into a sorority. In addition, Central High had gone to two shifts because of overcrowding, and all the other girls and boys I'd gone through grade school and junior high with were on the morning shift in high school and I was on the afternoon shift. I would walk to high school alone, eat lunch alone, walk home from high school after four, and sometimes the others would pass me, in their souped-up jalopies, on the way to Hunt's, the drive-in hamburger stand at the foot of Farmington Road, for Cokes or root beer floats, hot dogs or hamburgers, and they would be shouting or laughing and maybe not even wave at me. For some unaccountable reason—some terrible mystery of fate—I had dropped out of their world. Sometimes I would make a detour and go into the cemetery on the street behind our house and sit on a gravestone reading poetry, pretending I was Emily

Dickinson. But oh how much I would rather have been in that jalopy going off to Hunt's with my friends.

My sister never seemed to be as miserable as I was. I think she was more accepted. My brother, too, got along fine in school. I don't remember whether he actually got into a fraternity, but he seemed to be a very accepted boy. He was handsome and a very good athlete and is now a prominent businessman in Peoria. He could go home again. I couldn't. My ostracism by my high school classmates was too painful.

One afternoon, after they passed me in their noisy jalopy, I remember saying to myself, as I walked on alone, "They may not like me, but they are going to have to look up to me." I remember that afternoon very clearly, making that vow to myself. (And even if I fulfilled that vow, which I did, I wish it hadn't been that way. I distrust that motivation now, insofar as it may still drive me. It tarnishes, for me, the reality of the larger visions driving me now. I think it even gives me writer's block, and the activist's equivalent of writer's block.)

What I did, of course, was make other friends, who weren't in that sorority-fraternity clique. A new boy came to town, Doug Palmer, tall and blond and headed for Yale, where his older brother had been some kind of hero. We studied for college boards together. And with another boy, Paul Jordan, and two other girls whose names I don't remember now, I started a literary magazine, *Tide*. We got local businessmen to buy ads. We would walk up Main Street hill, Doug and Paul and I, after putting the magazine to bed in the print shop, and the sun would be setting, and I would feel blissful.

They both had girlfriends, went steady, in fact. They would say to me, "Even if you're a girl, you're my best friend." But it was the girls' dropping me, not getting into the sorority, that ate into me. Finally in high school, I made two new friends, girls, that made all the difference. Barbara Weir became my friend, as did Harriet Vance, whose mother had gone to Smith, and she and I realized we were both headed for that college. Her family belonged to the country club, she herself was an Olympic-class swimmer, and she also was very intelligent, Smith material, which was, I suppose, why she liked me. It was not very useful to be too intelligent, for a girl, in Peoria when we were growing up.

I remember telling my chemistry teacher one day that I had decided to go on and take physics, which not even the other college-bound girls were going to do, since it wasn't required. "Who do you think you are, Madame Curie?" that chemistry teacher laughed at me. In geometry class, I discovered it was more fun figuring out my own proofs than memorizing the textbook. My teacher was taken aback when it was my turn at the blackboard and I chalked up a different proof that clearly worked even if it wasn't the textbook one. She let me do it my way; there were good teachers then, in the Peoria public schools, in the Depression era, men and women. Our history teacher made us do real research papers; our Latin teacher, Mr. Hall, was brilliant, a strict martinet. I've always thought all that Latin, plus very strict grammar teachers, gave me the basis for a clean prose style.

In the beginning school had been such a pleasure, such a relief to be *good* at something, instead of a mess, clumsy, inadequate, bad, naughty, ugly, as my mother made me feel at home, no matter what I did. Plus the sheer delight of figuring things out, mastering the math, the Latin and French, the algebra and geometry. But now that pleasure, that relief, was clouded by the misery of being left out, not belonging to the sorority, being different. It wasn't just being Jewish, though by now I got headaches Sunday morning, playing tic-tac-toe through Sunday School class. I must have got the message that all those books and the long words and the original theorems also made me too "different" at school, even if the teachers gave me A's. I tried various crude defenses, whining to my mother in protest against the smocked dresses and plain loose sweaters and wool-pleated skirts from New York until she let me buy tight angora sweaters from Block & Kuhl, the local department store, like Marian Sweeney and the other sorority girls, and wear high heels to the dances. For some reason, those tight sweaters which I began to fill out and my new high heels infuriated my father. He used to mimic me, make fun of me, wobbling on high heels.

I also became publicly, openly "dumb" at the mechanical parts of physics class, the electric wiring and fitting of tubes together for the experiments. In fact, I made a deal with the football team: I did the math problems for all of us, they did the electric wiring and the tubing for my lab experiments, and they cheered at graduation, when I was valedictorian. I also remember writing and reading a long narrative poem at graduation, modeled after "The Highwayman" (or Edgar Allan Poe?) where I returned as a ghost to Peoria High School fifty or a hundred years later and found it haunted by our former selves. That poem was supposed to make my classmates cry with premature nostalgia and it did until my archenemy Merrill Klein, the other Jewish kid whose mother made him dance with me, made a jeering catcall.

By now I had some good friends, girls as well as those boys I edited the magazine with. I loved going home after school and staying for supper at Barbara Weir's, the atmosphere was so warm and loving—Barbara, her sisters and her mother, who was a widow and ran a travel agency, the only mother of any of my friends who had a job. Barbara started going steady with Ray Weeks, who was also "different," not because he was Jewish but because he was brilliant at science and not like the rowdy other boys. Another friend of mine, Janet Jacquin, was so "different" as a Catholic—she went to parochial school; in the Midwest then, anti-Catholicism was even more virulent than anti-Semitism— that all during our girlhood she stuttered terribly.

It was miserable, being "different" in Peoria. In some ways, it was dangerous. It doomed you to loneliness, isolation or worse. I remember one evening, in the depths of the Depression, my father coming home early from the store and calling us all into the front hall. "Your mother and I are going to vote now," he told us. "We are going to vote for a very great man. His name is Franklin Roosevelt, and he is doing things that will help people. He will get us out of the Depression. But you must never tell anyone that your mother and I voted for Roosevelt."

We knew about the Depression. One year we were told that instead of getting Christmas presents, we would take baskets of toys and food to a family of poor people, down below the Bluff. And we didn't move, after all, to the bigger house on a more elegant road on the other, more fashionable side of town. We no longer had a maid and a chauffeur. And the arguments between my mother and father over money got worse.

I had long since figured out that there was no Santa Claus. It had been exciting, hanging the stockings, wondering how he'd get down the chimney, standing at the top of the stairs at 7:00

a.m., until they gave us the signal we could go down and see what he'd brought us. We also lit Hanukkah candles, which weren't nearly as much fun: One year they set the dining-room curtains on fire. But despite the conspiracy with our mother, which usually worked, Daddy wouldn't let us have a Christmas tree.

My father would take me fishing with him. I remember the thrill, was it pike, was it bass, the sensation when a fish took the hook, and the rod bent down, and you jerked it up and began to reel in. My father taught me to cast. (I still love to go fishing. When I told that story to Kurt Vonnegut, he invited me to join him and his brother and their kids and grandkids in a fishing boat they chartered every September off Montauk. But that was like industrial fishing, those intricate fancy many-hooked rods and reels, snaring three, four, five fish at a time.)

One summer at the fishing camp, there was a boy from Rockford a few years ahead of me in high school. And he invited me to go fishing with him. I wasn't allowed to go. I had "talked back" to my mother, or something like that; it seemed as if I was always being punished for something I did or didn't do at home. That punishment really outraged me, since by now I was getting interested in boys. But not being in the sorority-fraternity crowd—in my not exactly voluntary solitary-introspective period—an actual "date" was a state I only yearned for. My mother and father would take us to the movies on Saturday night. I hated going to the movies with them on Saturday night. What if someone from high school saw me? Everyone would know I didn't have a date. (To this day, I feel uncomfortable, depressed if I don't have a date on Saturday night.)

After I got too old for camp, one summer I worked for the Peoria newspaper. Another summer I worked in Peoria's settlement house. And one year I gave lessons in English to one of the refugee German families who somehow got to Peoria in their flight from Hitler. The wife was supposed to teach me German. A lot of German was spoken in my household. When they didn't want the children to hear (*Schweigen für die Kinder*), my father spoke in Yiddish and my mother in the German she'd learned in college.

Peoria was the world then to me, and how I hated that world. It seemed so unfair to me, so unjust, to be barred from places the others enjoyed just because we were Jewish. I hated being different, an outsider. And yet I knew some of our different ways were better. The food at our house, where my mother always used fresh vegetables, and wonderful three-inch sirloin steak, served rare, seemed better to me than the canned peas and tasteless gray slices of beef at my friends' houses. As the Depression subsided, my mother would take us shopping in Chicago once or twice a year, and to the theater there. For my eighteenth birthday, they took me for a weekend in Chicago, and I saw Katharine Cornell in *Saint Joan* and Helen Hayes in *Victoria Regina.*

My senior year in high school, I won the Dramatic Honor prize for a five-minute walk-on part as the madwoman in *Jane Eyre,* our senior class play. That maniacal laugh—which I uttered offstage as the incarcerated Mrs. Rochester, and then appeared all deranged, for those few minutes—I practiced in our bathroom, with the door locked, making mad faces at myself in the mirror. My brother and sister would stand outside, listening. The bathroom, with the door closed, was also the only place I was allowed to sing.

But my ambition to be an actress suddenly gave way to realism. To be an actress, you had to be pretty, which meant pert and blond like Betty Grable. Well, of course, the actresses I really loved—Norma Shearer, Bette Davis, Katharine Hepburn, Myrna Loy—had character and strength. But they were also pretty in a way I knew I would never be.

I must have known I would have to leave Peoria. My favorite sound, as a child, was the sound of the train whistle and the clanking of the rails as the Santa Fe to California came within earshot of our house on its way from Chicago. I would stand at the window of the bedroom, waiting for the sound of the train. Another favorite game, in winter, was to open the window very wide and stand there in my nightgown until I couldn't bear the cold any longer. Then, I would burrow under the covers, exulting in the warmth after that cold.

So, wherever I have gone since my childhood in Peoria, I have exulted in the sense of warm community, especially a community that appreciated and welcomed difference. And if I didn't find such a community, I learned how to create one. But I expect I also learned the value of community in Peoria, not only because of the cold pain of being excluded from it but because of the way, in a town like Peoria, people organized the community to solve problems, provide services, innovate kinds of enrichment that were not always or only for profit. We had no trouble getting money from the Peoria merchants to start our high school literary magazine. I took delight in the Peoria Players, which people in our town who loved theater organized to act in or direct themselves when the Broadway shows stopped making those one-night stands in Peoria. Maybe they hired a professional director, but even then it must have been community-run, as was the symphony orchestra. When my high school friends came back to Peoria after the war—almost all of them came back but me—they also built an art museum, and made the Peoria Symphony a community pride.

I had no sense at all of my own future as a woman, growing up in Peoria. By the time I finished high school, it was seared deep in my gut that I didn't want to grow up and be like my mother. She wanted to run everything, she was always right, but there was never enough for her to run. The Sunday School, Hadassah, the women's division of the Community Chest. How much time could you spend shopping for clothes, especially if money was scarce? She would always win at the bridge games, the mahjong games. The only women in Peoria who had actual professions outside the home were a single mousy spinster woman doctor and the daughter of a widowed lawyer friend of my parents who dressed in men's clothes and went everywhere with her father. But I somehow sensed that if my mother had a profession that absorbed her, if she was really as strong and confident as she seemed, bullying us or the women's committee, she wouldn't make life so miserable for my father or us kids, she wouldn't find everything we did, every present, so inadequate.

When my father, in his fifties, started suffering severe heart trouble, and had to cut down and finally hand over to my mother the management of the store, she got much better. Literally, physically, she stopped having the colitis which all during our childhood would periodically send her to bed, screaming with pain, for days at a time. She stopped picking on us so much. She was too busy. But watching my father decline, I hated my mother. When I saw the play *The Little Foxes*, I recognized my mother. I felt that her demands, the constant battling, the way she sneered at my father for his accent and lack of education, the lack of support in our home—combined with the endless pressures of making the money that was never enough for her, even before and after the Depression—were what was killing him.

When Philip Wylie's book attacking the American "mom" came out, and I started studying Freud in college, I would say things like: All mothers should be drowned at birth. I wanted to be the kind of woman for my husband and children my mother wasn't. I knew even then that she had to feel better about herself as a woman; the problem was, she didn't. But I had no model at all of what such a woman could be. It was a woman, in a family, that I yearned to be, a warmer, more supportive, affectionate woman than my mother. Though I was consumed with dread of her and, I suppose, hate, and even finally a kind of revulsion, there was a desperate yearning underneath for the love she couldn't give me. And only now do I begin to understand the emptiness and fragility beneath her assumed superiority, perfectionism, and the constant unrelenting put-down of her husband, her children, her women friends. I was so repelled by her sugary sweetness on the telephone—"dear" this and "darling" that— and then the mean, vicious maligning of the caller after she hung up. (As a result I am, to this day, so abrupt on the telephone, just getting my business done, personal or political, and hanging up, that my lack of the usual preliminaries or terminating niceties adds to my reputation as a ferocious witch.)

"My dear sweet darling baby," she would begin letters to us from their occasional trips, or when we started going away to camp and school. But I cannot remember ever being *touched* by her, in the kind of spontaneous hug I delighted in with my own children. I must have longed so terribly for that touch, and despaired of it, and buried that longing so deep, that years later I would flinch when anyone unexpectedly touched me, woman or man, in a spontaneous gesture of affection. I had to steel myself to do the New York "kiss" on the cheek, to hide my shudder, shrinking away from it. Only when prepared for touch, in sex, could I accept it, and later when I had kids of my own to be mother to. I think my father was much warmer, but my mother created that family conspiracy with us which—along with the pressures and long hours of the store—kept him outside. I also can't remember that kind of touch from him. But I felt increasingly uncomfortable when my father made a confidante of me, and tried to get from me the intimacy my mother didn't give him. My mother was the one who ran the show, and at the time we still believed she was the heart and center of our family. I began to shrink away from him as he began to encroach on me, demand of me something I didn't want to give him. I'm not at all implying here the kind of incestuous sexual abuse it has become so fashionable in feminist circles to drag up against our fathers from buried childhood memory. But I knew he adored me and it made me uncomfortable. I didn't want that kind of triumph over my mother, it was my mother I really needed.

I remember how desolate, how empty I felt, sitting on the couch in our living room, by myself, without turning the lights on, on one of the rare times, after the Depression, when they went to Miami for a week in the winter. As if, despite the relief from the constant battles and the unrelenting detailing of my sins and inadequacies, life seemed to stop when they were gone. It was my mother I thought I missed. Only after my father died did I realize that without him there was no warmth, for me the world was cold. But I never gave much thought then to how the rigid cold narrowness of Peoria, the anti-Semitism, the discouragement of anything different, the narrow possibilities for the use of intelligence, creativity, adventurousness, must have affected my mother, growing up in Peoria. Why was my mother so intent on my trying out for the school newspaper? Why did she arrange for me to be in a dramatics class when I rebelled against the piano lessons? Why did she put it in my head to go to Smith, though it required even more desperate battles with my father, night after night? My mother was determined that I would get the good education—and the aspiration—that was denied to her. "She made it possible for you to have the advantages she didn't have," my father said once when I was putting her down. "She couldn't get out of here the way you can now."

Later, when I began to use psychology to deconstruct (as we would put it now) and denigrate everything my mother and father ever did to, for, us, I was very contemptuous, and then righteously furious, at the conditions that made mothers have to live through their children. At the time, it only made me uncomfortable. A psychologist who gave the new IQ tests had arrived at Bradley, the college six blocks from home where my mother had gone. My mother took us all to be tested. She never should have told us that my IQ was "genius" 180, my sister's a good deal lower, though still above average, my brother's superior, but not as high as mine. My sister still holds it against all of us, that she became the "pretty" one, that I was, exclusively, the "bright" one. All those years when my mother and I were so constantly in conflict, when nothing I did was right, did she resent the abilities she saw in me that she had never been able to use in Peoria? Did she resent, did maybe both my parents resent, the freedom they were giving me to make a larger life for myself? They gave me that freedom, consciously.

All I knew, at the time, was that in the world of the mind— school, the plays, the newspaper column, the literary magazine, and, as I got near to it, college—I was free, this was my world, my mother couldn't get at me there, my father couldn't make me cry anymore. Later I resented it, when my father stored my poems and columns and then newspaper reports of my college triumphs in the safe in the store, and took them out to boast to his customers. It made me cringe with embarrassment. I didn't do those things for him; or did I? Tired, finally, of psychological deconstruction, I would say today, for good or ill, my mother's frustrations, my father's importunities, the realities of growing up Jewish in Peoria, both strengthened me and scarred me. They also made it possible for me to get out of Peoria, to get on that train, on the Rock Island Railroad, change in Chicago, and take the sleeper to Northampton, Massachusetts.

TWO

Discovering the Life of the Mind

The summer after I graduated from high school, getting ready to go to Smith, I acquired a cough that wouldn't go away. I'd been admitted to all the colleges I applied to—Vassar, Radcliffe, Wellesley, Stanford, Chicago—but my mother had put it in my mind to go to Smith. And with my friend Harriet I had been to an alumnae tea in Chicago to get further indoctrinated about Smith. There were quotas then for Jewish kids in Ivy League colleges, 10 percent, I believe, but coming from Peoria and not New York was probably as much an advantage as my SATs and College Boards. I should have gone to the University of Chicago. Robert Hutchins's innovative required curriculum of humanities, social, biological and physical sciences appealed to me. But Chicago was too close to home, not far enough from Peoria. I knew, without saying so, that I had to get out of Peoria and that I wouldn't come back.

You had to take a sleeper then from Chicago to get to Springfield, Massachusetts, where you changed to a little train to Northampton. A few days after we arrived, the great hurricane of 1938 struck, trees fell down all over the beautiful campus, the power was out. My roommate, Natalie Tarlow, seemed nice enough, but by now the shell around me built up by the sorority girls' rejection, my imposed aloneness, made me too self-consciously inadequate to make friends easily. Something she said some days after we put our things away, set up our own desks and beds, made me ask her, with surprise, "Are you Jewish too?" "Who else would they give you for a roommate?" She was truly surprised at my naïveté.

In some ways, coming as I did from Peoria, though I had suffered the actuality of anti-Semitism, I didn't experience myself as Jewish with either the solid strengths or the expectations of rejection of the Jewish girls from New York or Chicago or Cincinnati. I was never part of a Jewish crowd, a Jewish community, a group of Jewish friends. Nor was I part of the WASP crowd in Peoria, though we didn't use that word then. I was a loner and I didn't like it.

At Smith, what had made me different in Peoria made me accepted, welcomed by the other bright girls, one of the crowd, finally, as I had longed to be, in spite of being Jewish. First, though, there was the thrill of marvelous new kinds of books to read— Virginia Woolf's *Mrs. Dalloway* and *A Room of One's Own;* Thomas Mann's *The Magic Mountain;* and James Joyce's *Portrait of the Artist as a Young Man.* New kinds of analysis, of conceptual thinking demanded of me in psychology, philosophy, history. I luxuriated in it, I reveled in it, such thinking was fun. And whereas I had been so inadequate at all the things my mother and the other girls did so well in Peoria—tennis, golf, volleyball, dancing, curly hair, makeup—I not only got A pluses but was accepted by the other girls, who, I guess, had also suffered from being too bright "for a girl" in their high schools. The WASP girls and Catholic girls, especially the ones who didn't need to social climb, they were the country club girls in their cities, but too intelligent; they were looking for something else at college.

I tried out for the college newspaper, of course, and coughed so much, taking my tryout stories down the hill to the student newspaper office, that when I managed to get back up the hill to Chapin House, I reported in sick and was sent to the infirmary. It turned out that I had burst my lung and the cough that wouldn't go away was asthma. They sent for my mother, and prayed for me, that Friday night, at the Jewish temple in Peoria.

I suppose, in the terror and pain of that night, I wanted my mother, but when I started to get better, I wanted her out of this new world of mine, where I was fine, okay the way I really was.

At Smith I was beginning even to be ebullient, to sparkle, to have fun, to feel finally like one of the girls, the bliss of that.

But also, that first year at Smith, I began to feel consciously the need to be authentic, and not to hide or deny or be ashamed of being Jewish, as my mother had been, as well as some of the Jewish girls I was meeting at Smith. One day in chapel, which was compulsory once a week for all two thousand of us, the president of Smith, William Allan Neilson, talked to us about Hitler and the invasion of Austria, Czechoslovakia, Poland, and the killing of the Jews. He proposed to send a petition to each house, to be voted on at the weekly house meeting, to ask President Roosevelt to relax the immigration quotas and give asylum to Jewish refugees, so we could bring to our college girls of our age and educational qualifications who could thus escape the Third Reich.

It was sometime in 1939 when this petition was discussed at the house meeting. I was a very new freshman, very conscious, coming from Peoria High, of the greater sophistication of the girls from New York and Boston, many of whom had been to private prep schools. When the petition was presented, a number of girls spoke against it, about not wanting any more Jews at Smith. Only two girls, one, Martina, a gifted musician, the other, Helen Dunaway, a very bright junior, a Protestant, a history or philosophy major, spoke in favor of the petition. And Helen also spoke of the dangers of fascism, of which I had known almost nothing. There were four Jewish upperclassmen in Chapin House, two from Cincinnati, one from Birmingham, one, I believe, from St. Louis, or was it Scarsdale. I expected them to speak up, but they didn't. Finally, despite being only a freshman from Peoria, I spoke, urging that we open our doors to those girls fleeing persecution.

The resolution was defeated, but the president of the house said the petition would be left on the hall table for anyone to sign as an individual. All that week, when I came back from the library for lunch or dinner, I would look at the petition. The several WASP girls who had spoken in favor signed it, I signed it, a few others. I kept looking for the signatures of the four other Jewish girls, the sophisticated upper-class girls, who wore their Braemar sweaters and white blouses with round gold circle pins and saddle shoes the way all the other girls did and never talked about being Jewish. I don't remember how I even knew they were, but I did. At the end of the week, the petition was taken away, with those few signatures. The four other Jewish girls never signed it.

By the fall of my sophomore year, on the newspaper now, I was happily at home at Smith. I had won the freshman honor prize, the news was sent home to the Peoria paper, my father kept the clip in his safe and showed it to all his customers. I seemed to lose my hayseed accent faster than Harriet, my WASP country club friend from Peoria. She was very proud of my exploits. I took a course in medieval literature, because the professor, Howard Patch, was supposed to be one of the most brilliant, and difficult, of all the professors. I learned about Catholicism in that course, and became friends with one of the brightest Catholic girls, Ruth Murphy, who was a part of the "secret society" group which, it seemed, ran, or tried to run, social life at Smith as the sororities and fraternities had in Peoria High. But the academic life, the life of the mind, and the life of music and art and theater and writing and social conscience was the important life at Smith, not the small world of social snobbery. And the girls who discovered and used their abilities in these worlds, and discovered and formed bonds with each other, were the ones that mattered here, and I was one of them.

I remember passionately arguing in and after philosophy class or history class about communism and fascism, about the war in Europe, about art as pure truth, value-free, or the necessary function of values. The kind of talk I'd begun to have with Doug Palmer and Paul Jordan, but now with other girls. And I got over that terrible self-consciousness about being different. Those other bright girls who were becoming leaders in our class now sought me out, even the girls in my house who had not signed the petition, the WASP and Catholic ones, but not those upper-class Jews. I couldn't get over their not signing that petition. Maybe they couldn't get over their discomfort at my being so openly Jewish, and yet not being held back by that, as they were, from proclaiming my new literary, political and philosophical passions.

I took a wonderful course in music history, and I learned how to listen to and analyze what Beethoven and Mozart and Debussy were trying to do. I began to love music, especially symphonies, which I thought I hated from the piano lessons, from not being allowed to sing. I took zoology to fulfill the science requirement—why, I wonder now, didn't I go on with physics and math, which had so challenged and intrigued me in the beginning in high school? On scholarship now since my sister Amy was also at Smith, I was offered a chance to make some money tutoring, first in psychology, then in zoology. I took a wonderful course in Russian literature with Miss Muchnig, and was totally enraptured with *War and Peace*. Some of the other girls may have read Tolstoy or Chekhov or Dostoevsky in prep school, but it was college that opened great literature to me. Flaubert's *Madame Bovary* made a great impression on me. Did it explain my mother? I wish now I'd taken Miss Chase's Bible as Literature, Miss Dunn's Shakespeare. I don't know whether it would have been possible then to take anthropology or archeology or genetics at Smith. I wish I'd taken astronomy. Your mind has to be opened to possibilities you know nothing of to know what you might like to study and explore. I didn't even know enough to take a course in sociology, though I've held professorships in that field in recent years.

In my sophomore year I read *Middletown* and began to understand the economic and political and social dynamics of Peoria, my hometown, where I had felt so miserable and alien. In Dorothy Douglas's economics class (she was the ex-wife of famed Senator Paul Douglas) I learned about capitalism, and communism and the rise of fascism. And she sent me off the summer after my sophomore year to be an apprentice at Highlander Folk School at Monteagle, Tennessee, where a writers' workshop and a school for labor organizers was held, and where later, as a center for organizers of the civil rights movement, the song "We Shall Overcome" originated. My father fumed, when I came home, "I send my daughter to Smith to go work for the CIO?"

By now I was news editor of the Smith paper. I started covering things that hadn't been covered before, like the conditions of the employees of the college. Later, after I became editor, I instituted a critique of all the courses and the professors who taught them, commonplace now but very daring then. I took a course in poetry writing, in short story writing, and started a literary magazine again with friends who would later become book and magazine editors.

I wrote a short story called "The Scapegoat" to lay bare and exculpate the experience of being an anti-Semitic Jew, which I had so hated in my mother and those girls from Cincinnati, and yet was also guilty of myself. There was another Jewish girl in our house, who was in my class but was never accepted by the others, as I now was. From the warm, safe haven of being "one of them," I watched with discomfort her growing sullenness, unlikable mannerisms, the deterioration of her whole personality. Was that what had happened to me in Peoria? I felt so free and easy now, accepted, approved of, "one of them." I even had a nickname, after falling and hitting my head on the walk home from the corner drugstore, where we would go for coffee after the library closed. They started calling me "Cussie," short for concussion, but I suppose also expressing a kind of ornery cussedness that I was free to express now, in the sparkling intellectual atmosphere at Smith, in my new role as crusading editor, using the long words I'd only found in books before.

With all my new ease and delight, basking in this newfound approbation at Smith, I didn't say a word to stop their ridiculing, sneering, isolating treatment of the other Jewish girl in my class. She finally left college. And I realized that I had been a silent party to her persecution, rather she than I. I freed myself, writing that story, from being an anti-Semitic Jew. But it was not until much later, after I found my own conscious authenticity as a woman, that I began to take conscious strength from my Jewishness.

But what strength I got at Smith, what delight and, yes, comfort, from the life of the mind. Do they use words like that anymore? Did my own kids, at Princeton and Columbia and Harvard, experience that kind of liberation? I loved my carrel in the library, free to roam in the stacks. I was allowed to take a graduate seminar on the French Revolution, even though I wasn't a history major.

I loved, with even greater passion, Pearce Hall, where the psychology labs and classes were held. I was drawn to psychology from the beginning. Psychology II was my favorite course. Harold Israel and Elsa Siipola did a brilliant job teaching us the scientific method, devising psychology experiments for us to do and analyzing the results in ways that made us *experience* scientific investigation and conceptual development. Later, I took experimental psychology with Eleanor Gibson and social psychology with Jimmy Gibson, and I began to understand the social dynamics of Peoria, and of the time we were living in, the Depression, the approach of war. I had been an art-for-art's-sake, truth-for-truth's-sake purist, not interested in politics. I never read newspapers until I went to Smith and started reading *The New York Times*. My first awareness of the Spanish Civil War was reading Hemingway's *For Whom the Bell Tolls*. And then I studied how and why it happened. I read John Reed, *Ten Days That Shook the World*, and studied the Russian Revolution. I studied about capitalism and the Depression we had just lived through in America. I was a pacifist myself, having learned about the evils of capitalism and how munitions makers profited from war. I learned about the rise of fascism in Germany and Italy and the appeasement of fascism in Britain and France.

Because I was editor of the Smith paper, I was invited to be on the board of the American Youth Congress. I was suspicious that the Congress was communist and wanted to use me as a front, so I refused to be on the board. But I decided to go as an observer to the march the Congress had called in Washington in 1940, or was it early '41? I didn't much like the American Student Union group at Smith—they were grubby, I was a snob. I thought they were communists. I kept my distance from them on the long train ride to Washington, where I stayed with my Peoria friend, Barbara Weir, who was going to George Washington University. And I stood on the sidewalk watching, as those thousands of students from all over the United States marched from the Capitol to the White House, chanting, "Johnny Wants a Job, Not a Gun." And then troopers (the National Guard?) started riding their horses down on the students. I stepped down off the curb and found myself also marching. I wasn't just an observer, a writer. Despite that shrinking dread I would always feel at such moments—the dread of sticking my neck out, the dread of any action that might seem unfeminine, immodest, aggressive, selfish, the dread of taking any action that would rock the boat—I marched. But I was also learning more about the evil of fascism. It was different from communism. There were now girls at Smith who had fled from Vienna when Hitler invaded Austria. I didn't know, none of us in America knew then, about the full reality of the concentration camps or the gulag.

I was invited to conferences of Ivy League newspaper editors at Princeton and at Yale. I was amazed, at those conferences, by the impressive surroundings, the paneled boardrooms, where my male counterparts edited their papers. Kingman Brewster was editor of the Yale paper then. I edited the Smith paper on an old kitchen table in the basement of the student building at Smith, even after I changed it from once to twice a week and got the advertising to justify it. I was no feminist, don't remember even studying the battle for the women's vote, only knew of suffragettes, with my new Freudian sophistication, as neurotic spinsters suffering from penis envy. However, it did occur to me, maybe not then but later, how, as editor of the Yale paper or the *Harvard Crimson*, I would have been expected to become, might have had the confidence to become, a big newspaper editor, or a college president and ambassador, like Kingman Brewster. I had no such power assumptions, or ambitions even, as editor of the Smith paper. I simply loved doing it.

I was called to the phone at one of those conferences at Princeton to come back at once to Northampton. My associate editors, including Priscilla and Aloise Buckley (sisters of William), had been caught after breaking into one of the girls' rooms at Sessions House, where the secret society records were kept. They had gotten away with the records, which were safely hidden. But the story had gotten into the local newspaper that this secret society, called the Orangemen, I believe, was going to be exposed. And a fraternal organization in Northampton called the Orangemen was marching on the campus in protest. The president of the college wanted to see me right away.

Neilson was no longer president. He had been followed by Mrs. Morrow, Anne Morrow Lindbergh's mother, as acting president, then Hallie Flanagan, who left to head the WPA theater program, and now a new one, Mr. Davis. He said, if you publish those secret society records, we will expel the Misses Buckley. By now I knew the purloined papers showed clearly how those societies, with support from alumnae, tried to exert snobbish control of Smith society, barred Jewish girls, and so on. But we couldn't let Aloise and Priscilla (Pitts, we called her) be expelled. I called a meeting of all my editors. I suggested that we bury the papers, but in the next issues of *SCAN (Smith College Associated News)* we leave a whole page blank, with the word "CENSORED," and that we let the story out by word of mouth what was censored. I wonder if Priscilla Buckley remembers where she buried those papers. Do those secret societies still exist at Smith?

After another conference, in December 1941, I stopped in New York to go, for the first time, to hear the Philharmonic. In the middle of the concert, a man came out in front of the curtain to announce that the Japanese had bombed our navy at Pearl Harbor and we were now at war. I rushed to Grand Central. By the time I got to Northampton, the whole college was meeting in the chapel, and the president was asking us to vote our support of the war by standing. I was already standing in the back, having come in late. Others were looking at me, because I had written strong pacifist editorials. I had gotten into bitter arguments with faculty members Mary Ellen Chase and Daniel Aaron, who had just come to Smith as young instructors and befriended us literary types. However, I kept standing. I would support the war. It was a just and necessary war, as I put it later, whoever profited from it.

I loved walking home from the library, the days our newspaper came out, and seeing girls sitting on the steps of the college houses reading the paper, hearing them argue about my editorials. I wrote some heady editorials supporting, for instance, a strike of the college employees, another, "Remember the Roses," about the unseemliness in war of Ivy Day, a traditional part of the Smith graduation, where the seniors in white gowns each carried a long-stemmed red rose. (Secretly, I must have grieved when they dispensed with the usual formal graduation ceremony altogether at my graduation in 1942, because that meant I wouldn't get to give the valedictory, which, ham that I was and am, I would have delighted in giving.)

By now we were the ones running things, my friends and I who shared a strong social conscience. Smith's heritage to us was that social conscience, that sense of personal responsibility for society and the future, as well as that passionate commitment to truth. We elected Mario Ingersoll head of student government; discovering how to run a political campaign, we easily outsmarted the secret society girls. Jane Kehnig was head of the Student Christian Association. Ruth Murphy was head of the Judicial Board, Franny Wilkinson head of Student Council.

I still suffered certain agonies, not having dates on weekends. Two boys from my class at Peoria High had gone east to college, Doug Palmer to Yale, Bob Easton to Harvard. Bobby had been my first "boyfriend," when we were in fifth grade, playing post office and other kissing games. We wrote each other letters when his father, Dr. Easton, went to Vienna for further medical study and took his family with him. Bob was going steady with Ruthie Short in Peoria, but was agreeable to come and be my escort at the Smith junior prom. As I remember, we had a very good time. As I remember, we drank a lot of a drink that was pink with applejack in it, called, I believe, a Jack Rose, but it was not a Shirley Temple drink. I got so sick that after he left, I had to go to the infirmary.

I discovered that, having a drink, I would lose that terrible feeling of self-consciousness that still plagued me with boys, although not any longer with girls. When Bob invited me to his Harvard house dance, at Dunster, I actually flirted with one of his roommates, Jim Lynch, thin and dark and handsome. After Bob dropped me off at the boardinghouse where girls stayed, Jim Lynch picked me up and took me to a party at one of his professors'. I felt it was legitimate to go off like that with Jim, since I knew I wasn't really Bob's girl (though later, we both realized, I could have been). That was my first experience sitting around, singing those wonderful songs: "No Pasarán," "We Are the Peat Bog Soldiers," "Joe Hill," "Freiheit."

Jim, I later learned, was an heir to the Heinz catsup fortune. He would come down to Northampton on weekends to see me, bringing me Thomas Wolfe's *Look Homeward, Angel* and *You Can't Go Home Again* and a bottle of Scotch, and a picnic lunch of watercress sandwiches and strawberries. And we would sit by Paradise Pond, that beautiful pond, and he would read Thomas Wolfe aloud to me. And at night we would go out to dinner and drink more Scotch. And we would "neck," as they called it then. But even drunk, I protected my virginity. I got so sick drunk, drinking Scotch with Jim Lynch, that to this day I cannot bear the slightest hint of Scotch in a drink.

One weekend he drove me down to Pittsburgh to meet his mother. I was afraid to stay with him, but one of my Smith friends lived outside Pittsburgh, I would stay with her, and he would drive us both down. He got very annoyed with me protecting my virginity. He had visions from Thomas Wolfe of a passionate Jewish mistress. I don't know what his mother felt, when her son brought home a Jewish girl. But the last I saw Jim Lynch was a final weekend in New York; he was off to England to join the American Field Service Ambulance Corps just before the United States entered the war. I was still protecting my virginity, which I surely regret now. I would get dizzy, even sick to my stomach, from all that sexual feeling, which I loved, but not "going all the way." When the United States entered the war, Jim Lynch became an officer and was killed in action.

Besides "The Scapegoat," my other college short story was called "Sex on Saturday Night." It told the way it was when we girls at Smith who didn't have dates on weekends would go down the hill to the movies and, swooning over Heathcliff, come back from *Wuthering Heights* past the parked cars where all the girls with dates were making out before our ten-fifteen curfew.

I was never any good at mixers. Bob Easton told me years later I looked like Bette Davis, only with dark hair, and that I was pretty. But Betty Grable, not Barbra Streisand, was the boys' pinup girl then. Someone fixed me up with a Jewish boy from Amherst. I think he also would have preferred Betty Grable. At the Smith prom I took him to, we were both pretty miserable. He had someone call to say he'd come down with measles to escape having to come back to Smith for the final picnic lunch. I went for a walk by myself, feeling my old don't-want-to-be-Emily-Dickinson misery—until, on my way back to Chapin, who do I see waiting for me on the porch but lovely tall, blond, handsome Doug Palmer. He'd dumped his Smith date, who was "boring," to come take me to Sunday supper at the tavern before going back to Yale. He even strongly hinted that we maybe could, should be "best friends" again even if I was a girl, even hinted that maybe I could, should be his "girl," but I reminded him that he was going steady with Ida back home. (Why was I never *able* to take a guy away from another woman, even to *expect* a guy to leave another woman for me, an analyst would, of course, ask later. But I was inordinately jealous, fearfully anticipating that any guy I liked would *leave me* always for another girl.)

During the week, men were not on our minds at Smith. What I loved most, besides the newspaper, was psychology. My junior year I was allowed to take Kurt Koffka's graduate seminar on Gestalt theory. My generation benefited as students from Hitler's book burning, driving so many great psychologists, philosophers, scientists and historians out of Germany, Austria, France to become our teachers at even a small college like Smith. I had Hans Kohn in history, Otto Kraushaar in philosophy, Kutschnig in government. But Kurt Koffka and the elegant conceptual structure of Gestalt psychology made me feel like some kind of mental mountain goat, leaping from peak to peak, perilously, behind that austere impassive guide. And I learned, forever, that the whole is more than the sum of its parts, that human behavior can only be understood in its cultural context, that our vision cannot be wholly objective.

The summer after my junior year, my psychology professors sent me off to Iowa City to work with Kurt Lewin on his early experiments in group dynamics. Very early, I saw proof of the inferiority of autocratic, authoritarian leadership as opposed to a participatory democratic model, not as a matter of ideological litany but tested in problem-solving experiments. I would have lunch or supper with Tamara Dembo, Lewin's longtime colleague, who in those hot, non-air-conditioned Iowa cafés would order dark bread and butter and radishes. I loved those radish sandwiches. I also started going out with some of Lewin's lab assistants, brilliant young guys from City College in New York getting their Ph.D.s. (They later went on to make group dynamics a government-sponsored science at National Training Laboratories.)

But my Peoria naïveté (or whatever psychological hangups kept that in place) couldn't handle their sophistication. I remember having dinner with one of them in the Iowa student union café. We were discussing one of the women who worked with him. He used the term "penis envy." I stared at him, uncomprehendingly. He repeated it, "Penis envy." I went and locked myself in the john for a half hour, waiting for him to leave. It was not feminist outrage at that term. I didn't know what it meant, had not yet read Freud myself. But for a man to say that *word* out loud, to a girl, to me, I was insulted, scared. When one of those graduate students drove down from Harvard to see me that fall, I went out the back door and hid in the library until he left.

A circle of psychologists and social scientists radiated around Kurt Lewin at that time, meeting for a week each year over New Year's to exchange ideas. That winter, 1942, they were planning to meet in Northampton, so they invited me along. I came back to Smith early from Christmas vacation and reveled in the lively, luscious, European-accented feast of ideas. Margaret Mead was there. She would come in to dinner, short, dumpy Margaret Mead in some nondescript dress, and behind her, her husband, tall, elegant-looking Gregory Bateson, in tuxedo, carrying her shawl. We called them "God the Mother" and "Jesus Christ." I made that one up—in words, at least, I was never a mouse, not bashful, self-conscious, or even decently modest. Mr. Patch, that brilliant professor of medieval literature, would finally protest, when I held my stand, disagreeing with him: "Miss Goldstein, you have no humility."

I was so happy at Smith I never let myself think beyond it. I climbed mountains for the first time there, not only mentally but literally, on Mountain Day. One day each fall when the leaves are in full color the whole college is dismissed to hike in the mountains. I had never even seen a mountain before I went to college. I had never had that experience of climbing those mental mountain peaks, as I did behind Kurt Koffka. No longer crippled by that shy self-consciousness, no longer isolated by that agonizing otherness, I had felt my own power, editing the newspaper. I had even allowed myself to risk my own honors degree, not starting work on my thesis until the very last minute, because of the absorbing challenge of the newspaper, as even our women's college adjusted to war.

For some strange reason I did not do my thesis on one of the group dynamics experiments I had tried. I did a thesis exposing "Operationism in Psychology," a derivative of logical positivism, forerunner of deconstruction, reducing complex human phenomena we needed to explore in all their complexity to simple, reified abstractions, which I saw as denying the very possibility of meaning. I had to stay at college through spring vacation to get that thesis done, precursor of a lifetime of meeting book and magazine deadlines.

My senior year I also studied the psychology of personality, Freud and Adler and Jung and their American followers. It fascinated me, obsessed me, scared me. It gave me new words to express my deep uneasiness about my own "normality" (or craziness). We learned how to give the Rorschach test and score it, by applying the manual to our own inkblot answers. I was given the test by Miss Siipola, who by now had married Harold Israel. (She kept her own name. I guess she must have been a feminist, but nobody used that term then.) I spent nearly three hours, I recall, dredging images out of those inkblots. When I analyzed them according to the manual, it seemed that I was either a hopeless schizophrenic or some test-breaking genius. I didn't want to tell anybody, I felt such panic about it. Because now I was beginning to feel some horrifying nameless unease, some scary indescribable anxious state, when I wasn't actually studying, taking a test, editing the paper. With honors exams approaching, I handed over the newspaper editing to my successor and tried to concentrate on studying. But, for the first time in my life, I couldn't concentrate, I couldn't think.

I would be graduating, college would be over. Nobody had ever really asked me, "What do you want to be when you grow up, little girl?" The boys were asked that. As for the girls, "You're a pretty little girl, you'll be a mommy like your mommy." But I wasn't a pretty little girl, and the one thing in the world I didn't want to be was a mommy like my mommy. *I did not want to be a woman like my mother.* (If I wanted to be a different kind of mommy, the one I always wanted and never had, there was no psychoanalyst to show me that then.) But what other kind of woman was there to be? Most of my women professors at Smith were spinsters or mannish, as were the one or two women doctors and lawyers in Peoria. Even at a college like Smith, women were not expected then to prepare for careers. We were expected to be responsible competent community leaders, good wives and mothers, and cultured patrons of the arts, hostesses for our husbands. I don't think I even heard the word "career" until "career women" became a term of opprobrium, imbued with nuances of Freudian penis envy. Of course, if you were a truly brilliant student in your field, your professors might steer you to graduate study, as my psychology professors did me. Or if you were a really good writer or editor as I was, you might get a job on *Mademoiselle* or as a Time-Life researcher, until you got married. But there was no future "career" in those jobs. At Time-Life, the boys out of Yale or Harvard could become reporters, editors. But girls like myself could only be researchers, doing the spadework for which the writers, the men, would get the bylines, and the promotions.

I couldn't see myself taking that kind of job. But it didn't occur to me, as it would my male counterparts editing the *Harvard Crimson* or *Yale Daily News,* that I might get a job on *The New York Times,* or some other city newspaper, much as I loved, more than anything I'd ever done, working on newspapers. My boy cousins went to Harvard Law School and became great lawyers. One of them, Milton Goldstein, came down to visit me one weekend at Smith, and scolded me for being so bumptious, obstreperous, compared to the sweet Smith junior his roommate was dating. But he let me come to class with him at Harvard Law, when he dutifully hosted me one weekend. The class, on torts or whatever, was taught by one of those ferocious brilliant monster professors that I so loved to be challenged by. His name, I believe, was Bull Connors, or something like that. (He was, I guess, the professional counterpart of that bull-whipping southern sheriff marshal.) I probably would have loved law school, might have ended up a judge myself with my passion for justice. But it never occurred to me to want to be a lawyer, because Harvard Law didn't even take applications from women then.

So I filled out the applications for graduate fellowships in psychology, and got recommendations from my professors. Because of the war, none of us could think, then, of a fellowship in Europe or a year of traveling after graduation. I was too young to apply for the Red Cross or other war service, though later I did, and was turned down because of my asthma. I didn't get the fellowships I wanted, at Harvard or Yale; I believe my short story writing professor, Al Fischer, had written a letter damning me as a troublemaker, untidy, obstreperous, whatever. Maybe I was obstreperous, and a troublemaker, but a *constructive* one, surely? (Al Fischer had just left, or been left by, his second wife, Helen Eustace, a former student of his who had become my friend. She later became a marvelous detective story writer. In her first book, I, the student editor, who was also herself, was the amateur detective whose life is seriously threatened by the great professor who is the murderer. Al Fischer's first wife was M. F. K. Fisher. I suppose he didn't like women like us.)

Still, I won a coveted fellowship in psychology at Berkeley as well as at Iowa, and danced an appropriate jig of joy when the letters came, though underneath I wasn't at all sure that was what I wanted to do, or be. I tried, once, when I was home for vacation, to express my uncertainty to my father. Maybe I should go to medical school; psychologists with Ph.D.'s then didn't get to treat people clinically like Freud. (I think by now I was driving my family witless with my unremitting new psychological jargon, analyzing their sins.) "If you're just going to be another doctor with a shingle, you might as well be a woman," he said to me. I knew enough psychology by now to be devastated with horror and dread and unspeakable shame by that remark, which I could never forget. Then, I wasn't a woman? He didn't see me as a woman? He wouldn't let me be a woman? If I became a psychologist, if I became a writer—which I know is what he dreamed of—I could not be a woman?

One of his friends, an eminent Jewish businessman of our town, had always admired me. I was going to ask him for advice. My father stopped me. "If you aren't sure of what you want to do, just keep it to yourself. Nobody wants to hear something like that from you. Don't you realize how proud we all are of your success?"

I knew how proud he was of my exploits. But every summer, when it came time to send in the tuition check ($500, and $500 for room and board), he would tell my mother, in my hearing, that he couldn't afford it. I couldn't go back to Smith, I'd have to stay home and go to Bradley. I knew he was just saying that to torture my mother and me. I finally screamed at him: "You know you're going to pay my tuition. I know how you show off news stories about me to your customers. You get your money's worth out of my education. So why do you put me through this each year?"

Back at school with the newspaper handed on to my successor and my thesis turned in, all I had to do was study for my two honors exams. But with the other pressures off, an ominous dread and anxiety about that Rorschach test took over like a gray fog obscuring some unnamed menace. I still went through the motions of attending class, going to the corner drugstore for coffee with my friends, the cozy routines and continuing political, philosophical bull sessions, and the movies on Saturday night, but one of my friends told Miss Siipola how worried I was about that Rorschach test. She took me off for a weekend seminar with Bruno Klopfer, one of the authors of the test, who not only clearly expounded its revelations and proper use but rescored mine. But even officially assured I did not have to worry about being schizophrenic, only about being a unique "genius," I could not shake off a brooding sense of doom.

I suppose, now, it was the jumping-off place, the end of college, that small world where I had done so well, become so comfortable, to an unknown where I had no idea at all of what, who I wanted to be, where I really wanted to go, what I wanted to do. Now, it's expected that young men or women may make several starts, try jobs, travel, change their minds in those years after college. But then, college was the *end*, unless you were clearly going to medical school or law school, an academic career. For most of the boys, it would have been back home and into business with their father, but now, it was the army. For most of the girls, college concluded with that engagement ring.

Exams, which terrified others, were actually fun for me. I loved the challenge of the kinds of questions our Smith professors gave us, though later when I threw such thought-probing essay questions at my own students, reared on multiple choice, puzzlement and even panic ensued. Even at Smith, I'd learned it wasn't wise to show too much ease and enjoyment at work others evidently found difficult. It seemed my first roommate literally couldn't study. And it made her worse, when, after ten-fifteen, and the final coffee bull session, I would sit down at my desk and write up my psychology experiment, or my essay for English class, or crack open the history text, and not come up for air until I finished. Like when I used to lie on my stomach on the living-room floor at home, reading my books, and never noticing when the family walked over me. I guess that kind of concentration annoys people.

But now, I couldn't concentrate either. I tried to review my psychology texts. It probably wasn't necessary. I'd loved that study, had absorbed it. But when I sat down for the exam and read the first question, just the kind of essay question I always loved to play with, my mind went blank. That cliché accurately describes it. Or rather, it went fuzzy gray. I couldn't focus. Usually, I would spend three minutes jotting down the main points of my thesis, if it was a long exam like this one, and then plunge in, writing hot and hard till it was done. Now, I just sat there. I literally could not think. Miss Siipola finally walked over and asked if I was sick. I shook my head. She pointed to the clock. I had been sitting there for an hour. The exam was half over. I think I went on and did the second question. But there was not enough time left to go back and finish the first question. Such a thing had never happened to me before. I think only once in my life did I receive less than an A on a test, a B+ in history. With my newfound psychological sophistication, I knew it would be good for me to let myself get a B now and then. But I never could. Now, well, maybe that Rorschach test did mean schizophrenia. Only after that gray foggy miasma did I realize the pure joy of my usual fine-tuned intellect. Physically, emotionally, in terms of looks or athletic ability or manual ineptness, I may have been a mess, but I always could count on my mind.

Now that there was no further possibility of high honors, I simply had to give a respectable performance on the final test. I sort of honed myself not even to try to show off the depth and breadth of my mastery of psychology theory and its historical development but to consciously pick off small easy pieces.

But I was to graduate *summa cum laude,* in spite of myself. My record-breaking grade point average, my thesis, which was later published in the *Psychological Review,* and the second exam were high enough, despite that first setback, to surpass the field. And my newspaper editorials won a college literary prize. Yet I did not feel the joy I was expected to feel, graduating with all those honors.

When I called to tell my parents the good news, my father told me he wouldn't be coming to my graduation. Since I'd been in college, his heart condition had steadily worsened. He no longer went into the store. He hardly walked now. But somehow, I didn't believe him when he said he wasn't going to come to my graduation. "You could use a cane or even a wheelchair," I said. I knew, suddenly, that my father not being there would take the whole joy out of my graduation. Did I try to tell him that? I only remember his saying: "Well, since I'm not going to be there, you and your mother won't have to be ashamed of my accent." It hurt, his saying that. Was it true? And, in fact, there was no joy for me in that graduation, somehow, even though my classmates cheered when I went up to get my degree *summa cum laude.*

A more minor matter also clouded my graduation. The night after all our exams were finished, my friend Mario Ingersoll and I went down to Wiggins Tavern to celebrate. We had mint juleps, which the Tavern was famous for. We had more than one. We suddenly realized it was past 10:15 p.m. We had missed curfew. I climbed in a window from the dark porch. But Mario, who was head of Student Government and very virtuous (she was engaged to marry an Episcopal minister), officially reported our violation of the college curfew to our friend Murph, who was head of the Judicial Board. Since both of us were of such high office as to be role models for the younger students, we had to officially expiate our crime. We were ordered to write five hundred times, "I will uphold my own good name and that of the college," and sign our names. I thought such a punishment was absurd, childish, and I wasn't about to do it. Mario got more and more worried. She had done hers. She said I wouldn't be allowed to graduate unless I wrote that motto five hundred times. In the middle of graduation weekend, I came back to my room and found my mother starting to write those five hundred lines. Mario had told her the problem, so I swallowed my pride and finished them.

But though I did an appropriate dance for joy when I got the news of my psychology fellowship at Berkeley, I didn't really feel that joy inside. Did I really want to be a psychologist? What, who did I want to be? I didn't have a clue.

The summer after I graduated from Smith, at home in Peoria before I left for Berkeley, the Sisterhood of Temple Anshai Eched, of which my mother had been president until, as usual, she got bored with it, asked me to give a lecture. Since the Smith publicity office sent press releases to hometown newspapers every time one of us won some award, there had been a flurry of stories about my intellectual exploits. Of course, my father clipped them all and kept them in his safe at the store. I was embarrassed to think how he forced them on his customers. But, not yet a psychologist, what kind of lecture could I give in Peoria?

In the summer of 1942, we were beginning to learn a little more about the Nazi treatment of the Jews, as Hitler's storm troops had moved from Germany into Austria, Czechoslovakia, Poland, then Holland, Denmark, France. We would not know the full horror of the concentration camps and the Holocaust until our armies liberated the camps in 1945. But I was beginning to think a lot about the persecution of the Jews. Applying concepts I had learned from Kurt Lewin, I saw what made some Jews identify with their persecutors, and attempt to wipe out or deny their own Jewishness. What I saw now, more clearly than ever, was the need to identify with our Jewishness, claim it, get strength from it in the face of this danger.

The first public lecture I gave was in the Peoria synagogue, confronting openly the anti-Semitism we all had experienced in our own town, and its deadly evil expression in Nazism, though we could not yet conceive of the unimaginable depths of the evil even then being carried out, systematically eradicating Europe's six million Jews, the Holocaust. I read newspapers now, I listened to Edward R. Murrow on the radio. Did they not know what was going on in those camps? Why didn't they tell us about it? Certainly, the Jews in Peoria did not know, or did not want to talk about it. They must have been uncomfortable when, with all that fancy Smith education, what I talked about was that unspeakable horror in relation to our own experience as Jews in Peoria, which they somehow never talked about at all. My father, who spent most of his time in bed now, got up to come and hear me. Did it give him pleasure, or did it make him uncomfortable too? I don't remember what he said.

I remember also that summer the beginning of what might have been my first grown-up love, and how mysteriously, inexplicably, I went dead before it could happen, just like I did on the honors exam.

It was a reunion picnic of our former Sunday School class, the few Jewish kids in our age group, home now from our various colleges. Betty Ottenheimer brought along a young Canadian doctor, doing his residency in the Peoria hospital. He was dark and handsome and bright, and I was feeling bright and pretty sassy myself, the spontaneous lighthearted joyous self that had been liberated in Smith which a few days back in Peoria hadn't extinguished yet. I actually flirted with that doctor, and in one of those taglike games where the boys chased the girls, he and a lot of other boys chased me. He called me up a few days later and asked me to go out with him his next night off. His name was Harry. That is my father's name.

In my fluster, I was still upstairs changing my dress when he came to pick me up. My mother was sitting on the porch, and she sat him down and entertained him. When I came down, she was engaging this Harry in vivacious conversation, exerting all that charm I could never emulate. After we got into his car and drove off down the hill to Hunt's for a hamburger, even though I was riding in a convertible with that handsome young doctor, I had become my miserable, self-conscious, paralyzed Peoria self again. I could no more talk to him, respond to him, than I could drum up from my memory the concepts I knew so well on that test. When he tried to kiss me, I was wooden, dead. He never called again. I was aghast, I couldn't figure it out. Why had I been that way, why had I turned him off, when I wanted so badly to turn him on? (Many years of analysis later, when I knew, at least consciously, the answer to that question, I still reverted to that wooden state when one of the by now many truly good and brilliant men who had become my friends came on in that different way to me.)

But I was quite uninhibited that summer, "necking" with another man I'd met on that picnic, who was dull and boring and didn't interest me at all. (Of course, not really uninhibited. I wouldn't get into the backseat. I let him take my bra off, but not my underpants.)

The bond of having all gone off to college together, and maybe something new in me or them, made me almost "one of the crowd" now back in Peoria, with my contemporaries who had run the high school in our time. The old sorority-fraternity thing no longer mattered. I gave a party, they all came. I've always liked giving parties; I got that from my mother. She always gave good parties. Despite my vow not to become a woman like my mother, in some ways I couldn't help it. But I was no longer bound by Peoria, it no longer had the power to destroy me.

THREE

Becoming Political, Becoming Sexual

I don't know where, when, how I first experienced political passion. I read somewhere that the essence of religion for a Jew is to use your life, not for some reward in heaven or punishment in hell, but a religious responsibility to live your own life in some way that makes life better for the generation to come. I don't remember anyone ever telling me that or teaching me that. Of course, growing up Jewish in Peoria gave me a passion against injustice, I know that. But my political passion is more mysterious than that.

At Smith, it was also inculcated in us, that same kind of personal, moral, religious responsibility. It was your responsibility to take a stand on political issues, to figure out where you stood, personally, on religion and politics, no matter what the faith or politics of your mother or father; and what you did or would do with your life would, could, must make a difference. We were not, then, given a clear sense of career possibilities at Smith, but a lot of us got a wonderfully clear, inescapable social conscience, an inescapable sense of political responsibility. When the president asked us to stand up and vote our support of the war, he meant it, and we had to mean it. As editor of the paper, I had to take a political stand on all such important questions shaping our future, and mean it—I would, could make a difference. And by the time I got out of Smith, having experienced the effect of some of my newspaper campaigns on my classmates, I knew I could make a difference. I also knew by then that I wasn't just a scholar, observer, writer. I had to march.

The first content of my political passion came from seeing Peoria and its injustices through the lens of class, political economy, and the great conflicts of democracy, communism and fascism that I was learning about in those years leading up to World War II: the dramas of Chamberlain's appeasement and Winston Churchill, the Popular Front in France and the Vichy collaborationists, the resistance movement in occupied Europe, the underground. But I was too young for the WAVES or the Red Cross, and my asthma was too severe. When the boys I knew were drafted, or enlisted, or went off to officer training camp, and then began to be sent overseas, I wondered how brave I would be if I had to go to war. I was certainly afraid of a lot of things. When I began to learn about the concentration camps, I felt ashamed of my own cowardice, my own appeasements, even though I talked in such big, brave terms.

The summer after I graduated from Smith, I had an internship in psychology at Grasslands Hospital in Westchester County, New York. I gave the Rorschach test to incoming patients. I was very lonely after the lovely sense of collegiality and community I had felt at Smith. I went off one weekend to be a bridesmaid for Mario, who was marrying Joe, an Episcopal minister, at her family's estate on the North Shore. Duck Island, it was called. With my new socioeconomic sophistication (by now I was reading Marx and Veblen) I sneered at the fake peasantry of building a band floor on the lawn for a square dance rather than have a regular dance in the ballroom; it was a very grand house. But Mario and her brothers and sisters were radicals now, as I was. That house was big enough to put up the dozen bridesmaids and ushers plus both families for a whole weekend of festivities. We bridesmaids were supposed to flit around, before the wedding march, picking our bouquets of flowers from the grassy field and putting them into the wide-brimmed hats we were given to carry. I wondered how they could be so sure the flowers would bloom on time. Those flowers weren't really growing there, they'd been put in the ground in little hidden containers the morning of the wedding.

Another friend of mine, Liz Roberts, had gotten married secretly our junior year to O'Brien Boldt, who was editor of the Dartmouth paper. The three of us became "radical" together. He had originally been a "conscientious objector" and was now stationed in New York. She had had to keep her marriage secret or she would have been expelled from Smith. The three of us, when I would come into New York on my days off from the hospital, would go to Communist Front meetings and rallies, and parties where you sat on the floor singing "Freiheit" and "No Pasarán" and "We Are the Peat Bog Soldiers" and "I Dreamt I Saw Joe Hill Last Night." Everybody I met who was interesting and idealistic and passionate about justice, as I was, and had managed to get away from their Peorias, or Montclairs, or Scarsdale suburbs, to the sophistication of those Greenwich Village apartments, was consciously and delightfully "bohemian" as to food and drink, dress and decor, and "radical" as to politics. Actually, we were college liberals trying hard to become radicals, with romantic visions of communism.

I now thought of myself as a revolutionary. I had loved studying about the French Revolution, the Russian Revolution. (Only much later, after reading Hannah Arendt, did I appreciate the unique nature of the American Revolution.) Actually, I knew very little of either wealth or poverty. When one of my Smith classmates invited me home for the weekend to Montclair, New Jersey, I said, are you sure you have enough room for me? She wore such ragged jeans (before they were chic), I was sure she was quite poor. The butler opened the door of what was a mansion: her father was an eminent banker. They served caviar when she announced her engagement to a union organizer and I didn't know what you were supposed to do with it.

For us, the big thing was to escape the "bourgeois" narrow world of our parents, "the middle class." It was, indeed, chic for our generation to be radical long before they dubbed it "radical chic." Being liberal was tame, timid, not really revolutionary. One day, before I left for Berkeley, I looked up the address of the Communist Party headquarters in New York and, on my day off from the hospital, went into their dark and dingy building on 13th Street and announced I wanted to become a member. The woman at the desk looked a little surprised. Maybe it was unusual for a well-dressed college girl, in Braemar twin sweater set, pumps and pearls, to come in out of the cold and announce she wants to be a communist, or maybe it was not. There was nothing illegal then in America, or even incriminating or subversive, about being a socialist or communist or Trotskyite. Of course, when I went home and told my parents, my father had a fit. "Is that what I sent my daughter to Smith for, to be a communist?" But I talked with such pseudo-sophistication then about everything. Using all those sexual words I'd now learned in psychology class, while still fighting the good backseat battle to keep my virginity intact.

My father was serious and loving, not angry, when I went in to kiss him good-bye, before my mother drove me to Chillicothe to catch the Santa Fe train for California. He meant it, truly, for my good future, when he said, "Don't come back to Peoria."

In those days it took two days and nights on the train to get from Illinois to San Francisco. You had to change in Los Angeles. On that train, riding now with that lonesome whistling sound, that romantic whistling sound I used to hear, yearning, from my bedroom window in Peoria, I flirted with GIs my age, going off to the war in their new uniforms. But when one tried to get into my upper berth, I screamed, and a porter came and pulled him down. I think he was evicted from the train at the next stop.

I didn't really fit in with the young radicals I met at Berkeley in 1942. I had applied to live at International House, but that letter from Mr. Fischer about my disruptive leadership qualities soured that. I got an advertised room in some private house, and my asthma got so bad I needed oxygen when I got off the Key train over the Bay Bridge to get to the doctor in San Francisco. Then I started going to radical meetings and learned someone was moving out of the house on Channing Way which was called the Red Castle, or something like that. Sophie and Esther and Evelyn and Mitch let me cook and eat with them. They kept avocados on the window sill and taught me how to make an avocado sandwich. But they made fun of me for being such a "lady." I wore stockings (with a garter belt, as I remember, or even a girdle). They wore bare feet and sandals and they didn't seem to wash or comb their hair all that much.

After Koffka, Lewin, and the work at Smith, I didn't find my psychology courses at Berkeley all that challenging. But I found wonderful professors. I loved Edward Tolman. Erik Erikson was a much better writer than a teacher, but his concepts were exciting. Jean Macfarlane was a few years into her mammoth longitudinal study of Oakland-Berkeley cohorts of children through adolescence. Danny Levinson, and Maria whom he later married, were graduate students with me. Else Frenkel-Brunswik was there, and Nevitt Sanford and Ralph Gandloch.

Jane Loevinger, who was about my age, was already an instructor. She had graduated from college in Minnesota at nineteen. We became good friends. We would go have lunch at the faculty club. I remember wonderful fruit salad, with fresh apricots and pineapple, avocado and cottage cheese. And we'd run into Tolman on our way back to the psych building, and he would tease us: "Here come the career women." And we would both cringe.

Freudian thought, which I had first encountered at Smith, was now invading Berkeley and the American theater. Kurt Weill and Moss Hart's musical *Lady in the Dark* was playing in San Francisco. We went to see it. The heroine, a beautiful gutsy magazine editor, falls in love with her handsome macho advertising manager. At first, she fights him. He doesn't want a career woman for his wife. He's a real man, he wants a real woman. And then she goes to a psychoanalyst and discovers that she really doesn't want a career after all. She will give up her job and marry him, become a real woman. That musical made Jane and me uneasy.

I was now dating her brother Bob, a physicist. He took me to real Chinese restaurants in San Francisco, not like the chop suey ones in Peoria. I went to various radical study groups. We sneered at "liberals," we wanted to be the real thing, communists. Earl Warren was governor of California, and Harry Bridges was the head of the longshoremen's union, and we joined the picket line against Earl Warren when he tried to break the longshoremen's strike.

The intellectual excitement for which Berkeley was famous was muted and distracted; all the professors seemed to wish they were elsewhere, working for the war. Since most of the boys my age were off to war, the ones left to go out with all seemed to be physicists. They would have to leave early, after supper, or go back to the lab after the meeting. They were all working on some mysterious project they couldn't talk about because it had something to do with the war. Their professor, "Oppie" they called him, J. Robert Oppenheimer, was their god. I didn't take them very seriously, my new physicist friends. No one did. They were sort of nerds, if we had used that word then. One of them, David Bohm, had a crush on me. I would look out my window on Channing Way at night and see him standing in the street, looking up at my window. He didn't make me nervous because he was even more shy and inhibited than I was. I was positively an extrovert compared to David.

I had presented my Smith honors thesis, "Operationism in Psychology," to the Berkeley faculty symposium, and Tolman told me that if I had only kept it to myself that it had been my Smith thesis, I could have used it for my M.A. or even Ph.D. at Berkeley. But by now, applying Gestalt thinking to Freudian theory, I had the ambitious idea of what we would today call "deconstructing" Freud's concepts of oral, anal and genital stages of development. I would use the data Jean Macfarlane was collecting in her longitudinal study of Oakland-Berkeley cohorts from infancy into adulthood to test those concepts, or translate them into the concrete observations they had to be based on, with suitable attention to cultural context. I remember, presenting that thesis proposal to the Berkeley faculty symposium, how embarrassed some of my professors seemed as the words "oral," "anal," "genital" were tossed off so blithely by me. They decided to recommend me for the biggest science fellowship at Berkeley, to take me straight through to my Ph.D.

Home for Christmas vacation, I went to Chicago for a few days to talk to Franz Alexander, pioneer in the theory of psychosomatic illness, about my thesis, and to use the university library. My friend Paul Jordan was a medical student now at the University of Chicago. He was no longer going steady with Harriet. After dinner, we went back up to my hotel room and he started to make love to me. We were no longer just good friends. I didn't feel like fighting this time. But, in the midst of lovely touching, he suddenly got up and washed his hands! My Peoria personality took over then, my virginity still intact, and I sent him off.

In Peoria, my father tried to talk to me about money. He was afraid of what my mother would do to the store if he left it all to her. Maybe he should leave it to me, in trust for us kids? This made me very uncomfortable. I don't want your money, I said, I can take care of myself. I did not even want to think of how my mother would feel, how angry she would be, if he did that to her. (Though, in fact, it had been a prosperous business. When she finally remarried and sold it, our shares amounted to about $7,000 each. I used mine to get psychoanalyzed!)

My father was out of his head now. Lying there in bed, his eyes glaring, his face all mean and twisted, he accused me of being a whore, of sleeping with Paul Jordan, of being a slut, etc., etc. I went out of the room and never spoke to him again. I didn't even go in to say good-bye before going to catch the Santa Fe. I was too numb. A few days later, on January 11, 1943, I was called out of a psych class in Berkeley to take a long-distance call. My father had died.

This time I flew home. I don't remember that first plane ride, I felt too sick. My father couldn't stand it when I cried, but I cried on that rocky plane ride back to Peoria for the first time since I'd made a conscious vow back in high school never to cry again. In the coffin, my father had that same grim unforgiving look. He seemed an old man, though he was barely sixty, and I suddenly felt this enormous hatred of my mother. I felt the pressures my father must have felt, with his business and Gentile customers and bankers, and the way my mother made him feel so inadequate, so inferior. Why couldn't she give him the love he needed? And if I didn't say so then, why couldn't I give him that kind of love? I swore again not to be the kind of woman my mother was. But something went dead inside me.

Back in Berkeley, I moved in cold calculation to sleep with someone, anyone, as my father had accused me of doing. It was a law student in my radical study group, whose deformed arm had kept him out of the war. I don't remember any joy, any feeling, except that he was appalled when he discovered I was a virgin.

And then it was announced that I had won the big science fellowship. It was the first time a psychologist had won it, not a physicist, chemist or biologist, and the first time a woman. And I pretended to be excited again. But my asthma attacks got worse, and I broke out in welts all over my body.

Bob, the physicist I was mooning over, took me for a walk in the Berkeley Hills, up behind the lab where they were working on their mysterious project, and he said, "It's over between us. I'm never going to win a fellowship like that." I don't remember what I said. But I guess it felt to me like, if I took that fellowship, if I went on in this academic world where it was so easy for me to be brighter than the boys, I would never be able to be the kind of woman my mother wasn't. I lost sight of the possibility that I had sensed even as a child, saying my prayers, that if my mother had a career of her own that made her feel good enough about herself as a woman she might have been better able to love her husband and children.

Like the heroine in *Lady in the Dark,* I would have to give up any idea of a "career," I would "just be a woman," as my father had taunted me. But that was hardly a reason I could give out loud, even to myself, for turning down that fellowship. I told my professors I was going to give up a career in psychology to work for the "revolution." Tolman, who respected political commitment himself, tried to dissuade me. Erik Erikson was sure this decision had something to do with my father's death. I went to see Steve Nelson, a Spanish Civil War veteran who was editor of *The People's World,* the West Coast communist newspaper, and offered my services. I knew I was a good enough newspaper reporter and editor, but this would not be a "career." He was very disapproving. "You could do more for the revolution if you went on and became a great psychology professor," he said. "How often do we find someone who can win a fellowship like that? Anyone can write for *The People's World.*" No, he would not offer me a job.

But I didn't want to stay in California now. My revolutionary friends still teased me for being a "lady." That sense of being part of something, a group, a community, which has always meant so much to me since the isolation in Peoria, was, I think, what drew me to the ideals of communism in the first place. But I didn't feel that community with the actual communists I was living with in Berkeley. To be honest, I was relieved when Steve Nelson turned me down. I would have been miserable working for *The People's World.* And I couldn't stand the communist prose style!

I had to get a job, of course. I felt morally obligated, out of my guilt for giving up that fellowship, to work either for the war or the revolution. I tried to get a job at the Office of War Information in Washington, but they took one look at my college editorials and decided I was too radical. Or, rather, they asked me if I was a communist—at the OSS, I think—and if I'd said yes, they probably would have hired me anyhow. But I wasn't a communist when I wrote those editorials and, despite my radical braggadocio, wasn't so sure I wanted to be one now. Still, I somehow couldn't settle for one of those "researcher" jobs Smith and Wellesley girls like me were getting at Time-Life.

Some of my friends from Smith—Maggie Comstock, Madelon Berns and Priscilla Buckley—had rented a little house at 17 Grove Street in Greenwich Village and wanted me to join them in New York. I moved to New York in 1943 and got my first job at Federated Press, a news agency serving labor unions and liberal and radical newspapers, because they were sure I was not a communist. They asked me, in the job interview, to analyze the difference between the AFL and CIO, and I said I knew one was radical and the other wasn't, but I didn't actually know which. In fact, I knew nothing about labor unions or economics, and it was a torturous discipline, great for my prose style, to eschew my long social scientist words for even starker simplicity than the usual newspaper who-what-how-why-when. I learned, I wrote, reporting the concrete detail, the actual experience. I covered the first major strike over race relations in Philadelphia. I was asked to find out if the AFL executive board was going to come out for Roosevelt, and I persevered until I had asked each one on the board where he stood, and they were so surprised, they told me. I had my second exclusive interview with Eleanor Roosevelt. My first had been at Smith, where Mary Jackson, my friend and fellow psychology major whose father was U.S. Attorney General, had me, as editor of the Smith paper, run the press conference when Mrs. Roosevelt came to Smith to campaign for her husband.

I was canvassing for Roosevelt in June 1944 when D-Day was announced, the victorious invasion of Nazi-run Europe. I went into a little French restaurant that night, and cried when everyone stood up and sang the *Marseillaise*. I conscientiously wrote sentimental V-mail letters to an officer, I forget his name, I'd met when he was stationed at Camp Ellis near Peoria. I served as a hostess every week at the Newspaper Guild canteen. Since all the boys were away at war, I had several "affairs" with married men, and

shared with one a summer house on Fire Island, which I loved—
so different from Peoria, no cars, no electricity then, kerosene
lamps, no country club.

I wrote a column for Federated Press called "Wartime Living." I had to print at least one recipe each time, but otherwise I'd
have fun translating concepts like "price control" and "inflation"
into language a union member's wife could understand. I got
into real trouble when, in one recipe, I called for a tablespoon of
salt instead of a teaspoon. The readers complained! I'd never
baked a cake myself, of course, but I'd never worked in a factory
either. Economics excited me more than cooking.

I voted, for the first time, for Franklin Roosevelt for president, in November 1944, in New York. He was, and is, my idea of
a great president, though later, when I learned he didn't do what
he might have done to bomb the rail lines to the concentration
camps in Germany and liberate the Jews, I was sad and disappointed. But the Roosevelt years were exciting and marvelous,
the way he recruited all the best intelligence of young and old to
come to Washington and make the U.S. government the dynamic
force it became, tackling the nation's seemingly insoluble problems—closing the banks, setting up the Federal Reserve and then
the minimum wage and forty-hour week, Social Security, WPA,
and murals in the post offices so artists wouldn't starve. And then
Lend Lease and the miracle of American war production, and
price control, and the new ways of teaching Japanese and German fast to the boys I'd gone to school with.

One morning I picked up the *Times*, and realized Dave and
the rest of the physicists at Berkeley weren't such nerds after all.
They'd actually made that atom bomb! It actually ended the war
in Japan! Though, very soon, they and other scientists had grave
reservations about the use of nuclear energy for purposes of war,
and even the development of the hydrogen bomb.

And now the GIs began to come back from the war, and were
entitled to take the jobs we women had been doing in their absence. One took my job at Federated Press, but I got another one,
as a reporter and editor on the *U.E. News*, the official publication
of the United Electrical Workers, one of the most progressive of
labor unions then. I would work for the labor newspaper for the
next six years.

Once, I covered a strike in New Jersey at a plant where almost all the workers were women. I discovered, with a strange sense of recognition as well as that excitement one always feels on the heels of a new story, that the women were getting paid much less than the men for that job. I interviewed the women and wrote such an unexpected story about their lives and the conditions they were working under that Julius Emspak, the head of the United Electrical Workers, had me turn it into a leaflet about the union fighting for women workers. There was nothing I had studied, at economics class at Smith or in the classes on radical economics I now took, along with other Smith sisters, at the Jefferson School of Social Science in New York—the educational enterprise run, I suppose, by the Communist Party—that explained or even described the special exploitation of women.

It would not be until much later, in the evolution of my own feminist thinking, that I realized the whole Marxist concept of labor and economic value was male. Women's work, and the nurture of the family, had no value. The "family" was a tool of bourgeois oppression, etc. Men and women would be liberated when true glory was given to their work on the factory assembly lines. That romanticizing of Ivan-the-tractor-driver swayed a lot of us to disdain our own intellectual abilities in those years when almost anybody who managed to escape their Peorias was a socialist, communist, Trotskyite or revolutionary. But the Marxist concept didn't really send me after I discovered the reality of women's lives, and men's, on those factory assembly lines.

To be honest, I was a snob, an intellectual snob certainly, probably the other kind too. Though I truly disdained the jargons and pretensions of pseudo-intellectuals and the emptiness and painful prejudices of country club snobbery, a part of me still wanted to be asked to join the country club and thus be truly free to disdain it. I probably would have been much happier as a society reporter on the women's page of *The New York Times* than covering workers' strikes for the *U.E. News*. But I learned a lot.

The *U.E. News* sent me to cover the Bretton Woods Economics Conference in New Hampshire right after the war. I hastily read several books on international finance, of which I knew nothing at all. The combination of my Smith education and being thrown into that unknown labor turbulence and forced to master it made me able to get on top of new questions, even welcome the challenge of change and new unknowns for the rest of my life. At Bretton Woods, trying to explain postwar international finance to my real non-college working-class readers, I sought out former resistance heroes, now there as delegates from the new Socialist countries. I was interviewing a Czech labor leader, a former partisan, in my atrocious Peoria high school French when his distinguished-looking compatriot offered to interpret for me. It was Jan Masaryk, whose later mysterious suicide-murder in Prague accentuated my growing distrust and revulsion in the face of real communism.

We were idealists, most of the people I knew who bought the Communist dream in those years of American depression and World War II. The Marxist doctrine that democracy, civil liberties and the freedoms of conscience and speech our parents and grandparents had come to America for was all a capitalist mask for oppression didn't sit easily, for me at least. But in those days I was still able to parrot accepted abstractions that belied my own experience.

Consider the matter of sex and abortion. As the big talker of sexual liberation at Smith and in Peoria (in the years when I was still a virgin myself) I was, of course, the obvious expert to consult, a sophisticated newspaper reporter in New York, when my Smith sisters got in trouble and actually needed an abortion. I would go out to lunch with the group—fortyish, over draft age, "Front Page" editor-types, Travis Hedrick, Al Larke and the others, who taught me to down a three-martini lunch and then go back and write a pithy lead—and ask them for help. "I have a friend who seems to be pregnant [did we say "knocked up" then?]. I need to help her get an abortion." And they would give me an address up in Harlem, and I would go with my friend and wait, terrified, in the dingy reception room, hearing her screams, and take her bleeding back down to the Village in a cab. Six months later, and then again the following year, when I had to ask them for another abortion address for a friend—the first one had been shut down—Al and Travis began to look at me very strangely. It was only later that I realized they thought I was getting all those abortions.

As a loudly self-proclaimed radical revolutionary now, reveling in the bohemianism of the Village and yet made uneasy by it in my Peoria-bred insecurities and proprieties, I disdained the conventionalism of my Smith sisters. Of course, while I was proclaiming sexual license, they quietly had their new diaphragms in their dressers, underneath the Braemar twin sets. I remember one morning during the war, when I was sleeping late, before or between jobs, the doorbell rang at 17 Grove Street. Men from the FBI, checking on Maggie or Pitts Buckley, who'd applied for jobs at Naval Intelligence. They had given me as a reference; after all, I was the one they had all looked up to at Smith, what better reference? In my pajamas and bathrobe, I stared intently into the eyes of those FBI agents, attesting to my friends' sterling characters, while pushing *The Daily Worker* on the floor back under the couch with one bare foot.

I was beginning to get very restless writing those labor stories. I missed the stimulation of my psychology studies. Maybe I should go to medical school and become a psychoanalyst. I would need college chemistry and physics to get into medical school, so I enrolled to take those courses at night at New York University. But now the war was over, and the GIs were home, and here I was almost twenty-five and not married. Then, if you weren't married by twenty-five, forget it, you thought you'd be an old maid all your life, a spinster aunt.

The first man (unmarried) I went out with after the war was a South African financier. The second was a dentist. The third was a blind date with a labor press colleague's (Fred Zeserson) Boston childhood chum, Carl Friedan. He'd been director of the Soldier Show Company in the European theater of World War II—Paddy Chayefsky and all that gang—and was trying to make it as a summer theater producer and little theater manager before Off-Broadway. He brought me an apple on our first date, and made me laugh.

By now I was living on my own in a basement apartment, made out of a big old-fashioned kitchen behind the furnace of a brownstone on 86th Street, off Central Park West. The "group" from Smith had given up that lovely little house at 17 Grove—it was conventional then for people like us to move every year in New York, but the postwar housing shortage changed all that. The other Smith girls had got an apartment on Waverly Place, and

I moved in with friends from Berkeley, first on Seventh Avenue South, then up to the West Side. With this new life beginning with men, roommates were a drag.

That first night, we went to a deli called Barney Greengrass and I ordered a sturgeon sandwich. It was expensive, over $2.00. Carl looked a little concerned. He was living on the GI Bill at the time. He never made a date ahead of time, so every night I would sit there waiting for the phone to ring. And, of course, every night he would finally call, and come over, and we would go to a movie or something, and go to bed. I began to be very happy with Carl in my life. After a bit, he stopped going back to his apartment on 105th and, in effect, moved in with me. But he was very busy, organizing his first summer theater at Lake Hopatcong in New Jersey. I don't know how or why we started talking about getting married. I'm sure I wanted to. But he would always talk about looking for just the right man for me to marry, not him. Once I found a letter he was writing to his parents about a girl who wasn't very pretty but so sharp, she'd always be able to support him or somesuch. When he took me up to Boston to meet his parents, I had a major asthma attack, brought on, I'm sure, by his mother, Tillie. I should have known, my body did know, that mother's son would have a problem all his life with any woman he depended on. But it was when my mother objected—not a bit happy at the idea of coming to New York and hosting a wedding for her older daughter—that Carl, always contrary, decided we would indeed get married, before the opening of the summer theater.

Our wedding would have to be in Boston, though my mother, of course, would pay for it, because his mother wasn't well enough to come to New York and all his relatives, cousins, uncles, aunts, were in Boston. It also had to be a proper Jewish wedding under a *huppa,* which certainly horrified my mother. He teased me that I'd have to take a bath in sour cream. What did I know? The first time I ever had a bagel, much less lox and cream cheese, was in my twenties, in New York. I didn't really enjoy that wedding at all.

But the Boston wedding wasn't our real wedding anyhow. Because of his schedule, getting the summer theater ready, and my job, we didn't want to take the time needed in Boston to post banns some days before actually getting married. So he picked me up at the newspaper office the Friday afternoon before our Boston wedding, and on June 12, 1947, we went to City Hall to get married with Fred and my colleague Katherine Beecher as witnesses. (I think he got cold feet just before we got married. He was supposed to pick me up at four, and at ten after four I came down in the elevator and he was walking away. But he turned around and came back.) Afterward, we all repaired to our favorite bar and drank stingers. (I noticed recently, when we became friends again twenty years after our divorce, Carl still orders stingers. They're too sweet for me now.)

My daughter Emily says I try to deny now that I ever loved Carl. I did, of course. I can still see his fast, nervous walk, slightly bowlegged; he was very thin then and always in a hurry. I'm a slow walker, my legs are too short, I was always about ten paces behind. He made me laugh. I loved going to bed with him. I loved our sex. We were silly and cozy, had pet names for his cock and my diaphragm. I loved giving myself over to sex, letting him take over. Later, the feminist critique of heterosexual sex seemed crazy to me. It denied my own experience, certainly. I loved kissing, and when he put his tongue hard down my throat, I loved the whole melting feeling, not just the clitoral orgasm. I never felt oppressed or demeaned by sex, when I went to bed with someone I really liked. (Once, with one of those soldiers from the Newspaper Guild canteen, and then again later, in the subway, when I tried to run away after a terrible argument with Carl, I had to fight off rape. That is another story. But I was able to talk them out of it.) Sometime after we were divorced, I sat next to a friend of Carl's at a dinner party, and he told me that my husband boasted that I was a wonderful lay. Should I have been insulted? I was, in fact, quite pleased. I also liked snuggling afterward, spoon fashion, or my head on his heart and his leg over my body, or vice versa. Much nicer than sleeping alone.

We couldn't afford a fancy honeymoon. I think I was making $35 a week, and when the GI Bill ran out, everything he made went back into the summer theater. But my friend Mario lent us a car equipped with a tent, two sleeping bags, a charcoal grill and detailed maps of New England. Carl's first summer theater, before the war, had been in western Maine at Rangeley Lake. So we set out on a camping trip—slept on the beach in front of an elegant old hotel in Ogunquit, closed then in September. We climbed Mount Washington in sneakers, with an orange in each of our pockets. I liked the climb up, but it was sunset when we got to the top. So we hitched a ride down on a truck. I listened to the guys on the truck talk about a car the day before on which the brakes had failed and everyone had been killed. I got terrified when the truck we were riding in began to slip out of gear occasionally. I made Carl jump off with me and walk the rest of the way down, even though it was dark. We could see the road clearly enough, but it took longer than the trail up. And we canoed through Sebago Lake and the Saco River, and camped on the shore and thought we heard bears, and I was happy.

Now we were officially ensconced in my basement apartment, husband and wife. Carl made a bar out of a barrel to hide the little sink in the corner of the living room (also kitchen) where we washed ourselves and dishes. There was a tub in the long narrow hall leading to the bedroom, but the cold water faucet didn't work, so you had to fill the tub at least a half hour early for the water to cool. We gave parties—we always gave great parties. But his theater friends, with their "dahling" this and that, ignored me when they found out I wasn't in the theater. Carl was managing a theater troupe, but this was before Off-Broadway or Off-Off-Broadway, and there was no money to be made. The troupe put on a great production of Clifford Odets's *Waiting for Lefty*, I remember. And then, for a while, he actually got paid, as assistant publisher to Alexander Duce at *Theater Arts Monthly*.

When we went home to Peoria in the fall of 1947 for my brother's wedding, sitting up all night in coach since we couldn't afford a sleeper, I wore an elegant gray flannel New Look suit with a jacket trimmed with black braid, and a long swishy skirt. I bought it in the junior department at Henri Bendel, the one store where I had a charge account. (Friends of my parents in Peoria knew the owners then, and sent me there.) When "Aunt Elsa," as we called our parents' friend, complimented me on my elegant suit (the New Look had not yet come to Peoria), she said: "I thought you were supposed to be a communist now." "I am," I said. "Nothing is too good for the working class."

But I was getting more and more uneasy about communism.

The stories of gulag atrocities, the invasion of Hungary, rumors of anti-Semitism, all this could be dismissed as Trotskyite or capitalist propaganda lies. But I didn't like the authoritarian tactics of the party commissars in the United States. One of our friends, Fred, I think, was brought up on charges as a racist and expelled. He wasn't a racist, he simply had to fire someone who wasn't a good enough photographer. I covered the House Un-American Activities Committee trial of the Hollywood Ten for the *U.E. News*, and was outraged at the persecution of guys like Ring Lardner Jr., who had written some of the best movies of the war years. Most of the people I knew who were communists then were motivated by the same idealistic visions as I was. Still, I didn't like the commissar types, though surely the "capitalist oppressors" were worse. I stopped going to meetings. I didn't want anyone telling me how and what to write.

Using Freudian terms (and Jewish theology) to understand my original embrace of Marxism, I think, looking back, it gave first shape to my superego, my Jewish existential conscience, that sense which always seems to drive me, though I dread its appearance, that I have to use my life to make the world better, have to protest, step off that sidewalk and march against injustice. I wouldn't be the first Jewish thinker—in a long line of prophets and social theorists, up until now mostly male—to have applied that existential imperative, which may or may not stem from those tablets Moses brought down from the mountain or our personal experience of injustice as Jews, to the widest possible class of humanity of which we are part. If, growing up in Peoria and experiencing injustice as a Jew from the country club crowd, I now identified with the working class, also oppressed by those masters of the universe, so be it.

I remember the sharp distinction I had learned in my economics classes at Smith where I studied communism, fascism, capitalism—that fascism was capitalism carried to the extreme, absolute power to those who owned the industries and banks, no freedom of the people to organize or express dissent. No unions allowed to strike against workers' oppression, no social thinkers allowed to be critical of the system, burning of the books—and the Jew as a scapegoat for the growing frustration, fear and hate the people could no longer express against those who profited from their suffering. In our classes at the Jefferson School, we learned that communism was a system that put the interests of the people first and in which private profit from the exploitation of workers was abolished. The government organized housing, production of food and clothing, medical care and education; the arts were not for profit but for use by the people. With Spain as an example, I also learned that communism, to protect that revolution from its capitalist enemies, at home and in the world, had to suspend the freedoms of speech and the press and other democratic rights we hold dear. We were told that under capitalism democratic freedoms, like religion, are "opiates" for the masses, serving the interests of profiteers by keeping the people diverted and quiet. We were told that both political parties in America were controlled by big business and their networks, newspapers, the arts, etc.

A germ of truth can be found in almost all of it. But confusing inconsistencies bothered me as, for instance, when word began to get out about anti-Semitism in Russia and Poland, the collaboration between Hitler and Stalin, the perversion of psychiatry in Russia to suppress dissent, and the atrocities of the gulag. And, of course, I knew from my own experience in Peoria, at Smith and in New York, that people could and did organize in America, the strikes that were run in the Roosevelt era, the very organization of the CIO unions, the social innovations like earlier compensation and Social Security and antitrust laws and other curbs on big corporations. I knew also of the dissenting voices heard in our press, radio and television despite its control by big business.

A book that had an enormous effect on me when I was confronting this confusion was T. W. Adorno's *The Authoritarian Personality*, which had essays written by Nevitt, Sanford, Else Frenkel-Brunswik and former colleagues in the psychology department at Berkeley—an elucidation of the conditions and kinds of personality that can turn any revolutionary "ism" into authoritarian dogma, and stifle the free human spirit and democratic expression necessary for society to evolve. Another was Hannah Arendt's essay "On Revolution," which gave me the insight that, unlike other revolutions, which resulted in overthrow or transfer of power from one group to another, the American Revolution resulted in a structure which continues in perpetuity the *process* of revolution, the democratic process embodied in our Constitution, giving it continued rebirth, the continuing process of questioning, of confronting problems, new challenges, new ideas, reaffirming truths to meet changing conditions. The authoritarian personality couldn't tolerate that kind of flexibility, freedom, change.

None of this, of course, at that time had anything to do with women. When I thought about politics, which I did a lot in those days, it was not about women at all. It was about people who suffered and were oppressed—blacks, Jews, workers—by capitalist bosses and Nazi dictators and, to my horror, communist commissars. But later this struggle to make sense of it all made me wary of any tinge of authoritarianism in the women's movement, and the danger of perversion of feminism by its own extremists.

Above all, I began to feel an aversion to any and all political dogma that didn't seem to come from real life. The politics I got involved in and thought through for myself, in the communities where I lived, seemed so much more real and vital than the abstractions of Communist revolution. It was such small stuff though, compared to world revolution. But in the America where I lived, abstractions of that world revolution of the masses didn't seem all that real, didn't really *work*, didn't actually change real life.

On that trip back to Peoria for my brother's wedding, Carl and I went to see my friend Harriet, who was living in Peoria now, married to our former classmate, John "Parky" Parkhurst, with a new baby, Van. We thought that baby was heavenly. I was nearly twenty-seven, Carl was twenty-eight. Shouldn't we have a baby? (Well, we shouldn't have. We had no money. Neither of us had secure professions. What on earth were we thinking of?) I think I must have gotten pregnant the first night I left my diaphragm out after we got back from Peoria.

Seven months pregnant, with my belly out to here, I covered the Progressive Party convention that nominated Henry Wallace for president in August 1948 in Philadelphia. By now I was getting interested in what I thought was a different kind of politics from that of the communist commissars. The cold war was beginning, but committees were being formed of artists, writers and other professionals still committed to peace and the ideals of Roosevelt and the New Deal. I had got active helping to organize such a committee on the Upper West Side, near our apartment. Then it became the Progressive Party, and the communists took over. By now I recognized the tactics and knew they were ruining something that could have been good.

I worked until the middle of September; the baby was due in October. According to the Newspaper Guild contract, I had six weeks paid maternity leave but could take up to a year unpaid. Since Carl had a good job with a theatrical publisher, I was determined to take that year off and get used to being a mother. Carl was also a good carpenter, from all those years of building summer theater scenery. While I was in the hospital having Danny, he turned a closet into a proper kitchen, brought our bed into the living room, built shelves around it, and fixed up the bedroom as a nursery.

I would have liked to have natural childbirth, but it was just beginning to be talked about. My pregnancy had been so easy, the sheer pain of labor took me by surprise. Despite the exercise class I took at Planned Parenthood or wherever, I couldn't seem to get on top of that labor. My water had burst on the way to the movies. The enema after we got to the hospital was torture. That labor went on and on, it took so long for me to dilate, I remember, and then the head wouldn't come down. But still, I was horrified when they said they were going to do a Cesarean. I seem to remember they asked Carl's permission, not mine—could that be right, or is it a later feminist reconstruct?

Carl was not instructed to coach my labor and join in it, as fathers are now. Trying to be helpful, he brought me a martini. I couldn't stand the taste of martinis or avocados (two of my favorite foods) when I was pregnant. He got drunk, from terror, I suppose. But I was sure that doctor was going to do a Cesarean because he wanted to get home for Sunday dinner. I wanted to keep on trying, despite the pain. But the baby's head wasn't coming down because it was too big for my pelvis, and all the labor was doing was banging that baby's head against my bones. (So, okay, maybe the doctor was right to do the Cesarean. He did turn out to be a genius, my firstborn, Daniel.) I breast-fed Danny, though there wasn't much encouragement then from the hospital nurses. Tired as I got during those first few months of his life—I was all thumbs diapering, giving him a bath in our bar-sink—I'll never forget the sheer indescribable thrill, wheeling him home in the baby carriage one night after a meeting, when I looked down and his eyes were open, and he smiled at me.

Carl invented some rockers to put under the crib, and we bought a rocking chair. We also rigged a system where, if the baby wouldn't stop crying, we'd put him in the baby carriage with a long rope attached to the handle, and from our bed we would push the carriage sailing down the long narrow hall, past the bathtub, and then pull it back by the rope. The baby thought we were taking him for a walk, I suppose. Anyhow, he slept! And we fell asleep election night with the radio on and Dewey was president, but when we woke up it was Truman.

Danny was a beautiful baby, and so blond, Carl's genes, I suppose. People would look at me, dark and ordinary-looking, wheeling this gorgeous blond baby in a stylish carriage we surely couldn't afford, and think I was the nursemaid. That summer I was also accused of baring my breasts to nurse him on the front steps of the summer theater, in West Newbury, Massachusetts. It wasn't true. I always went inside and nursed him in one of the backseats of the darkened theater during rehearsals.

I'd planned to go back to work, after my year's maternity leave was up the end of September 1949. But they called me in Massachusetts from the paper and said I had to come back the last two weeks in August or nobody else could take a vacation. I had to start Danny on bottles, and leave him in the care of the farm girl that we used as a baby-sitter, under Carl's supervision. But Carl was too busy running the theater to watch over the baby. Later, when Danny had problems with his girlfriends or otherwise seemed too lonesome and unhappy, I blamed it on that first forced unprepared desertion by his mother. After I found a fine motherly nursemaid in New York, I took the baby back with me while Carl wound up the theater season. I remember the terrible tantrum of Danny's crying on the plane; I wondered what had been happening while I was gone.

We had a wonderful pediatrician in New York, Dr. Lewis Fraad, who kept assuring me that despite what Dr. Spock said, it did not have to hurt my baby that I went back to work. I had no choice. Carl didn't make enough money in the summer theater to take us through the winter. The *Theater Arts* job was on again, off again. It's all mixed up for me, in my memory as it was in real life, that new mix of marriage, motherhood, job and politics. At that time in my life, there's no question that motherhood came first, though there was also no question for me that I wasn't committed to my job or that I wouldn't do it well. I made new rules for myself, get in by 10:30 a.m. (the men often came in that late, stopping for breakfast en route), skip lunch if necessary, and get my errands and shopping done, then leave by 5:00. And since by now I was a good, fast writer, no one could complain I didn't get my work done. But I wasn't so enthusiastic anymore about covering stories I had to fly to. In fact, I have to admit I was terrified then of flying.

That bohemian basement apartment behind the furnace no longer seemed so interesting. It wasn't comfortable. But the postwar housing shortage was still with us, and there were no apartments to move to. We worked a three-way swap: my old physicist friend Bob Loevinger, now working in New York, wanted to get out of his studio in the Village. He took our apartment. A widow on upper Riverside Drive close to Harlem moved into his Village studio, and we moved into her proper two-bedroom apartment in an old building on Riverside Drive near 145th Street. Carl fixed it up again, the floor, the walls, bookcases. But it wasn't good for us. Our friends from his theater and my paper and my old Smith buddies wouldn't come all that way uptown to visit us. And Danny, going on three, needed other kids to play with whom I couldn't seem to find on weekend visits to the playgrounds nearby.

One day I read a story in the *Times* about a wonderful cooperative nursery school, in a community built for the United Nations out in Queens called Parkway Village. Although that village of garden apartments was built for UN personnel, the article said vacancies were also open to ex-GIs and to newspaper correspondents. I took the subway out there my next lunch hour, and brought Carl out that night.

I loved the concrete daily life of that community, Parkway Village, the politics of it, the bonds we formed with other parents at the nursery school. By now I was no longer interested in abstract Marxist politics. I remember wheeling Danny in the grocery cart, shopping in the supermarket (so new, then, the supermarket, after the war) and the phenomenon of his actually talking to another little boy in a neighboring cart's basket. So, of course, Danny's mother introduced herself to Roddy's mother, and our group began.

We were ecstatic about our garden apartment, with real wood floors and French doors, opening off a central green lawn. We could sit in deck chairs, and barbecue hamburgers, and Danny could play with neighbors' kids. So our friends Dick and Gladys, Fred and Ruth, also with kids now, got apartments there too. And at nursery school we became friends with Tom and Peggy Wolf. Tom worked for ABC, Harold and Dick worked for *PM* and its later derivatives. Gladys, like me, worked for a labor union news agency. But she quit when Nancy was born. We became an extended family for each other, but we also made close friends with Mexican and Iranian families, and French and Swiss we met. All of us were so happy in that community.

I always liked fixing up an apartment, a house, rearranging the furniture. We went to the exhibit of modern architecture, the Japanese House in the garden of the Museum of Modern Art. We bought the first Eames chairs and a red plastic Eames rocker and a free-form three-corner Noguchi dining table which we later cut down to a coffee table. I even liked experimenting with cooking. Our first party at Parkway Village, I served a Swiss fondue but put in a cup of Kirsch instead of a tablespoon and it was inedible. I loved our family backyard barbecues. And Danny loved the cooperative international nursery school. My upstairs neighbor met me once, on my way home from work by bus and subway to take Danny somewhere, and she said in annoyance: "You go to work every day. You don't take care of your child all day long the way I do. So how come you don't have problems with your child the way I do with mine?" And, for sure, we could hear the hysterical frenzy of those problems, night after night, through the thin walls of our garden apartment.

Danny, none of my kids, were ever "problems" for me. They were a sheer delight, so beautiful, so bright, so funny, so themselves. They seemed like a *bonus* in my life, an unexpected, maybe undeserved, marvelous bonus. Well, of course, they wet the bed, and had to be toilet-trained, and I had to insist that the maid spank Danny when he went out into the street, because it was dangerous. But, I have to admit, it was delicious for me being a mother. And I think Carl also felt that way about our kids.

But I was no longer so happy in my marriage. Carl's lack of a job, our lack of money bothered me. And he had become distant. In fact, once I became a mother, Carl actually turned away from me sexually, and I grieved and didn't understand it, and was miserable in bed at night, where I used to exult so in our togetherness. That word "togetherness" was a word that the women's magazines were beginning to use a lot in those years of idealized marriages, post–World War II. But the friendship of our group filled a lot of the loneliness.

The move to suburbia was beginning all around us. But in our UN community, we had a better idea. We would join together, several hundred families, get land—we found some wonderful acres on a hill above Ossining on the Hudson—and build a truly future-minded cooperative community, each with our own houses, but a common library, pool, tennis court, as well as nursery school. We had wonderful meetings off hours in the UN General Assembly chamber debating the question of bidets. But our dream of a utopian international community on the Hudson, bidets and all, came up against violent opposition from the Ossining and Westchester town fathers—such a community would, of course, be interracial.

Danny was nearly four now, and we didn't want him to be an only child. I was thirty-one, but when I told the doctor we intended to have another child sooner or later, he said, well, you'd better do something about it. It might not be so easy this time, you're not so young anymore. Of course, I got pregnant the first week I left the diaphragm off again. Only this time, there were unexpected consequences. Carl began calling from the office to say that he wasn't coming home to dinner. (I later learned he was having an affair with a former girlfriend. I knew who she was. I sensed that they'd been seeing each other and I felt desolate, deserted, betrayed, all those things. He admitted it and said he would stop. I never could take that, other women. When I started bleeding one night, a possible miscarriage, it was Tom Wolf who took me to the hospital.

And then, in maybe the fifth month of my pregnancy, I was told that I was fired from my job on the union newspaper. They didn't give me any reason. My work, I knew, had been good. I wrote practically every story in the paper. I'd even taken a course in photography at a famous left-wing photo school so I could take my own pictures, doing the inquiring reporter interviews on picket lines in Dayton or Elmira when a photographer was unavailable. A colleague finally explained, they weren't prepared to let me take another year's maternity leave, as I'd done the first time.

I was angry. I went to the Newspaper Guild. I was being fired because I was pregnant, not because my work wasn't good. That wasn't fair. But Jule, our hard-boiled, chain-smoking "Front Page" type copy editor, who was head of the Guild unit, said: "It's your fault for getting pregnant again." There was no word for sex discrimination then, no law against it. But I bitterly felt the injustice of it, being fired because I was pregnant.

Still, in a way, it was a relief, because all those negative books and magazine articles about "career women" were beginning to get to me. I'd been too indoctrinated in psychology, Freudian psychology and its derivatives sweeping America in the years after World War II, to easily dismiss the pejorative that women who worked, had professional careers, were losing their femininity, undermining their husbands' masculinity, and destroying or stunting their children who wouldn't somehow grow without the twenty-four-hour care of the mother. I read Helene Deutsch's two-volume *Psychology of Women*. The only true fulfillment for a woman was through serving her husband and children. And much was made of B. F. Skinner's studies of animals separated from their mothers in isolation cages, who didn't grow properly, and John Bowlby's babies left in orphanages in wartime London who never really matured right. Besides, I was feeling more and more alienated in that labor press job, partly because I was no longer so politically naive and idealistic about it all. And partly because, though I wouldn't have put it that way at the time, as a woman on those jobs I wasn't really accepted. My opinions were never sought on policy or political questions.

So, I dispensed with the nursemaid and took Danny along with me on trips to town to collect unemployment insurance. You could hardly look for another job then, with your belly so pregnantly swollen. I took on the unpaid job of editing the Parkway Village community newspaper. One of the UN officials from Africa said to me once, after a meeting of the community association, "Why are you at home, playing around this way? In my country, we couldn't afford to let a woman like you not use her training and ability."

Now Carl had to carry the whole financial burden. If only he'd been able to make himself apply for a job, with his theater experience and advertising–public relations knack, he could have been on the ground floor of television, along with his friends Arthur Penn and Paddy Chayevsky. Instead, with *Theater Arts Monthly* now folded and summer theater too risky, and no money yet for Off-Broadway, he decided he'd have to leave the theater altogether. He had this idea with Fred of starting some PR advertising venture with drug companies, creating newspapers or magazines that could be read in waiting rooms, sent to all doctors for free. And he also went after other advertising accounts. He was very good at it, he had an office on Fifth Avenue and 57th, and a secretary. But he wouldn't even try his hand at one of the big advertising agencies, even when some of those early projects were taken over by them.

It didn't seem right for me to be doing no work. Or rather, for me, housework, cooking, taking care of the kids, wasn't somehow "work." The only thing that really seems like work to me, ever, is writing. One of the husbands, hearing Gladys and me discuss this one night, said we should try freelancing for magazines. We decided to write a two-part piece about staying home with our kids. I'd write, "I'd rather work," and she'd write, "I'm happy staying home." Dick, who had graduated from *PM* to article and book writing himself, gave our article to his agent, Marie Rodell, and she sold it to *Glamour*. And so, with Marie also my agent now, I embarked on a surreptitious, unadmitted career as a freelance writer.

First, I took a course at nearby Queens College in fiction writing. I've always had a thing about the greater truth of fiction. I also was reading women's magazines, which had bored me before. Nobody was yet talking about "the new journalism," in fact, it hadn't yet been invented. But I'd figured out for myself what was needed. As Jim Skardon, an editor at *Good Housekeeping*, later put it to me: "Don't say they did it, describe them doing it." I also saw, reading those magazines, that the articles and the stories were about children, marriage, sex, houses, clothes and, sometimes, improving communities. These were things that also interested me at the time. Besides, after Jonathan was born in 1952 and with two kids now, I wasn't so interested in flying off to cover strikes or infiltrate neo-fascist meetings as I'd been doing before.

So, I wrote a profile of the dress designer Clare McCardell. I called Fergie—Charles Ferguson—the wonderful *Reader's Digest* editor I'd interned for at the Highlander Folk School writers' workshop, and sold him on an article about my friends who all went home to Peoria after the war and were cleaning up the town. "You Can Go Home Again," I called it. (The photographer later told me he'd been accosted in the lobby of Peoria's Père Marquette Hotel by one of the prostitutes the article said no longer operated in the red light district so notorious in our childhood.)

I had a pact with myself: I had to make enough money to pay a maid (we weren't grand enough to call her a "nanny" as they do now) three days a week so I could get out of the house to do my interviews and research, and some of the writing, on an unused desk in Carl's office. But Carl clearly had to support the family, as I clearly was responsible for taking care of the kids and the house. That was the way it was then. In fact, before I was fired when I was carrying most of the earnings ball, I several times lost my wallet in the subway on Friday, payday. It made me uncomfortable, then, earning more than he did. But when I stopped earning and he had to carry the whole burden, it created terrible tensions in our family, the worries about money and my unspoken disapproval of what I sometimes considered his slightly far-fetched deals. One had something to do with tropical fish; all we got out of it was a fish collection. Then too, though he didn't speak much about it, there was some bitterness at not having the freedom anymore to try things like those Off-Broadway theaters that wouldn't make enough to support a family.

It wasn't good for our family, playing those old traditional roles, I now see. My asthma reappeared, severely, after I was fired from my newspaper job for being pregnant and entered on my housewife life. I had to resume therapy, which I'd started those first months in New York when my asthma got so bad I had only one-fourth of my lung capacity. My asthma had gotten much better in the years when I was doing newspaper work and getting happily started as a wife and mother. But bodies don't lie. I was determined to be happy and fulfilled as "just a housewife," but even my therapist, who knew something of my background, didn't buy it. "Why are you pretending to be just a housewife? Didn't you graduate *summa cum laude* in psychology? Aren't you a writer?"

I had a dream that I went to a movie with my women friends, the other mothers in our group, and they all had tickets but I didn't. I had another dream about John Hersey, who'd recently quit *Life* to write books. "You should take yourself more seriously," Dr. Menaker said. "Maybe you need to be a more serious writer."

But, of course, I wasn't that serious, couldn't be, writing for those women's magazines. It's strange, how one thinks one's given something up, made a terrible mistake, an irreparable loss, and yet one uses it, uses everything in the end. I said good-bye to any thought of "career" when I turned down the psychology fellowship and came to New York. The labor newspaper jobs I didn't consider "career" at all. They were just something I could do, liked doing. If I had taken myself more seriously, I'd have tried to get a job on *The New York Times* like my fellow Ivy League editors. I would have loved that. I still identify more as a journalist than anything else. But I didn't have that kind of confidence then. I did the labor union reporting as a kind of political duty or penance. It didn't serve any career advance, surely, even if I'd been thinking of journalism in those terms. And yet I learned so much, interviewing those workers, writing my "Wartime Living" column, being thrown into the economic ocean and forced to swim in real waves, deep water where neither classical economics nor Marxist abstractions could keep me afloat very long.

Writing for women's magazines I never thought of in "career" terms at all. I'd given all that up to be a fulfilled wife and mother, had I not? But I learned a lot, writing for women now—ordinary American women, middle-class wives and mothers like myself, writing for the magazines I used to disdain in my intellectual days, though I sneaked a peak under the hair dryer at the beauty parlor. I learned a lot that I used later, from the very absence of seriousness toward women on the part of the male editors that used to frustrate me so.

For instance, I wanted to do an article about Beverly Popporos, a woman sculptor. I read a little item in *Time* magazine about this hotshot woman advertising executive—a real freak in that era of the vanishing career woman—who, after Freudian analysis, gave up her career, went to Italy, married a struggling writer there, had a baby, and became a serious sculptor. She was having her first show in a New York gallery and she was coming out with a cookbook on how to make good tasty meals with an Italian flavor that would still leave you plenty of time for your serious work, like her sculpture.

Marie Rodell was dubious. She warned me that the editors would say that American women couldn't possibly identify with a woman who was a serious sculptor. And, in fact, that's what the editors of the magazines I usually wrote for—*McCall's, Ladies' Home Journal, Redbook*—did say. I don't remember which magazine finally gave me the go-ahead, maybe one of the supermarket magazines, on the basis of the cookbook. But in the article itself, I showed in lusty detail Beverly cooking, painting her kid's crib, sculpting a luscious basket of vegetables for a party decoration, her love affair with her husband, Bill, and her flamboyant dressing, pink and orange with flaming red hair. The paragraphs about her serious work and her sculpture—massive works which now decorate some of New York's largest buildings—were deleted.

I also learned a lot, following my new interest in moving out of the city, into a house, looking for a community. In 1956 I was pregnant for the third time, by unconscious "accident" this time. After three martinis I thought my diaphragm was still in from the last night, but it wasn't. On the other hand, the accident was timely—four years between each baby; as a child of the Depression, I didn't want to have two kids in college at the same time. (Little did I bargain for the reality of their college years, dropping out and then back in, graduate school, medical school.) With a third kid, which I so hoped would be a girl, that simple Parkway Village garden apartment wouldn't be big enough. We could have moved into a three-bedroom duplex, like Tom and Peggy's, but by now we were also succumbing to that dream of a suburban house.

Well, of course, I hated suburbia at first sight; somehow Westchester reminded me too much of Peoria, and the country club conformity and snobbery. I realized later that the kinds of community bonds that had sustained our otherwise "dysfunctional family" in Parkway Village, and our extended family of friends as I would call it now, were more important than an extra bedroom and a view of the Hudson River in Rockland County.

But in my writing, I sensed a truth that the new conventional dream of suburbia kept me from realizing in our personal life. I did a whole series of articles, for *Redbook, Reader's Digest*, etc., on "To Get a House, They Built a Community." One was about young couples like ourselves who, in Westport, Connecticut, had bought a tract of land, on a waterway leading to the Sound, and built their houses, each to their own taste, but with common land for swimming pool, tennis court, nursery school, and club house. In the midst of my pregnancy, I did another story about couples who had gotten together when they were in graduate school at Columbia on the GI Bill, and, living in Shanks Village, ex-barracks in Rockland County, had built a community they called Hickory Hill in Tappan, New York. Milton Carrow, the lawyer who led the group, elicited my immediate admiration for his wisdom, principles and pragmatism. (Forty years and several lives later for us both, we are still friends and dreaming of new projects.) So Carl and I started seriously exploring Levittown and contemplating the plans for wondrous factory-made techbuilt houses somewhere in Massachusetts and looking at barns in Rockland County on weekends and scanning the real estate ads.

We read books like *The Exurbanites* and *Mr. Blandings Builds His Dream House*. We pored over the plans of architect George Nelson and the writings of William A. White and Buckminster Fuller about the relationship between space, architecture, the house and the community. Later, I went with the kids to live for a week in Moshe Safdie's house of the future in Habitat at the Montreal World's Fair, hoping to do an article about it. But where was the community? Finally, in the basement I found plans for community facilities, but they required a much denser population than the small model in Montreal. But we didn't really have the money to buy and fix up a barn in Rockland County.

And then one day we saw an ad for an old stone barn to rent on the Hudson in Sneden's Landing, three bedrooms, and no more rent than moving into a three-bedroom apartment at Parkway Village. I seem to remember it was under $500 a month and it was the most romantic house I could ever dream of living in. It belonged to Charles Christian Wertenbaker, chief *Life* correspondent in Europe, and his wife, Lael. And so, with some fear and sorrow, for we were leaving our extended family and wonderful community that had been more important for our own stability and happiness than even we realized, we said good-bye to Alice, Harold, Tom, Peggy, Fred, Ruth, Gladys, Dick and all their kids who had cut their baby teeth with ours, and headed across the Hudson River.

It was strange, that lemming impulse to leave the city for suburbia that struck so many of my generation in the 1950s. I think now that for me, and perhaps other women, once we gave up or were forced out of jobs and careers by the returning GIs or were fired as I was for being pregnant—once we were no longer part of that mainstream—we didn't want to be reminded of it. I remember how miserable, uneasy, it would make me, when I went into the city to visit my old colleagues on the paper. In a personnel crisis they got me to cover a strike again, and I wrote a great story about it, which I think was published later by *New Masses* under a pseudonym. But I was no longer part of that world. In fact, with McCarthyism now becoming virulent in America, I wanted to forget I'd ever been part of that world.

I really wanted to be a happy, fulfilled suburban housewife, and soon-to-be mother of three. But I remember, in those first months in Rockland County, going on a hike as a family on some church group's Sunday mountain outing, and again, at a supermarket mall parking lot, a sudden inexplicable, terrifying panic attack. It was worse than asthma.

FOUR

A "Happy" Suburban Housewife

The house in Sneden's Landing was magical. The downstairs, except for a brick-floored carriage-room entrance gallery, was still stable—stalls and all. The living was on the second floor—a great long stone-walled living room with a long facade of glass French doors going out to a balcony overlooking the Hudson, a dark dining room with a balcony where I put my desk, and some more of those long windows in front of which we put the dining table; a homey kitchen with, I recall, a sort of benched alcove to eat breakfast in, and in the bath off the master bedroom a bidet, and in front of the toilet a coffee table with bullfight tickets under the glass top and a great view of the next-door estate lawn. A French oil painting hung over the fireplace. I'd never even dreamed of a bathroom like that.

But it was midwinter when we moved in, I was pregnant, and that stone barn was *cold*. I wore gloves, typing my articles, because every time I turned the furnace up, I could hear dollar bills going up in flames. It became clear almost immediately that we couldn't really afford a house, so many more expenses than our apartment. We had to take out charge accounts at the grocer and the butcher, it was before you could live on credit cards. And there was no cooperative nursery school, no nearby children one could safely send Jonathan and Danny out the garden door to play with.

I formed a play group with a woman geologist up the hill at Lamont Geological Observatory who had a kid Jonathan's age, and we took turns watching them, mornings. Danny went to the little Palisades elementary school, and made friends with a boy whose father was a television writer and playwright. We made friends with them immediately, but when we suggested they join the Sneden's Landing tennis club, to which we were admitted as a result of living there, they gave us a strange look. When we proposed at the next meeting of the club that the Elmans be asked to join—did they know he had a new play running Off-Broadway?—we got the same strange look. It seemed that wouldn't be "appropriate." Because they were Jewish, I wondered, realizing suddenly that most Snedenites were WASP? No, it seemed that they simply wouldn't do because they lived on the wrong side of 9W in a rather ordinary house, not one of the wonderful old decaying heirlooms lining the Sneden's road down to the river. "But it's only a highway," Carl and I said incredulously, to each other, this "in" or "out" depending on what side of 9W.

Even with all that romantic stone barn, we missed our friends, our Parkway Village group. At least I did, terribly. I was now almost completely dependent on Carl for grown-up companionship and support. And I really had to do those articles now, to help pay our expenses. I must have gotten sharper with Carl about his deals, when we were so behind on our bills, or his not getting home for dinner. I seem to remember a sense of unspeakable horror, fear; I felt numb, until, one night, he hit me. And he cried afterward, that first time.

I had to drive again in Rockland County. I never really liked to drive. My mother made me so nervous teaching me, it's a wonder I ever got a license. After I bumped into our garage door in Peoria, driving our new car, I virtually stopped driving. When we lived in the city, I didn't need to. Carl drove. In Parkway Village, I used bus and subway. I mislaid my license, it lapsed. My geologist friend's husband offered to coach me through the new test I had to take to get my driver's license back again. He was mortified when three times I got notices that I didn't pass the test. (That's what happens to bright girls when they get the word it's not smart to be smart. Once I decided to be "dumb" about electric wiring, and let the football team do my lab experiment, I somehow became "dumb" for good about machinery. I never learned to run a washer and dryer, not only because I resisted the role and wrote articles so I could pay someone else to do the laundry or send it out but also because I was *scared* of such machinery. It took me the longest time to agree to buy a dishwasher. I'm probably the last living American writer to resist a word processor. Get on line, get on line, my men and women friends keep telling me, get with it. However, I'm positive I'd press a wrong key, and all my deathless prose would vanish.)

I found a wonderful woman to clean and watch over the kids when I was writing, except she couldn't speak English. Eva was Haitian, so I taught the kids a few words of French. My boys were so delicious now, so different from each other, becoming little persons themselves. I loved Jonathan's sensuousness. I can still remember the lovely warm feeling when he'd climb on my lap and cuddle. Danny was more standoffish. (I'd worry, was that a lasting scar from leaving him with that farm girl at that summer theater when I had to go back to work? But I can still remember his excitement when I'd pick him up at nursery school.)

I was frantically finishing an article for *McCall's*, or was it the *Ladies' Home Journal*, about Julie Harris, and how her natural childbirth had matured her art. It was one of those miracle article ideas I got that turned out to be golden. I'd read an item in *Time* magazine about Julie Harris. She had just had a baby by natural childbirth and claimed it gave her new warmth and depth in her acting. I longed to have natural childbirth myself, but it was impossible. Jonathan's head had also been too big for my pelvis, so I'd had a second Cesarean, and natural labor was not deemed possible after two Cesareans then. After a third Cesarean, they tied the tubes, even at a Catholic hospital. It was considered too dangerous to have another. I suppose it reassured me, reliving vicariously Julie Harris's natural childbirth. She was appearing then on Broadway in *The Member of the Wedding* and in Christopher Isherwood's *I Am a Camera* at the movies. I saw both in a single day, and then had three interviews with Julie, the kind of interviews that are pure gold, because we really dug each other. She could see how I empathized with her and, of course, she could see I was about to give birth myself. So she told me, as perhaps a dramatist might, in all the concrete, dramatic, colorful detail I needed, about her natural childbirth and how she felt about it, showed me pictures of her baby.

I hastily did another article during that pregnancy about a "poor little rich girl" former actress married to Huntington Hartford, heir to A&P. I did it for *Cosmopolitan*, just for the money, really. I figured with two articles' fees, I could take a hiatus from magazine assignments after I got home from the hospital, take care of the kids myself, and concentrate on breast-feeding the baby. (That second article taught me nothing except the arrogance of the very rich. I'd get there in the morning at the agreed-on time, she'd keep me waiting an hour while she bathed, dressed and had breakfast. Interviewing her after all that wait, I visibly got nauseous—the way one sometimes does in pregnancy—but she wouldn't even offer me a piece of toast. Finally, I took along my own crackers.)

In desperation, I called my mother, living in Chicago now with her third husband, and asked her if she'd come and stay with the kids while I was in the hospital. The last thing I needed was my mother around to make me feel inadequate again, as she always did, just when I was about to have *three children* (as, of course, she had). But I couldn't leave those little boys in that stone barn all day with someone they couldn't communicate with, and Carl was in New York.

My mother came, and somehow didn't appreciate the romantic glamour of the stone barn. Everything was so dusty, "dirty" (nose turned up), my lovely oiled dark wood barn floors. She seemed falsely sweet, artificial with my adorable little boys. Had she been that cold with me?

This time, I was conscious during the Cesarean. I had a spinal, and heard the doctor and nurse exclaim, "How sweet, what a sweetheart," and on May 23, 1956, I had a little girl at last, my Emily. I can still remember how unmistakably she looked like a girl, in the little white gown they swathed her in.

When we brought Emily home, things were very tense between my boys and their Granny and Eva, the Haitian housekeeper, was ready to quit. It seemed that Mother had hired an exterminator for a year (at our expense) because she'd actually seen two mice (well of course there were mice in that old barn—they didn't bother anyone). She kept making the kids wash—

which I never did, unnecessarily—punished them for things they said and did they never knew were wrong (because they weren't), made Eva peel the tomatoes for salad every night, and ordered a 25-pound prime rib roast beef for the neighbors who would come to meet her and admire the new baby. Well, we didn't know that many neighbors, we never cooked prime rib ourselves, and threw most of it out when she finally left, unable to tolerate another night in our old barn.

While I was still in the hospital (new mothers weren't kicked out of the hospital then the day after giving birth by Cesarean), I used the corridor pay phone to call my agent and she informed me the *Journal* had turned down the Julie Harris story. It was too graphic about natural childbirth, women readers wouldn't identify with all that serious stuff about Julie's art as an actress.

So I had to do another article right away. We were too behind in our bills for me to take a hiatus. And yet I was determined to breast-feed Emily. I remembered that the geologist mother at Jonathan's play group had told me about a recent discovery at Lamont Observatory, the carbon dating of cores they'd brought back from the floor of the Antarctic Sea indicated a warming of that glacial sea which portended another ice age coming. I could do a story about that, I thought, go up to Lamont mornings to talk to the scientists—I'd finally gotten my driver's license—and get back in time to breast-feed Emily. I wouldn't have to go into the city at all.

My agent thought I wasn't qualified to do such a serious scientific story (Marie was also Rachel Carson's agent), but I insisted I was. After all, I'd loved chemistry and physics, loved the whole adventure of scientific detection. And in all those years of labor reporting and freelance magazine writing, I had learned to master any field enough in twenty-four hours to understand and ask the right questions on the cutting edge. (That's why journalists— at least the serious ones—have made as much or more of a contribution to social theory in America as formal academic social scientists. They aren't hampered by the old assumptions built into the jargon. They can cut to the cutting edge.) Anyhow, over breakfast every morning, I'd pore over a geophysics textbook. I hadn't studied physics since high school, and had never studied geology at all, but I'd followed intently the new scientific break-

throughs in that era after World War II, the nuclear developments, genetics, molecular biology. And then I'd go up the hill
and interview Maurice Ewing and his colleagues. The piecing together of evidence of a coming ice age, from the carbon dating of
the ocean floor cores, was, as I titled the story, a "True Scientific
Detective Story." *Collier's* folded in 1958 just as I was finishing the
article, but it ended up as a cover story in *Harper's* and in *Reader's
Digest.* A few years later it was anthologized in *Gentlemen, Scholars and Scoundrels: A Treasury of the Best of Harper's from 1850,* one
of only two scientific articles (though I was still described as a
"housewife writer"), and has since been anthologized in other
books of science writing.

When George Brockway, head of the W. W. Norton publishing company, read the article, he asked me to come into the city to
see him. He wanted me to turn that article into a book. I refused.
The subject wasn't my field, the discoveries weren't mine. And
besides, with three little kids, how could I write a book? However,
I was losing my stomach for women's magazine articles. I was
getting tired of being told American women wouldn't "identify"
with any story, for instance, about the development of the hydrogen bomb, or nuclear testing in the Pacific, unless it could be done
in terms of concern for their husbands or their kids. Besides, those
dollar bills going up in flames to keep the furnace running in the
stone barn were making me too nervous to write. We needed a
house of our own that we could afford to keep warm.

The one we found on a little hill across the street from the
Hudson River, on River Road in Grandview, a mile below the
Tappan Zee Bridge, looked gloomy from the outside, that winter
day. It was a big old Victorian house with French doors opening
out onto a front porch the length of the house, overlooking the
river, with a boxwood maze in the front yard. An area of mostly
ivy and woods went behind the house and up the hill to old railroad tracks. It had a beautiful big living room, an octagonal dining room, four fireplaces, a graceful stairway, all covered with
coats and coats of hideous paint.

Carl recognized it just as I had—the way you know, at least I
always do, when a house is yours. Believe it or not, broke as we
were, we could buy that house on a GI-FHA mortgage for
$25,000, with $2,500 down (all that was left of my inheritance

from my father when my mother sold the store) and a mortgage of $2^1/_2$ percent, I believe.

It was a beautiful, beautiful house, beneath all that old paint, and I, unmechanical I, spent hour after hour with paint remover, until I got down to the original marble on the fireplaces and the lovely old wood on the stair banisters. Now Carl made me really angry, night after night, when he didn't get home for dinner. I believed in families having dinner together. I kind of enjoyed cooking, though the boys would grumble "gourmet" when I gave them anything much beyond hamburger or chicken. (They like to remember now that they only had TV dinners, but that came much later, in the city, when our marriage was truly breaking up.)

On weekends, we would go to auctions. Antique dealers would come out from the city to Tippy's Yonderhill Auction. Living right there, and not caring what period, as long as I liked it and could get it for less than $50, I got wonderful furniture, most of which I still have. I bid $35 for a signed, oversized Victorian love seat (the twin of one in the Museum of the City of New York, I later learned) and a little side chair to match it for $7.50. Someone told me they'd be worth six figures now.

Afternoons I would take Emily out in her stroller and canvass for Adlai Stevenson and our next-door neighbor John Dow, an idealistic, principled man who was running for president for the second time against Ike. And, of course, I got involved in education for our kids.

It became clear very early that there was something unusual about Daniel, that he was some incredible genius at mathematics. It worried me when his teacher punished him for doing his arithmetic problems in unconventional original ways at a much earlier age than when that happened to me. When the first sputnik was due to fly overhead, we woke him up in the middle of the night and went down into the boxwood maze to watch. It was a strange, marvelous, awesome moment. And I said to that serious little blond boy who now knows so much more than I do about what science can make happen, and thinks about his super-string theory in mathematical symbols I don't understand: "Maybe you'll go to the moon in one of those someday, Danny." And he was so matter-of-fact about it, he already took it for granted that he would.

I didn't believe in private schools, there wasn't a good one then in Rockland County anyhow, but he needed more real challenge in school. They skipped him, of course, but I didn't like that, I'd suffered too much myself when I'd skipped a grade. It occurred to me that, with sputnik raising everybody's interest in science and education, maybe we could organize a pool of the scientists up at Lamont, and artists and writers, anthropologists and architects and planners and professors living in our county across the river from Columbia University, to work with the kids on Saturdays, on real scientific experiments, or murals, or law cases. And I called my friend Milton Carrow and his Hickory Hill community gang in Tappan, New York, and some of the scientists in Lamont, and the artists and writers and architects I was getting to know around Grandview. I went to the board of the Rockland Foundation, which sponsored art shows and art classes by local artists, and got them to sponsor a discussion series on the new thinking demanded by the sputnik era. Everyone had been so afraid of new thinking since McCarthyism. I'll never forget, back in 1956, watching television with my kids, when Welch finally said to Joe McCarthy, "Sir, have you no shame?" But it took longer than that to get over the stultifying effects of McCarthyism on American thought and education.

Jim Fitch, brilliant soft-speaking architectural historian at Columbia, who chaired the Rockland Foundation at the time, took me personally to meet Vernon Eagle of the New World Foundation, who said he would give us a grant for my Intellectual Resources Pool if we got a more indigenous community group to co-sponsor it. He said I would have to run it, for which I'd actually get paid some money from the grant. And so we got the PTA to co-sponsor it and renamed it the Community Resource Pool. Even those who opposed school budgets and sex education in the schools wanted their kids to get into college.

I continued to write more and more magazine articles, though it was hard in those days for a woman to take herself seriously, as a writer, an artist, any kind of thinker. For instance, after a few years freelancing, when I was selling four or five articles a year, my agent got me to join the Society of Magazine Writers. I went into the city every month to meetings, to get the feeling of being a real, honest-to-goodness magazine writer. I loved the shoptalk and editorial gossip. But I felt sort of invisible at those meetings. Most of those writers then were men, though freelancing was a great solution for women, then and now, combining young children and writing, as I was doing. I asked a new friend, Jean Libman Block, who later became a top editor at *Good Housekeeping*, why there were so few women. (I don't think I added, out loud, "and why don't they ever call on us at meetings?") "Well, it's hard, you know, for a woman," she said. (A lot of the leaders of that society became my great friends—Bob Heilbronner, Maurice Zolotow, Bernie Asbell, Alvin Toffler—and helped me a great deal, once I did become visible to them, but that was later.)

But then, women were more or less invisible to themselves. I remember the census taker coming to our house in Grandview one morning while I was having coffee with an older woman neighbor, an eccentric, determined, unpublished writer whom I'd met on the Rockland Foundation board. After the census taker left, my neighbor asked me: "Why did you identify your profession as 'housewife'? You are a writer, a professional, a published writer. You should take yourself more seriously." But it was hard.

Like many writers, I used to suffer the tortures of the damned every time I handed in an article, day after day waiting for the phone call, the letter from the editor, would he like it, would it get printed, even though it was almost always accepted, usually with enthusiasm. I conscientiously studied what the women's magazines were printing before I went in to pitch my own ideas to an editor, just as some of my men friends did who had also moved from newspaper to freelance magazine writing. I got the picture that to write about serious political concerns, or serious women in any field, wouldn't play. But I was somehow losing my zest for those conventional women's magazine articles and I couldn't make myself consciously write to fit a formula.

I remember one very offbeat article I wrote for *Coronet* magazine, of all places, about an excellent psychiatric facility, Hillside Hospital. The guy doing pro bono public relations for that hospital, a friend of Carl's, thought I might be interested because of my psychology background. I went out there, and found two patients with the most marvelous love story. They had both been seriously depressed, I think one of them didn't even talk, and, as they got better, they began to really talk to each other, and ultimately both recovered, and now lived together, in the real world again.

My interviews with them, once again, were "gold," as I call it. After writing it all in the usual magazine format, which somehow dulled the magic, I got inspired to write it as a free association narrative, first her talking, then him, the writing technique I had learned from Jim Skardon, then editor at *Coronet*. When I sent the article to my agent, however, she was shocked. "Who do you think you're writing this for, *The Yale Review?*" Marie said.

I told her to send it to Jim at *Coronet* anyhow, and if he turned it down, she could try *The Yale Review*. (Why didn't I ever try writing for one of the more highbrow magazines? Because I was in no position to write for $300 when I could get $3,000, that's why. My agent always said—and rightly so: "It takes as much time and energy to write for little magazines as for big ones; it makes more sense to go for the money.") But *this* article was so emotional somehow, and hit some deeper chord, so that I suffered even worse tortures than usual, anticipating its rejection. I had really exposed myself this time, risked—risked what? The editors of *Coronet* loved that offbeat article and made it a cover story, "With Love We Live." Later it was even sold to the movies, though it seemed they just wanted the title; then it was optioned for a television series.

Television was really taking off at that time, and my friend Ted Apstein, one of the Golden Dozen along with Robert Alan Arthur in the days of Hallmark's "Great Stories" adaptations, got me invited to join a professional workshop which he and other television writers like Arthur Penn were running to teach writers from other fields how to write plays for television. I was—and still am—very fond of Ted and his wife, Pat, who had taken over our lease on the stone barn when we bought our house in Grandview, and elated that someone was taking me seriously as a writer. But it turned out that the workshop was going to meet on Tuesday nights, and Tuesday afternoons were when Danny's Cub Scout troop, of which I was now assistant den mother, had its meetings. I couldn't run the meetings and get a bus for the city in time to make the workshop. Or, at least, I couldn't every other week, since the chief den mother and I alternated leading the Cub Scout troop.

Now, don't get me wrong. Nobody pressed me into being a den mother. I'd loved being a Girl Scout myself, especially the hikes, and the Cub Scouts troop was a place where Danny might make more friends, though the rote lessons, plans and games for the meetings, which came down from National Headquarters, seemed boring and dumb. When it was my turn to lead, I took the boys for hikes on High Tor and the other magical historical little mountains bounding Rockland County. But the first two times I skipped Cub Scout meetings to take the bus into the television writers' workshop, I got an asthma attack. And not going every week, I didn't really feel part of the program. I mapped out a script, okay, but I never really wrote it. It was more important to be a good mother and stick with the Cub Scout meetings, wasn't it? And so, I finally called Ted and said I couldn't go on with the workshop. He sounded kind of annoyed, and really sorry that I was turning down this opportunity. Some months later, Danny said to me, "Mommy, Cub Scouts is so boring, do we really have to do it next year?" He'd been humoring me, pretending to enjoy it! But it was too late by then. Ted and some of the others had moved to Hollywood.

I almost quit writing altogether, but not because of Ted. I was downstairs talking on the telephone, not to an editor or agent actually, but to some local school board politician, and Emily started screaming upstairs. I got off the phone to investigate. She had climbed into the bathroom sink and turned scalding hot water on. I got her to the Nyack hospital, where they told me she had second-degree burns on her foot. I sat by her bed, overseeing the IV apparatus—that hospital didn't have a very good reputation—feeling so scared and *guilty*. When I got home, I told my agent I wouldn't take any more magazine assignments; I needed to devote myself more completely to my children.

And that wouldn't have been a terrible sacrifice, if it had been really necessary. But the fact was, the boys were both in school now most of the day, and with them gone, it was too lonesome for Emily just to hang around with me. I tried a play group with another mother down the street, but after the Parkway Village cooperative international nursery school (whose teachers were now running Bank Street College), I knew that a good nursery school was what Emily needed, whether or not I wrote articles. And, it turned out, there was a good one several miles down the road. I liked doing things with my kids. But it wasn't necessary twenty-four hours a day. And besides, when I wasn't writing articles, I simply spent more time on school board politics, community, the Resources Pool, volunteer stuff, though I really didn't like most of the organized volunteer stuff women did then, bake sales and auctions, addressing envelopes for the Women's Division of the Democratic Party, teas and those rote programs sent out from National Headquarters to the local League of Women Voters. To be blunt, they assumed American housewives were pretty dumb, unable to think for themselves. My heart wasn't really into a lot of the volunteer work I was doing because I felt I should be making money. And I was way behind in my writing income at the end of the fifties, because I'd wasted a year on an article which, for the first time in my life, *kept* getting rejected.

My book grew out of a Smith alumnae questionnaire I was asked to do for our fifteenth college reunion in 1957. I felt so guilty, somehow, that I hadn't done the big things everybody expected me to do with my brilliant Smith education—giving up the fellowship in psychology, getting fired from my newspaper job for being pregnant, writing too many mundane, inane women's magazine articles. It wasn't just a shame at not living up to others' expectations of me. It was also, I now believe, an existential guilt, which I have to this day when I'm just coasting and not using my powers to meet serious new challenges.

The reason I agreed to do the questionnaire was because of a widely debated book that had just come out, *Modern Women: The Lost Sex,* by Marynia Farnham and Ferdinand Lundberg, two Freudian psychoanalysts who said something was terribly wrong with American women—they'd had too much education and it was keeping them from "adjusting to their role as women." A noise of diffuse angst, discontent, anger was coming out of those ideal suburbs where between the hours of 9:00 a.m. and 5:00 p.m. nothing stirred over three feet tall. If American suburban housewives weren't "happy" taking care of their children and running appliances other women only dreamed of, their education must be the problem.

Now, that made me really angry. I bought all that Freudian

stuff about the role of women, of course. After all, hadn't I given up my big psychology fellowship, my newspaper "career" to be fulfilled as a wife and mother myself? But the concept that educating women had negative consequences for themselves and their families was going too far. I *valued* my Smith education, valued it a lot, even though I felt guilty about not using it very well. I knew my Smith classmates were doing great things in their own communities, and having a great time, as I was, fixing up their houses, getting their kids educated, though most of their husbands' careers were probably grander than my husband's. Surely, education made us *better* wives and mothers, as Adlai Stevenson had said in his commencement address to the Smith class of 1955:

> Women, especially educated women, have a unique opportunity to influence us, man and boy . . . [yet] once immersed in the very pressing and particular problems of domesticity, many women feel frustrated and far apart from the great issues and stirring debate for which their education has given them understanding and relish. Once they wrote poetry. Now it's the laundry list. Once they discussed art and philosophy until late into the night. Now they are so tired they fall asleep as soon as the dishes are finished. . . . They had hoped to play their part in the crises of the age. But what they do is wash the dishes.
>
> The point is that whether we talk of Africa, Islam or Asia, women never had it so good as you. In short, far from the vocation of marriage and motherhood leading you away from the great issues of our day, it brings you back to their very center and places upon you an infinitely deeper and more intimate responsibility than that borne by the majority of those who hit the headlines and make the news and live in such a turmoil of great issues that they end by being totally unable to distinguish what issues are really great.
>
> [Woman's political mission] to inspire in her home a vision of the meaning of life and freedom . . . to help her husband find values that will give purpose to his specialized daily chores . . . to teach her children the uniqueness of each individual human being. . . . This assignment for you, as wives and mothers, you can do in the living room with a baby in your lap or in the kitchen with a can opener in your hand. . . . I think there is much you can do about our crises in the humble role of housewife. I would wish you no better vocation than that.

I decided to use that Smith questionnaire to write a major magazine article refuting *Modern Women: The Lost Sex* and proving education didn't make American women frustrated in their role as women. Why couldn't we appreciate our true political part in the "crises of the age" as wife and mother? I pitched the idea to *McCall's*, and they wanted it.

I spent an inordinate amount of time on that questionnaire. I asked two friends of mine, Mario Ingersoll Howell and Anne Mather Montero, to work on it with me. So Mario and Anne came out to Rockland County once and we met several times in the city and dreamed up open-ended questions as well as the usual ones. I realized later that we were putting into words questions that we had not asked ourselves out loud before. We included the following in our list of questions:

About "Your Marriage" we asked: Is your marriage truly satisfying? How does it compare with your expectation of marriage? How does it change with the years? To what extent do you talk to your husband about your deepest feelings? Do you believe the same things are important? How do you make major decisions (together, or which his, which yours)?

About "Your Sex Life": Is your sex life less important than it used to be? Getting better and better? At 35–37, do you feel almost over and done with sexuality? Or just beginning to feel the satisfaction of being a woman?

About "Your Children": Did you plan your children's births? Did you enjoy pregnancy? Were you depressed after birth? Did you fear childbirth? Exult in it? Take it in your stride? Did you breast-feed? How long? Did you try? Do, or did, you have problems with: Eating? Toilet training? Discipline? Do you have fun with your children? As a mother, do you usually feel: Harassed? Martyred? Contented? Do you try hard to be a good mother? Or just let it work itself out? Do you feel you are a good mother? Or guilty that you aren't?

About "Your Home": Does your home reflect your taste, your husband's, or what? How much time do you spend on housework? What major household appliances do you have? Do you put the milk bottle on the table? Use paper napkins? Are you a good cook? What part of housekeeping do you enjoy? Detest? Does your husband complain about your housekeeping? What does he do around the house? How is your home different from your home as a child?

About "Your Finances": Who manages the family finances, you or your husband? Do you worry about money? Live above your income?

About "The Other Part of Your Life": Did you have career ambitions? What? Are you pursuing it actively? Have you given it up? Or postponed until kids are older? If you work, is it mainly for the money? Or because you want to? Or both? What does it cost you to work? What is your arrangement for children and house while you work? Do you feel guilty about leaving the children? If you don't work, is it: From preference? Not qualified? Would feel guilty about kids? . . . If your main occupation is homemaker, do you find it totally fulfilling? Are you frustrated? Have you managed to find a satisfying interest outside your home? Do you find volunteer work as satisfying as professional? Please describe any "professional" volunteer work—over and above routine or occasional volunteer tasks.

We asked about "Your Intellectual Life": How many books have you read in the last year? Do you read a newspaper every day? What television programs do you watch regularly?

About "Your Political Life": Do you vote: Regularly? Occasionally? Straight Republican? . . . Democrat? Or cross party lines? Do you take any active part in party politics? Are your politics the same as your husband's? Have you ever taken a public stand or done anything about a controversial issue or unpopular cause in your community?

We asked about "Your Religious Life": Which church? How often do you go? Do you believe in a personal God? Or in religion as a system of human values and social ethics? Or does religion have no place in your life at all?

We asked about "Your Social Life": How do you spend most of your evenings during the week? Weekends? How much time do you spend alone? Enough? Do you feel your life is too fragmented? Do you feel that in most social situations you or others "never really say anything" except empty chitchat? Or is there real communication? Are there things you do because everybody else where you live does them, that do not reflect your own individual values? What do you do—little or big—because you or your family want to, that is *not* exactly "the thing to do" in your community?

And, finally, we asked about "You, Personal": How has your appearance changed? Clothes less important to you? More? Have you had psychotherapy? Your husband, or children? Do you feel you need it? In what ways have you changed inside, as a person, since college? What difficulties have you found in working out your role as a woman? What are the chief satisfactions of your life today? The chief frustrations? What do you think of as the best time in your life? How do you visualize your life after your children are grown? Are you doing anything about that now? What? Do you hate getting older?

We sent out the questionnaires and received two hundred responses. When the results were tabulated, I realized they raised more questions than they answered. The ones who seemed to value their education the most, who seemed the most zestful and healthy about their lives, were the ones who didn't *exactly* conform to "the role of women" in the sense that it was then being defined—wife, mother, housewife, living through husbands, children, home and so on. The ones who really seemed to be doing only that were either depressed or outright frustrated. But the ones with many other interests and activities—like the kind I couldn't quite stop doing myself—seemed to be *enjoying* their children, their homes their marriages more. Maybe it wasn't education that was the problem, keeping American women from "adjusting to their role as women," but that narrow definition of "the role of women."

And, for sure, the noises then coming out from those idyllic suburbs belied the image of the happy, happy suburban housewife. The "woman problem," it was now being called. There were strange, undiagnosed diseases that sent those women to doctors, who somehow couldn't find a cause or cure for their "chronic fatigue syndromes."

When we went to the Smith reunion in June 1957 to report on our questionnaire, for the first time since we'd graduated I didn't feel uneasy with my former college classmates. They had expected such great things of me, looked up to me so, and here I was, "just a housewife" as almost all of them were now. But I was onto something, something I already sensed might be important.

That feeling was underscored when Eli Chinoy, professor of sociology at Smith, got in touch with me before the reunion and asked to see the questionnaire and its results. He also thought it might be important. We became great friends. He had done pioneering studies of auto workers on assembly lines in Detroit. It turned out he was married to Mike Krich's sister, Helen, who was a professor in the theater department at Smith—Mike, the one who looked like Humphrey Bogart, with whom I was so in love in my labor press days, when we all shared a house on Fire Island one summer.

The night after we presented our questionnaire results, to the great interest of the Smith class of '42, in our late thirties now, almost all of us married, mothers, housewives—and serious community leaders—and a few of us, despite everything, doing professional work, we got back late from drinks at Wiggins Tavern and found Hubbard House, where we were staying, locked. Did Smith still have a curfew? A few graduating seniors were also locked out and joined us, waiting for the janitor to come to the rescue. I started talking to those lovely young graduates. "What are the courses you get excited about now?" I asked them, remembering how in the heady intellectual excitement of my days at Smith, we would linger outside Hans Kohn's history class, or Otto Kraushaar's philosophy class, or Kutschnig's on government, arguing about communism, fascism, democracy, war and peace, capitalism and workers' exploitation, and the future. What were students arguing about in 1957? And those young women, in their white dresses and black robes—who had walked with their red roses through the ivy chain as we had not, in the foregone Ivy Day of World War II—looked at us as if we were aliens from another planet.

"We don't get excited about things like that," one explained. "I'm going to get married right after graduation. I spend every weekend with my fiancé. What I'm interested in is where we're going to live and his career. I want to have four children, and live somewhere where I can spend a lot of time ice-skating with them." Try as we might, we, who were reveling in being together again, in the college where we had acquired our taste for a life of the mind and a passionate commitment to politics, a sense of personal responsibility for our society, for making it better, and had gotten an authentic taste of what that might be like, running the student government, the college paper—try as we might, we couldn't get these fifties seniors to admit they had become interested in *anything*, at that great college, except their future husbands and children and suburban homes.

I sensed something strange going on here, juxtaposing these young ones' carefully *limited* dreams with the results of my own class's questionnaire. I didn't think Smith education could have deteriorated that much; a lot of the faculty that had inspired me was still there. And Eli and Helen and their friend Peter Rose were obviously superbly qualified in their own fields, inspiring teachers. It was as if something was making these girls defensive, inoculating them against the larger interests, dreams and passions really good higher education can lead to. Did lead to, with me and my classmates, even if we felt we weren't doing justice to it, living up to it, in our current suburban life. It was as if these young women weren't going to let themselves have those larger passions and trained abilities that might indeed be frustrated by suburban housewife life.

And so I went home and wrote my article for McCall's—"Are Women Wasting Their Time in College?"—suggesting maybe it wasn't higher education making American women frustrated in their role as women, but the current definition of the role of women. *McCall's* turned it down. (I learned later that the male editor of *McCall's* had been "shocked" at that article, though the women subeditors had tried to get it in. I'd never had that experience before.) Then the *Ladies' Home Journal* rewrote it to say the opposite of what I'd found, and I took the article back. I wouldn't let them mess with my findings that way. I'd never done that before either. And then Bob Stein at *Redbook* wrote my agent: "Betty has always done good work for us before. But she must be going off her rocker. Only the most neurotic housewife will identify with this."

Each time my article got turned down, I'd do more interviews. I interviewed doctors and counselors and did group interviews among my own suburban neighbors in Rockland County, in Westchester. And increasingly, I knew it wasn't just overeducated Smith graduates I was writing about.

It was on an April morning in 1959 that I listened to a mother of four, having coffee with four other mothers in a suburban development fifteen miles from New York, say in a tone of quiet desperation " 'the problem.' " And suddenly I sensed that they all seemed to share the same problem. "I'm Jim's wife, and Janey's mother, a putter on of diapers and snowsuits, a server of meals, a Little League chauffeur. But who am I, as a person myself? It's like the world is going on without me." And I identified what I later called "the problem that has no name."

Women were being blamed for all kinds of "problems" then—their children's bedwetting, their husbands' ulcers, not cleaning the kitchen sink white enough, not pressing their husbands' shirts smooth enough, their own lack of orgasm. But the "problem" they kept bringing up and others always recognized had nothing to do with children, marriage, home, sex. And there was no name for it, in all the words being written by the experts, telling women how to catch a man and keep him, how to breastfeed children and handle their toilet training, how to cope with sibling rivalry and adolescent rebellion; how to buy a dishwasher, bake bread, cook gourmet snails, and build a swimming pool, how to dress, look, and act more feminine and make marriage more exciting. Truly feminine women did not want careers, graduate degrees, political rights. Educated, middle-class women were being taught to pity the neurotic, unfeminine, unhappy women who wanted to be poets or physicists or presidents.

"If a woman had a problem in the 1950s and 1960s, she knew that something must be wrong with her marriage, or with herself," I had written in the magazine article. "What kind of a woman was she if she did not feel mysterious fulfillment waxing the kitchen floor? She was so ashamed to admit her dissatisfaction that she never knew how many women shared it."

On a bus, taking my kids into the city to go to the dentist, I opened a letter from Marie Rodell, about yet another editor turning down my article, and I knew that editor was wrong. All those editors were wrong. I'd wasted nearly a whole year on this article. But I knew now I was really onto something. I also realized, suddenly, why all the editors had turned it down, why it never would get printed in one of those big women's magazines. It wouldn't, because what I was finding out, from answers to the questionnaire—from new interviews with my own suburban neighbors and other real suburban housewives—and what I'd started to write in my article somehow threatened the firmament they stood on, the very world the magazines were defining for women, the whole amorphous, vague, invisible miasma around "the role of women," "feminine fulfillment" as it was then defined by men and psychological followers of Freud, and taken for granted by everyone as true. Maybe it wasn't as true as it seemed. I hadn't yet called it "the feminine mystique," but, taking my kids to the dentist that day, I stopped at a pay phone and called my agent and told her not to send that article to any more magazines. I was going to write it as a book.

FIVE

The Mystery of My Writing The Feminine Mystique

I never set out to write a book to change women's lives, to change history. With three little kids and that big Victorian house, still writing "housewife" on the census blank, each magazine article a traumatic chore, I wonder now that I had the nerve to write a book, then, at all. I'd turned down even the suggestion of one before. And that would have been a pretty safe, objective book about someone else's work, scientists' work. The book I actually wrote, though objective in its technique and search for evidence, came from my personal truth, my personal, objective-subjective participant-observation of my own and others' experience, and from my repudiation of so-called accepted truth, social scientists' truth, psychiatric truth, when it didn't ring true to my own observations, my own following of clues to a new, larger truth about women.

When people later said, you must have had a hard time getting a publisher, they were wrong. Serendipity was the magic sesame, every step of the way. My agent said, "Go see George Brockway at Norton. He wanted you to write that book about the coming ice age." For some mysterious reason, George Brockway listened very intently, didn't seem at all incredulous, while I told him about the Smith questionnaire and my later interviews of psychologists, mental health counselors and other women—and how the women who were living most completely within the confines of what I would soon come to call "the feminine mystique" seemed in many ways worse off than the frustrated, rebellious ones. He later told me that his wife, a brilliant Bryn Mawr graduate, had just given birth to their thirteenth child. He *understood* what I was talking about. (My book hit so close to home, to *his* personal truth, it seemed to me, he had a hard time really pushing the book after it came out. A few years later, though, his wife went back to school and got her Ph.D.) In any event, he gave me a $3,000 advance. I figured writing the book would take me a year. It took me five.

Before that questionnaire, I had virtually decided to stop my magazine writing altogether. I was going to be a housewife, yes, a suburban housewife, period. I'd stopped going into the city to use one of the extra desks in Carl's office; he'd moved to a more impressive building on Fifth Avenue, and it didn't really have room for an itinerant journalist. Anyhow, I'd stopped looking for magazine assignments. But this was serious, a book. Where, how, was I going to do it? It just didn't seem possible to write at home, with the kids underfoot, even if I hired a housekeeper again.

But, serendipity again. At the very moment of my need I read in the *Times* that the New York Public Library was opening a new room, the Frederick Lewis Allen Room, for writers who were working on worthy books. I immediately applied. Emily was now in nursery school. So, three or four days a week, I'd take the bus to the city in the morning right after the children left for school, and get back in time to get supper. At the Allen Room I had a carrel, I could order books from the Reading Room or anywhere in the library and they'd be delivered to my carrel, and no telephone. There's something about a place like that, with other writers working, that is really great for getting writing done. Some day before I die, I'd like to try Yaddo or MacDowell, but I never have, because, first, kids, and then lecture commitments, or so many books and mounds of paper research notes to ship, I didn't even try.

The other writers in the Allen Room then were mostly men— James Flexner, Tom Flanagan, Sid Offit, Charlie Flood. We'd have lunch together in the cafeteria in the library basement. They were writing biographies, novels, a children's book about baseball, but I soon gave up trying to tell them what I was writing about. They thought it was a big joke, a book about women. They kidded me about it, ceaselessly. I don't like talking about what I'm writing anyhow, it makes me nervous, takes the edge off, somehow. But I didn't enjoy their jokes. Sometimes I'd pretend to be so busy that I didn't notice it was lunchtime, and let them go without me.

Two things I did right away, once I knew I was going to do the book. I arranged to stay for four or five days at Smith, living in one of the houses, getting to know some of the undergraduates, to test my hunch about their *resisting* the kind of intellectual commitment and excitement I had received at college. And when I had confirmed that hunch, I spent a few days at Yale to be sure what I was seeing was really about women and not just college life in general. Tom Mendenhall, master of a college at Yale, had just been appointed the next president of Smith. He was happy to host me and was intrigued by my questions. In fact, at lunch at Yale, trying to explain to Tom Mendenhall what I was investigating, I used for the first time the phrase "the feminine mystique" to describe that miasma of traditional and sophisticated Freudian assumptions about "femininity" that was preventing the women he was about to shepherd from intellectual commitment. And when I heard him feed back that phrase, "Then, becoming an astronaut, for instance, or a physicist, would defy the feminine mystique?" I said, "Yes, that's it, and remember you heard that concept from me." I didn't see it yet as the title of my book, too highfalutin' intellectual. But I began to write to that concept: the mystique of feminine fulfillment.

I was also interviewing groups of suburban women. Nothing systematic about it, just wanted to be sure I had enough geographic and ethnic diversity. I was, admittedly, investigating a middle-class phenomenon, dealing with educated women in the suburbs, and in those days, such women were assumed to be white. Through various contacts, I interviewed women in New Jersey, Westchester, as well as Rockland County, around Boston and Chicago; I couldn't afford to go to California. It wasn't a scientific standardized sample. But large enough, diverse enough, to make sure I really was dealing with a widespread phenomenon. Something happened, then, to answer this concern more definitively than any sampling I could have done. My old editor, Jim Skardon, now working for *Good Housekeeping,* called me: "I hear you've been doing some deep interviews of suburban housewives. How about doing an article for a special issue we're going to do about the state of American women today?" But I was doing those interviews for my book, and I was nowhere near finished, I told him. However, I'd already spent more than a year, and most of my $3,000 advance had already been spent in wages for the housekeeper. They didn't want my *book* for the magazine, just what I was learning from those interviews with the women.

So, using my first interviews, I wrote an article in 1960 about "the problem that has no name." To my mortification and puzzlement, *Good Housekeeping* didn't use it in its special issue. I was paid, fine, but I was told my article was "too strong," that it would negate the rest of the issue, that it would be used later, separately. I didn't believe them. Maybe it wasn't any good, after all, though I was getting more and more sure about it, the more interviews I did, the more I started putting it down on paper. That special *Good Housekeeping* issue on women was yet another celebration of the happy fifties suburban housewife. But when, some months later, the magazine ran as a cover story my "Problem That Has No Name," the letters they got, from women all over the country, and not always college graduates either, confirmed all my hunches. I was allowed to keep those letters, and they were great supplements to my own interviews.

Another crucial piece came to me from the magazine world I'd served my apprenticeship in, via one of the other nursery school mothers. Peggy had been in one of the first group interviews I'd done of my own suburban neighbors. She also was making desultory stabs at freelancing for women's magazines, but short stories, not articles like mine. She told me that in going over back issues, to find out what they wanted, she'd noticed a sharp change in the heroines from the thirties and forties to the fifties.

I spent the next few weeks in the Periodicals Room at the New York Public Library, going over back issues. I soon saw that demarcation she'd noticed. So I did a study of the heroines—taking one month in 1939, 1949 and 1959, I believe, in the four major women's magazines (*Ladies' Home Journal, McCall's, Good Housekeeping, Woman's Home Companion*)—and also, while I was at it, surveying a general sense of change, if any, in format and article content. And the result was startling. The prevailing image of women in the thirties was that of the adventurous, attractive, self-reliant woman marching toward a vision or personal goal—becoming a pilot, a geologist, an advertising copywriter—and meeting her supportive hero along the way. The heroines were almost never housewives. By 1949, the image was blurring. Only one out of three heroines in the women's magazines was a career woman and inevitably she was shown in the act of giving it all up for the more "fulfilling" career as housewife. By 1959, the career woman had vanished altogether. I went through issue after issue of the remaining three women's magazines, *Woman's Home Companion* having folded, and didn't find a single heroine who had a career, a commitment to any work, art, profession or mission in the world, other than "Occupation: housewife."

Well, you really do use everything. If I hadn't been so immersed in the women's magazine world after I got fired from my newspaper job, if I hadn't been so aware from the inside of what you *couldn't* write about for women in the 1950s, what American women weren't supposed to be able to "identify" with, if my own article in defense of higher education hadn't been turned down so summarily by those magazines, I wouldn't have become so sharply aware of "the feminine mystique" in the first place. And now, tracing its development through those back issues, like carbon-dating a core of mud from the ocean bottom, like analyzing the inkblots of a Rorschach test, the analysis of the change in the mass media image of women led me to further questions about that image's relationship to reality, cause and effect. (And ever since, in times of change, dealing with questions that aren't being asked, that need to be asked, I want to see how the accepted media image fits or doesn't fit the reality of women's lives.) Then I went back to interview some of the editors I used to write for, and got a spelling out of the feminine mystique.

I was nonplused, at first, when they showed me market research data that they said *proved* that American women were only interested in their husbands, children, homes, clothes, sex, and could relate to any other question only if it could be tied to husbands, children, home. But, of course, as my new research showed, if women were forever being warned against other interests, what else could that market research show? Especially if such interests and a variety of role models no longer appeared in those magazines read by millions of housewives.

To get behind the facade of the feminine mystique, to dig out its origins and the base of its appeal, I had to go beyond that women's magazine world. I had to dig deep into my intellectual roots in psychology, and into the misery, the mystery, of my own flight from it.

My training as a psychologist and social scientist and my experience as a journalist enabled me to follow these clues, and gave me the confidence to pierce through the conceptual armor that kept the feminine mystique in place, even when it denied many women's personal reality. Later, a deconstructing male historian would try to dismiss my credibility in writing *The Feminine Mystique* by claiming it was all a communist plot, starting with my Smith student days and my labor immersion, and insisting that I never was a real suburban housewife. But that isn't true. My experience with Communist dogma had given me a healthy distrust of all dogma that belied real experience, while Smith had given me the conceptual ability to take on the feminine mystique, and my training by the psychological giants of the day plus my training as a hands-on reporter gave me a third ear to hear pieces of new truth behind denials and defenses and rigidity. That ability to follow leads, clues from many different fields, was invaluable once I truly committed myself to solve this mystery. As I would write in the preface to my book:

> Gradually, without seeing it clearly for quite a while, I came to realize that something is very wrong with the way American women are trying to live their lives today. I sensed it first as a question mark in my own life, as a wife and mother of three small children, half-guiltily, and therefore halfheartedly, almost in spite of myself, using my abilities and education in work that took me away from home. It was this personal question mark that led me, in 1957, to spend a great deal of time doing an intensive questionnaire of my college classmates, fifteen years after our graduation from Smith. . . . The problems and satisfactions of their lives, and mine, and the way our education had contributed to them, simply did not fit the image of the modern American woman as she was written about in women's magazines, studied and analyzed in classrooms and clin-

ics, praised and damned in a ceaseless barrage of words ever since the end of World War II. There was a strange discrepancy between the reality of our lives as women and the image to which we were trying to conform, the image that I came to call the feminine mystique. . . .

And so I began to hunt down the origins of the feminine mystique, and its effect on women who lived by it, or grew up under it. My methods were simply those of a reporter on the trail of a story, except I soon discovered this was no ordinary story. For the startling pattern that began to emerge as one clue led me to another in far-flung fields of modern thought and life, defied not only the conventional image but basic psychological assumptions about women.

I wrote the first two chapters, "The Problem That Has No Name" and "The Happy Housewife Heroine," in the Allen Room, and sent them to George Brockway, who was quite positive about them. But by now I had so many papers, books and notes for the rest of the book, I didn't like leaving them in the Allen Room. All the kids were in school. I could work at home during those hours and then be with them after school and save the two hours on the bus every day. I'd already outstayed my term at the Allen Room, anyhow. The first curator, a wonderful old guy named Camm, had given me a second term without my asking when he saw me so concentrated I didn't even go out for lunch some days. Evidently, he didn't think it was a joke that I was writing a book about women.

Up to now, I'd written on my old typewriter, which I'd taken to the library. Once I'd finished "The Happy Housewife Heroine," I had to confront the question of what gave the feminine mystique its *power*, why did American women like myself go home again—even though they had the education, the opportunities, rights? I had to move to a deeper level, into my own being, *my* personal truth. I still remember that night clearly. I'd had dinner with the kids and put them to bed, Carl wasn't coming home until late again. And I sat down on the couch in the living room in Grandview with a legal-size pad. I'd been going through books on the psychology of women—Helene Deutsch's two volumes— but it was all feminine mystique stuff. I'd been thinking about some of the new psychological concepts that intrigued me—Erik

Erikson's "identity crisis," Abe Maslow's "self-realization." However, they seemed to have been applied only to men.

And then I thought about my turning down that fellowship which would have led to a Ph.D. in psychology at Berkeley. I remembered my reluctant, shrinking reaction when I won that first fellowship my senior year at Smith. I remembered my panic, as college was ending, that blank I felt, *not knowing at all who or what I wanted to be,* only that I didn't want to be a woman like my mother. On the living-room couch, I started writing the third chapter of *The Feminine Mystique,* "The Crisis in Woman's Identity," applying to myself, and the women I'd been interviewing, basic concepts about the self, and identity crisis, as they had not been applied to women. And I got to such a different level of thinking, writing by hand on the yellow legal pad that night—the crucial chapter in *The Feminine Mystique,* where I spelled out how it had happened to me personally, a truth that other women could identify with—that I literally have not touched a typewriter since, let alone a word processor.

I went up to Boston for a few days to interview Andras Angyal, a psychiatrist who'd written a book that intrigued me about character development over a lifetime, outward and inner forces, that also had not been applied to women. I also had an appointment with Abe Maslow, whose human potential psychology was beginning to be widely read and discussed but, again, not applied to women.

I had an hour to kill between the two appointments and went into the Ritz Hotel, at around four in the afternoon, to have a drink. I went into the bar and ordered a whisky sour. The bartender said, "I'm sorry, madam, we can't serve you here." "But you're open," I said, noticing a man or two at the bar or a table. "We do not serve women at the Ritz bar," he said. And then, noticing, I suppose, that I was a "nice" woman, not a hooker: "If you will go into the Ladies' Lounge and make yourself comfortable there, I will bring your drink in to you." And so I drank my whisky sour in the ladies' room—in a little adjoining lounge with a couch and a mirrored dressing table—before I went to talk to Abe Maslow about how his concepts about "self-realization," the *need* to develop one's human potential, might apply to women.

I think it most generous now, quite wonderful, that Maslow

had me come back the next day, that he spent hours with this unknown "housewife" writer, discussing the possibility that "self-
realization" for a woman might go beyond natural childbirth,
breast-feeding, and being a good wife to a successful professor or
doctor, a good mother to babies or teenagers. He waved away my
apologetic, even guilty admission that I'd turned down the fellowship and never had gotten my Ph.D. in psychology. "It's a
good thing," he said. "You'd have been too imprisoned by the
rubrics to write such a book." (When I sent him an advance copy
of my book, he called me in the middle of the night, in great excitement at my use of his concepts, and, after that, sent his women
graduate students to discuss their theses with me.)

But if you think some lightbulb went off in my mind—from
not being served a drink in the Ritz bar because I was a woman,
about *why* that need to develop one's human potential was not
being applied to women, about why women, even psychology
students like me, didn't apply those concepts to themselves—you
give me more revolutionary credit than I deserve. It was only
later that I would make that link.

Then, I was going to dismiss feminism in four paragraphs,
explaining why the first feminists had every reason to suffer from
penis envy, even want to be men, and why that whole century of
the battle for women's rights had been stopped in its tracks, because most women still wanted to be, had to be, wives and mothers. Burton Beals, my brilliant young editor at Norton, suggested
that I find out about those feminists, who they really were. So I
read Eleanor Flexner's *Century of Struggle.* I read biographies of
Susan B. Anthony, Margaret Fuller, the Grimké sisters, Elizabeth
Cady Stanton, Lucy Stone. And in the process I discovered the reality of the "passionate journey" those women, our foremothers,
started in the century past and the reality of their political passion.

That reality was more complex, and yet quite simple, than
the Freudian mystique which had dismissed them as neurotic
spinsters suffering from penis envy. But it says something about
the power of the feminine mystique, already blotting out the historical reality of women in the 1940s, that this particular *summa
cum laude* graduate of Smith had never *studied* the documents,
records, biographies of any of those feminist foremothers in all
my years at that best-of-all American women's colleges. I wasn't

a history major but was certainly interested enough in history—
especially revolutionary history—to apply and be admitted to a
graduate seminar studying the French Revolution in my junior
year. The college faculty then, in what I can only sense as reaction
against their own feminist origins, did not push and, in fact, may
not even have offered the study of women's unfinished revolution. As I wrote in *The Feminine Mystique:*

> It has been popular in recent years to laugh at feminism as one of
> history's dirty jokes, to pity, sniggering, those old-fashioned femi-
> nists who fought for women's rights to higher education, careers,
> the vote. They were neurotic victims of penis envy who wanted to
> be men, it is said now. In battling for women's freedom to partici-
> pate in the major work and decisions of society as the equal of men,
> they denied their very nature as women, which fulfills itself only
> through sexual passivity, acceptance of male domination, and nur-
> turing motherhood.
>
> But if I am not mistaken, it is this first journey which holds the
> clue to much that has happened to women since. It is one of the
> strange blind spots of contemporary psychology not to recognize
> the reality of the passion that moved those women to leave home in
> search of new identity, or, staying home, to yearn bitterly for some-
> thing more.

To understand what drove those early feminists, I drew on
all I'd learned about modern psychology, beyond Freud: the ego
psychologists, Erikson and the identity crisis, Maslow and the
drive to use one's human potential, to become fully human. I was
beyond apology. I saw those feminists as "pioneering on the front
edge of women's evolution."

> They had to prove that women were human. . . . They had to prove
> that a woman was not a passive, empty mirror, not a frilly, useless
> decoration, not a mindless animal, not a thing to be disposed of by
> others, incapable of a voice in her own existence, before they could
> even begin to fight for the rights women needed to become the
> human equals of men.
>
> Changeless woman, childish woman, a woman's place is in
> the home, they were told. But man was changing; his place was in
> the world and his world was widening. Woman was being left be-
> hind. . . . They also had the human need to grow. But the work that

fed life and moved it forward was no longer done at home, and women were not trained to understand and live in the world. Confined to the home, a child among her children, passive, no part of her existence under her own control, a woman could only exist by pleasing men. . . . She was, at that time, so completely defined as object by men, never herself as subject, "I," that she was not even expected to enjoy or participate in the act of sex. "He took his pleasure with her . . . he had his way with her," as the saying went. Is it so hard to understand that emancipation, the right to full humanity, was important enough to generations of women, still alive or only recently dead, that some fought with their fists, and went to jail and even died for it?

I discovered it was "a strangely unquestioned perversion of history" that the fire of the feminist movement came from "man-hating, sex-starved, embittered, castrating spinsters" who burned with such envy for the male organ that they wanted to take it away from all men, "demanding rights only because they lacked the power to love as women." I discovered that Mary Wollstonecraft, Angelina Grimké, Ernestine Rose, Margaret Fuller, Elizabeth Cady Stanton, Julia Ward Howe, Margaret Sanger not only loved, were loved, and married, but often seemed "as passionate in their relations with lover and beloved in an age when passion in women was as forbidden as intelligence, as they were in their battle for a woman's chance to grow to full human stature. But if they and those like Susan B. Anthony, whom fortune or bitter experience turned away from marriage, fought for a chance for woman to fulfill herself, not in relation to man, but as an individual, it was from a need as real and burning as the need for love."

I began to get beyond that dismissal of feminism as penis envy. Identifying with them, I realized quite simply that

The feminists had only one model, one image, one vision, of a full and free human being: man. For until very recently, only men (though not all men) had the freedom and the education necessary to realize their full abilities, to pioneer and create and discover, and map new trails for future generations. Only men had the vote: the freedom to shape the major decisions of society. Only men had the freedom to love, and enjoy love, and decide for themselves in the eyes of their God the problems of right and wrong. Did women want these freedoms because they wanted to be men? Or did they want them because they also were human?

I also figured out that it was hardly a coincidence that the struggle to free women began in America on the heels of the Revolutionary War and grew with the movement to free the slaves. I pointed out that the women who issued the first Declaration of Women's Rights at Seneca Falls, New York, in 1848 met each other when they were shut off behind a curtain in the balcony at an anti-slavery convention in London, that the cadences of the Seneca Falls Declaration came straight from the Declaration of Independence. I finally realized:

> What the sexual terminology hides is the fact that the feminist movement was a revolution. There were excesses, of course, as in any revolution, but the excesses of the feminists were in themselves a demonstration of the revolution's necessity. They stemmed from, and were a passionate repudiation of the degrading realities of woman's life [then], the helpless subservience behind the gentle decorum that made women objects of such thinly veiled contempt to men that they even felt contempt for themselves. . . .
> Of course they envied men. Some of the early feminists cut their hair short and wore bloomers, and tried to be like men. From the lives they saw their mothers lead, from their own experience, those passionate women had good reason to reject the conventional image of women. Some even rejected marriage and motherhood for themselves. But in turning their backs on the old feminine images, in fighting to free themselves and all women, some of them became a different kind of woman.

From the lives of Wollstonecraft, Fuller, Stone, I saw how such women became free finally to love and be loved, passionately, by men as fully equal human beings. They all rejected the early marriage common then and did not, in fact, marry until in their battle against slavery and for women's rights they had begun "to find an identity as women unknown to their mothers." Lucy Stone kept her own name, I realized, "in more than symbolic fear that to become a wife was to die as a person." I saw the miracle, finally, of that first century's struggle for women's rights.

> They held women's rights conventions every year after 1848, in small towns and large. . . . They could talk until doomsday about the rights they did not have. But how do women get legislators to let them keep their own earnings, or their own children after divorce, when they do not even have a vote? How can they finance or organize a campaign to get the vote when they have no money of their own nor even the right to own property?
>
> The very sensitivity to opinion which such complete dependence breeds in women made every step out of their genteel prison a painful one. Even when they tried to change conditions that were within their power to change, they met ridicule. . . . When they decided to petition for married women's rights to own property, half the time even the women slammed doors in their faces with the smug remark that they had husbands, they needed no laws to protect them. When Susan B. Anthony and her women captains collected 6,000 signatures in ten weeks, the New York State Assembly received them with roars of laughter. . . . The wonder is that the feminists were able to win anything at all—that they were not embittered shrews but increasingly zestful women who knew they were making history. . . .
>
> In their own lifetime, such women changed the feminine image that had justified woman's degradation. At a meeting while men jeered at trusting the vote to women so helpless that they had to be lifted over mud puddles and handed into carriages, a proud feminist named Sojourner Truth raised her black arm: "Look at my arm! I have ploughed and planted and gathered into barns . . . and ain't I a woman? I could work as much and eat as much as a man—when I could get it—and bear the lash as . . . I have borne thirteen children and seen most of 'em sold into slavery . . . and ain't I a woman?"

I also understood that the image of empty gentility was challenged by the growing thousands of women who worked in the red brick factories and mills, and even fought their terrible working conditions. But I no longer bought the Marxist illusion that the working class "were the only ones capable of revolution." Those women who after a twelve- to thirteen-hour day in the factory had to take care of their housework and children lacked the education, even literacy, to see through the prejudices which had justified women's degradation and to put their dissenting voice into words. Uncovering that first century of women's struggle in America, I saw no need to hide or apologize for the fact that most who led the battle for women's rights, early and late, "shared more than common intelligence fed by more than common education for their time." They were, mainly, middle class, educated, white women.

I drew on what I had learned covering the labor movement and meetings of the National Association of Manufacturers to figure out why business and industrial interests so bitterly fought women's final campaign for the vote in the twentieth century. This was the time of the battles for social reform of Jane Addams and Hull House, the rise of the union movement, the Triangle Shirtwaist fire and the strikes against intolerable working conditions for women and children in the factories.

> Behind the cries of "save femininity," "save the home," could now be glimpsed the influence of political machines, quailing at the very thought of what those reforming women would do if they got the vote. Women, after all, were trying to shut down the saloons. Brewers as well as other business interests, especially those that depended on underpaid labor of children and women, openly lobbied against the women's suffrage amendment in Washington.

I also detected the zest, the joy, the sense of excitement, the freedom finally that exhilarated those who fought and won the battle for the vote in 1920, before I was born. "They cast off the shadow of contempt and self-contempt that had degraded women for centuries."

I quoted the savory reminiscences of an English feminist, Ida A. R. Wylie, of her "years of wild and sometimes dangerous adventures."

> I worked and fought alongside vigorous, happy, well-adjusted women who laughed instead of tittering, who walked freely instead of teetering, who could outfast Gandhi and come out with a grin and a jest. [We] slept on hard floors . . . were often tired, hurt and frightened. But we were content as we had never been. We shared a joy of life that we had never known. Most of my fellow-fighters were wives and mothers. And strange things happened to their domestic lives. Husbands came home at night with a new ea-

gerness. . . . As for children, their attitudes changed rapidly from one of affectionate toleration for poor, darling mother to one of wide-eyed wonder. Released from the smother of mother love, for she was too busy to be more than casually concerned with them, they discovered that they liked her. She was a great sport. She had guts. . . . Those women who stood outside the fight . . . little women, hated the fighters with the venomous rage of envy.

Did women really go home again as a reaction to feminism? From my own generation's experience, I knew that to women born after 1920, feminism was dead history. "It ended as a vital movement in America with the winning of that final right: the vote," I concluded then. In the 1930s and 1940s, the sort of woman who fought for women's rights was still concerned for human rights and freedom—for Negroes, for oppressed workers, for victims of Franco in Spain and Hitler in Germany. But no one was much concerned with rights for women; they had all been won. And yet the man-eating myth painted by the enemies of women's vote prevailed. " 'Feminist,' like 'career woman,' had become a dirty word. The feminists had destroyed the old image of women, but they could not erase the hostility, the prejudice, the discrimination that still remained. Nor could they paint the new image of what women might become when they grew up under conditions that no longer made them inferior to men, dependent, passive. . . ."

I also realized that most girls growing up during the first two decades of the twentieth century when feminists were "eliminating the causes of that denigrating genteel nothingness, got their image of women from mothers still trapped in it. These mothers were probably the real models for the man-eating myth; the shadow of the contempt and self-contempt which could turn a gentle housewife into a domineering shrew also turned some of their daughters into angry copies of men." And, in fact, the first women in business, medicine and law were treated as freaks. I surmised that "insecure in their new freedom, some perhaps feared to be soft or gentle, love, have children, lest they lose their prized independence, lest they be trapped again as their mothers were."

But the daughters of my generation who had grown up with the rights the feminists had won "had come unknowing to the turning point in women's identity. They had truly outgrown the old image; they were finally free to be what they chose to be. But what chances were they offered? In one corner the fiery, man-eating feminist, the career woman—loveless, alone. In another corner, the gentle wife and mother, loved and protected by her husband, surrounded by her adoring children."

Now I had to figure out the intellectual and societal origins of the "mistaken choice," and also the reasons I and so many other women had fallen victim to it. I doubt if I'd have had the nerve to take on the Freudian basis of the feminine mystique if I hadn't had that rather unusual theoretical (read "useless," read "irrelevant" in the sixties) training by the great Gestalt psychologist Kurt Koffka, and by my other professors at Smith, by Kurt Lewin at Iowa and Erik Erikson at Berkeley. For one thing, I was in Freudian therapy myself, as a result of my asthma. It was becoming known at that time that asthma was at least in part psychosomatic.

I can't remember too much about that first bout of analysis in my early years in New York, except lying on a couch and talking endlessly about how I hated my mother and how she had killed my father. I was also very lonely in those years, quite miserable often with that hair shirt I'd put on, choosing to write for the labor movement instead of *Time* or *Life*—and finding it so much harder to write in *simple* words than the intellectual jargon I'd learned in college and graduate school. But I finally began to enjoy writing about *what I observed as a reporter,* and got rather good at it. It was then that I began to feel less lonely, quite happy, in those first years of my marriage and motherhood. With my asthma "cured," I stopped analysis. But when I was fired from the newspaper job, my asthma came back. In fact, it threatened to interrupt my pregnancy. When I tried to go back to my Freudian analyst, I discovered he had died.

A new one, William Menaker, had been trained by Anna Freud herself. But, I later learned, he had some revolutionary ideas about human evolution, which he saw working itself out in some symbiosis, or symbiosis-breaking, between an individual's ego and the culture. To my surprise, since I knew he was a Freudian, he kept questioning my "playing the role" of suburban housewife. When I had that dream about John Hersey, who'd gone on from magazine writing to write such classics as *Hi-*

roshima, he didn't dismiss it as penis envy but as a message to take my own writing more seriously. When I myself used the Freudian rationale to consider giving up my writing altogether to seek total "fulfillment as a wife and mother," he didn't somehow encourage it. And when the women's magazines kept turning down that article, he wondered why I didn't think beyond that kind of writing.

When I had got the contract to write the book in 1958, I knew I'd have to take on the Freudian basis of what I now called the feminine mystique, but I knew I didn't have the necessary expertise to do that. I was afraid of all the psychoanalysts and Freudian followers who now dominated the burgeoning profession I had left. I was no longer in therapy myself, but I went back to see Menaker to see if he might consider collaborating with me. It would give the book more authority, I thought, the reputation of an analyst actually trained by Anna Freud giving intellectual weight to an unknown "housewife," writing from her experience as a women's magazine writer, making that image, and living according to it, with the other wives and mothers. We met several times for an hour between patients in his office and at one point he gave me invaluable advice: "When what the woman says and is doesn't fit the book, listen to the woman." But most of the notes I made there were not in my own voice, the one I finally hit on, on that couch in my living room with the yellow legal pad.

To my amazement and relief, George Brockway was not at all interested in having this eminent male psychoanalyst collaborate on the book. He wanted me to write it. He did not want another book written by a psychoanalyst. In retrospect, I would have found it difficult to disagree with Dr. Menaker. A collaboration would have dampened my own spontaneity. (I understand now why psychoanalysts don't think it's such a good idea to have sex with one's patients.) Perhaps Dr. Menaker was also relieved. But there was no evading the necessity of taking on the Freudian basis of the feminine mystique, the old prejudices—that women were less than human, born merely to breed children and serve men—which science and the feminists had seemingly dispelled but which reappeared at midcentury in Freudian disguise.

The new mystique is much more difficult for the modern woman to question than the old prejudices, partly because the mystique is broadcast by the very agents of education and social science that are supposed to be the chief enemies of prejudice, partly because the very nature of Freudian thought makes it virtually invulnerable to question.

How can an educated American woman, who is not herself an analyst, presume to question a Freudian truth? She knows that Freud's discovery of the unconscious workings of the mind was one of the great breakthroughs in man's pursuit of knowledge. She knows that the science built on that discovery has helped many suffering men and women. She has been taught that only after years of analytic training is one capable of understanding the meaning of Freudian truth. . . . How can she presume to tread the sacred ground where only analysts are allowed? . . .

But I do question, from my own experience as a woman, and my reporter's knowledge of other women, the application of the Freudian theory of femininity to women today. I question its use, not in therapy, but as it has filtered into the lives of American women through the popular magazines and the opinions and interpretations of so-called experts. I think much of the Freudian theory about women is obsolete, an obstacle to truth for women in America today, and a major cause of the pervasive problem that has no name.

Not Freud nor Marx, nor their interpreters, could explain or even recognize that problem with no name I was hearing from the women I interviewed, and that resonated in my own gut. I knew the problem was *real*. But I had also learned, back in the days of my own serendipitous education by the Gestalt psychologists, that a social phenomenon must be seen in its cultural context and that perception is never wholly objective, that it is determined often by one's mind-set, what one is trained or expects to see. Freud's "truths" about men and women were based on his observations of the middle- and upper-class men and women who were his patients in Victorian life in Vienna. He translated those observations into the scientific language of his day as timeless, biologically determined entities. He reified his observations into biologically determined instincts.

I had learned a lot about the development of scientific theory and the dangers of reification way back at Smith. And so I began to dare to question Freud's concept of "penis envy," focusing on what he observed in those women and their dreams, in terms of their own lives back then. With my twentieth-century understanding of the scientific paradigm which dictated his conceptualization of those observations, and convictions based on my observations of the lack of relevance of his concept to American women today, I laid down a challenge:

> The concept of "penis envy," which Freud coined to describe a phenomenon he observed in women—that is, in the middle-class women who were his patients in Vienna in the Victorian era—was seized in this country in the 1940s as the literal explanation of all that was wrong with American women. Many who preached the doctrine of endangered femininity, reversing the movement of American women toward independence and identity . . . not the few psychoanalysts, but the many popularizers . . . could not have known what Freud himself meant by penis envy. One needs only to know what he was describing, in those Victorian women, to see the fallacy in literally applying his theory of femininity to women today.
>
> Freud, it is generally agreed, was a most perceptive and accurate observer of important problems of the human personality. But in describing and interpreting those problems, he was a prisoner of his own culture. . . .
>
> The knowledge of other cultures, the understanding of cultural relativity, which is part of the framework of social scientists in our own time, was unknown to Freud. . . . Much of what Freud described as characteristic of universal human nature was merely characteristic of certain middle-class European men and women at the end of the nineteenth century.

Searching for what he had seen beneath those abstract concepts, I was helped by the publication, around this time, of Freud's letters. In his letters to his wife, and then in Ernest Jones's voluminous biography, I could see, as I wrote in my chapter on "The Sexual Solipsism of Sigmund Freud," that

> to Freud, even more than to the magazine editors on Madison Avenue, women were a strange, inferior, less-than-human species. He saw them as childlike dolls, who existed in terms only of men's love, to love man and serve his needs. It was the same kind of unconscious solipsism that made man for many centuries see the sun only as a bright object that revolved around the earth. Freud grew up with this attitude built in by his culture—not only the culture of

Victorian Europe, but the Jewish culture in which men said the daily prayer: "I thank Thee, Lord, that Thou hast not created me a woman," and women prayed in submission: "I thank Thee, Lord, that Thou hast created me according to Thy will."

I could see that with his wife, as earlier with his mother and sisters, Freud's needs, "his desires, his wishes, were the sun around which the household revolved." When the noise of his sisters' practicing the piano interrupted his studying, "the piano disappeared, and with it all opportunities for his sisters to become musicians," Anna Freud wrote years later.

I figured out that Freud had translated his own psychological observations into the language of genetically determined biological "instinct." His observations of his patients' sexual behavior, symptoms, dreams, and his own unending psychoanalysis of himself were the basis of his theories. But what he observed in his women patients—that they envied men, that they dreamed of having a penis, that no matter how he analyzed their dreams and neuroses, they did not seem able to *develop* as men did—he ascribed to ordained biological instincts. He did not see the lack of education for girls, the lack of opportunity for them to develop and use their abilities in any respected occupation of society, the attitude that perceived women as something *other*, less, than a full human being "as a problem or cause for any problem in women. It was woman's nature to be ruled by man, and her sickness to envy him."

I wrote that Freud's letters to Martha, his future wife, written during the four years of their engagement (1882–86), have the fond but patronizing sound of Torvald in *A Doll's House*, scolding Nora for her pretenses of being human. Freud was beginning to probe the secrets of the human brain in the laboratory of Vienna; Martha was to wait, his "sweet child," in her mother's custody for four years, until he could come and fetch her. From those letters, one could see that to him she "was defined as child-housewife, even when she was no longer a child and not yet a housewife," defined by

Tables and chairs, beds, mirrors, a clock to remind the happy couple of the passage of time, an armchair for an hour's pleasant daydreaming, carpets to help the housewife keep the floors clean, linen tied with pretty ribbons in the cupboard and dresses of the latest fashion and hats with artificial flowers, pictures on the wall, glasses for everyday and others for wine and festive occasions, plates and dishes . . . and the sewing table and the cozy lamp, and everything must be kept in good order or else the housewife who has divided her heart into little bits, one for each piece of furniture, will begin to fret. . . . Are we to hang our hearts on such little things? Yes, and without hesitation. . . . I will let you rule the house as much as you wish, and you will reward me with your sweet love and by rising above all those weaknesses for which women are so often despised.

I read a letter Freud wrote on November 5, 1883, deriding John Stuart Mill's views on "female emancipation and the woman's question altogether" for its failure to conclude that "women are different beings—we will not say lesser, rather the opposite—from men. . . ."

"I believe that all reforming actions in law and education would break down in front of the fact that, long before the age at which a man can earn a position in society, Nature had determined woman's destiny through beauty, charm, and sweetness . . . in youth an adored darling and in mature years a loved wife." Freud's biographer, Jones, respectful of Freud in every page, called Freud's attitude toward women "rather old-fashioned." It would certainly be going too far to say that he regarded the male sex as the lords of creation . . . but it might perhaps be fair to describe his view of the female sex as having their main function to be ministering angels to the needs and comforts of men.

I thought a lot about his remark to Marie Bonaparte: "The great question that has never been answered and which I have not yet been able to answer, despite my thirty years of research into the feminine soul, is, what does a woman want?" Freud did not try to understand women in terms of himself, as he did in all other aspects of his psychoanalytic theory, for he simply did not, could not, see women as human beings like himself. Accepting the limitations society imposed on women as natural and inevitable, he postulated his concepts of the "castration complex"

and "penis envy" on the "assumption that women are biologically inferior to men."

What did Freud observe in women that led him to postulate
the universality of penis envy? I asked myself.

> Even those who realize that Freud could not escape his culture do
> not question that he reported truly what he observed within it.
> Freud found the phenomenon he called penis envy so unanimous,
> in middle-class women in Vienna, in that Victorian time, that he
> based his whole theory of femininity on it. In Freud's own words,
> in a lecture on "The Psychology of Women," after a girl "notices the
> difference and, it must be admitted, its significance" she feels her-
> self "at a great disadvantage . . . and falls a victim to penis envy,
> which leaves ineradicable traces on her development and charac-
> ter formation, and even in the most favorable instances, is not over-
> come without a great expenditure of mental energy. That the girl
> recognizes the fact that she lacks a penis does not mean she accepts
> its absence lightly. On the contrary she clings for a long time to the
> desire to get something like it. . . ." He felt that penis envy could
> even drive a grown up woman to come to analysis with the hope
> that it might give her "the capacity to pursue an intellectual career"
> which "can often be recognized as a sublimated modification of
> this repressed wish" (for a penis!).

I found reference after reference to Freud's "impression
which one receives over and over again in analytical work"—that
not even psychoanalysis can do much for women, because of the
inherent deficiency of femininity and the "exhaustion" of her
possibilities in the difficult process of overcoming her penis envy.
In his lecture on "The Psychology of Women," he had put it quite
clearly:

> A man of about thirty seems a youthful, and, in a sense, an incom-
> pletely developed individual, of whom we expect that he will be
> able to make good use of the possibilities of development, which
> analysis lays open to him. But a woman of about the same age fre-
> quently staggers us by her psychological rigidity and unchange-
> ability. . . . There are no paths open to her for future development
> . . . it is as though . . . the difficult development which leads to fem-
> ininity has exhausted all the possibilities of the individual . . . even

when we are successful in removing the suffering by solving her neurotic conflict.

"What was he really reporting?" I asked, in the blasphemous chapter on Freud.

One sees simply that Victorian culture gave women many reasons to envy men: the same conditions, in fact, that the feminists fought against. If a woman who was denied the freedom, the status and the pleasures that men enjoyed wished secretly that she could have those things, in the shorthand of the dream, she might wish herself a man and see herself with that one thing which made men unequivocally different—the penis. She would, of course, have to learn to keep her envy, her anger, hidden to play the child, the doll, the toy, for her destiny depended on charming men. But underneath, it might still fester, sickening her for love.

And what could she do with her life, then, even after analysis, except have more children, since most professions were not open to women? It was not that most American women had read Freud, but certainly they were exposed to his dogma, as it was accepted unquestioningly in that era and taught by psychologists and sociologists, and in those ubiquitous courses on "Marriage and the Family" which sprang up in every college. Studying census statistics—the same census that registered me as "housewife"—I saw that college graduates in the 1950s were more likely to have three, four, five children, than women who had only high school education or less. Always before, more educated women had had fewer children. I traced the academic dissemination of Freud's feminine mystique by Margaret Mead and the functional sociologists. It was fascinating to go back through Mead's early writings and see how her finding that every culture—from Samoa to the Aropesh—ascribes different traits to male and female, but that if tenderness is female and assertiveness is male in one tribe, it can just as easily be male and female in another. Those of us influenced by Margaret Mead's early work came away with the realization of the enormous plasticity of the human condition, male and female, our amazingly large, various and, in the end, similar human potential.

And then I found, clear as a line in the carbon dating of those

2

My father, Harry Goldstein.

My mother, Miriam Horwitz Goldstein.

Miriam Goldstein with her children: *(left to right)* Amy, Harry, and Betty.

3

4

ABOVE: With my elementary school class in Peoria (I am fourth from right in the first row).

RIGHT: With Paul Jordan *(left)* and Doug Palmer *(right)* at our high school radio station, spring 1938.

5

BELOW: Posing for the camera.

7

With Paul Jordan *(left)* and Doug Palmer *(right)*, cofounders with me of *Tide,* our high school literary magazine.

6

8

ABOVE: At Smith College.

LEFT: A group of friends, including Harriet
Vance (*front center*), another Smithie
from Peoria.

BELOW: In a college play.

10

11

As a bridesmaid at Mario Ingersoll's wedding in the summer of 1942 *(front row, second from left)*.

Carl and I in 1947.

With Carl in the early years of our marriage.

With baby Daniel, October 1949.

Playing with Daniel.

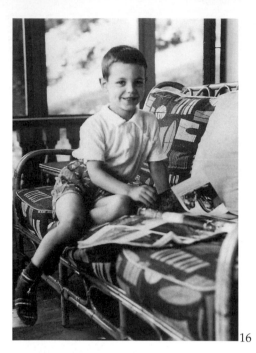

16

Daniel.

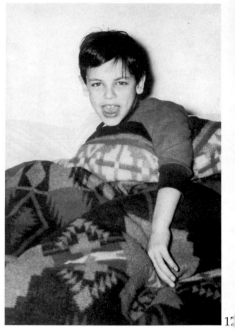

1

Jonathan.

Emily.

The children with their dog.

18

1

A photo that appeared in the October 2, 1963, issue of *Life* magazine.

From the October 2, 1963, *Life* magazine feature. 21

Lecturing in 1963 after the publication of *The Feminine Mystique*.

22

With Carl.

With Emily after my trip to
India.

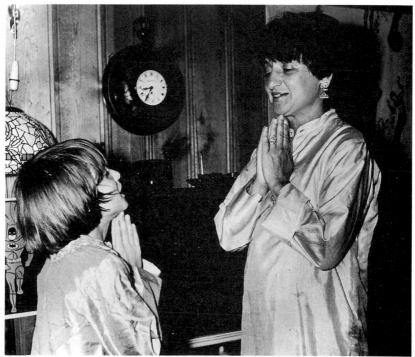

With Kay Clarenbach at the second annual NOW Conference in November 1967.

Meeting with students in 1963.

At a 1970 fundraising event hosted by Ethel Scull at her East Hampton home.

Left to right: Gloria Steinem, New York lawyer Brenda Feigen Fasteau, NOW president Wilma Scott Heide, and I at a 1972 meeting of NOW's National Policy Council.

28

ABOVE: With Indira Gandhi.

RIGHT: Speaking at a New York City women's lib rally in 1971.

ABOVE: Exchanging gifts with Pope Paul VI in October 1973.

RIGHT: A session of the International Women's Conference held at my New York apartment. Yoko Ono appears at bottom right.

33

In a discussion with an unidentified woman at the 1975 International Women's Year Tribune in Mexico City.

34

From left: Jacqui Ceballos, Pat Burnett, me, Dorothy Haener, and Wilma Scott Heide at a NOW conference in the late 1970s.

With the Indian, Kenyan, and Egyptian delegates to the 1985 UN Women's Conference in Nairobi, Kenya.

35

LEFT: Playing charades with the Long Island commune. *(Susan Wood)*

BELOW: With David Manning White in my Sag Harbor garden. *(Susan Wood)*

LEFT: David and me. *(Susan Wood)*

BELOW: With Daniel, Emily and Jonathan. *(Susan Wood)*

40

41

ABOVE: Jonathan and his bride, Helen Nakdimen, under the *huppa. (Susan Wood)*

ABOVE RIGHT: Daniel preparing a feast.

RIGHT: Carl and I escorting Emily to her wedding ceremony.

BELOW: Three generations of Friedans in 1993. *From left:* Carl, Daniel holding his son Benjamin, Agga *(behind me),* Jonathan holding his daughter Tya, Helen with sons Rafi *(left)* and Caleb *(right),* Eli, Emily with daughter Isabel and son David. *(Susan Wood)*

42

43

44

Grandchildren Tya,
Rafi, and Caleb.
(Susan Wood)

Holding Rafi.
(Susan Wood)

45

cores on the bottom of the Antarctic Sea, a demarcation after Mead's exposure to Freud and psychoanalysis. What followed was an assertion of the suddenly ineradicable boundaries of female fulfillment through a woman's biological capacity to have a child and her warning of a dire fate to society when an individual defies or denies that ordained female destiny. All this time Margaret Mead was adorning her own brilliant career, marrying three husbands and accompanying them on anthropological expeditions that she might not have been able to get to on her own. And when she finally gave birth to her one daughter with her third husband, Gregory Bateson, she took her along in the sling or backpack to demonstrate to the next generation of feminine mystique mothers that they need not be parted for one minute from their babies.

I was bemused then, and now, by how Margaret Mead—like those first female analysts trained by Freud, Anna Freud, Helene Deutsch, Lou Andreas Salomé—had to *deny* her personal experience as a woman and her own intellectual achievement to preach and practice the Freudian feminine mystique. It had shocked me. I read every page of Helene Deutsch's two-volume bible *The Psychology of Women* only to discover that she indicted as "penis envy" any expression by women of intellectual discovery, any research other than handmaiden help to a male scientist (an acceptable feminine substitute for motherhood and passive servility). I felt again, in my gut, the necessity that any doctrine about women must come from, and be checked against, life's experience.

The concepts that gave the feminine mystique its intellectual authority distorted and twisted a particular time- and culture-bound phenomenon into a universal, irradicable, permanent, biologically determined destiny, perpetuating the inferior housewife woman in Victorian Vienna, reincarnated in the glorified suburban housewife of post–World War II America. I wonder now I had the nerve to take on Margaret Mead and Talcott Parsons. But like the child who blurts out that the emperor wears no clothes, reading functional sociology texts and the later Margaret Mead, I saw how they took the craze for motherhood and suburbia and repudiation of career in those fifteen years after World War II and converted it into a "functional" absolute: man the breadwinner, woman the housewife, man the doer, woman the be-er. Sociologists and psychologists were confirming as absolutes what generations of priests, rabbis and other preachers and philosophers had ordained as God's will.

And the irony was that this message was sending several generations of educated American women back to the home for "feminine fulfillment" just as their new eighty-year life span, and the evolution of work, made it almost impossible to live most of their lives only as housewives and mothers and now offered new challenges and opportunities for women to lead more multifaceted lives in society.

But how had that dogma, the feminine mystique, got its power to so affect women's lives that, in great numbers, my generation of educated women and the one after it did go home again and try to make careers of three-, four-, five-child families? And how was it that a younger generation even gave up college or quit in the middle to take a secretary's job and put their husbands through law school, to get those husbands, children and houses in the suburbs—which now defined the limits of feminine ambition—even sooner?

I saw the direct line of that socio-psycho dogma when I examined the statistics showing that the great majority of sociology students were now women, but even fewer than in other fields were going on to graduate degrees. I traced the popularization of those ideas in "Marriage and Family" textbooks, and imagined myself, as a young girl considering graduate work, fearfully, ambivalently finding a rationalization in functional sociology, Freudian psychology, *not* to risk, not to make the effort.

I know now that my empathy for that girl came from my own personal truth. Ever since psychologists have been doing such studies, girls in America, until very recently, *did not want to be like their mothers,* might have even liked to be boys. (One of the wondrous results, since the women's movement, since the changes in women's lives, is that daughters whose mothers combine motherhood with work in society do want to grow up to be like their mothers.) "Who was your role model?" reporters asked me later. I *didn't have a role model.* Almost none of us did then. Women in 1950s America, like those in Freud's Vienna, didn't have any map at all of what women could be, or even want to be, from their mothers or other women in their towns, or in movies or magazines. We had the housewife heroines—Doris Day, June Allyson. Everyone, everything was selling us the glories of suburban domestic bliss, the backyard barbecue.

I did enough research to assure myself that the feminine mystique was affecting all women, not just a few overeducated Smith girls. I made no attempt to make my basic study anything other than middle class. My early political experience writing for the so-called working class had taught me that ideas, styles, *change* in America comes from the middle class. I also knew that whether our fathers and mothers started out as Peoria peddlers, farmers, doctors, housewives, laundresses or even millionaire bankers, we all want to be accepted and achieve "success" in middle-class terms.

In those years, "success," even for sophisticated middle-class women, was to be a "happy housewife." But after I traced down the roots of that feminine mystique, figuring out the ambivalence that made my generation of women susceptible to it, even realizing what a welcome escape that suburban backyard was for women and men from the ugly currents of the McCarthy era, I was still dissatisfied. What pushed it all? What gave that mystique its seeming inevitability, its overwhelming irreversibility, so that each woman thought she was alone with "the problem that has no name," never realizing how many other women were not having orgasms waxing the family room floor?

I remember sitting on the porch of my own suburban house in Grandview, contemplating that the business of America is business. What was blanketing women's minds with that "happy housewife" image were the television commercials, and *Ozzie & Harriet* and *I Love Lucy* and *The Brady Bunch,* and those women's magazines that made "career women" into monsters and chided housewives for even dreaming of other pursuits.

Of course. The companies retooling from war production needed housewives to *buy* all those appliances and soap powders they were turning out. Even in my labor press days I did not believe in conspiratorial theories of history, but I decided to go see some of the "motivational researchers," the market researchers who advised companies on strategies to create and sell the markets they need.

To my incredulous amazement, I found, if not a "conspir-

acy," a seemingly conscious campaign on the part of those running American industry then to *keep* those housewives busy,
busy, and never entirely free of guilt.

Ernest Dichter, one of the early social scientists who hired
himself out to industry to do "motivational research," as it was
then called, boasted of it all in his headquarters in a Hudson River
suburb. He explained to me how you could sell women cake
mixes that required no brains or work. But you had to give them
something to do, like break an egg, to make the project somehow
seem demanding enough that they'd feel they were accomplish-
ing something. And you had to keep making a woman feel guilty
so she'd buy even more of those appliances.

I was talking to my neighbor Si Goode, an eminent sociologist, about this. I asked, how come, with all these new labor-
saving household devices, the suburban women I've been
interviewing always say they're so busy, doing housework that's
never finished? That's all they have time to do, they say. With all
these new machines, shouldn't they be spending much less time
on housework than their mothers and grandmothers? He was intrigued and said he'd assign the question to his graduate students. To our amazement, a review of the data showed American
women in the 1950s, with all their dishwashers, washers, dryers,
vacuum cleaners, floorwaxers, were spending *more hours* on
housework than their mothers and grandmothers. And so, I figured, "housework expands to fill the time available."

But then I got carried away, and wrote the one chapter in *The
Feminine Mystique* I now regret, "The Comfortable Concentration
Camp." I had found figures from Donald Wood at MIT on two
characteristics of the suburbs, as compared to the city: the women
were more educated, and fewer of them were in jobs or professions than in the city. I'd been reading Bruno Bettelheim on the
psychodynamics of the concentration camp, how the will to resist
was eroded, the will to escape self-destroyed. I am ashamed of
that analogy. To resist, escape the concentration camp, risked
death; there was no way out for most of the Nazis' prisoners. The
American suburb was no concentration camp. That analogy, it
seems to me now, was an insult.

I am also ashamed because it denied my personal truth. During my years as a suburban housewife and mother, I had many

happy hours with my kids, my husband, my friends and neighbors, fixing up our Victorian house, chauffeuring the kids, running educational projects, despite an underlying uneasiness and an occasional panic of "the problem that has no name." I remember the deliciousness now of Jonathan, at eight or so, starting "business" after business with his friend Peter. All those shoes he collected for his shoeshine business, and then didn't remember who they belonged to. The contraptions that kept coming to the house that he'd ordered to "sell," that had to be returned. And going to Danny's basketball games in junior high, until all the other boys, older than he, got so much taller that even his brains didn't help enough. And switching him to the Nyack school, where teachers didn't penalize him for solving math problems in original ways. And the joy, when he found enough boys and girls on his wavelength at that larger school to make really good friends to have adventures with. And my daily walk with Emily, after she got back from nursery school, kindergarten, second grade, where we'd hold hands and sing a song we made up as we went along with every verse beginning "Swing High, Swing Low," and we'd swing our hands *high* then *low*. "It's off to Nyack we go," "the twenty-sixth letter of the alphabet is O." And our "lady lunches" at the Plaza, after I'd given her *Eloise* to read, when I'd take her shopping or to the dentist in the city. The sheer loveliness of my daughter—the doctor—as a little girl!

I was having terrible fights with Carl. We were always worried about money. We always owed too much to the butcher. But we had good sex and gave great parties together, and took the kids camping on an island in Lake George, and put up a tent on the beach at Cape Hatteras, money or no money. I would put my writing aside when the kids came home from school, until dinner was over. I no longer got so hysterical when Carl came home late. I got on with my writing. He thought *I* was having an affair!

But it was mysterious, awesome, the way the writing of *The Feminine Mystique* took me over. It's as if my whole life, including the mistakes, the pains, the paths not taken, had prepared me for this. When I think about it now, it seems almost like a religious experience, as if some divine hand were guiding me, if I believed in such things.

Sometimes when I'd get stuck, I'd take a martini out on my

neighbor's dock to muse. I still sort of hid my writing, like secret drinking in the morning, since none of the other mothers on River Road "worked." Part of me wanted still to be one of them, accepted as a "happy suburban housewife." I remember once when Emily, around five or six, was making a play date with her friend Diana. "We can't go to my house this afternoon because my mother is waxing the family room floor," Diana said. "Let's go to your house, your mother never does any work." "My mother is doing her footnotes today," Emily protested.

I had an "office" or "study" in whatever bedroom wasn't being used on the second or third floor. But I merely stored my notes and books and papers there. I put a table under the china cabinet in our lovely octagonal dining room, facing the river, in the center of the house. I'd write there, or spreading out if I was dealing with notes, on the dining-room table. As the pages accumulated—all of them in my awful handwriting, on yellow legal-size pads—I cleared out the bottom shelf of the china cabinet and stored my manuscript there.

As one clue led to another, from all my different, unused or unappreciated study, work, and life experience, I became more convinced that I was right, that American women had been sent home again and that it was bad for them, and not only for them but for their families. Was it healthy that 60 percent of women were dropping out of college to marry by the end of the 1950s, that women were getting married at ever younger ages—the average was twenty and going down—that the birthrate was ballooning, especially among college-educated women who were now having four, five and six children where once they'd had two?

I was realizing how my conclusions went against what everyone else accepted as basic, unshakable truth. I wondered, "Am I crazy?" Still, it did add up, it fitted together, it got clearer and clearer. But I didn't know how to end the book. If I was right, and there was something very wrong about the way American women were living their lives, what should they be doing instead, what was the answer?

You can't really see around a corner like that. I wouldn't have put it that way then, but breaking through the feminine mystique was a true paradigm shift: women no longer being defined, defining themselves, solely in relation to men, as wives, mothers, sex objects, housewives, but defining themselves instead as *people* in society. The *personhood of women* sounded revolutionary then. Well, my "New Life Plan for Women" was hardly revolutionary. My own thoughts then were themselves limited by the feminine mystique. I suggested simply that women *plan* to use their abilities in society, their lives as men do, in ways that fit with marriage and children, not the either/or which was the first feminists' undoing. So, I concluded, in college, they should be advised to major in fields or disciplines they could use in whatever city their husbands' jobs might take them to. It would have been impossible to conceive that in only twenty years, husbands and wives would make such decisions together, sometimes in terms of her job first, or, with equally serious commitment to jobs and family, even embark on periods of living in different cities, commuting father or mother.

I had no idea that my book would start a revolution. Until that revolution actually came—the women's movement—new possibilities for women's lives weren't visible. But I did understand that what I had figured out—that the feminine mystique was no longer a valid guide to women's lives, that it was *obsolete*—implied monumental social change, and that my text would be very threatening to those who couldn't deal with that change, men and women. In the way that you sometimes know more than you know that you know, I wrote in the preface: ". . . my answers may disturb the experts and women alike for they imply social change. But there would be no sense in my writing this book at all if I did not believe that women can affect society as well as be affected by it; that, in the end, a woman, as a man, has the power to choose, and to make her own heaven or hell."

I remember now that my publisher made me take out several pages comparing the situation of women to the situation of blacks in America. George Brockway said, "This book is going to be controversial enough. Why bring that in? It's not really relevant."

After I finished the book in 1962, while it was at the printers, I decided to go back to school and get that Ph.D. in psychology I'd given up in the first of my own feminine mystique mistaken choices. With all the kids in school now—Emily was in kindergarten—I decided I'd better do something more serious about a career of my own than my hit-or-miss freelance magazine writing. So I sent for my Smith undergraduate transcript and my Berkeley fellowship records. And thus armed—along with W. W. Norton's announcement of my forthcoming book—I went to see the head of the social psychology department at Columbia.

I told him I wanted to come back and get my doctorate in psychology and that I would need a fellowship. I mentioned the fellowships I'd won at Berkeley, that I'd studied with Erikson and Tolman, as well as Koffka and Kurt Lewin. I gave him a reprint of the *American Journal of Psychology* article based on my Smith honors thesis "Operationism in Psychology." And I showed him Norton's announcement of my forthcoming book, *The Feminine Mystique.*

He dismissed it all. Psychology had changed so much in the years since I studied it, had become so professional, he said patronizingly, I wouldn't be able to master it now. For instance, I would have to deal with very complex statistics. Well, I told him, I had to draw on some of the latest theoretical developments in psychology in writing my book, and I had to dig into and use some very complex statistics. Since I'd gotten an A in statistics when I was doing graduate work at Berkeley, I was sure one refresher course would do it.

But you would have to do serious research to get a Ph.D., he replied. I explained that I had to do some serious research using my own interviews to write *The Feminine Mystique.* "Well, you seem to have been doing useful work as a volunteer in the community," he said. "I just don't think it's possible for you to get back into the profession after all these years. But it sounds as if you're able to keep yourself busy without a professional degree, so just keep on doing what you've been doing."

I took the bus back to Rockland County, diminished. I felt humiliated, embarrassed, depressed, more angry at having made a fool of myself than mad at him. Maybe it was a silly idea, anyhow. Graduate work at Columbia would cost a lot of money. Even if I persisted and got admitted, they would never give me a fellowship. So how would I pay the fees? (It did not occur to me that I would actually make money from writing that book.) And if someone as aggressive and with as good a record as I had couldn't get taken seriously applying to go back to graduate school, what was going to happen to others after they had broken through the feminine mystique to try to become more than housewives or secretaries? I didn't yet perceive it, but I was beginning to understand that something would have *to change society* in order for women to be able to become all they could be. It wouldn't be enough just for the woman herself to break through the feminine mystique and want something more.

On a plane, around that time, another passenger was reading a book (or was it a pamphlet?) proclaiming "the first step in a revolution is consciousness." If I could have foreseen then the revolution that my particular breakthrough in consciousness would set off, much less the changes in my own life, would I have hesitated? Probably not. That mysterious thing always drives me on, despite my dread.

SIX

"It Changed My Whole Life"

I still feel a mixture of awe, pleasure and rue when women stop me on the street, or at a conference, after a lecture, in a restaurant, to say, "It changed my whole life," and even remember, thirty-odd years later, where they were when they read *The Feminine Mystique*. Well, of course, it changed mine too, but not like-a-flash-of-light from the sky. I just prayed the book would be reviewed in *The New York Times*. But part of me *knew* it was more important than that. All through the research and writing, I had felt this calm sureness, as if in tune with something much larger and more important than myself that had to be taken seriously. But I seemed very alone at first in that awareness.

Marie Rodell resigned as my agent after I sent her the manuscript. Marie was also Rachel Carson's agent and *Silent Spring* had just come out, but I think she was threatened by my book, as many women were. She was a great devotee of Freud and she wanted me to throw out the whole chapter on Freud. I didn't take her advice, or anyone's really, when I was writing *The Feminine Mystique*, except for Burton Beals, the superb young editor at Norton then, who cut and rearranged my 1,000-page manuscript to get rid of repetitions. He was right when he suggested that I flesh out my few paragraphs on those early suffragettes into a whole chapter, even though I resented having to go back and do more research.

Still, George Brockway evidently didn't have much faith the book would sell. I think Norton's first printing was 3,000 copies. They upped it to 5,000 when, besides *McCall's* publishing an excerpt, *Ladies' Home Journal* and *Mademoiselle* also decided to do so. I was amazed because, after all, the book was an attack on the image of women perpetuated by those women's magazines, and to my knowledge they never printed excerpts of the same book. (*McCall's* had rejected the piece I'd written five years before based on the Smith questionnaire, and *Ladies' Home Journal* had taken it but rewritten it.) I'd brought a bunch of page proofs with me to a dinner meeting of the Society of Magazine Writers (which I took the bus in to attend every month so I could feel like a "writer" and not "just a housewife"), and Peter Wyden, the new articles editor of *Ladies' Home Journal*, sensed something in the way I was talking about the book and insisted on seeing those messy proofs.

I guess the first person who saw *The Feminine Mystique* was going to be a big book was Carl. I hadn't shown it to him, or anyone, when I was writing, which is strange considering my constant need for reassurance when I was writing magazine articles. But part of me, this time, *knew* what I was doing, and I didn't want anyone else tampering with it. Carl started reading my page proofs on the bus into the city. He called me from his office and said, "It's great. It's going to be a very big book."

Reading my galleys, maybe the *seriousness* of it all did scare me. I remember going into a fancy beauty parlor in New York and saying, "I want to dye my hair blond." Remember that ad: "If I have one life to live, let me live it as a blonde"? The people at the beauty parlor said, "Madam, we can't do that, you have virgin hair." "Don't be silly," I said, "I have three children." "But you have never dyed your hair." So they dyed it an "auburn" red. I felt a little strange, but a few weeks later, out at Fire Island with the kids, my hair suddenly turned green! From the sun. I had to go back to the beauty parlor and get it dyed back to its original dark brown.

At first, it seemed as if I was going to have a hard time getting another agent. What agent would take on an unknown housewife-writer for what was probably going to be her only book? Besides, a new agent would have to split her fee with Marie. I called a lot of agents in vain. (Some months later, when *The Feminine*

Mystique was beginning to sell those millions in paperback, they called me back.)

I was pleased when Martha Winston of Curtis Brown agreed to become my new agent. Martha had been sent my book in manuscript by Burton Beals and had stayed up all night reading it, she told me. I remember Hilary˙ Rubenstein, an up-and-coming British publisher, calling me from the airport on his way back to London. He'd read a chapter on George Brockway's desk. Later, when we had become friends, he told me it was the first important book he'd bought.

I felt a kind of sacred commitment to get that book *out* and taken seriously. And my fellow writer friends—almost all men then—took me aside, one by one, and told me I couldn't rely on my publisher or anyone else, it was *up to me* to get that book taken seriously. I sensed then, and acted on it but guiltily, that writing the book is only part of it. From some of my former newspaper-magazine colleagues who had gone into books ahead of me, I'd learned that you can't take for granted that your publisher will make the book surface. You have to get to the media or the book can die, stillborn. I guess some writers are born knowing that now, but it was a revelation to Al Toffler, Bernie Asbell and myself in the early sixties, as we helped each other and egged each other on.

But that was proving very difficult for me when the book came out in February 1963 since all the New York newspapers were on strike. It was not reviewed in *The New York Times,* and because of that, wasn't listed the next Christmas among the 100 best books of the year. I remember getting up the nerve to call Dave Scherman, an editor of *Life,* who had married my Smith friend Rosemarie Redlich. They came to dinner, or Carl and I went there, and I told Dave about my book. A few weeks later a *Life* photographer and writer—Jane Howard, who became my beloved friend and neighbor later in Sag Harbor—came out to Rockland County and took lots of pictures of me and Carl and the kids. (They were quite taken with my plaster-of-Paris bust of Abraham Lincoln that I'd gotten at auction, which had come from some city hall.)

Norton ran a few small ads in *The New Yorker,* but it was Carl who persuaded them to hire an outside publicist and send me on a publicity tour. They got Tania Grossinger, a member of the famous Catskills resort family, who had publicized the excerpt for *McCall's*. Author tours were relatively unknown then, but Tania got me on a lot of talk shows. I remember one television program called *Girl Talk* with this horrible host named Vivian something who kept telling the viewers how much more fulfilling it was for "girls" to be housewives than to have a career, and, in my case as a writer, to have a byline. So I turned directly to the camera and said: "Women, don't listen to her. She wants you out there doing the dishes or she wouldn't have the captive audience for this program, whose byline she evidently doesn't want you to compete for."

I was surprised at first that my book was more threatening to some women than to men. Later it turned out that many men whose wives had made those feminine mystique career renunciations had bought the book for their wives, and encouraged them to go back to school or work. But then, of course, it was threatening to women who'd made those painful choices and had to get up the courage to take themselves seriously in a new way. A woman in Detroit called in to the television program I was on there to tell me "to stop putting ideas" in her daughter's head. Women wrote to accuse me of being more of a threat to the United States than the Russians for questioning their "sacred role as housewife." But a trickle of letters which would turn into a flood came from women who were tired of feeling "like an appliance" or "brain dead" or "so depressed that it nearly drowns me." There was no doubt that the book was striking a nerve—if you could find a copy.

Carl met me in Chicago in the middle of my book tour and gave the publisher hell when he made the rounds of the bookshops and found no copies. I got very uneasy, *embarrassed,* when he would call the publisher and *scream* at them for only printing 5,000 copies. And here I was getting all this wonderful publicity on *The Kup Show,* and from Studs Terkel, from the women reporters at the *Sun-Times* and the *Chicago Tribune,* and once the newspaper strike in New York was over, reviews by brilliant women I'd long admired—Virginia Peterson, Marya Mannes. It was interesting, a few male columnists and older women's page editors were shocked by my book. But on the whole I got wonderful coverage from those undervalued women reporters and editors.

I'd get on the best-seller list and then fall off because there were no books in the stores. (The people at Norton told me later they thought Carl was buying all the copies.) Norton printed another 1,000, which didn't come close to being enough. Interest in the book was spreading by word of mouth. A woman called me one night from Pittsburgh to ask how to get hold of the book. She'd heard about it, knew she had to have it, had looked for it in all the bookstores in the city. Now she had her kids in their foot-pajamas in the station wagon, driving through the suburbs, couldn't I help her *get hold of the book.*

Cartoons began to be run of women holding this red book— it had a beautiful red cover, that first edition—and moving! Because each woman who had thought only she, alone, had these doubts, in her supposedly happy happy suburban housewife's life, now knew she shared that "problem that has no name" with all those other women. It was such a relief, they would tell me, so *empowering.* "It changed my whole life," they said then—and still say. "I decided to go back to school." "I decided I would be more than a secretary." "I told my husband, you're not the only one around here that counts. I'm a person, too."

A lot of things began to change, but not right away. Sid Offit, one of those guys in the Allen Room of the library who used to tease me for writing a book about women, ran down 64th Street yelling, to throw his arms around me. He told me later that he and a number of the guys from the Allen Room had a meeting to analyze how come the book they'd so scorned had made it bigger than theirs.

Mort Hunt told me later he went out every Saturday night to get the *Times* to see if I was still on the best-seller list, annoyed when I was. He had decided, when I was still writing *The Feminine Mystique,* to do a book on women himself and he'd asked me to meet with him and determine who was going to deal with what so we wouldn't get in each other's way. He was surprised when I wouldn't do it. He was a much bigger magazine writer than I was, and also much faster. My heart sank when I realized he was covering the same territory because I knew he'd finish first. But I never would let anyone else mess with that book. I *knew* what I had. And, of course, *Her Infinite Variety* came out when mine was still at the printer and made some of the same points I did. Hunt was a pro as a researcher and magazine-book writer. But, I guess, his book lacked the passion of personal truth.

I was beginning to get invitations to lecture. Martha Winston sent me to a lecture agent, Bill Leigh, of W. Colston Leigh, and I soon discovered that I got paid much more for lecturing than for writing an article. Writing was *work*, but lecturing was not. I enjoyed the feedback from the live audiences, women and men—that suppressed actress who was not pretty enough, the ham in me, out in full voice now. Cornell University, one of the first to invite me, scheduled the lecture for the living room of one of the dorms. So many people were lined up outside, refusing to go home, they moved it to the chapel.

I put in the contract that after whatever lecture I did, I wasn't to be committed to do another for at least two weeks, because I didn't want to be away from my kids too much. It wasn't that I had problems with the kids. I never had problems with my kids. I just missed them. Daniel was already showing signs of his mathematical genius but also making the basketball team in junior high, despite not being all that tall; Jonathan, with all those businesses he and his friend Peter would start, and get bored by. Those kids were, are, the great undeserved bonuses of my life— so beautiful, so bright, so *themselves*. "I'm my own me," I remember Emily saying to me one day, when I was telling her to do something. "But Daniel Friedan is only twelve years old," I remember telling the physicist calling in search of "Dr. Daniel Friedan" to discuss some mathematical matter.

I considered my husband and my kids the most important part of my life then, and that was not just "feminine mystique." They were the core of my life. But writing that book, and the feeling when I held the first bound copy in my arms, *was* important— carrying my life forward, realizing my potential, finally. All I knew was, suddenly I could fly! I was no longer terrified when the plane took off. (They say it's only when you haven't fully lived that you're afraid to die.)

It was great, at first, having enough money to go to Antigua, to take the kids to Caneel Bay in the winter, to rent a nice house on

Fire Island for the summer. But as I began to get asked to lecture around the country, and go on radio or TV, I became some sort of leper in Rockland County. Carl and I loved to entertain, we liked having people to dinner Saturday night, or going to their houses, but suddenly, nobody invited us anymore and nobody wanted to come to our house. I was fourteen in Peoria again, the girl that didn't get into the sorority because she was Jewish. Now I was being kicked out of the sorority because I was becoming famous.

There was no way I could protect my professional life from, I guess, the jealousy of my friends and neighbors and even my own husband. I'd always kept my serious writing kind of hidden—my magazine articles, my book—but it wasn't possible to keep my life secret anymore once the book was out and I was all over radio and TV.

When it was my turn to drive our kids to dancing or art class and I had an interview to do, I'd sometimes have to use a taxi now. And the other mothers didn't like that. None of them had jobs, professions or careers, though those near my age might have started out with such intentions. Some of the younger ones hadn't even finished college. It was from interviews of women like them—I'd done my first interviews with my neighbors—that I'd begun to conceptualize "the problem that has no name." I guess it must have been threatening to see a book that questions the life you're living become a best-seller, to recognize yourself in it, to begin, inevitably, to ask new questions—and where did she get off, anyway, your own neighbor (and onetime friend), the nerve to write such a book and go on TV.

The first money from that book, after paying off the debts, went into our lovely run-down Victorian house overlooking the Hudson. It was always beautiful, with its lovely long porch overlooking the river. But it had been so in need of paint and repairs, those years when we could barely pay the butcher bill each month. Now we had it painted—a purple living room, red flocked wallpaper in the dining room. If my memory serves me, I did our bedroom in red, too. We re-covered the old mismatched furniture I'd bought at Tippy's Auction, the oversized Victorian love seat, whatever else I had got for under $50 or $100.

I tried a decorator, but everything she suggested was *beige.* I dispensed with her after one day. I didn't go for beige. I found some wonderful paisleylike Jack Lenor Larsen fabric for the big pieces, and got the smaller chairs re-covered in velvets of the blue colors in the paisley. I didn't have the patience for a decorator. I still have that wonderful old furniture, which people now admire as my "collection," and it's been re-covered twice more in fabric by Jack Lenor Larsen, who is now my friend and neighbor.

It was a relief to be out of debt and able to spend money, and the fame was exciting at first, but I wasn't really enjoying it. If Carl was mad at me, or cold, I was miserable. If I went out of town to lecture even for only one night—which was usually all I would agree to do then—he would go berserk, and call me long distance in the middle of the night, obscene phone calls. I remember once, when I was lecturing in Seattle, I stayed with a new acquaintance whose husband was the symphony orchestra conductor. I was embarrassed to learn what Carl had said over the phone to them—he had a rich four-letter vocabulary from his GI days, which I acquired. (I think it disconcerts people now to hear this dignified white-haired grande dame saying "fuck.") Sometimes, when I got back home, I would discover my old red suitcase missing. He would let me know that he had lent it to a lady friend he started having liaisons with when I went out of town, and I was devastated.

It was embarrassing, and worse, when someone at a party would introduce Carl as "Betty's husband" and he would sock the guy in the jaw! And then, I don't remember how it began, but he started beating up on me. It seemed as if I never went on a television show in those days without a black eye I had to cover over with makeup. I realize now he must have been desperate with rage and envy because he, after all, had started out as a showman. He had loved running his summer theaters. He'd given all that up to go into advertising to support us when I got fired for being pregnant. And now here I was, on television, lecturing, getting all the applause and the limelight. He had used his own showman instincts to get my publisher to promote the book. But, then, he had carried that to such an extreme that they refused to take his calls.

But if I was angry, as I must have been, that Carl wouldn't let me enjoy it—the fame, the *satisfaction* of the spreading fire I had started—all I let myself feel was guilt. It got too impossible, this life in the goldfish bowl of suburbia. One night, when Carl was trying to throw me out of the car as we were driving home from some meeting, our friend Milton Carrow was driving by and made Carl stop. He was a lawyer and handled divorce cases.

But I couldn't contemplate getting a divorce, myself. No one I knew personally had ever been divorced. And also, I couldn't bear the thought of having to go to places, parties, wherever, alone. For years I was terrified and would do anything to avoid being alone. But as friends, my publisher, my agent couldn't help but be aware of some of the difficulties in my marriage, they'd keep reminding me, "It's so important for your book that you are a good wife and mother." They even had me take along pictures of my kids when I was on television or giving a lecture.

Underneath, I guess I began to realize I would have to get a divorce. That wasn't conscious, when I started suggesting we move into the city. But it surely would have been much more difficult for me to get along without him if I'd stayed in the country. However, divorce wasn't really in my mind yet, because the summer we bought our apartment in the Dakota, we also bought a house on Fire Island.

A friend in the real estate business told us about an apartment in that beautiful, famous old building. It hadn't been painted in twenty-five years. A minister who had just died had lived there for decades. We bought it for $17,000 (it's now worth a million and a half, they say) and Carl got it painted and put in some bookshelves while I was out on Fire Island with the kids. I remember picking out a beautiful deep blue-green tile for the kitchen floor. We also bought some wonderful old oriental rugs in some secondhand place and went down on our hands and knees to color the white spots with a Magic Marker.

I'd loved Fire Island in my single reporter days, when my friends and I rented a cottage in Ocean Beach with gas lanterns. That summer of 1963 after my book came out, we rented Teddy White's house in Fair Harbor, and then bought a wonderful old brown shingled house in Lonelyville. I remember seeing an ad in the paper that Lord & Taylor was carrying a fabric with prints by Picasso on heavy linen. I went and got several yards of it—very expensive, then, $12 or $13 a yard—one with a clown, one with bullfighters and a big panel with ladies in purple, blue and green and feathered hats riding horses. Those Picassos decorated our beach house at Fire Island, then the kids' college rooms, my various sublets in California, and now the purple ladies ride over my long hall wall in Washington and the clown and the bullfighters over Emily's stairs in Buffalo.

The kids loved Fire Island. Emily could ride her bike by herself to her friends' houses, with Mervin, her dog, in the basket. The boys learned to sail. I bought them a Sunfish. I asked their teacher, a college boy on vacation, to give me a few lessons during the week, when Carl was in the city. I'd always loved to go sailing, or be taken sailing, by our neighbor Frank Bang on the Hudson when we lived in Grandview. But after a few lessons, the boy took Jonathan aside and said: "I know your mother is supposed to be very intelligent, but it's a waste of her money, paying me to teach her to sail. She's never going to learn to sail." All those years of making myself dumb on mechanical things couldn't be overcome. He'd say, "Sail into the wind," and my mind would go blank. Emily earned money clamming and I bought sixty thick white soup bowls at the Bridge, a restaurant supply shop, and we gave great clam chowder parties.

But there was really nothing for grown-ups to do at Fire Island but swim and drink. So, we did too much of that and the physical violence got worse. My asthma had come back, severely. Dr. Menaker was dead now, so I went to see another analyst, Carlos Dalmall, a beautiful man of Puerto Rican origin. I was in the "can this marriage be saved?" mode still so I wouldn't listen to his subtle pointing me to the truth, that I had to get out of this marriage to save myself. But he did get me to stop drinking because I was beginning to have blackouts. I remember the *inanity* of cocktail party conversation that summer, when you have to get through it cold sober. And I remember a disastrous trip to Peoria.

In June 1963, my Peoria High School class of 1938 was having its twenty-fifth reunion. The following week I was giving a lecture in Kansas City. Our kids had often been to Boston, where their father grew up—but never to Peoria. Carl hadn't been to Peoria either, so I decided the whole family should go for my high school reunion, stopping off for an adventurous night in a

Chicago hotel, and then Carl would take the kids back to New York and I'd go on to Kansas City. I thought it would be great for Carl and the kids to see Peoria (though not experiencing the pain of growing up in Peoria, they still might not understand where I came from). By now *The Feminine Mystique* was a best-seller, but the rest of the gang that had run high school life wasn't doing too bad. Parky was a Republican state senator, Bob McCord an insurance tycoon and Republican kingmaker, John Altorfer had made a lot of money on some Chicago business, Bob Easton had come home after Harvard and Yale Medical School and was now the Peoria pediatrician. They had all married the people they'd gone steady with in high school—Harriet and Parky, Bob and Vicki, Bobby and Ruthie.

My brother Harry, now a prominent businessman in Peoria, had a big house on Grandview Drive, but when I wrote that I was coming, he did not offer to put us up. We stayed at Bob Easton's, a few houses away. But when, almost immediately, I took my kids over to meet their cousins, I sensed a strain. Harry's kids were leaving almost immediately for their grandfather's farm. Harry's father-in-law, Louis Cohen, my father's friend, who had gone from peddler to furniture tycoon as my father had to jewelry store owner, was taking his grandchildren to the farm lest they be contaminated by their radical aunt. I always had been a bit too big for my Peoria britches. I used to talk a big radical game—politically and sexually—when I came home from college at Christmas and summers, and I suppose it got back later that I was working for labor union newspapers. And now I was a successful best-selling writer and, I suppose, with all the excitement being stirred up by *The Feminine Mystique*, I was by far the most famous member of our class. Not bad for Betty Goldstein, who didn't even make it into a sorority in high school, who spent those dusky afternoons reading Emily Dickinson on a gravestone. Yet surely now they couldn't snub me anymore, and since the war, anti-Semitism wasn't so popular, even in Peoria.

But the hostility from my former classmates that weekend was such that Carl got drunk and had to be restrained from knocking some of them down. "You can't treat my wife this way, she's famous!" he shouted. The next morning, toilet paper was spread all over the trees in Bob Easton's front yard. So, you can't go home again? I remember how small our big house on Farmington Road looked now, a run-down rooming house for nearby Bradley students, my father's store on South Adams Street long since gone, only the big clock remained.

But I was part of a larger world now. Peoria no longer had much power to hurt me, though it did hurt and embarrass me that weekend that my own kids, who had never experienced anti-Semitism for one moment in their lives, should see their mother as pariah in her own hometown. We were against racism and bias of any kind in our family. We supported blacks marching in the early sixties with Martin Luther King Jr. We took the kids to Washington on one of those marches and watched the "I Have a Dream" speech on television.

After Peoria, we stopped off in Chicago on our way home, where Carl and I went to see my uncle Ben, a brilliant lawyer who had won the first million-dollar law case in Illinois against Bell Telephone. My father had pawned diamonds to send his youngest brother to Harvard Law School. Uncle Ben didn't marry until he was almost fifty, a much older wealthy widow he called "Mommy." Now, they were divorced and he was living alone in the Drake Hotel, looking disheveled and distraught, his hotel suite crowded with rows of planks on sawhorses holding books. I wonder today if he had Alzheimer's. I heard he married his nurse and went to Arizona.

In Kansas City, I gave the keynote speech to the American Home Economics Association. How amazing, I thought, home economists, who you'd think would be really threatened by my attack on the feminine mystique, welcoming me, hungry for more, like those women's magazines. What capacity American culture has to absorb and welcome social criticism. In later years, meeting Latin American or Russian poets and philosophers whose lives were endangered when they so much as implied a critical political note, I realized how wonderful a society like ours is, which makes celebrities of its critics, gives them prizes and honors, fame and fortune.

The seed I was sowing with *The Feminine Mystique* was sprouting in so many places I couldn't keep track of them all. Dean Emma Baines of Southern Methodist University invited me to Texas to speak after the Home Economics convention. They'd never had a woman speaker there before. I decided later that Emma must have paid my lecture fee out of her own purse. In one day, she had me speaking to the business school, the theological school, the law school, the YWCA and several undergraduate classes before my evening lecture. When I asked her secretary on the way to the five o'clock session with business school students if we couldn't stop at a bar for a drink (I'd resumed drinking, but in moderation, except when Carl and I were fighting), she looked distressed. Well, of course, it was dry! At the end of the session, Emma appeared and beckoned to me. "A little birdie tells me you'd like a drink. My secretary will take you to her house where she has some whisky. And then she will give you some Sen-Sen. This is the first time in history we've had a woman speaker at Southern Methodist so we must be careful, mustn't we?"

It's hard to remember now how "careful" women had to be, taking those first steps thirty years ago. I remember having lunch with those girls at the YWCA, and meeting sorority and student groups, and one girl after another telling me how "careful" she had to be, *she* wasn't going to get engaged and married right after college and start having kids like the other girls, she was, well, maybe not planning on having a "career" but thinking of going to law school. Of course, she would never let on to the other girls anything "serious" like that. By the end of my visit, I was telling those young women, each thinking she was alone in her ambitions, that they should start a new support group—"Career Women Anonymous"? "Serious Girls Anonymous"?

The Kennedy administration was at least giving the impression of taking women seriously. Eleanor Roosevelt, encouraged by women's organizations like the AAUW (American Association of University Women) and BPW (Business and Professional Women) had persuaded President Kennedy in 1961 to set up a President's Commission on the Status of Women to review women's progress and to make recommendations. The commission's 1963 report, *American Women,* detailed the discriminatory wages women were earning (half the average for men) and the declining ratio of women in professional and executive jobs. Among its recommendations were calls for the end of sex discrimination for government employees; paid maternity leave for women workers; flexible academic requirements and financial aid for mothers to reenter the workforce; child care centers and other services to enable women to combine motherhood and work; and counseling programs for women to "lift aspirations beyond stubbornly persistent assumptions about 'women's roles' and 'women's interests.' "

For all the valuable information, however, the commission was given no teeth to implement its own recommendations, and the report seemed destined to be filed and forgotten. Only pressure from women's groups and a small group of women who worked for the government convinced Kennedy to extend the commission's work through an executive order (one of the last two he issued before he was assassinated on November 22, 1963) and to endorse the creation of similar commissions on the status of women in each state.

As I began to attend some of the meetings of the extended Commission on the Status of Women, I began to suspect that the real point of the Women's Bureau at the Department of Labor in Washington and other government agencies now beginning to be assigned to women was simply to keep the women quiet. The contempt which even those now publicly addressing "the women problem" felt for women themselves shocked me. And no one really expected the reports being issued by that commission to be taken seriously. Margaret Mead wrote the introduction to the commission's national report and attacked its own conclusion. If all women were going to be off making new discoveries, practicing professions, creating works of art, who was going to be home to bandage the child's knee or listen to the husband's trouble? "Honestly," I thought, "what a hypocrite, that Margaret Mead!"

I remember Johnson & Johnson hiring me as a consultant to tell them why Band-Aids weren't selling, or rather their ad agency brought me in to tell them about the new American woman. I told them the new woman might be interested in teaching the child how to put a Band-Aid on his own knee.

At a lecture in Seattle at a western regional conference called by the presidential commission, I listed all those segments of the new women waking up and moving beyond the feminine mystique—the students who would no longer quit school to put their husbands through law school but go themselves, the couples who would take turns supporting each other, the women who would no longer leave their jobs or graduate studies when they got married or started having kids, and all the women now with children in school who would go back to school themselves or back to work, and an even younger generation planning careers of their own without interruption, perhaps deciding they wouldn't get married or have kids. There was a certain urgency for the women who would have to live that paradigm shift.

I was supposed to have lunch with George Brockway in 1964 to discuss my next book. I had been embarrassed, at first, when Carl kept giving Norton hell for not printing more copies, but now that I had begun to take my work seriously, I was fed up with the gentility of Norton, playing well-bred British publisher— why print more books to stay on the best-seller list? Besides, Norton had decided early on to sell the paperback rights of *The Feminine Mystique* to Dell for $35,000, though I knew it was too soon. My then agent, Marie Rodell, had told me I was lucky they were offering that much, and Brockway told Jim Silberman, who was then working at Dell, that he thought Dell had *overpaid*. I was the only one who knew it was too little.

George Brockway hadn't even thrown me a book party, my husband did. Our friend Fred Zeserson, who had first introduced Carl and me, lent us his apartment in the city, because we didn't think people would come all the way out to Rockland County. We had the kids come in. I remember Emily in white kneesocks and Mary Jane shoes. She was in first grade then, just learning to write. Later I framed one of her first compositions on "What do you want to be when you grow up?" "I want to be a book writer," she said.

It was Don Fine of Dell who put *The Feminine Mystique* on the map in 1964. The paperback sold by the millions and was the number one best-selling non-fiction book of the year. Even now, *The Feminine Mystique* is on every list of the top ten books that have changed life in our century and has sold countless millions in foreign-language editions in countries around the world.

I couldn't know that then, of course, but I did know I was mad at Norton. So in the middle of lunch I said, "George, I'm going to another publisher. You make me feel Jewish for wanting to sell books." Bennett Cerf, the president of Random House, and his wife, Phyllis, took Carl and me to a lovely French restaurant in Connecticut for lunch and Random House became my new publisher. Random House had just hired Jim Silberman away from Dell, and he became my new editor.

My next book was supposed to find the new, post–*Feminine Mystique* patterns in the ways women and men were living their lives. "You've said no to the way women are living their lives now," George Brockway had said, even while I was still working on *The Feminine Mystique*. "But what then is the way they should be, will be living in the future?" But my own mind, and women's actual lives, were still so bounded by the feminine mystique, I simply couldn't visualize, then, the new pattern which, only a generation later, our daughters simply take for granted.

I was lecturing all over the country, still with two weeks in between. I would ask my hosts to arrange group interviews with women in their towns who were combining marriage, motherhood, and job or profession beyond the home—a job with some career commitment, "not just secretary," I would say, since I sensed the cutting edge was this kind of complex pattern—transcending the either-or, motherhood vs. career split that, to my thinking, had finished off the first century of women's struggle for equality and paved the way for the feminine mystique. The interviews I'd done, and the letters from women, confirmed that such an either-or damaged not only the majority who lived the feminine mystique but the small minority who didn't buy it, became "career women" and, for the most part, abjured marriage and motherhood.

But my interviews didn't really reveal any new patterns. Most of my generation was still home, bringing up the baby boomers. And the younger women were giving up their education in the middle of college or after high school to put their husbands through school. If husband, children and that suburban home defined the limits of feminine fulfillment, what point in wasting time and energy on different education? Never in history had educated women married so young and had so many babies. It was still the assumption that if you wanted a career, you wouldn't marry and have kids. The few women who made it into *Who's Who* had mostly not married or had children. The very few who lived busy lives combining family and career were older than I was. There didn't seem to be any *patterns*, except keeping it from the boss when they were pregnant or staying home with a sick kid. I did notice that these women who worked looked much more vital, alive, even their skin, eyes, hair, than the suburban housewives I had interviewed for *The Feminine Mystique*, who were always so "tired."

I was surprised when, to my idle question about menopause, many of these older women who had combined career and family said they didn't have any menopause. When this happened several times, I wondered if I was stumbling on biological freaks. But, no, it turned out they had stopped having menstrual periods but didn't *think* they had menopause because it wasn't any big deal. Menopause, then, was supposed to be the end of your life as a woman. But these women didn't take to their beds with depression or suffer "involutional melancholia," which filled mental hospitals. It wasn't the end of their lives as women at all. Sometimes they didn't even remember when it happened.

My mental Geiger counter clicked at these interviews. Why were these women in effect defying age? I went to see psychiatrists and obstetrician/gynecologists to find out what this might mean. They weren't much help. Menopause, the end of one's reproductive sexuality, was, had to be, traumatic for women. (And it was, when women were defined in those terms, and certainly it had been when their lives hadn't extended much beyond their reproductive years. After all, at the opening of this century, women's life expectancy was only forty-six years.) It wasn't until much later that I followed through on the questions my Geiger counter had alerted me to. That was the seed that germinated thirty years later into *The Fountain of Age*.

But it was hard for the women who were now trying to go back to school or take their jobs more seriously. It wasn't all that easy to take yourself seriously, to be taken seriously, after all those years as "just a housewife." The community colleges were starting up and a lot of women who otherwise could not have afforded to go back to school were saved thereby. They couldn't have taken serious tuition out of the household budget—perish the thought. Have to save for the kids' college.

I remember my disappointment when I approached Mary

Bunting, who was winning such acclaim for her work advising women, as president of Radcliffe. She had established an institute where educated housewives could go back for a year of supported study which might enable them to brush up their qualifications or prepare themselves to be admitted to programs, or finish their Ph.D.'s. I asked her why not pioneer at Radcliffe patterns whereby qualified women with kids could study and work toward their Ph.D.'s part-time, weekends, nights, summers, etc., instead of having to quit in the middle as so many did then. Heavens no, she said, shocked at the idea that Radcliffe would change the traditional standards of Ph.D. study to accommodate women's childbearing.

I did find a few interesting new patterns. Helen Kaplan, a brilliant young psychiatrist (who would become one of the world's leading sex educators and my close personal friend), had persuaded the medical school dean at Mount Sinai, then her husband, to make a pattern for women to do their residencies in two years instead of one, on a different schedule of hours that would permit them to be home with their kids before and after school and on weekends and vacations. But there still weren't enough new patterns to support a second book. "The only thing that's changed so far is our consciousness," I wrote one-third of the way through the book which I never finished, because the next sentence read: "What we need is a political movement, a social movement like the blacks."

Then Clay Felker, a great magazine editor, who had just left the *Herald Tribune* and not yet started *New York* magazine, called and said he'd been hired as a consultant to modernize the *Ladies' Home Journal* and he thought *The Feminine Mystique* showed the new direction women were seeking. Would I edit an issue of *Ladies' Home Journal* that would break through the feminine mystique?

I was supposed to meet Clay for lunch in the Oak Room of the Plaza. I'd often gone there for drinks with Carl after work since it was across the street from his office. But when I got there that noon and asked for Mr. Felker, the waiter said he was not there yet and refused to show me to a table to wait. "Madam, we do not serve women in the Oak Room," he said. But, I insisted, I've been here often at night with my husband. "Madam, we do not serve women under any circumstances at lunch in the Oak Room." He suggested I go to the Edwardian Room, which I did. But when Clay arrived, I hardly listened to his proposition. I didn't take it seriously, he couldn't really mean he'd let me edit the magazine. I was suffering from the lack of self-confidence that, for centuries, has kept women from having the chutzpah to say no to existing truth, to even dream of a "new yes." When I told my agent, Martha, she phoned them and then assured me that they *did* want me to edit a special issue.

Leaving their offices the next day, I remember stopping at the ladies' room and shaking my head at myself in the mirror, incredulously. The editors were treating me so differently now than I'd been treated before as a *woman* freelance writer. Writing that book had made me a *person!* I remember too my amazed delight, a few months after *The Feminine Mystique* hit the best-seller list, when suddenly I was *recognized* at the meetings of the Society of Magazine Writers when I raised my hand to speak. I was even shown to a table at the Press Club from my own place in line. Before, it always seemed as if they took care of all the men first. Maybe they had thought I was someone's wife waiting for him.

I wrote a long cover piece for *Ladies' Home Journal* called "Women, the Fourth Dimension," claiming the new possibility *over time*, in an eighty-year life span, of transcending the either-or of family and career. I used interviews of these older women who had gone back to work after their kids went to school, or a few younger ones who were *trying* to get through law or medical school or internships and residencies that were structured in terms of the lives of men whose wives took care of the details of life. But there still wasn't enough for a book. In effect, that second book on new patterns beyond the feminine mystique never got written, by me at least. My real "second book" was the women's movement that made new patterns possible.

For that special issue I got really first-rate writers—Doris Lessing, for one—to write short stories, the great black poet Gwendolyn Brooks to write a poem. In addition to my cover story on "Women, the Fourth Dimension," I commissioned a serious article, beautifully illustrated, on the best kinds of child day care for mothers working or going back to school. The cover showed a schizophrenic split: a woman with two heads, the pretty, conventional Doris Day–type housewife, and the emerging new career woman.

The circulation manager told me that that issue had done well in college towns and in the big cities and suburbs with younger women. But it raised such a ruckus among the magazine's older readers that the editors reversed themselves. The next issue featured a celebration by Phyllis McGinley of women devoting themselves to husband, children, home—even running the author's byline as "Mrs. Stuart Udall."

About that time, I also did a magazine piece for *TV Guide* on television and the feminine mystique. Interviewing network executives and producers, I found out that their image of the American housewife they were selling their soaps to was so miserable, drab and dumb, living only in desperate hunger for a man, that the young and older intern-doctor heroes of their soap operas could only have romances with a patient dying of leukemia, in order not to threaten the housewife's fantasy of him as her man. Betty Furness told me Frigidaire had instructed her to dumb herself down or she couldn't do their commercials anymore. She came over too smart for American housewives to identify with! (When she couldn't make herself dumb enough for Frigidaire, she moved on in 1967 to become President Lyndon Johnson's special assistant for consumer affairs and chairman of the President's Commission on Consumer Interests.)

Actresses were told there were no good parts for them on TV. If you tried to show a woman doing anything beyond those endless housewife chores, "American women won't identify with her." But I knew now, from all those letters, that I'd hit a chord with perhaps every woman.

I tried, without success, to convince publishers that a new magazine that *took women seriously as people* would sell. The great back-to-school, back-to-work movement was getting underway. Over one-third of women were in the workforce by the early sixties, and of those women, about one-third were married. All those baby boomer mothers were seeing their children off to school now, kindergarten, high school, college. And the "girls" who were never asked before were now asking themselves, "What do I want to be when my children grow up?"

But it was too early. Maybe my demographics weren't convincing enough. The men from Hearst, Newhouse and others were courteous, but they didn't get it then, as they would a few years later when Gloria Steinem proposed *Ms.* The magazine I had in mind was not a trumpet blast from the feminist barricades. (I did not think of myself as a "feminist," that word was not yet used. As I found out, the feminine mystique had made it a dirty word, like "career women.") I would still have covered clothes and food and home decor, and raising kids, and marriage, the women's magazine staples, because I believed women were still and will be concerned with these matters. But I would cover them in a *context* where the woman is her own person, has concerns besides those traditional ones, is involved in the larger world, ambitious in that world, concerned with her place in it. (I think such a magazine does not yet exist.)

As I was to learn soon enough, the whole Gestalt does change when a woman becomes fully recognized as a person in her own right. If I had known what it would do to my own marriage, would I have worked as hard as I did to make that big red book famous? I laugh at myself now, writing this—what a woman would have been expected to ask herself then. In reality, it was my mission, my *duty* to get that book read. I knew that despite that *dread* again.

The money I was earning was creating problems between Carl and me. We had a joint account. He could take money from that account, now that there was money in it, for his mysterious business "deals." He was a sucker for con men, those deals never did make money. So for that next book, while I had gotten, as I recall, a six-figure advance from Random House, I had it specified in the contract I would only get paid $10,000 a year.

In my search for new patterns, I went to Washington to see a woman psychiatrist who, I'd heard, was training housewives without an M.D. or Ph.D. but "equivalencies" in life experience to be some new kind of counselors. She put me up for the night and thus was witness to one of those phone calls from Carl. "It is possible to get a divorce, you know," she said bluntly. I suppose she overheard, or could figure out, what he was saying or threatening from the other end of the line. But, of course, I did not consider, would not even think about getting a divorce.

I suppose, however, I must have been getting madder and madder that because of Carl, I couldn't enjoy my new fame and fortune. I didn't sense it yet, the freedom my new fame and fortune could give me. I was only concerned with keeping it from "interfering" with my marriage and motherhood. That's the way it was then: If a woman does work or tries to have a career of her own, she must first make sure it does not interfere with her marriage or family, has no effect on her husband and kids. Get home on time to make dinner, or leave it ready to heat up in a casserole.

But I *knew better* intellectually. After all, I'd written those chapters on Freud and the lady analysts, apologizing for their own daring to have such careers themselves by dubbing it rationalizations of their penis envy. I never for one moment believed that aspirations of my own—hard as they were for me to *affirm*, carried out despite myself, one hand not letting the other know what it was doing, the two-headed lady—came from penis envy. Who would want the constant having to *get it up*, to prove oneself that way? But it wasn't really or mainly because of the kids I took such pains to stay home two weeks before setting off on a lecture again; it was Carl.

He had begun Freudian analysis now, and was full of bitter accusations of my castrating him; that's why I'd become famous and he still was no big success himself. But was I really responsible for his problems? Why didn't he try to get a job on the ground floor of television? It's true he'd had to support our family. I used the little money my father left to make the down payment on our house, I made enough money with my freelance articles to pay for part-time help, my own shrink and clothes, and help pay some of the bills. But in those days women were not even supposed to help support the family. I was *embarrassed* when I made more money than Carl, even if it was only $35 a week, in those early days when he was in the theater or on GI unemployment insurance.

I had given up any idea of a "career" when I gave up the fellowship in psychology. I did newspaper writing because I love newspapers, but I never thought of it as a career. And certainly I didn't think of the freelance magazine writing as a career. And I only wrote *The Feminine Mystique* as a book because no magazine would publish it as an article. And I was discouraged when I tried to go back and get my Ph.D. in psychology. So, I never did have a "career." But, after the book, I stopped feeling guilty about it—I put it all together finally, all the pieces of my life. And it was awesome, as my grandson would say now, how other women, after reading my book, were *taking themselves seriously and changing their lives.*

UCLA, not knowing quite how to handle all the housewives who were applying to go back to college, decided to take a bunch on a retreat to Lake Arrowhead to help them find out "what women really wanted" and invited me to be the keynote speaker. I described the new vistas of what women might be, might aspire to, if they took themselves seriously, as they must now, to take full advantage of their new eighty-year life span. I was followed by Dr. Philip Rieff, a Freudian analyst who was or had been married to Susan Sontag. He warned the women against false prophets (like me?) who were playing on their frustrations and discontents and giving them new ideas about careers. He told them these were dangerous threats to their fulfillment in their roles as women. Besides, he warned, they wouldn't be capable of actually carrying out any such dreams. After all those years of helping their kids with fourth-grade math, let them stick to the PTA, and maybe improve the teaching of fourth-grade math.

Ordinarily, I'd leave a conference after my speech. But after Rieff's speech, I heard the members of the faculty reporting the long lines of women at the phone booths, anxiously calling home to make sure the kids were all right. Were they really supposed to take such women seriously as students? It made me mad, all over again. So these women were anxious; some had never left their kids overnight before. It was feminine mystique time, remember, and maybe they were even more anxious because they were stepping outside of the feminine mystique, taking themselves seriously again, becoming students themselves, capable of something beyond fourth-grade arithmetic. Wanting to defend those first of the new women stepping out for themselves again, with all their vulnerabilities, from the contempt of Dr. Rieff and the faculty, I stayed for the whole conference, taking on and working off any notes of condescension or contempt from the faculty, supporting more boldness from those new housewife-students themselves.

But I surely wasn't getting much of anywhere, looking for patterns beyond the feminine mystique. I remember after one group interview, when I was lecturing at the University of Oklahoma, the educated women telling me how they were prisoners, forever grading freshman English papers, doomed never to get beyond instructor's pay or title because they were married to the doctor or dentist or lawyer practicing in that town and not about to leave. And when I got back home, there were long-distance calls: "Please don't use what I told you. They'll recognize me. I'm just lucky to have the job at all."

Instead of new patterns, there was all this talk, talk, talk about women and no action. I remember Esther Peterson, deputy assistant secretary of labor, calling me from the Democratic Convention in Atlantic City in 1964 to ask me to be on a women's committee to elect Lyndon Johnson. It was a farce, of course, everybody knew women voted like their husbands (and they did then, there was no "women's vote"). We all got to sit around the table where the cabinet met and have our pictures taken, but it didn't mean anything. Betty Furness and I can't even remember who else was there. Not many women had yet surfaced to be recognizable names in the United States at that time. I think I sat in the secretary of labor's seat.

It was cute, letting a few of us women on the women's committee sit in cabinet secretary seats, but that seemed to be about all it was. I remember that it was the beginning of a holiday weekend and I was stuck in the airport on a Friday night trying to get back to New York. I became friends during that long vigil with Marlene Sanders. She was working for ABC News and later became the network's first woman vice president.

Only Esther Peterson seemed determined something would come out of the women's committee. She invited me to the first event ever, analyzing the media's image of women and what it was doing to girls. But the housewife still prevailed, in those women's magazines, on television in *I Love Lucy* and *The Brady Bunch*. I remember Muriel Fox, then head of American Women in Radio and Television, inviting me to talk about television and the feminine mystique. It seemed to me many of those few women then working in that medium were made uneasy by my critique of its image of women. Muriel herself was one of the few women with a really big job in that field, executive vice president of the big PR agency Carl Byoir. Well, surely, an establishment woman like that would be very threatened by my message! But she passed me a note, quietly, just before I left: "If you ever start an NAACP for women, count me in."

I paid no attention to it. I never did think of myself as an organization woman. I was too impatient. The Women's Division of the Democratic Party just seemed to be collecting furniture for auctions and I didn't even have the patience for the League of Women Voters. I was a writer, not a political activist.

I remember a dream I had about that time. I was behind the curtain on an empty stage, peeking out, and I saw a whole big audience of women out there, waiting for the curtain to go up. It was time for the play to begin. What was holding it up? They were waiting for something, they were ready to move.

After those McCarthyite conformist fifties, when we all huddled over our backyard barbecues shutting our minds and hearts to dangerous political thoughts, social protest, social conscience, social change was springing up again, all over the place. The black civil rights movement—what did we actually call it then?— was *happening*. When those ministers, priests and rabbis went down to Alabama, when they marched with the blacks, when that sheriff Bull Connor with his bullwhip hosed down those protesters in Alabama, everyone saw it on television, paving the way for Lyndon Johnson to push the Civil Rights Act of 1964 through Congress.

I read about the passage of the new law in the newspapers in the summer of 1964, and saw with mounting excitement that Title VII of the Civil Rights Act not only banned racial discrimination but sex discrimination as well. Here was a real, new pattern, or the possibility of one. A law guaranteeing equal job opportunity for women would mean that bosses could no longer refuse to hire or promote women, fire them for getting married or pregnant. Illegal now, against the law! But just as the national report from the Commission on the Status of Women was being buried in bureaucratic drawers, so, evidently, were the equal opportunity guarantees for women in Title VII.

Soon afterwards I saw an item buried on an inner page of *The*

New York Times that a Yale Law School professor named Pauli Murray had told the convention of the General Confederation of Women's Clubs that unless women were prepared to march on Washington as the black people had done, the sex discrimination provisions in Title VII would never get enforced and women would lose their historic chance. And my inner Geiger counter clicked again.

I knew in my gut that the new pattern had to transcend that no-win either-or of marriage and family versus career, that a profession, job, outside the home was what every woman needed now. And those words "sex discrimination" suddenly threw light onto the murkiness, the seeming difficulty surrounding women's movement into such jobs. When I was fired for being pregnant, there were no such words as "sex discrimination" in my vocabulary. I knew now that "jobs" were the issue for women. I read that item in the newspaper with a sense of recognition. I tracked down Pauli Murray at Yale and made a date to meet her. And I started down the road that would lead to the women's movement.

SEVEN

Starting the Women's Movement

When I've written before about starting the women's movement, starting NOW, it's been with a breathless incredulity that we, ordinary American women—suburban housewives, League of Women Voters volunteers, nuns, trade union members, guilty career women, back-to-school community college students and educators, frustrated women government bureaucrats— started a revolution that transformed society. And as I look back now, tracing small parts that became greater than the whole, I still feel in awe.

Pauli Murray, later to become one of the first women to be ordained as an Episcopal priest, and a member of the original President's Commission on the Status of Women, was very impressive. She turned out to be a brilliant lawyer and articulate black woman who was frustrated, as were the impatient women in Washington and Detroit I met through her, by the burial of the commission's recommendations and the trivializing of Title VII. I shared that same frustration. And once again, my Geiger counter began buzzing.

The women Murray led me to in Washington were bureaucratic insiders, a small cadre of senior women working for the government who were getting just plain tired of all the talk, talk, talk about women and no one really intending to do anything about it. Pauli introduced me to Mary Eastwood, then working in the Office of Legal Counsel in the Department of Justice (the two were writing an article entitled "Jane Crow and the Law: Sex Discrimination and Title VII"), and to Catherine East, executive secretary of the Commission on the Status of Women, who had worked for the Women's Bureau for years and had come to the conclusion that in spite of its records and statistics on women's employment, health and the like, its main function was to keep women quiet.

They in turn introduced me to Marguerite Rawalt, a lawyer who had headed the legal task force for the national Commission on the Status of Women and was then working for the IRS, and to other women from the Labor Department and other agencies supposedly doing something about women. They had done the staffwork for the national Commission on the Status of Women and had fought all the way, in vain, for teeth to implement the commission's recommendations. My new Washington friends were all at the same point of impatience.

I called this network of women I was meeting my "underground," which made them laugh. They thought I was romanticizing their small network with a revolutionary term like "underground," but they liked it. And oh, how they welcomed me, could be open with me where they were used to being secret for fear of losing their government jobs. It was the end of the McCarthy era and you could still be fired for organizing anything openly. Catherine, who was middle-aged then, older than I, divorced and putting her daughter through college, didn't dare do anything that might cause her to lose her job at the Women's Bureau. (But then, and through the years to come, she served as a formidable one-woman research and support system, supplying those of us who were free to do what needed to be done with the statistics and data we needed.) That "underground" of women maneuvered me into place all right, recognizing that I, famous for writing a controversial book about women, could do publicly what they could only do underground: organize a women's movement.

I went down to Washington nearly every week in 1965, supposedly to research my next book, and spent two or three days at the wonderful old and slightly seedy Jefferson Hotel. Actors and actresses stayed there while their plays opened or had trial runs in Washington, and I knew about it from Carl. Those days at the Jefferson were a welcome escape. I was entering the last years of my marriage and things were pretty stormy at home. Almost every time I got ready to go to Washington, and especially when I returned, Carl and I would get into an argument and he would start beating up on me.

But for reasons that are still unclear to me, I still wasn't considering divorce. I didn't confront Carl. That's the reason I've always been uneasy, politically, about the battered wife issue because I knew from personal experience that it wasn't that simple. When it was happening to me, if I am honest about it, I think I colluded in it. I think if I had made it clear to Carl that I would leave him if he didn't stop hitting me, he probably would have stopped. But I didn't. I know I am blaming the victim, even if the victim was me, but I think I accepted the abuse because I didn't have the nerve, somehow, to get out, or make it clear that I would get out.

Was Carl really a vicious wife-beater? Or, taunting himself as he must have when my fame became just too much, did the slightest hint of taunt from me, when we were both drinking as much as we were drinking then every night—a martini or two or more before dinner, and brandy after—bring out pent-up rage? Looking back on it now, I was so into what we would surely call denial that I didn't want to admit how much I really enjoyed my new fame or how angry I was at Carl for not letting me enjoy it. Guilty of all that, I suppose, I taunted him into finally beating up on me and giving me those black eyes, giving us both something to feel guilty about to make up for that incredible unearned fame (unearned? I *earned* it) that he couldn't really share.

But I would not consider getting divorced. Not only that nobody I knew, nobody in my family, ever had. But Smith women don't give up—the divorces in the Smith *Alumnae Bulletin* are still much lower than the national average. And I *liked* being married. And so, despite the concern of my friend Milton Carrow, who had seen Carl smack me around in the car, despite the support and concern of my shrink, who was worried about permanent damage to my face if I let it go on (I still have some scar tissue), despite my own embarrassment in having to seek shelter from Carl with my friends or at the Jefferson Hotel, the marriage continued.

My political education in Washington was turning out to be stormy as well. I was still theoretically looking for "new patterns beyond the feminine mystique" for my second book, but the patterns I found in Washington were all turning out to be a little phony. Lyndon Johnson was making a big fuss about naming women to high positions in the State Department, prompted by a subliminal awareness of the potential of the women's vote. But the highest jobs women were being promoted to had titles such as "Assistant to the Assistant Secretary of State" in charge of flower-arranging or picking out paintings to decorate the embassies. One woman, given an impressive new title at one of the government agencies, told me she had been sitting there for three months, with no orders to do anything beyond memorizing the agency's internal phone book.

A cousin of mine, who was married to a distinguished judge, David Bazelon, was working as a volunteer in the poverty program with Marie Ritter. But when I went to see Sargent Shriver, the head of the poverty program, I discovered that there were no women in decision-making posts, and no programs or job training at all for women, even though women, and children supported by women, made up 80 percent of the welfare rolls. The poverty program didn't include "girls" in their figures for high school dropouts or unemployed youth. "Why should I worry about computer training for a woman who would rather be my wife and mother of my children?" Sargent Shriver said to me. Maybe it was my own bias, but I was not impressed by a poverty program in Detroit that was offering girls a course in beauty parlor techniques.

I started nosing around the Equal Employment Opportunity Commission (EEOC), the agency empowered to oversee enforcement of Title VII outlawing racial as well as sex discrimination in employment. Everyone was very polite to me, but they didn't exactly regale me, as I had expected, with stories about companies and whole industries forced to hire and promote women where they never had before, or to work out parental leave policies. Finally, one young woman EEOC lawyer, Sunny Pressman, shut her office door. "Nobody ever appointed me to represent women and I'm not a feminist," she told me, "but I can't stand what's going on here. It's like some secret order has been given not to do battle on the sex discrimination part of Title VII. We're getting hundreds, thousands of complaints, but nobody is supposed to do anything about them. You've got to expose it."

Sunny was married, at the time, to an economist working for the Johnson administration. Taking seriously President Johnson's promise to bring women into government, she'd researched and made a file of openings that existed in government jobs that might be filled by women. When she'd gone with her husband to the president's annual tea in the Rose Garden and it was her turn to shake the president's hand, she'd told Johnson about the list, which could save him a lot of time in making those appointments. The next day her husband was warned by the White House to tell his wife to shut up.

Then I met Richard Graham, a Republican appointee on the EEOC who'd emerged as a real fighter for women. But his term was about to expire and the expectation among my underground informants was that he wasn't going to be reappointed because he took the new law against sex discrimination seriously. Among the thousands of complaints being filed with the EEOC in the first year of Title VII were many from "stewardesses," as flight attendants were called then, who charged the airlines with violating Title VII by hiring only women and not men for the job, and forcing them to resign if they got married, became pregnant, or reached the age of thirty-five.

Dick Graham wanted the EEOC to hear the stewardesses' case and to take action as well on help-wanted ads which also violated Title VII. Though the new law specifically made illegal discriminatory advertising like "Help Wanted, White" for all the good jobs and "Help Wanted, Colored," for shoeshine boys, newspapers were continuing to run "Help Wanted, Male" for all the good jobs, and "Help Wanted, Female" for sales clerks, housemaids and Gal Fridays. Behind closed doors again, Dick Graham told me that the commission was about to issue a waiver exempting newspapers from the ban on sex-based help-wanted ads as long as each newspaper put a disclaimer in the upper-left-hand corner—"Each employer subscribes to equal employment opportunity."

If that happened, Dick Graham told me, it would be a signal to employers everywhere that they didn't really have to do anything about sex discrimination, didn't have to take Title VII or the

EEOC seriously. They could continue firing women because they got pregnant, or like the stewardesses, make them resign at thirty or thirty-five or marriage, or say, "I wouldn't take a woman in management training."

Dick Graham was convinced that a new organization was needed to speak on behalf of women—that "NAACP for women" again—or women would lose their historic chance. But when he'd gone personally to urge the heads of the League of Women Voters, the AAUW, and other women's organizations with national headquarters in Washington to exert pressure on the Johnson administration to get Title VII enforced, they had been appalled at the very suggestion. "We're not feminists," the head of the League of Women Voters at the time told him. "We're just not concerned with issues like that."

Of course, the League of Women Voters, after its feminist origins in the battle for women's right to vote, had become if not anti-feminist in the years of the feminine mystique, then feminist-denying. The League was very chaste and pure now in fighting for "good government" in non-political, non-threatening ways and not especially concerned with women at all. Such a dirty word "feminist" had become in those years that it seemed almost obscene, surely "strident."

Then my phone began to ring in the middle of the night with calls from suffragettes, dauntless old women now in their eighties and nineties who had chained themselves to the White House fence to get the vote. These leftover feminists who refused to die were seen as a joke and a nuisance by Washington political observers, even by the underground concerned with jobs and Title VII. But now these ancient fighters were calling me and saying in their wavery voices: "You've got to do something about getting Title VII enforced."

Why me? I guess because I didn't have anything to be afraid of, was known for championing women, and most important, didn't work for the government and didn't have a job I could be fired from. I was free. And because I was well known and they were not, I could attract attention. "Go to the White House or call a press conference and warn Lyndon Johnson that he will betray women if he allows the ban on sex discrimination in employment and advertising to be weakened," they told me.

Surely the progressive unions like the United Automobile

Workers (UAW) and the CIO were working to get that law against sex discrimination enforced. But my underground, who often came up to my hotel room at the Jefferson after dinner and somehow started me making lists of key women I had met in my research around the country, showed me cases where the unions were actually siding with the bosses against the women. They got me to go out to Detroit, where I met Dorothy Haener and Caroline Davis, who were in charge of the "women's department" for the UAW. They, at least, with their training and tradition of fighting for workers' rights, were now, with UAW president Walter Reuther's approval, evidently putting their full attention to the millions of invisible women working on the assembly lines and organizing them and fighting for their rights and needs in union contracts. And so the underground grew.

It was through the union women in Detroit that I got to Martha Griffiths, the intrepid congresswoman from Michigan, and learned the magnificent story of how Title VII actually got into the Civil Rights Act of 1964 and why it didn't get taken out. When it became clear in the heady days after Martin Luther King's March on Washington that nothing could stop the law that would make racial discrimination illegal, she told me, Congressman Howard Smith, an avid segregationist from Virginia, had tried a last-minute tactic to kill the bill by proposing the addition of sex discrimination—as a joke. The House almost had to be recessed in the hysterical laughter that followed. But Griffiths and the few other women in Congress swore to make those men stop laughing; they demanded a roll call vote in the House. In the Senate, Margaret Chase Smith of Maine, the only woman senator, demanded the same of Everett Dirksen, the minority leader. Though nobody took the women's vote seriously yet, some sound instinct told those male congressional leaders that they better not be counted in a roll call vote against the ladies, so the "joke" stayed in Title VII of the Civil Rights Act of 1964.

But the law, at first, was still considered a joke. When Franklin Roosevelt, Jr., the first chair of the EEOC, was asked what he was going to do about sex discrimination at a 1965 press conference at the first White House Conference on Equal Employment Opportunity, he'd replied: "Oh, sex discrimination? I guess we'll have to insist that boys can be Playboy bunnies."

The Washington underground pressed their campaign to get me to start an NAACP for women in the spring of 1966. The third annual conference of the various commissions on the status of women was going to convene in Washington in June. All the commissions from the fifty states were invited to report, but my Washington friends were less than hopeful about the result. Three years before, they had watched in dismay as the president disbanded the national commission, with thanks, and filed its report to be forgotten. Didn't I realize the same thing was happening now in every state? Though it was clear that something had to be done, the commissions were not going to do it. The men and women appointed by their governors to those state commissions could be counted on not to rock the boat, my friends told me, because the only power the delegates had came from the governors. Even if some of the members were outraged about the status of women, there was nothing they could do because the commissions were set up with no power to act.

The women presiding over the final conference were also handicapped. Senior women, among the very few in government at the time, the majority from the Women's Bureau, they were charged with carrying out the administration's policies, not challenging them. Any dissent could derail their careers, even cost them their jobs.

The group was pressuring me to have a press conference at the meeting in Washington to raise a public outcry. They knew that Title VII was an opportunity that might not happen again, and that the inclusion of women in the law had to be taken seriously and enforced. I agreed with them that there *needed to be* an NAACP for women, that we must use that law now that we had it, that we must not let it be destroyed. But the NAACP analogy never seemed quite right, even at the time. We were talking about a *revolution*, and though the NAACP fought for black people (not like those women's organizations so afraid of being called "feminist"), the NAACP wasn't considered a radical organization at all. So I said no, I couldn't hold a press conference and sound the call for action, but I would get a press pass to cover the two-day conference. I'd never been an organization woman. I'd never been a member of any women's group. I was a writer who had written about women.

"Instead of starting an NAACP for women," I said, "we should get those fifty Commissions on the Status of Women to demand that Title VII be enforced, and repudiate the attempt to weaken it in the 'help-wanted' ads. And they should tell the president that he has to reappoint Dick Graham. And if that is not enough, strong women from *all* the states will be there to get an NAACP for women started."

Though I resisted sticking out my own neck, the urgency my Washington guides were conveying about the threat of losing Title VII and the whole new road that would be possible with sex discrimination outlawed struck home to me. I knew that jobs were what women needed now, *real* jobs, not just temporary, secretarial "until-I-get-married" jobs or teachers' certificates in case their husbands died.

I had known since I was a child the frustration that my mother felt, with no job, no role in society except as my father's wife or our mother, and that it had made her angry and bitter and disappointed. I knew in my gut how important jobs were for all those women who could no longer plan to live an eighty-year life span as "just a housewife." And I knew it would take a revolution to move beyond the feminine mystique, that men and women both would have to transform society. And I understood that it was in the question of jobs that the issue would be joined.

I ran into Dorothy Haener and Pauli Murray on the escalator at the Washington Hilton the first morning of the conference and I remember, with that dread I should recognize every time I start down a new road, that I agreed to invite whomever we met who seemed interested in organizing women for action to my hotel room that night. I invited Kay Clarenbach, head of the Wisconsin Commission and director of continuing education at the University of Wisconsin, after hearing her biting analysis of how little had been done about women, despite the talk. I thought she was ready to move, as impatient as I was.

We were bused over to the White House that afternoon, where Lady Bird gave us tea in the Rose Garden and LBJ patted us figuratively on the head. The members of the state commissions must be so happy, the president said, now that the reports were in and the job was done. It was time for us to go back home and resume our volunteer work, distributing grocery bags to the poor and helping the children with their homework. There was not one word uttered about Title VII and job discrimination against women.

The women met that night in my hotel room, around fifteen to twenty of them. Kay Clarenbach was there, and Catherine Conroy of the Communications Workers of America, several members from the California and Wisconsin commissions, Dorothy Haener and Caroline Davis from the UAW, and Pauli Murray, Catherine East from the Labor Department and Mary Eastwood from the Department of Justice, among others. Catherine and Mary had made up most of the list of the key women in the room, but Mary at first hadn't dared show up herself. It was too dangerous.

It is not surprising that there was a certain timidity in that crowded hotel room. The idea of starting a women's organization seemed radical, especially to those of the official establishment, women whose job was to keep other women quiet. How could we trust each other? Kay's presence was greeted with particular suspicion by the underground. She was "the darling of the Women's Bureau," one warned me, the federal agency we all agreed was so threatened by the idea of a real women's movement that they would do anything to stop it.

We argued until after midnight. Everyone was concerned about the betrayal of Title VII and everybody wanted to get Richard Graham reappointed. But nobody, except for the members of the underground and me, wanted to start an independent organization. In fact, there was a lot of talk about why we should *not*. The others wanted to work within the system, and were nervous at the thought of starting an organization independent of the government.

I was very disappointed at their lack of fire, for some reason not recognizing my own dread in others. I remember Kay Clarenbach being particularly hesitant, seeing me, I'm sure, as a rabble-rousing New York radical. The consensus at the end of the meeting was that Kay would introduce a resolution on the floor of the convention the next day to be voted on demanding that Dick Graham be reappointed and that Title VII be enforced. The idea of starting an organization for women was put on hold, probably to be discarded altogether.

I remember Pauli Murray, Dorothy Haener and me looking at each other and shrugging—*Women*. What can you expect? I thought the battle was over before it had begun. I also remember going to bed relieved at least that the Washington underground would stop pestering me now. And then, in the morning, the phone started to ring.

Kay had been blocked from introducing the resolutions, members of the underground told me. The conference leadership not only had ruled resolutions "out of order" but had told her that this conference on the official status of women had no power to take any action, not even on sex discrimination. Kay was outraged, as were many of the other women who had held back the night before. "We've taken a table for us all at lunch to start the NAACP for women," the underground told me.

The phone rang again. "What are you doing here, stirring up the women, rocking the boat?" said Mary Keyserling, head of the Women's Bureau and one of the conference leaders who'd ruled against Kay. "You'll get us all in trouble."

The lunch took place on June 29, 1966, under the noses of the members of Johnson's cabinet who were praising us for our good work and urging us to go home. I wondered whether they knew that the fifteen or so of us seated at the two front tables, rudely and agitatedly whispering to each other, and passing notes written on napkins, were laying the groundwork for one of the most profound social revolutions of the century. We had to work fast because most of us had plane reservations that afternoon. We had to get back home in time to make dinner for our families and get the kids ready for school on Monday.

The name of the modern women's movement, we decided, would be the National Organization for Women, NOW. It wasn't going to be women against men; men had to be included, though women must take the lead. I wrote the first sentence of NOW's Statement of Purpose on a paper napkin: "to take the actions needed to bring women into the mainstream of American society now, exercising all the privileges and responsibilities thereof, in truly equal partnership with men." Actions, not just talk.

We would meet in Washington in October to organize NOW formally, we decided. We'd all invite women and men we knew we needed to get the organization going. Kay Clarenbach, who at least had an office and a secretary in Wisconsin, would run the operation over the summer. Before rushing off to the airport, we all agreed to chip in five dollars a person. As the word got around, those five-dollar bills kept coming at us, one from Eleanor Roosevelt's granddaughter, Anna.

Catherine East and Mary Eastwood came out to Fire Island to see me that summer. "You have to take leadership of the new organization," they said. "I'm sure Kay wants to be president, and everyone does respect her," I replied. But they insisted that I had to do it, that this organization had to dare in ways previous women's organizations had not dreamed of really fighting for women.

At the century's end, understanding how the women's movement transformed our whole society, I see us then, starting it all with incredible chutzpah, knowing somehow that we were accepting the challenge history was giving us to take up that unfinished revolution for women's equality that the suffragists had carried forward, but that had nearly sputtered out in those years of feminine mystique. "The time has come to confront, with concrete actions, the conditions that now prevent women from enjoying the equality of opportunity and freedom of choice which is their right, as individual Americans, and as human beings," I wrote in that first draft of NOW's Statement of Purpose.

NOW officially began on October 29, 1966, with some three hundred charter members. Around thirty of them came to that organizational meeting in Washington in the John Philip Sousa community meeting room at the *Washington Post*. Among them were two nuns: Sister Mary Austin Doherty, and Sister Mary Joel Read, who later became president of Alverno College in Milwaukee. Labor women came—Caroline Davis and Dorothy Haener of UAW, Catherine Conroy of the Communications Workers, and businesswomen such as Muriel Fox.

There were men, like Phineas Indritz, a civil rights lawyer in Washington who supported us from the beginning. Members of the state commissions on the status of women attended, like Virginia Allen, a Republican appointee and an intrepid, correct WASP who never wavered in her clearheaded championship of women's rights. Sociologists Alice Rossi, then at Goucher College, and Carl Degler, chair of the history department at Vassar, were there, and Janey Hart, the wife of Senator Philip Hart, who had a pilot's license and was an outspoken advocate for women in NASA's fledgling space program.

There was this *sense of history* we all shared as we began to make it happen. Here women, for all these years, had done volunteer work and helped organize and support causes of anti-fascism, of the plight of the poor, organizing for everything but women themselves. But now, finally, we were doing it for ourselves—for women. It was a heady business, as if we were moving to this enormous chord. There were only thirty of us but we were certain we spoke for millions.

The timing was indicative of the way movements happen in America. In 1848, Elizabeth Cady Stanton and the other early feminists decided that they had to have a movement to emancipate women, not just slaves, after they'd come back from an abolitionist congress in London where they were forced to sit in the balcony behind curtains. Just as the first women's movement came on the heels of the black movement to abolish slavery, so did the modern movement we were starting come soon after the March on Washington for the blacks and the passage of the Civil Rights Act of 1964. Liberation was in the air and it would have been surprising if women didn't apply it to themselves.

NOW's Statement of Purpose was adopted at that first meeting as I'd drafted it, with one exception. I had wanted to confront the issue of abortion but was advised not to include it because it was too controversial. (It wasn't until its second year that NOW confronted the issue.) But the statement, which included many of the comparative statistics about women that Catherine East had put together, addressed far-ranging concerns, including inequality in the workplace. Though almost half (46.4%) of all American women were working outside the home, the statement pointed out, 75 percent were either in clerical or factory jobs or they were household workers, cleaning women and hospital attendants. Earning only 60 cents for every dollar earned by men, half of all full-time women workers earned less than $3,690 a year! College-educated white women earned less than high school–educated black men, while African American women (or Negro women, as they were referred to then) faced the double discrimination of race and sex: Almost two-thirds of Negro women were in the lowest-paid service occupations.

Women were underrepresented in every profession and were losing ground. Though women made up 51 percent of the population, they accounted for less than 1 percent of federal judges, less than 4 percent of all lawyers and 7 percent of all doctors. They were just as underrepresented in the institutions of higher education. In 1966, only one out of three B.A.'s and M.A.'s were being earned by women and one in ten of the Ph.D.'s.

The statement called for equal opportunity and the end of job discrimination for women and other deprived groups, the end of quotas against the admission of women to graduate schools, equal representation for women in the committees and leadership of political parties, the end of the "false image" of women portrayed in the mass media, the end of the "protective" policies and practices that deny opportunity for women.

We were clear, forthright and firm about our objectives. Fighting for women's rights and knocking down the barriers that kept women from moving into the mainstream of society was a legitimate goal now, which it had never really been before. "We organize to initiate or support action, nationally or in any part of this nation, by individuals or organizations, to break through the silken curtain of prejudice and discrimination against women in government, industry, the professions, the churches, the political parties, the judiciary, the labor unions, in education, science, medicine, law, relationships and every field of importance in American society," the statement read. Mary Eastwood had us all sign the document, which she later put in the National Archives.

We also voted on a proposed slate of national officers and board members at that first organizing conference. Richard Graham, who had not been reappointed to the EEOC despite our efforts, would be vice president, Caroline Davis would be secretary-treasurer, which would give us free access to the UAW's printing and mailing facilities. The leadership positions would be shared by Kay Clarenbach and me.

At a previous meeting I'd persuaded Kay that to avoid a fight, why didn't we split the leadership; she'd be chairman of the board, I'd be president, because it made more sense to run a national organization out of Washington or New York than Wisconsin. And we turned out to make a solid team. Kay was more radical than she had seemed, had good organizational skills and was a more patient parliamentarian than I. I'd have my big ideas, but I'd never act on any of them without consulting Kay, who usually just spurred me on.

I knew that we would have to make the decisions of the organizing conference public, so shortly before the meeting in Washington I had asked several friends over to my apartment in New York to discuss "public relations"—Betty Furness, who was now a consumer advocate, Marlene Sanders, who was about to be made vice president of ABC News, and Muriel Fox, the business executive who'd first sent me a note saying, "If you ever start an NAACP for women, count me in." "You've got to come over and take charge of the PR," I told them. "We're going to start a woman's movement."

Muriel, then a vice president of the huge Carl Byoir outfit and the top woman in PR in America, said she'd be happy to "consult" with us (for free, of course) and tell the staff what to do. Well, there was no such staff, of course. Muriel ended up bringing her husband, Shep, a doctor and also a founding member of NOW, and their two infants to Washington for the organizing meeting. That night, after we adopted the Statement of Purpose, Shep baby-sat the kids while Muriel and a half dozen women economists and lawyers stayed up all night writing and running off the first press release on Janey Hart's husband's senatorial office mimeograph machine and hand-delivering them to the newspaper offices.

But the real public launching of NOW was the press conference after our first board meeting in the winter of 1966 in my apartment at the Dakota. We had our women board members there, among them our nuns in their habits. (They were liberated nuns who were personally moving more and more out of wearing their habits, but I used to insist they wear them when we visited members of Congress or had our pictures taken and they agreed for the cause.) All the networks, the newspapers, and the wire services came. A woman's movement was being organized that was reported from the beginning as big news, that was seen as history.

At the beginning, there was the columnist and a couple of prissy women's page editors who were afraid of being called "feminists." But on the whole we got terrific media coverage from male reporters as well as women. We had to worry about being taken seriously. I knew that there was no way we could start a national movement of women in our great big America without the mass media. Some of our group considered reporters enemies and wanted to bar them—certainly male reporters—but I would have none of that. I was never afraid of the media, I came from the media. I would tell my sisters, "If you want to change consciousness, and isn't that what we are doing, you need to use the mass media to get the story out to this huge nation of ours. You can't do it otherwise. There is no reason to be afraid of the media. The way to control it is by giving them something to report, by what you do and what you say." We did use the media and we got the story out.

This was a period when everybody was liberating themselves and liberation was news. You had the SDS, the student movement; you had the anti-Vietnam War, the peace movement; you had the grape pickers striking and Cesar Chavez fighting for field workers; you had SNCC, the black student movement. It was an era of social change, revealing the power of ordinary people to organize and make demands and reshape society. It all seemed very possible. Maybe it was a younger generation coming of age in great numbers, I don't know. But there was this powerful feeling that you didn't just have to go along and accept things the way they'd always been and put on a few timid Band-Aids. It was in the air that you could—and should—start a real movement to change your position if you were in an oppressive situation. The students were doing it. The blacks were doing it. It was time for us.

I knew there were all those women out there, waiting. Over three million copies of *The Feminine Mystique* had been sold and I was still getting all these letters telling me "it changed my life." I also knew from my own experiences, from the research I was doing in Washington and Detroit for the second book I never wrote, and from the increasingly large audiences at my lectures, that women needed a movement to break through the visible and invisible barriers they faced.

Title VII, the provision against sex discrimination in employment, was the defining moment that made the women's movement possible. Now, finally, we were going to *act*.

EIGHT

Out of the Mainstream into the Revolution

When people ask me now—"Did you realize you were starting this huge revolution?"—the answer is yes and no, no and yes. It seems to me that we knew what we were doing and that it was important beyond what it could seem at the time with only thirty or so founding members, but I'm not sure we ever dreamed how big it was going to become. Yes, we were going to transform society, the political agenda, all of it—and we did. But did we realize it at the time? Underneath, there was a sense of dread and yet a sense of existential necessity. Like I didn't plan it, I just knew what had to be done and the next thing that had to be done. We didn't have a grand blueprint. We just invented it as we went along and that's the way it happened. There's no question, however, that the women's movement was and *is* the second chapter of the American Revolution.

Our first order of business was to make it clear to Washington, to employers, to unions and to the nation that someone *was* watching, someone *cared* about ending sex discrimination. So our first official acts were to petition the EEOC to rescind its guidelines allowing discriminatory help-wanted ads in newspapers and to issue a finding of sex discrimination in the long-delayed case of the stewardesses. How could it not be sex discrimination to fire the stewardesses as soon as the first lines appeared around their eyes while allowing pilots to marry, have children, and age in the sky?

We had no idea what a high-stakes game we were in until the EEOC finally decided to vote on the stewardesses and the airlines moved to block whatever decision was reached. Because Aileen Hernandez, the only woman commissioner at the EEOC, was also a member of NOW, the Air Transport Association invoked "conflict of interest" and managed to get a restraining order from the courts on the propriety of her participation in the EEOC determination. Aileen was subsequently subpoenaed to appear in federal district court on the West Coast, as was I, in New York, on Christmas Eve, 1966.

This was the first case that I really got involved in, not ever having been subpoenaed before, but I felt secure enough. I was getting the equivalent of a law school education in the early years of organizing NOW and the women's movement because I had to. And I knew my rights. When the high-powered attorney representing the airlines, a man so famous that even I had heard of him, demanded NOW's membership list, I refused to give it to him. We had all agreed to keep the membership secret to protect the officers and charter members from being fired, or, with the advent of the first right-to-life groups organized by the Catholic Church in 1965, excommunicated.

Still, I remember wondering why the airlines were spending a fortune hiring all these expensive lawyers and dragging us to court to give affidavits on Christmas Eve. And then I began to see that sex discrimination was big business. The real reason the airlines wanted to force the stewardesses to resign at thirty or thirty-five or marriage was so they wouldn't ever get enough seniority to get good pay, good vacations, good pensions, good smarts to fight the company. It was in the airlines' best interest to fight the enforcement of Title VII because women were a reliable source of cheap labor.

Our frustration grew after the judge ruled for the airlines, leaving the EEOC decision on the stewardesses lingering for over a year, and there was no word at all from the EEOC on our petition for a public hearing on guidelines for the help-wanted ads. So I said, "Well, we'll have an action." Our first was in February 1967.

Looking back on it now, I marvel at our nerve. There were so few of us, but we organized simultaneous demonstrations at EEOC offices all over the country and tipped off the television networks. In view of the cameras, we dumped newspapers all tied up in red ribbon tape at the feet of the government agents. I went with my bag of papers to see the head of the EEOC in New York and demanded that a hearing be held on the help-wanted ads and that the law be enforced on behalf of women. He thought we were cute and was utterly condescending, reacting to women speaking out as if he were hearing a dog talk.

I was so annoyed at his attitude that I borrowed his secretary's phone and called Mary Eastwood at the Justice Department.

"Mary, can you sue the government for not enforcing the law?" I asked.

"Yes," she said.

"How do I say it?" I asked her.

"Demand a *writ of mandamus,*" she said.

I'd never heard of a *writ of mandamus* but I went outside to the television cameras, threw down the bundle of newspapers wrapped in red tape, and announced that the National Organization for Women was demanding a *"writ of mandamus* be filed against the U.S. government for not enforcing Title VII on behalf of our sex." The legal action being taken by NOW, I went on, was an expression of women's "acute outrage" being demonstrated by "our sisters" all over the country. No matter that we only had two members in Atlanta, six in Pittsburgh, a dozen or so in Chicago and California and not too many more in between visibly doing the same action. If there was one thing I learned early on, and we had great people like Kathy Bonk who made an art of it, was to use chutzpah and mirrors. We may only have had six women at a press conference and not that many more at our first national action, but we knew we were speaking for 600,000 or 6,000,000 and we acted accordingly and made our point.

The men at the EEOC weren't used to anything like this from women and didn't know how to respond. But their eyes were opened wide, as it were. (Later I would meet these guys from the EEOC again, the head of the EEOC in New York then was a Puerto Rican I think, and they would tell me that they thought we were really the nuts.) But we had to use any tactics we could to be taken seriously and improvise, if need be, as we went along. And in this case, it worked.

Union women and some men as well testified on behalf of the enforcement of Title VII at the hearing we forced the government finally to hold in Washington in the summer of 1967, as did some male publishers and advertisers. Martha Griffiths, who had castigated the EEOC's ruling on sex-segregated want ads on the floor of Congress as the "peak of contempt," took on the airlines. "Do you think people ride the airlines because the stewardesses are nubile or so they can get to Chicago on business?" she said. "If you are trying to run a whorehouse in the sky, then get a license." And finally, finally, the EEOC began to mandate the law against sex discrimination.

Though it would take another year, a complaint filed by the New York chapter of NOW with the Human Rights Commission in New York, the *writ of mandamus* filed against the EEOC, and several coordinated NOW demonstrations against sex-segregated job advertising (NOW members in New York staged a widely publicized picket line in front of *The New York Times* office, which the paper was forced to cover as a news story), a few key newspapers including all four in New York finally capitulated in 1968 and began to advertise jobs alphabetically and without gender. The American Newspaper Publishers Association (ANPA) would make one last stand in 1969 by challenging the authority of the EEOC regulation in federal court, but ANPA would lose.

Nothing gave me greater pleasure than to pick up *The New York Times*, whose business manager had told us patronizingly on that first day of national actions that it would be suicidal for newspapers to change their sex-segregated advertising, and to see "Help Wanted—Male-Female: Wall Street Bank Reconciliation Supervisor, Warehouse Supervisor, Buyer/Sales Person, Lunch Counterperson"—not exactly singing poetry, but the early fruits of herstory.

And though the case of the stewardesses would also linger at the EEOC and in the courts until 1968, stewardesses were finally allowed to grow up and still fly. For many years afterward, when I was on an airplane, I would get a kick—and still do—out of seeing stewardesses with lines around their eyes. Often they recognize me and ply me with champagne.

We didn't have money in the early years for an organizing staff or an office staff or even supplies. The staff was me, sometimes Emily, an adolescent in kneesocks, whom I paid 50 cents an hour to help get our first mailings out from my dining-room table in New York, and a few of NOW's first organizers who took full advantage of their paid employment opportunities to get our work done. I have no idea whether Carl Byoir ever knew that they were doing our printing or whatever, or whether Walter Reuther knew that the UAW where Dorothy Haener worked was sending out our mailings. One employer knew for sure. Until Dolores Alexander, a prize-winning reporter at *Newsday*, left the paper to be my assistant (Dolores would soon become NOW's first national executive director), several women moonlighted after their day's work as secretaries at W. R. Grace. One day I called one of them at the office and the boss answered the phone. "I'm getting quite a kick out of helping you organize your movement," Mr. Grace told me.

The ideology of those of us who started the women's movement was not sexual or political. I would have said, then, we had no ideology. It was simply the idea of equality, of American democracy. But when applied to women by women in terms of the grit and substance of their real lives and daily duties as women, it became a different kind of revolution from any before. This was not a mere matter of an oppressed group seizing power from its oppressors and oppressing them in return. This was a revolutionary and unique new concept—a women's movement for equality in truly equal partnership with men.

The first national board met in cities around the country to decide on everything from policy and actions to membership dues. Should the dues be $25 or scaled even higher according to ability to pay so we'd have money in the treasury to hire the services that were taking so much of our time—or should we reduce them to $5 so the women in direst poverty could join NOW?

We crammed everything we had to do into the shortest possible time so we wouldn't waste time or spend money on hotel bills. In retrospect, it's sort of a miracle it all happened. Nobody had any money. The women on the board who had jobs did not have the kind of jobs that had expense accounts for travel and the women who volunteered at women's organizations were housewives. They couldn't take the grocery money or the school lunch money to pay for food and hotel bills. I don't remember eating at all at those early board meetings. There was so much to be done in so little time that we scarcely took time to go to the john. I emerged from those early years of NOW leadership with a bladder like a camel!

I hated the procedural wrangling at board meetings or national conferences and regarded any time spent on structure or details of internal housekeeping as time wasted, time stolen from the business of the women's movement. I began to get headaches and to start impatiently tapping my foot under the tables when our finicky lawyers felt it necessary to change the by-laws yet again, or to describe the endless red tape we still had to negotiate to get tax-exempt status for our legal defense fund. (It wouldn't come through until 1971!) I just wanted to get out there and *do* it.

The necessary thing, I realized, as the *idea* of a women's movement began to sweep the nation—it was soon impossible to keep up with it, to even try to control it, as the letters and phone calls poured in—was to envision actions women could organize in their own communities without the treasuries, staff and resources feminist organizations sit on top of now. Because we didn't have the resources to answer all the letters and calls, I would use my lecture dates to leave a NOW chapter behind. At the College of Home Economics of Syracuse where I was invited to give the commencement address, I had a chance to respond to the many inquiries from Karen DeCrow, then a secretary, later a lawyer. She immediately started a local chapter in Syracuse and would serve as president of NOW in the seventies. In Pittsburgh to deliver a lecture, I finally contacted another persistent caller, Wilma Scott Heide, a sociologist and journalist, who not only started a local NOW chapter but joined the national board of directors and went on also to become a president of national NOW herself in the seventies.

I recruited wherever I went and often accepted lectures and journalistic assignments in places we were weak. Before I went to Florida to cover the Republican Convention in 1968, I called an army officer's wife named Roxy Bolton who had written me all incensed at the practice of using women's names to name hurricanes. Did she want to use my presence in Florida to start a new chapter? She hesitated, saying that she was seven months pregnant. "Nothing wrong with that," I insisted. In fact, a pregnant army captain's wife was perfect. The myth of bra-burning femi-

nists was beginning to circulate in the press after some members
of New York NOW went to Atlantic City that year to demonstrate
against the Miss America Beauty Contest and dumped girdles
and other restrictive underwear in a garbage can. But that's all
it ever was—a myth. I certainly would have known, then, if
anybody was burning a bra in the name of feminism. And nobody was.

I was very eager that the women's movement be organized
by black women as well as white, especially in the South. I remember lecturing at Agnes Scott, a women's college in Atlanta,
where I met enthusiastic white women who wanted to organize a
NOW chapter, but I didn't want NOW in Atlanta to be organized
just by white women. So I went to see Coretta King and got her to
agree to be on our first board, and also Julian Bond's sister, Jane, if
I remember correctly, and got her to agree.

I wanted young black women as well, so on that same trip to
Atlanta or maybe another, I met with students with their new
afros at the headquarters of SNCC (Student Nonviolent Coordi-
nating Committee), an organization of black college students
formed in 1960 by Stokely Carmichael to end segregation peace-
fully in the South through voter registration drives and sit-ins.

It was hard to convince those young black women to join
NOW. I remember sitting on the floor and talking with all these
young women and some men and the women saying to me: "We
don't want anything to do with that feminist bag. Black women
have been too strong. It's the black MAN who should get his
power now. Then they'll take care of us." Well, I wanted to spank
them, but they learned soon enough. They eventually came in.

It was true, of course, that black women were already strong.
They were forced to be because they could get jobs cleaning
houses and taking care of white children, when black men
couldn't get any jobs at all, except for shining shoes. Because
black women were essential to their family's survival, they never
had the "luxury" of the feminine mystique—that belonged to the
white middle and upper class. Even daughters of the black
upper-middle class like my brilliant psychotherapist friend Margaret Lawrence, who started the mental health clinic in Rockland
County, Jane Wright, dean of a medical school, Eleanor Holmes
Norton, prominent civil rights attorney and future congress-

woman, never really bought the feminine mystique. They couldn't afford to. They had progressed from their slave great-grandmothers, laundress grandmothers, teacher mothers to distinguished careers as doctors and lawyers, never diverted by the feminine mystique while most of my white Smith classmates were writing "housewife" on the census blank. So I understood why there seemed to be no great interest in feminism in the black community and never had any quarrel with it. For a black person, the battle against racism took priority.

But black women suffered the same sex discrimination as white women did, and I couldn't buy the line that equality was for white women only. To me, black women, especially the radical ones, were being given a special African American version of the feminine mystique, which held that black men were hurt by the excessive strength of black women. I used to have long discussions with Gwendolyn Brooks about this. "But it isn't black women that castrated black men, it was white society. Surely they know that," I would protest.

"Well, it doesn't make it any easier at home," she'd say.

Male chauvinism was indeed color-blind. When Muriel Fox and I went to see the men at the NAACP Legal Defense Fund to ask their help in setting up such a defense fund for women and in getting NOW into the Leadership Conference on Civil Rights, we were told, "Women are not a civil rights issue." I disagreed. I had committed NOW unequivocally against racism from the very beginning and saw the battle for women's rights as part of the struggle for human rights. But black male leaders seemed to resent the women's movement and made black women feel guilty about joining it. "The only position for women in SNCC is prone," Stokely Carmichael, SNCC's leader, had declared at an organizational staff meeting in 1964. With attitudes like that among some black leaders, it was hard for black women to join us.

Let it not be said, as it often is, however, that the women's movement was only a white, middle-class movement. While it is true that the majority of the first organizers were white because that's the way America is, we had exemplary black leaders as well. Pauli Murray, after all, was a distinguished legal scholar. Aileen Hernandez, who left the EEOC in frustration and became the executive vice president of NOW in 1967, had a background in the civil rights movement and the trade union movements. Phineas Indritz was with us from the beginning, as was Dr. Anna Arnold Hedgeman, an early board member who worked with the National Council of the Churches of Christ. In fact, the black women who were in from the beginning were more advanced in their thinking than we were because they never had bought or been able to buy the feminine mystique. But there's no denying that the early NOW leadership was mainly white as America is mainly white.

Black and white, we were all middle class and, for the most part, well educated because the ability to lead requires having had enough education or public leadership experience to raise your voice on the issues, to have enough sense of power to organize a national movement. So, except for the women who came out of the organizational leadership of the unions and were not formally educated, we were all middle class and educated from the beginning, regardless of race.

Not all the early members of NOW shared my determination to make the movement as large and inclusive as I did. Some of them were old-timers who had gotten their ideologies from men, and some of the old suffragettes were, I think, racist. Schooled in the battle to free the slaves, some of our feminist foremothers had later turned bitterly against the blacks in their own frustration that women were not added to the amendment that gave black males the vote. This time many of us, but not all of us, were determined not to let the women's movement and black civil rights be pitted against each other. But it wasn't that easy in the beginning.

Some of my NOW sisters also did not approve when I began publicly to protest the Vietnam War, much like the criticism leveled at Martin Luther King, Jr., for his opposition to the war from within the civil rights movement. This was beyond the fight against racism and beyond the fight against sex discrimination. And some of them certainly did not approve when, at a NOW board meeting in San Francisco, I went out to Berkeley to try to recruit women members of the leadership of the SDS (Students for a Democratic Society), the radical student movement led by Tom Hayden.

I wanted the young, radical women in NOW and was more concerned with getting them in than I was establishment women.

The movement had been started by women in their forties, fifties, sixties, even some from the suffragette remnants of the old battle for the ERA, and we needed the young. At this stage of the game, in the 1960s, the radical student movement at Berkeley and at Columbia was going strong and I sensed that the young activists on both coasts were ready to see the need for a separate women's movement. They were getting sick, they told me, of their male co-revolutionaries giving them the spaghetti to cook, and delegating them to shifts on the mimeograph machine, and calling them "chicks." I wanted these young radical women in our movement, just as I wanted the Catholic nuns and the League of Women Voters and the members of SNCC and the PTA housewives who had been afraid of being called "feminist" in the beginning.

There were many different lifestyles involved here, different ages, agendas and biases, but somehow we held together. I'll never forget one press conference in my apartment in the late sixties where seated next to each other on the same couch were a bare-breasted member of the radical group Redstockings nursing her baby; my friend Beulah Sanders, a black welfare reform activist who was easily over 200 pounds and had arrived late because she had to see someone off to jail; and proper Michigan Republican Patricia Burnett wearing a hat and nail polish.

Some of the radical women looked at Pat and said, "What do we want her for?" and I said, "We *do* want her." I wanted the hats and nail polish and pumps as well as the hippies and the welfare mothers. The movement had to speak for *all* women, not just a few, to succeed. I always welcomed the establishment women like Pat who supported NOW, the women who were glamorous like Ti-Grace Atkinson, an early president of New York NOW whose Main Line accent, red fox fur and ladylike blond good looks were perfect, I thought, for raising money from those mythical rich old widows we never did unearth, and Gloria Steinem, whom I had first met in the early years of the anti-Vietnam movement, and who was working with Cesar Chavez and the migrant workers and Bobby Kennedy. In the early years of the women's movement, women like Pat, Ti-Grace and certainly Gloria helped give it glamour, and that's a good contribution.

The different ideologies, however, were difficult to assimilate. The young radicals were more separatist than I was. They tried to make an ideology of their feminism by copying the black movement of Black Power and advocating Woman Power. They were making too literal an analogy to class warfare and racial suppression. The relationship between men and women is much more complex and interdependent certainly than between black and white or even between boss and worker. I always saw the women's movement as a part of a profound sex role revolution, not women *versus* men, but women *and* men breaking out of obsolete sex roles that prevented both of us from being all we could be.

But sexual politics, a new ideology of women's liberation, was coming into play. Though I understood women's long-pent-up anger, I became increasingly apprehensive that the frustrations now surfacing among the women so determined not to be trapped as their mothers had been were being siphoned off into a war of women against men. "Let's face it, men are here to stay," I would half-joke in some of my speeches as first president of NOW. "We have to live with them, work with them, have kids with them, love them if we can. And if they won't change, walk out if we can afford to and make it better for our daughters."

I did not agree with the message some were trying to push— that to be a liberated woman you had to make yourself ugly, to stop shaving under your arms, to stop wearing makeup or pretty dresses or any skirts at all. I always made a point of looking well groomed and "feminine." What was the shame in going to the hairdresser or wearing makeup?

I was particularly concerned when some extremists began using abusive language and a style that alienated the middle-class women from the establishment and the church with their sexual shock tactics and man-hating, down-with-motherhood stance. Here we were, trying to organize a massive women's movement that would cross lines of class and race and really speak for the majority of women, and the majority of women still chose to marry men and have children.

It made me very uneasy when *New York* magazine did a huge cover story on a woman who took her little daughter away from her father and their comfortable suburban home to join a feminist commune and described her as a "feminist heroine." I also objected to the media's description of another "feminist heroine," a woman named Valerie Solanas who shot and almost killed Andy Warhol in 1968 and issued what she called a "SCUM [Society for Cutting Up Men] Manifesto," declaring war to the death on all men. Well, Valerie Solanas was no feminist heroine. We'd never heard of her and that's not what feminism was all about—cutting up men. Muriel Fox and I tried to disclaim this as feminism for the media, but we were all very careful, in those early years, about attacking other women or disagreeing in public. We had discovered our power as a whole movement and we didn't want to open fissures that would weaken that power. It was more important to preserve the ambition that "Sisterhood Is Powerful."

We had to repudiate Ti-Grace, however, when we learned that it was she who had smuggled the SCUM Manifesto out of the mental hospital where Solanas was confined and she began not only to spout theories of an Amazonian army of women advocating absolute separatism from men, but, at a joint symposium of New York NOW and the National Conference of Christians and Jews, announced that the only honest women were prostitutes. When Ti-Grace urged the "dishonest prostitutes,"—i.e., the married women at the conference—to join the women's movement to work for better conditions for the honest prostitutes, they began to leave. And so, soon, did Ti-Grace from New York NOW when it became clear she was not going to be reelected president. But, then again, this was the era of real radicals and I always got a kick out of Ti-Grace.

Like any organization, there were radical cells inside NOW, probably a heritage from the Communist era, so there were whole lists of politically correct issues having to do with foreign policy and the redistribution of wealth and God knows what, but I didn't want to mess up the burgeoning movement with all this extraneous stuff. I felt women had to organize on the issues that were then of major importance to them. Of course, I almost immediately did escape those limitations, both personally and politically.

In my own thinking, almost from the beginning, I realized you couldn't have too narrow a focus. The economy was of enormous importance to women, as was what our nation did in war or peace, the plight of people in poverty, whether or not they were women, the conditions that create and continue poverty, and the critical need for federally mandated child care facilities on the same basis as parks, libraries and public schools. New forms of communal housing and domestic arrangements to accommodate the women who were increasingly carrying their share of the work in the world particularly interested me, especially after I read an article about just such a visionary community at the World's Fair in Canada called Habitat, designed by a famous architect, Moshe Safdie, who became my friend. Women's leadership style also interested me, especially after I went to India to interview Indira Gandhi for the *Ladies' Home Journal* and in the process made a lifelong friend.

It had been Carl who urged me to go to India in 1966 to cover the first woman to be elected prime minister. I was certainly curious to see for myself how Ms. Gandhi would use her power. One of the problems we faced as women in America was our lack of experience with the realities of power. "Power may corrupt, and absolute power may corrupt absolutely, but absolute powerlessness is worse," I used to joke. Because we had had little or no direct voice in the decisions of the world, we often wielded too much covert power in the family, which wasn't healthy for anyone. So naturally, I was very interested in Indira Gandhi, who was just three years older than I.

I'd never been out of the country before. Here I was, forty-five years old, and I'd never even been to Europe. When I would originally have gone hosteling or whatever after college, World War II broke out. And then, when the war was over and I would have loved to go traveling, I was having babies. And then we didn't have any money. So the first time I actually stepped on European soil was en route to India, though I don't remember where the plane stopped. All I remember was how eager I was to interview Indira Gandhi.

Ladies' Home Journal had offered me something like $3,000 to cover the first woman prime minister. If I got an interview with her, the price would double. And if I got an exclusive, triple. Needless to say, I had rushed around before I left, frantically getting names of people who might help get me to her. But the world press was descending on India to cover her ascent to power and I had no idea whether she would see me.

"Bet-ty Friedan. Bet-ty Friedan." I'll never forget the excited way her press officer pronounced my name with the sound of many "t's" and the rolling "r." "The prime minister wishes to talk to you." Perhaps it was the revolutionary red cover of the first edition of *The Feminine Mystique* that I had brought to give her which stood out at the 5:00 a.m. ceremony for the dead we both attended on the banks of the Ganges River. Or perhaps it was because I was the only woman among the press gathered in New Delhi. But not only did I get the interview and the exclusive with Indira Gandhi, she invited me to travel with her.

Tony Lukas, who was covering India for *The New York Times* and later became a very good friend, told me that all the other reporters were furious that I was the only press person allowed near Indira Gandhi. You know—where did I get off? All I'd done was write this book. The American ambassador, Chester Bowles, was so amazed that he sent for me and had the embassy staff brief me right down to what I should and shouldn't eat. The sense I had was that the Americans there were operating in a cocoon. I wanted to be in India and do as the Indians did, which is why I was staying in an Indian hotel with a bedroom as big as a ball-room and a big swirling fan. In fact, before I was finished, I was wearing saris and brought a lot home which I ended up using as table covers.

Her name may have been Gandhi, and her father Nehru, but there was no question, none, that she exuded her own sense of authority, which I found very impressive. We didn't have role models like that at the time. Golda Meir, who would soon become Israel's first woman prime minister, seemed to have a more male political style. Maybe she was a good role model for someone like Bella Abzug, a tough lawyer and politician I knew in New York, but to me, Indira Gandhi was both feminine and authoritative in a style indubitably different from men's. I saw a woman dealing with the complexities of India, and sensed a style of thought and action that is different from win-or-lose, yes-or-no solutions.

When she spoke to what seemed like a boundless sea of women in the garden of the Maharani College in Jaipur, she did not talk about the problems of women, but about the problems of food, poverty, backwardness, peace, problems I realized that would not be solved unless women took their place equally in the world with men. I listened to her scold the members of her own

ruling Congress Party at their national convention for not knowing their own strengths, and for not finishing the work they had
to do, urge the millions of people she spoke to on her tour to criti-
cize themselves and to have confidence in themselves and in
India, and snap finally at the Western correspondents who kept
asking her how it felt to be India's first woman prime minister.
"As prime minister, I'm not a woman—I'm a human being," she
retorted in exasperation.

The only tension between us—and it was mine, really—was
over my Rudi Gernreich cape. I had bought the reversible cape on
sale in the junior department at Henri Bendel (that was the only
charge account I had because the family who owned the store had
been friends of my family) and I loved it—black on one side,
camel on the other, with a wonderful, irregular line. But the prime
minister evidently loved it as well. "Tell me," her secretary said
over the phone to me on the last day of my three-week trip to
India, "do you have more than one coat with you? The prime
minister so admires your cape." The invitation was clear, but it
was the first designer thing I'd ever bought and I wasn't going to
give it up. They borrowed it to copy and at the last minute, returned it to me at the airport wrapped up in brown paper.

When I got home, I called Rudi Gernreich, who was quite
tickled to hear about his cape and the prime minister. I managed
to persuade him to send her his last remaining cape over his
protestations that it was last year's model and only a size 6. A few
months later, when Indira Gandhi came to Washington to seek
aid in her country's famine, I went to the White House to lend her
moral support. She got off the helicopter wearing our cape and as
she passed the press on her way into the White House and saw
me wearing mine, she gave me a big broad wink.

The last time I saw her was much later at some international
conference and she said, "How would you like to come back to
India?" I told her I'd love to, but then she was assassinated. And
then her son, Rajiv, invited me to India for a commemoration of
his mother and I was going to go, and he was assassinated. Indira
Gandhi left a lasting impression on me. I was beginning to think
about women's political style and women's leadership style
when I first traveled with her in India, and it was from her that I
came to realize that women did not have to become like men, or

assume a male political style to be effective leaders. There could be plenty of authority and autonomy within feminine definition when women really began to assume the leadership roles they were entitled to assume as 51 percent of the population.

I wanted to enlarge my vision of what feminism and its applications should be. The next year, 1967, I traveled to Finland, Sweden and Czechoslovakia. I had been invited to come speak by the industrial leaders of Finland, but once I got there, I felt that I should go see how feminist thinking and its application had evolved in Socialist countries. Socialism had been the ideal in my left-wing youth, and though I had been disillusioned by the strong anti-Semitism in Eastern Europe, I was full of bright-eyed, naive certainty that I would find the new domestic arrangements and communal services I was looking for. With women earning pay equal to men's, and expected to work instead of spending all day making dinner, it stood to reason that there would be new and innovative household solutions. I was to be disillusioned again.

The commissars in Prague who were showing me around looked at me as if I were crazy when I asked them to show me any form of communal housing. The best they could come up with was just another drab version of public housing like the "projects" in New York and Chicago which had become havens for crime. They didn't have anything in Prague I was looking for. The women were working in the factories all right, but they were still standing in line to buy the food and they were still cooking the food and, as far as I could see, the men were still putting their feet up, watching television. "Surely it's on your books that you're going to have new, innovative communal housing," I said to the commissars, but it turned out that they didn't have anybody who was even thinking about it.

The Swedes were at least thinking about communal housing and had some model cooperative projects. But these were no more part of the society than were the few communal projects we had back home in New England or out west. What service housing there was in Sweden, which had been built in an earlier era of Socialist dreaming, had buildings set aside for communal child care, cooking and eating, and was very popular with the people it served. The Swedes had plans on the books to build more service housing and even to make communal services available to towns; but there was no real thinking or even experimentation on what services people would be comfortable sharing, the kind of research I would think that such a country could do. I don't know how far those plans ever got, but the idea, which had been strong earlier in utopian socialist thinking, had disappeared. The culture of materialist greed that we're certainly in today was growing rapidly and the cooperative ideas were on the wane.

The Swedes were much further along in their feminist thinking than we were, however, and had set up really good child care throughout the country. The motivation to provide child care was not very altruistic, not because they loved women, but out of necessity. In America, we had the luxury of waves of immigration to replenish the labor pool, and the idea of women being needed in the labor force emerged only in war. But in Sweden, industry needed women to be working. I had learned from reading Gunnar Myrdal, and learned again while I was there, that the Swedish government had made a conscious decision to use and train women or else they were going to need immigrants from the South that they didn't want. The realization followed that they had to make arrangements for women to be trained to be a vital part of the labor force, hence the impetus for quality child care.

If there was just one thing I learned from the Swedish feminists in 1967, it was: "Without child care, it's all just talk." Convincing others, however, was next to impossible. Child care was considered very radical then in the United States and to some extent, still is. We are probably the only advanced nation beside South Africa that doesn't have a national child care system, despite evidence that children in Sweden, in France, in Israel, have thrived in subsidized care. I've never understood why it's considered better for children in their preschool years to be tied to the apron strings of their mothers when there is ample research that says it is very good for children to be in creches or nursery schools for part of the day.

Perhaps the resistance to child care in America was because it was relatively new for women to begin to work in great numbers outside the home from a combination of necessity and choice, not merely from family tragedy or desertion as it had been before World War II. But for some reason, though other advanced

nations were making the innovations and institutional adjustments to the fact that growing millions of women were going to
be working even when their children were little, the United States
did not. There was little or no recognition that the working job
structures in an advanced industrial nation like ours, and certainly in the capitalist world, were obsolete. They were based on
the lives of the men of the past who were the workforce then and
whose wives took care of the details of life.

Instead, there were years and years of research in this country trying to prove that mothers working was bad for children.
There was much cited research out of England about the develop-
mental difficulties of children separated from their parents during World War II. Well, the children had problems because they
felt abandoned, for God's sake. And in the States there was Skinner and his box theory and the presumption that a woman dropping her child off at a child care center was the equivalent of
putting her child in solitary confinement in Sing Sing where he or
she would have no interaction with other human beings and
therefore, without loving attention, would not grow. That may
have been true of the orphans in state-run institutions in countries like Romania, where the children were never touched, but it
was not the same thing as children of reasonably loving parents
going to a day care center or nursery school some hours a day. It
was really ridiculous stuff. But no matter how much positive research came out, people in the States were still trying to prove
that you were deserting your children if you worked. And the
bias remained.

I couldn't even convince the members of NOW to make child
care a priority, or even an issue. Though what I'd learned in Sweden—without child care, it's all just talk—was engraved on my
consciousness, in those early years of the women's movement it
sometimes seemed that it was only me and one woman from
New Jersey, Florence Dickler, who were interested in child care. I
think it might have been because the older feminists had either
rebelled against that domestic role, or had done their time taking
care of children and that was the last thing that interested them
now, and because too many of the younger feminists were
putting their minds to careers and all too often choosing not to
marry and have children at all. To my mind, such "either-or"

thinking among the young was a throwback to the one-dimensional status of women that the movement was trying to overturn, and I didn't agree with it, though it made sense, I guess, for the younger feminists to rebel against the feminine mystique which had defined women solely in terms of their role as mother or their sexual relations to men. But for women to take their equal place in the work world, there had to be arrangements to take into account pregnancy, maternity and child care. And there had to be thinking about getting beyond the mother as the one solely responsible for the children. Still, it sure as hell didn't get much thinking about in those early years.

The first board of NOW had created a series of task forces, including child care, and I put Florence in as head of it. But it was a lonely job. Even after I stepped down as president of NOW in 1970, I would get calls from Florence every now and again, saying, "Betty, I can't even get child care on the agenda." Among the many pressing and equally controversial issues in the sixties, child care was never the priority it should have been.

While child care seemed an obvious issue for NOW to champion, other issues presented themselves quite unexpectedly. One such early and unanticipated issue became one of our most successful consciousness-raising actions—and all because we couldn't get a drink.

We were having a board meeting in New York at the Biltmore Hotel in 1967 and we talked about going down for lunch, but everybody was always dieting so we decided to go to the Biltmore Men's Bar and Grill to have a salad and a drink. When we arrived, however, the bartender said, "I'm sorry, ladies, but we don't serve women."

"What do you mean, 'you don't serve women'?" I asked him. "We want something to eat and a drink."

But he refused to serve us, just as the Oak Room at the Plaza had refused to serve me a few years before and before that, the bartender at the Ritz in Boston when I was researching *The Feminine Mystique*. I had never forgotten how humiliated I felt having to have my drink served to me in the little anteroom off the ladies' john. And now, here it was again at the Biltmore Men's Bar where they weren't going to serve us lunch *or* a drink.

I was furious. So we went back upstairs and I said: "Look, I know this is not as important as some of the other things we're dealing with, but here we are right here in this hotel and they say they don't serve women lunch at all in the Grill and lunch is when a lot of business deals get made and here this is right under our noses. Shouldn't we protest? Shouldn't we do something about it? This is like the segregated lunch rooms in the civil rights movement."

We had a long discussion about how important, really, is a bar. Is this a frivolous issue? Being turned down for lunch and a drink is not as important as being turned down for a job. On the other hand, they aren't unrelated. If you can't have lunch where everybody else is having lunch in the business world, you miss out. We decided to tip off the media, adjourn our board meeting early, and go down and insist on being served.

What we hadn't reckoned on was a Judas in our midst. In those very early days, we let people bring their friends to our board meetings and some *fink* of a husband tipped off the management, we later figured out, because when we went down to the Men's Bar and Grill at 4:00 p.m., it was locked. Obviously we couldn't have our sit-in, but we picketed anyway and gave interviews to the reporters against the backdrop of the "Closed" sign on the Men's Bar and Grill.

Back upstairs, we decided to hold a national day of action against sex discrimination in public accommodations and scheduled it for Susan B. Anthony's birthday, the day after Valentine's Day. Karen DeCrow coordinated demonstrations in men-only bars across the country, including New York City, Syracuse, Colchester (Conn.), Pittsburgh, Washington, D.C., Atlanta, Chicago and Los Angeles. With the television cameras whirring, our sisters in Pittsburgh staged a sit-in at Stouffers Grill, while others in Los Angeles picketed the Polo Lounge at the Beverly Hills Hotel. In New York, a group of us invaded the superjock McSorley's Old Ale House, while another group, armed with signs made by our children, and led with great satisfaction by me, picketed the Oak Room at the Plaza.

Everyone could identify with that action. At that time, most women in America were housewives—only one out of three held jobs—but virtually every woman had experienced or known someone who'd been told, "No, we don't serve women." So job discrimination was where the bar discrimination issue was joined—and that was important as far as I was concerned because the demeaning insinuation that all unescorted women wanting a drink or a meal in a bar and grill were hookers struck a universal chord. I remember a black politician telling me that his wife had cheered when they saw the protests on television.

Far from frivolous, the action against male-only bars turned out to be an enormously important consciousness-raising tool, though it was not a term we used then. Later there would be a lot of consciousness-raising groups in church basements and people's living rooms, but we never had time. We were raising our consciousness through action and through the law, and the action against the male-only bars would achieve both. Title VII forbade discrimination in places of public accommodation on the basis of race, color, religion or national origin, but not on the basis of sex. After our national action, measures were introduced in Pennsylvania, New York, and elsewhere to ban sex discrimination in public accommodations.

It was at a national board meeting of NOW in 1967 at the University of Chicago Theological Conference Center, in the middle of a howling blizzard, that I put the issues of abortion and the Equal Rights Amendment on the table. We debated both issues around the clock. We were not only trapped by the storm unable even to go out to eat but both issues were a source of controversy—especially abortion.

The year before, I had been advised by friends like Carl Degler to take a woman's right to control her own body out of NOW's Statement of Purpose. "You're doing something controversial enough," he'd told me. "Don't put abortion in there." But I was very aware of that issue, and along with some other board members had decided since that we, as an organization for women, had to confront it.

Though I had never had an abortion, I had intimate knowledge of what the right to legal abortion might mean to women. As president of NOW, I knew we owed it to all women, and especially to the young women we wanted to bring into the movement, to take a stand on decriminalizing abortion.

Ideologically, I was never for abortion. Motherhood is a

value to me, and even today abortion is not. I would be the happiest woman in the world if RU-486 or something equivalent would make abortion unnecessary, and I think that's going to happen very soon. But the issue had to be confronted. You couldn't have woman's equality without her own control of the reproductive process. The time when biology was destiny and women's lives were defined mainly by their reproductive function was over as far as the women's movement was concerned. The personhood of woman required the emergence from passivity and biology and men's laws. So abortion was a very important issue, though the rationale was skewed. I believed passionately in 1967, as I do today, that women should have the right of chosen motherhood. For me the matter of choice has never been primarily the choice of abortion, but that you can choose to be a mother. That is as important as any right written into the Constitution.

Still, I was very nervous that if NOW gave serious consideration to the abortion issue, it would scare away the Catholic women. Before the board meeting in Chicago, I had sought the advice of Janey Hart as a senator's wife, a Catholic and mother of seven. "Don't be silly," she told me. "Catholics are doing some serious consideration of such questions themselves." Nonetheless, I didn't want to alienate Catholics or create a problem for the wonderful nuns on our board. I needn't have worried so. After a long debate during the blizzard, one of the sisters finally snapped at me: "Betty, don't palm it off on the Catholics. We're agonizing over the issue ourselves. If your conscience tells you that this is what the women's movement should do now, do it, and we'll act according to our consciences." It was a great relief to me when she said that.

I remember Alice Rossi saying that we *had* to confront the abortion issue because those of us who had started this movement were an older generation, but reproductive rights was going to be an important issue for younger women. She reinforced what I and many of us believed: that we were doing all of this not just for ourselves but for the generations of women to come.

Putting the Equal Rights Amendment (ERA) on the table for the board's consideration made me just as anxious. The amendment in some form or other had been introduced into Congress every year since 1923, spearheaded then by the National Woman's Party, which had continued the feminist movement

after women won the vote in 1920. The labor unions had stead-
fastly opposed it. Throwing our weight behind the ERA now was
a risk. As I'd worried about alienating the Catholics and making a
problem for the nuns on our board with the abortion issue, I was
worried that NOW's support for the ERA would compromise the
labor women like Dorothy Haener from the UAW and Catherine
Conroy from the Communications Workers of America who were
so important in organizing the movement.

The controversy about the ERA centered on the concern that
the constitutional amendment would supersede or make invio-
late the so-called protective laws for women which, in different
states, restricted the weights women could lift (I think it was
something like 15 pounds in Utah and 35 pounds in Michigan),
the jobs they could hold—women couldn't be bartenders or min-
ers—even the hours they could work. Overtime was out for
women in some industries, working at night in others.

I thought those laws were probably important and necessary
laws in the era of Eleanor Roosevelt, and I understood why some
of the women then who were the champions of reform and
women's rights had looked with disfavor on the ERA. In the beginning I too had dismissed the amendment as an abstraction
that was not nearly as important as equal job opportunity. I had
accepted the argument from the labor unions that the ERA would
destroy the laws that protected women. But either through the
tutelage of my underground network of lawyer and government
friends in Washington or through my own experience with Title
VII, it had become clear to me that at this stage of the game, the
protective laws were standing in women's way and denying
them equal opportunity.

It stood to reason that if the so-called protective laws were
needed for women, they should also be applied to men. Men hurt
their backs or got hernias, after all, from lifting heavy weights. On
that basis, the laws should apply to health and not sex. Restricting the hours women could work also hurt men. Not only did the
restrictions compel men to work overtime to support their families, but denied women the ability to contribute to their families'
support through overtime pay or promotions. And so I had concluded that instead of protecting women, these laws were being
used to keep women out of good jobs.

By the time of the board meeting in Chicago, NOW's Legal Committee was already challenging the protective laws in court as a violation of Title VII. Headed by Marguerite Rawalt, the committee (there were at least thirty members of NOW who were attorneys and judges) had already filed a brief in support of factory workers in California who were being denied the opportunity to earn time and a half for overtime and opportunities for promotion because the law there "protected" them from working any more than eight hours a day or forty-eight hours per week. The NOW board had also authorized the Legal Committee to assist an appeal by women at Colgate-Palmolive Company in Indiana who were confined to lower-paid jobs because they were "protected" from jobs requiring them to lift more than 35 pounds. The Legal Committee was about to take on Southern Bell for similar weight restrictions.

Title VII had proven a potent weapon for fighting sex discrimination in employment and public accommodations, and was far more effective than the protective laws. But as much as it had proved effective, it was a law and a law could be changed or repealed. I began to realize that we should get the ERA into the Constitution once and for all and be done with it. What you needed, to ensure equal opportunity for training and promotion and all the rest of it, was the constitutional end of sex discrimination.

I began to think of the practical and legal implications if we got the ERA. Could you take legal action against a company that not only made women quit at pregnancy or childbirth but didn't provide child care facilities? Shouldn't that be construed as a denial of equal opportunity under the law? The ERA would give us the basis for all kinds of creative interpretation of the law that now didn't exist on behalf of women. After all, if the Bill of Rights and the Constitution had been written by women as well as men, the right of women to decide whether, when and how many times to bear a child and to get whatever medical help was needed like abortion would be an inalienable right. And so would women's right to equal employment.

Still, I worried that NOW's potential support for the ERA would get labor against us. I had built a wonderful coalition of people from labor and I wanted to move ahead in a way that wouldn't get them in trouble. But as with the nuns on abortion, it turned out I had the union women with me on the ERA. I remember a call in the middle of the night from friends in the labor movement. "Listen, Betty. You do what your conscience says is right on this. Don't worry about us. We'll deal with it." So the national board decided to support the ERA as well as abortion rights.

I was quite nervous when the second annual national NOW convention convened in Washington in November 1967. We were up to just over a thousand members in our first year and 105 men and women had come to what could be a historic occasion. If we voted to support the legalization of abortion, we would be the first national organization to do so. If we voted for the ERA, which many of the young members hadn't even heard of, we risked losing support from the unions.

There were many other issues on the agenda as well, though less controversial. The board members and I had put together a Bill of Rights for women which included not only the right to choose and the simple words of the Equal Rights Amendment— "Equality of rights under the law shall not be denied by the United States or any state on account of sex"—but our demands for paid maternity leave, federally mandated child care facilities and a tax deduction of full home and child care expenses for working parents, the elimination of sex discrimination in admittance to academic institutions, and job training equal to men for women on welfare and in poverty programs.

The various NOW task forces had their own revolutionary resolutions to present to the convention delegates. Sounding a battle cry for the upcoming 1968 presidential election year, the Task Force on Political Rights and Responsibilities called on women to become politically active at the local, state and national levels, to elect women to the national party conventions, to refuse to do the "traditional menial work of sealing envelopes, ringing doorbells and raising pin money" unless men did their share, to demand equitable representation on all policy-making boards and commissions of political and governmental agencies, to get NOW's Bill of Rights for Women into the hands of the platform committees and the leading candidates of the national parties and for women to cross party lines to vote for candidates who accepted our goals. Though it would take over ten years for the "gender gap" to be officially recognized as a factor in elections, what I called the New Woman power bloc was born in 1967.

The recommendations from the Task Force on Religion were equally radical, calling for the opening of the priesthood and ministries to women and the removal of sex segregation in religious organizations and church-sponsored schools. So were the goals put forth by the Task Force on Education, which called for identical curricula and encouragement for boys and girls, the integration of student facilities including dormitories, and instruction in contraception and family planning. There were recommendations that seemed just as wild at the time from the task forces on employment, on the image of women in the mass media, on the family, on women in poverty, from the Legal Committee which was already establishing a separate NOW Legal Defense and Education Fund to better handle the growing number of inquiries and sex discrimination complaints coming in from women all over the country. There was no doubt in our minds that the women's movement was about to explode.

But to me as well as other members of the NOW board, the Equal Rights Amendment and abortion were and are issues essential to real security, equality and human dignity for all women, whether they worked at home or outside. The delegates had already received a long, detailed memorandum from the Legal Committee on the history and potential effect of the ERA on state labor laws, family law, criminal law, social benefits law, and service to the nation. The memo explained that the ERA would supersede the laws in some states that either excluded or relieved women from serving on juries, and might require women as well as men to register for the draft.

The two issues were so important and so potentially divisive that I had the NOW convention go into a committee as a whole for a day to argue and discuss them freely before we would take action. It was so clear that I favored ERA and women's right to choose that I stepped down from the chair during the debate. At least I think I did. I had enormous influence on women then, and what I said should be done or should not be done was fairly important. And I'm no poker face. I must have handed the gavel over to Kay Clarenbach because I remember addressing the convention as a member of NOW. Looking straight at the old suffragettes in the front row, I spoke of our responsibility to take the torch of equality from these valiant women who'd kept it lit alone all these years. And I remember looking at the young women and speaking of our responsibility to them and to the generations coming up to take the torch from us.

My NOW sisters from the unions had called me at five that morning to say that if NOW took a stand on the ERA, we would lose the UAW facilities for our mailings. But as the issue was debated, those same women—Dorothy Haener and Catherine Conroy—both argued that equal opportunity was more important.

As I listened and watched the women who spoke, I saw that very few were opposed to taking a stand on the ERA. The very young women were energized by the proposal as they had not been on narrow job issues. They listened raptly to the suffragettes. Abortion rights drew support as well, not only from the young women but from square and middle-aged housewives from Indiana and points south. The Catholic women seemed to be abstaining rather than opposing.

I remember having a distinct feeling when we agreed to support and fight for the ERA. I felt gooseflesh, I felt that we were accepting the torch from the early fighters and passing it on. I felt the same thrill when we decided for women's right to birth control and abortion. We were aware that we were making history. And we had an utter confidence that came from that. Whether there were ten women or one hundred or one thousand—and there weren't more than that at the time—we understood that we had the authority to speak for women over the generations. We weren't thinking about our place in history every minute, and maybe some of us didn't at all, but I certainly had a sense that history was engaged. Later people would say, "Oh, it must have taken so much courage," but it didn't.

There was some price to be paid, though it was relatively small. The members who were the most uncomfortable with the abortion issue would leave NOW in 1968 to form a spin-off organization, the Women's Equity Action League (WEAL). The members of WEAL would continue to work actively toward our goals of equal opportunity in employment and education, but would sit out our fight for abortion rights. I respected their decision.

Predictably, the unions opposed our support of the ERA. Not only did Caroline Davis of the UAW have to resign as secretary-treasurer, but we were forced to find our own printers and mailers in New York. It would be a year before Dorothy and Caroline convinced the national board of their union, the UAW/CIO, to change its stance and officially support the ERA.

Dedicated to action and not just words, we held a press conference right after the convention and issued a press release detailing our new Bill of Rights for Women, including, of course, our support for the ERA. The next day, as many of us as could afford to spend another night at the hotel in Washington went to Capitol Hill to deliver the NOW Bill of Rights to a representative from the Johnson administration and to Senators Robert Kennedy, Charles Percy and Eugene McCarthy, as well as to our own senators and congressmen. We had $1,000 in the bank from membership dues and contributions. We needed to take dramatic actions to get national attention for our unfinished revolution. From that moment on, as I lectured more and more, I promoted the ERA as well as the many other NOW demands in our Bill of Rights for Women.

I volunteered to campaign for Gene McCarthy in the Democratic presidential primary race and went out west to do so in 1968. I was part of a writers' contingent for McCarthy, along with Wilfrid Sheed. We were never quite sure what we were supposed to do. We were just supposed to be celebrities, I guess, and give *éclat* to the campaign. But I had great hopes for McCarthy's candidacy.

I knew that McCarthy, in addition to leading the opposition to the Vietnam War, had introduced the Equal Rights Amendment in the Senate in 1967 along with thirty-seven co-sponsors. So I was completely morally and politically justified in supporting him on both counts. I used Gene's championship of the ERA to drum up support for him from women, though I think it was just basically his wife, Abigail. I don't know how much he knew about the ERA—ever.

His campaign staff did not want me to include his championship for the ERA in the campaign literature I helped to write, or in my speeches for him in primary states. They and other "liberals" of the time, including some of the women on McCarthy's staff, did not see the political relevance of the issues of women's equality. On one flight in California on the campaign plane, Tom Hayden, the revolutionary founder of the SDS and the editor of *Ramparts*, a far left magazine, scolded me for wanting to bring up "irrelevant" women's issues like equal rights.

The strength of the "women's" vote had not emerged in American political consciousness yet. The sheer simple fact that a majority of the population was women and that women voted in greater numbers than men had not sunk in. Women until then were still presumed to vote like their husbands, but this was beginning not to be the case. The issue that would flush out that gender difference in 1968 was war and peace, the divide between support or opposition to the Vietnam War, not just women's rights. That's why it is wrong to take a narrow view of what feminism was or is or can be. Politically, the horizons were always beyond that.

Even I, had I been asked then, "What are the main issues that concern you or are important?" wouldn't have said, "Discrimination against women." Nor would I now. It still seems to me that opposing the war in Vietnam, or later, the growing income discrepancy between the haves and have-nots, transcends the situation of women.

We women were part of a larger movement in the sense that we had to have a political response to what was happening around us. That gave us the vision and the reality of engaging in a battle bigger than our own lives, larger than our own careers. Energies that in an earlier or other era I might have spent in my own corner on economic injustice now were going into the women's movement. It was never a narrow issue for me.

I felt it incumbent upon me as a leader of women to come out against the Vietnam War. I may or may not have been influenced by the fact that I had sons at or approaching draft age. Women have always been interested in real life, not abstractions, and I'm convinced that if we'd had anywhere near 50 percent of Congress, America would have been out of the Vietnam War. Joining the anti-war movement was, for me, the first connection between the women's movement and mainstream politics. With the nation corroding in the war in Vietnam and with my own sons near draft age, I couldn't separate my concerns as a woman from the larger political agonies of the nation. My sisters wanted NOW to focus solely on feminism, and I understood that. There had been so many years of women being against slavery, *against* this, *against* that, but never *for* themselves. But we couldn't be that narrow. We had to use our growing political strength.

Women were no longer a malleable political bloc. It used to be that women were conservative and could be easily riled up to oppose any really progressive political movement. But that wasn't true anymore. Once women organized politically for their own rights in their own voice, they were no longer as susceptible to being manipulated. The post-election polls would show that new, independent political voice for the first time, in women's opposition to the war.

It wasn't a coincidence that the women who were opposed to the Vietnam War were also inclined toward working on women's rights. I met a lot of them in the anti-war movement. Gloria Steinem was on a committee of writers against the Vietnam War. I met others at a 1967 protest meeting in Chicago organized by Al Lowenstein. (I had read about the meeting in the paper and called Bella Abzug to ask if she knew anything about it. When I got a telegram inviting me, I went.) It was at that meeting that I met friends and colleagues I would march with through the years. Women such as Sarah Kovner, a progressive Democratic political leader in New York, and Ronnie Eldridge, who was working then with Bobby Kennedy.

Many of us were at the 1968 Democratic National Convention in Chicago. I had a broadcast assignment from Group W and was also going to cover the women's angle for *Newsday*. I was going to use various press assignments to get me into the Republican Convention as well. My real motive was not covering the conventions but garnering support for the ERA and to otherwise jazz up the women who were there on women's issues. I also wanted to take my place among the good people I had met from around the country who were opposing the Vietnam War.

I remember at the 1968 Democratic Convention marching down Michigan Avenue carrying torches in a candlelight procession against the war. That's where I ran into Arthur Herzog, McCarthy's campaign manager in Oregon, who was another writer who was getting involved politically. I walked behind John Kenneth Galbraith, the economist and diplomat, who was so tall I couldn't see anything beyond him. I remember the bitter disappointment I and many others felt when the old order prevailed and Hubert Humphrey won the Democratic nomination over Gene McCarthy. But mostly I remember the students.

I was waiting in line for the restroom at the hotel in Chicago when I heard someone shout, "They're beating up our kids!" On the television we saw cops in helmets and gas masks clubbing and gassing the kids who had come to Chicago to protest the war. The students were carrying signs like "Make Love, Not War" and "Johnny Wants a Job, Not a Gun" and the cops were beating them up. My own son, Danny, was out there somewhere among them.

A woman in the line said: "You shouldn't allow your kids to be involved in protests," so not all women thought alike. But I've never felt such outrage. I can still remember the stink of the tear gas that night in the room I had in the Conrad Hilton Hotel.

The violence against the students is a searing political memory—the men on horseback, the cops mowing down the kids. Danny had his head laid open in the melee. It always triggers my political anger that such force was turned on our children. I did not anticipate then that those same forces would be used against us.

NINE

The Enemies Without and the Enemies Within

The women's movement was becoming a force by the late sixties and with it came the rise of an organized, well-financed opposition. Change has always been threatening to keepers of the status quo. It's not surprising really that instead of considering new ways to restructure the workplace and to treat women equally rather than as a separate, lesser species in need of special protections, institutions from corporations to government agencies continued to resist and even subvert the movement. I guess the powers that be in America always get nervous when there are big movements capable of changing the ways they have arranged things and the women's movement was beginning to do just that.

Our newfound collective strength, coupled with the potency of Title VII, was overturning laws and challenging corporate giants. Women took to the streets in 1968 after the courts upheld Colgate-Palmolive's right to "protect" women by confining them to lower-paying jobs that didn't require them to lift more than 35 pounds. NOW called for a national boycott of Colgate-Palmolive products, and for five days straight, members in New York picketed the company's headquarters on Park Avenue carrying such signs as "Down the Drain with Ajax" and "Cold Power versus Women Power." Within a year, a higher court reversed the Colgate-Palmolive decision and ruled that any weightlifting test should be applied equally to both men and women, clearing the way for women to rise through the ranks.

NOW would win another major court victory in 1969 in the class action sex discrimination case against Southern Bell. After a NOW attorney exposed the telephone company's protective weightlifting limit of 30 pounds for women as the red herring it always was—the company had no qualms about requiring secretaries to lift their 30-pound-plus typewriters but barred them from higher-paying jobs as switchmen—the U.S. Court of Appeals ruled that the policy was a violation of Title VII. We won millions of dollars from the telephone company in back pay for the telephone workers who had never been allowed to apply for jobs beyond chief operator, and could not get into management training programs.

More and more women were learning to amass their collective power to effect that "threatening" change. While I and other NOW members demonstrated at the White House and at cities across the country in 1969 demanding "Rights, Not Roses" on Mother's Day, the National Coalition of American Nuns was forming to support the civil rights and anti-war movements and to press for women's equality within the Catholic Church. Virtually every institution in America was becoming aware of the women's movement, spearheaded by NOW. I was invited to lead a weekend women's retreat in Ithaca, New York. As a result, the first accredited course in women's studies was added to the curriculum at Cornell University at the instigation of the newly formed NOW chapter I left behind. The first Women's Caucus in a professional society was established in the American Sociological Association by Alice Rossi, and Congresswoman-elect Shirley Chisholm, a NOW member, was sworn in as the first black woman elected to the U.S. House of Representatives.

The fight for abortion rights was picking up real steam and real enemies across the country. The word "abortion" was only just beginning to be spoken aloud in the late sixties. I remember clearly the first time I saw the word printed in the newspaper. New York State was adopting a new constitution and I went to Albany by bus along with Ti-Grace and Cynthia Epstein, an up-and-coming Columbia University sociologist, to testify for the inclusion of NOW's Bill of Rights, and women's right to safe, legal abortion. Ephraim London, a prominent civil rights lawyer, had given me the wording: "The right of woman to control her reproductive process must be established as a basic, inalienable, civil right, not to be denied or abridged by the state—just as the right of individual and religious conscience is considered an inalienable private right in both American tradition and in the American Constitution." However impressive the words, I almost didn't get to deliver them.

When my turn came to testify, I followed some male politician who had gone on and on and on. Everybody was supposed to have fifteen minutes but the man who preceded me had spoken for twenty-five minutes or more. When I got up to testify, I wasn't three minutes into my speech when whoever was head of the legislative committee stated, "Well, Mrs. Friedan, we know what you're going to say, so you can sit down." I must have protested, I must have said I was going to finish what I had to say. I can't really remember. But it was just shocking. The establishment didn't want women to be talking like this. It was a miracle during the early years if we got to say anything *at all*. When women were listened to at all it made headlines.

We were insulted again at another New York State hearing on the question of abortion, this one in New York City. We were told that testimony was by invitation only and it turned out that the only woman who was invited to testify on abortion was a Catholic nun. All the other "witnesses" were men, which seemed obscene to me then and still does. Why should they have been the only ones heard on the question of women's bodies and the reproductive process, on what happens to the people who actually bear the children in this society?

Women were still all but invisible, even among some male supporters. We had joined forces on the abortion issue with a dissident group at Planned Parenthood who wanted to fight for the repeal of the laws which made abortion a crime and were unable to get Planned Parenthood to commit to that. Larry Lader, a fellow magazine writer, was one of the main reformers from Planned Parenthood who wanted to come out for abortion rights and, together, we decided to form a coalition of abortion activists. I never thought that NOW alone could do justice to all the issues women faced, so in 1969, Larry and I helped found NARAL, the organization known today as the National Abortion Rights Action League but which was then called the National Association for the Repeal of Abortion Laws.

It was at the organizational meeting for NARAL in the Drake Hotel in Chicago that it was demonstrated again how women still had to struggle to be taken seriously. While I was sent off to drum up publicity for NARAL on television, Larry and the others wrote the charter and a statement of purpose for the new coalition. When the preamble of the charter was read aloud the next day at NARAL's first national conference, it had absolutely nothing in it about a woman's right to control her own body. Instead, it was all about the right of a doctor to perform an abortion without going to jail.

I was horrified. For all that we were grateful to the doctors who put themselves at risk, we in the women's movement were not sticking out our necks on the issue from any great interest in the doctor's right to perform abortions and earn a lot of money without risking jail. Indeed, we were beginning to question whether doctors were even necessary. A self-help women's abortion underground in California had started their own clinic and were successfully and safely performing what is really a very simple procedure in the first trimester.

There was nothing to do but take the floor mike and propose a new preamble for the NARAL charter with women, not doctors, as its core. The new coalition had to recognize that it is a *woman's* inalienable human and civil right to control her own body and reproductive process, I told the first national convention of NARAL, and to decide, according to the dictates of her own conscience, where, whether and how many times to bear a child and therefore to have unlimited, safe, legal medical access to all forms of birth control and abortion, if necessary.

I shot down the possibility of merely reforming the laws instead of repealing them altogether, a compromise that was circulating. Reform meant that someone other than the woman would still have control over her body and that was totally unacceptable. "Don't talk to me about abortion reform," I said. "Abortion reform is something dreamed up by men, maybe good-hearted men, but they can only think from their male point of view. For them, women are passive objects that somehow must be regulated; let them only have abortions for Thalidomide, rape, incest. What right have they to say? What right has any man to say to any woman—you must bear this child? What right has any state to say? This is a woman's right, not a technical question needing the sanction of the state, or to be debated in terms of technicalities—they are all irrelevant."

It seems unbelievable now, but some of the leading abortion reformers and Planned Parenthood types lined up at the microphones to dismiss my arguments for women's rights. "Abortion is not a feminist issue," one said. Another added: "What have women's rights got to do with abortion?" A line of women formed behind me—a Baptist woman minister from Philadelphia, a white-haired, older woman from Chicago NOW, and any number of young women I'd never seen before. And together, we overturned the objections of male abortion politicos and medicos and inserted the right of women into the preamble as the basis of the abortion movement.

I remember the shock of even the most benevolent abortion reformers—the ministers, civil libertarians, liberal doctors, the liberal wing of Planned Parenthood—when we publicly demanded the repeal of all criminal abortion laws, and so moved the issue from the obscurity of an unspeakable dirty sexual secret to a proud political symbol and a final essential right of full personhood for women. In fact, it was when women took up the issue of abortion that it became a really big issue. We changed the terms of the debate. The whole dynamic changed. We did then get great support, as we have now in America a consensus that it is a woman's right to choose.

Abortion, of course, was still illegal and there was one protest march after another in cities across the country. The young radical feminists were using the phrase, "Free Abortion on Demand," a slogan I never liked. I would not permit such placards in any march I organized. It made me uneasy. We don't have free medical care in this country, and that slogan made it sound like a spoiled child demanding a lollipop. I thought it was a distortion really, to make abortion too light a matter. Abortion was and is a much more serious decision for a woman and I always insisted our message be a woman's civil right to abortion and a woman's right to choose.

We would win that right in New York in 1970 when the state legislature there became the first in the country to approve a bill removing all restrictions on abortion during the first six months of pregnancy. The legislative chamber in Albany was packed with the women who had marched and lobbied for the fundamental right to control their own bodies, and who were given clear credit for the bill's passage. It was a historic moment, coming only three years after I'd spoken in favor of the issue at the NOW convention in Chicago, and sitting in that packed chamber, I felt the same thrill of history being made.

The emerging power of the no-longer-quite-so-silent majority was being felt from state governments to the corridors of Congress. And in 1970, I found myself in front of the Senate Judiciary Committee testifying against a sexist nominee for the U.S. Supreme Court. It was Catherine East from the feminist underground in Washington who had tipped me off that President Nixon's nominee for the court, Judge G. Harrold Carswell, had a long record of sex discrimination as well as race discrimination, having been a prime mover in a racist country club. Civil rights groups and liberals in Congress would have been the logical coalition to try to block Carswell's nomination, but they had fought so hard to prevent the ratification of Nixon's prior nominee, Clement Haynesworth, that they were exhausted. So the historic challenge of using sexual discrimination for the first time to contest a judicial candidate fell to NOW and me.

Few members of those liberal activist groups thought women would have the political clout to influence enough senators to block Carswell's nomination. Certainly the southern senator presiding over the hearings did not. I'll never forget the way Senator James O. Eastland of Mississippi gazed down at me in disbelief as I laid out NOW's case against Carswell. I might as well have been from Mars. "It's the first time ah evah heard of anybody objectin' to a Supreme Court justice for discrimination—against wimen!" he marveled later to a reporter. But we had a strong case.

Judge Carswell, a member of the Fifth Circuit Court of Appeals in 1969, had voted against rehearing the sex discrimination case brought by a mother of young children against the Martin Marietta Corporation for violating Title VII of the Civil Rights Act of 1964. He evidently found it legally acceptable that the mother, Ida Phillips, had been refused a job by Martin Marietta because she had preschool-age children while men with small children were eligible to be hired. Judge Carswell justified his decision for Martin Marietta by applying a peculiar "sex-plus" doctrine which held that discrimination that did not apply to all women, but only to women who did not meet "special standards"—standards not applied to men—was not sex discrimination.

Well, of course it was. Not only had Carswell flouted the law that was designed to end job discrimination, he had opened the escape hatch for other employers to fire the 4.1 million working mothers who had children under six. Such an "unusually blind judge in the matter of sex prejudice," I told the Senate committee, would make it impossible for him to "judge fairly" the cases of sex prejudice that would surely come before the Supreme Court. I didn't spell out those cases, but they were crucial ones for women, including abortion.

Having never testified in Congress before, and sobered by the pessimism of the civil rights politicos, the liberals and the insiders, I was nervous about the outcome of my testimony. On the way back to New York from Washington, I decided to hold a press conference and call on women everywhere to put pressure on their senators to block Carswell's nomination. (It was that press conference, in my living room in New York, that drew together the nursing hippie woman, the welfare mother and Patricia Burnett, the pretty Republican model of the establishment from Michigan.) And by God, it worked! The unexpected pressure from women made a crucial difference in votes no one had expected and from states where the blacks and civil rights forces hadn't been that strong. Instead of Harrold Carswell being appointed to the Supreme Court, it would be Justice Harry Blackmun.

In what can only be divine justice, the Supreme Court would hear *Phillips v. Martin Marietta* in 1971, the very sex discrimination case that Carswell had refused to reopen two years before. It would be the first Title VII case to come before the Court and our first victory—employers could not refuse to hire women solely because they had small children, the Court ruled, unless they also denied employment to fathers of small children. Abortion would also work its way through the lower courts to the Supreme Court.

I would be invited to be in the Court on that January day in 1973, my first visit to the High Court, when it handed down its ruling in *Roe v. Wade*, legalizing abortion. In a satisfying irony, it was Justice Blackmun, Carswell's successful successor as Supreme Court nominee, who wrote the historic majority decision guaranteeing women the constitutional right to privacy in determining the outcome of their own pregnancies.

We faced increasingly organized opposition in the long and often nasty fight for abortion rights. Our greatest opponent was no less formidable than the Roman Catholic Church, which had established the National Right to Life Committee in 1970 to block the liberalization of abortion laws. Our support of sex education in public schools was also coming under concerted attack from the John Birch Society, the Christian Crusade and another right-wing group called the American Education Lobby. And there was the emergence of Phyllis Schlafly, who attacked us for just about everything.

Phyllis Schlafly grew up in Alton, Illinois, just a few miles from my hometown of Peoria. She still lives there. As conservative as conservatives can be, she had done research for Joe McCarthy in the early fifties and had been defeated in a bid for the presidency of the National Federation of Republican Women in 1967 as liberals tried to recapture the party from the right wing. I guess she never got over it. That same year, she began publication of *The Phyllis Schlafly Report*, which would attack NOW and everything the organization stood for for years to come.

According to Schlafly and women of her ilk, the members of NOW were either man-haters or they wanted to be men. We were socialists, if not communists, for demanding that the government fund community child care centers. They preached that childraising was a woman's highest calling and that it required her to remain at home, a dictate which never took into account the numbers of women who had to work to support those children. Their list of grievances went on and on, as did their hypocrisy.

Though Phyllis Schlafly insisted that women's place was in the home, she left hers and her six children to travel the country rousing public sentiment against us. While she decried our efforts to open career opportunities to women, she seemed to embrace our efforts by taking herself off to law school at the age of fifty. I've never understood why the opponents of the women's movement were so rabid. Under sweet smiles, one could feel their hatred, especially on the question of the liberalization of abortion laws. On one occasion, some women tried to stick a fetus in my face.

I got death threats. I had been invited to lecture at Catholic Loyola College in Chicago and I was doing a radio broadcast before going on to the campus when the host beckoned to me and said the lecture was being canceled because of a bomb threat. Another time I was invited to a lecture and book signing at Dayton's department store in Minneapolis and the day before the book signing I got a hate letter addressed to "Betty Goldstein Friedan." "You communist Jew, you set foot in Dayton's and we'll bomb the building," it read. I reported it to the police and the FBI was immediately at my door. I went to Minneapolis very nervous. When I got to Dayton's, police dogs were sniffing out the place and then the whole building was evacuated because a man had leaned over a counter and said: "There are bombs in this building and if that woman speaks, they will go off." Needless to say, the talk and book signing were canceled.

The Minnesota Women's Newspaper Association asked me to come back and hold a press conference to be joined by all the leaders of the local women's organizations. So that was great, really great. Then I got asked again to lecture at Loyola. "You do know my stand on abortion," I warned them. "Are you going to cancel it again because you'll get bomb threats?" "We'll take care of that. Don't worry," was the reply. "And we do know your stand on abortion. But you will talk about other things than abortion, won't you?" "Of course," I said. I certainly didn't *not* mention abortion, but you didn't, at that stage in history, dwell mainly on abortion if you were speaking at a Catholic college. Still, we did get to the point where at that lecture or another I was sitting in a circle of Catholic nuns, and the subject of abortion came up, and we were all able to talk about it in a perfectly reasonable and rational way. And I was asked to speak by several Catholic institutions, including one in the Diocese of Pittsburgh and at Jesuit Boston College.

The major threats and disruptions were, of course, from the

right wing or from anti-abortion people. But there were an increasing number of threats and disruptions from within the movement. I began to be suspicious that the women's movement was being infiltrated, which may sound paranoid, but wasn't really at the time. It was an era of great suspicion about everything and everybody and the leadership of NOW was certainly not immune.

It was at a wild conference in New York in 1969 that my suspicions were born. I had persuaded the national board to forgo our next board meeting and instead to organize a "Congress to Unite Women" in each of the cities where we were organized. The point was to bring together a broad coalition of feminists—the radical groups like Redstockings, New York Radical Women and WITCH (Women's International Terrorist Conspiracy from Hell), students, black women, women on welfare—with NOW members to see if we could get together on the specific issues of the greatest importance for women. I didn't think we should attempt to get all the groups into NOW. It seemed to me that problems of difference in style would be insurmountable, not to mention issues of structure. Our collective strength, however, could be politically crucial.

Over five hundred feminists in the Northeast came to the "Congress" in New York, which was a terrific turnout. What I had not counted on was an apparent coordinated effort by the radicals to take over and divide the meeting. To me, and to others, their tactics suggested sabotage.

The women at the Congress had voted to close the meeting to men and to the media. We were meeting behind locked doors of a public school, but somehow Bill Baird, an abortion-rights activist, and a male television crew managed to break in, prompting a group of young women studying karate to try to physically eject them. It was mayhem. "If you were a CIA agent trying to bust up the movement, wouldn't this be just the way to do it?" said the young woman sitting next to me.

The chaos continued that night when a group of radical women took over the stage and, urged on by a group called Cell 16 from Boston, cut off all their hair. I found the women's performance quite amusing to watch, really, but it took on a rather sinister proportion when I got a phone call in the middle of the night from Marlene Sanders. Marlene, who had persuaded ABC News to do a documentary on the movement, told me that someone had stolen all her cans of film. I called a meeting the next day to demand the film be returned immediately, but got nowhere. Though Marlene assured the women that she wasn't going to use the haircutting footage (women in the media were actually very protective of the movement and often saved it from its excesses), the radicals were adamant that dealing with a male-dominated television network, or the women who worked for one, was immoral. It was rumored that the cans of film ended up on the bottom of the Hudson River, which was a shame really. In light of disruptions to come from radical lesbians, I would have liked to have seen who was egging on the haircutters.

Whispers about lesbians in NOW had begun early in the movement. I didn't listen. My attitude was I don't want to know, sort of like the current military policy toward homosexuals of "Don't ask, don't tell." I come from Peoria, Illinois, after all. I was very straitlaced and the whole idea of homosexuality made me profoundly uneasy. The only homosexual I think I knew in my growing-up years was married and had kids, but he was also an expert in dress design, which was very unusual for Peoria, and he had a chic clothing shop. So when people started to tell me this one or that one in the movement was a lesbian, I didn't want to know. I felt it was not my business. I thought all of that should be private.

An increasingly militant group, however, was determined to make it public. Lesbians, or people claiming to be lesbians, started disrupting the lectures I was giving in the late sixties and demanding equal time to further their agenda. I was attracting very large audiences because of the tremendous interest in the exploding women's movement, the fact that I was president of NOW and the author of *The Feminine Mystique*. I did not take kindly to the extremists who tried to take over the stage and insist on talking about lesbians. I didn't want to discuss lesbianism. And neither did the audience. The audience had come to hear about the issues and changes facing all women.

But the disruptions continued. At one point, someone called me in advance of one of my lectures at a college somewhere to threaten me into sharing the stage with a lesbian. "But I am being paid to lecture here, not you," I told the caller. "If the college wants to have a lesbian lecturer, let the college pay her for another time, but not on my time. Homosexuality is not an issue on which I am an expert and it is not, in my opinion, what the women's movement is all about." "Well, we insist that you share the stage with us or we will disrupt," the caller said. I didn't, and they did.

Fortunately there were no television cameras at the lecture that night so there was no coverage of the disruption. The press just covered my press conference at the airport. But I knew if these interruptions continued, they would do harm to the organization. We had to get control of the situation. I called Toni Carabillo, one of the most effective leaders of NOW, and told her what was going on. "I want you to have some really responsible people fill the first rows when I lecture to prevent these disruptions or to drown them out," I told her. "This is very bad business for the women's movement."

Here we were, trying to organize a massive movement that would cross lines of class and race and speak for the majority of women. I didn't want to exclude anyone, but I wanted the movement to speak to and for and from the mainstream. If you really wanted to change society for all women and organize a large enough movement to do that, that was radical enough. Others, obviously, did not agree.

I remember Dolores Alexander coming to see me one night and telling me that the lesbians were planning to take over leadership of the New York chapter of NOW and perhaps the national, though they wanted me to keep on doing what I was doing because they liked using me as a front. I should be careful, she said.

I immediately called the chair of NOW, Kay Clarenbach, in Wisconsin. I didn't spell out any of the details Dolores had told me over the phone. Instead, I told her I was on my way to lecture out west and would stop in Madison if she would come meet me at the airport. There was a bad snowstorm in the Midwest at the time, which, looking back, shouldn't have surprised me. I have a lot of blizzardy memories about the early years of NOW. But Kay made it to the airport and was quite appalled, though not as much as I had been, when I told her about the pending takeover. I also had a real bad case of flu on that trip, but after I told Kay and felt some support, at least that somebody else knew about it and would help me, my flu got better.

I don't know how they did it, but the responsible leaders of NOW managed to stop or at least diminish the disruptions. There would be no takeover of the national or state chapters. Toni Carabillo somehow put a stop to it in California and Muriel Fox organized effectively in New York and kept the New York chapter a mainstream organization. Though some in the NOW leadership were themselves lesbians, they were part of that mainstream movement and they didn't want it to be primarily a lesbian movement either.

The women's movement was not about sex, but about equal opportunity in jobs and all the rest of it. Yes, I suppose you have to say that freedom of sexual choice is part of that, but it shouldn't be the main issue, the tail that wags the dog. I was worried mainly about it being a divisive issue for NOW, which it was. Though I don't deny that it was an issue then that made me squeamish, I just felt that NOW *had* to speak for the majority. You didn't have to speak *only* for those women, but you certainly had to speak for them.

The question was, who was provoking the disruptions and pushing the lesbian agenda? There certainly were lesbians within the movement, but the shock tactics of the radical fringe made me suspect outside agents. The attempt to equate feminism and the women's movement with lesbianism had always been a favorite device of those who wanted to frighten women away from it. What better way to divide and weaken the women's movement than to infiltrate and immobilize it politically? It may seem paranoid to have suspected *agents provocateurs* being planted within the movement. But it turned out that it wasn't.

We didn't know at the time, but found out later, that the FBI had initiated an investigation of the women's movement in 1969 for subversive activity. The truth would begin to surface during the Watergate hearings in 1973, when it was revealed that government agents had tapped the phones of American citizens during the Nixon administration and that the CIA had launched "Operation Chaos" to disrupt and divide the liberal movements of the New Left by infiltrating agents. It was those agents, though the extent was never clear, who engineered much of the violence and shock tactics that would alienate the most radical of those antiwar, student and civil rights groups from mainstream America.

When the Freedom of Information Act was passed in 1975,

NOW began its own investigation into the documentation of government surveillance of its activities and members. I hired a lawyer to get my file from the FBI, but all that came back was a bunch of newsclips. The FBI's rationale said it all. The rest of my file was still classified, I was informed, so as "not to endanger agents still on active duty."

Just who these agents were within the movement, we'll never know. But they were quite effective. I suspect that the origin of the bra-burning myth at the Miss America Beauty Contest protest which trivialized the movement was the work of *agents provocateurs*, as were the disruptions by radical man-haters at the Congress to Unite Women and the disruptions by the radical lesbian fringe.

I had my suspicions about the identities of those "agents," centering on those early officers of NOW who didn't seem to have any visible means of support. Several of them appeared to me to be good candidates. They were also among the ones pressing for provocative actions or messing up things.

In 1969, I finally summoned the courage to get a divorce from Carl. The tension and the violence between us had not stopped during those early years when I was organizing the movement, working with Gene McCarthy, protesting the Vietnam War, blocking Carswell's appointment to the Supreme Court, creating NARAL, fighting off the radical lesbian fringe. All these momentous events of 1967, '68 and '69 were going on in my public life at the same time I was still getting beaten up by my husband in my private life. I could no longer be the two-headed woman I'd written about in the *Ladies' Home Journal*.

Here I was acting like Joan of Arc while at the same time I was a disgrace, really, to the women's movement by being such a worm at home and accepting, maybe even inviting, abusive treatment. I was finally too embarrassed. How could I reconcile putting up with being knocked around by my husband while calling on women to rise up against their oppressors? On one hand, I was strong. Nothing ever fazed me in organizing the women's movement. Even the bomb threats didn't really terrorize me. Divorce, however, did.

Divorcing Carl was very painful for me because of the children. We both really loved our kids and Carl was a good father.

Our marriage may have gotten bad in terms of each other, but we never took it out on the kids. I don't think that all that beating-up stuff was good for them, but I also believed then and still do that divorce is often bad for kids. That would always leave me with some degree of guilt. But I had to get out or risk further injury. I had to get over my irrational fear of being alone if I was going to get on with my life. I had made pacts with myself—if I could do such-and-such, I could get a divorce. But I never did it. I had been almost at the point of resolution when I got back from interviewing Indira Gandhi in India. I'd managed to travel halfway around the world by myself and actually enjoy it. But when I got back, I remember getting undressed and Carl coming in and putting a fur coat he'd bought me on my nude body. So I put off my resolution and didn't say anything that time about a divorce.

I made another pact with myself in 1965 when I was asked to lecture at Ghost Ranch in New Mexico. The Presbyterian Church owned this ranch in Georgia O'Keeffe country where they held leadership workshops and Dean Lewis had invited me to lead a workshop for ministers and lay leaders of the church. It was the year before we organized the women's movement, but Dean Lewis, in charge of education for the church, had already decided that the next great civil rights issue was going to be women. So I accepted his invitation and took the kids with me to Ghost Ranch. The test came when Carl met us there and we went on to the Grand Canyon.

When I was a girl I loved horseback riding, but I had been thrown a couple of times and after that I was nervous that the horse never knew who was boss. I was also terrified of heights, which formed a deadly combination for me but a perfect pact. If I could go down the Grand Canyon on a mule, as scared as I was of heights much less horses, and get back up alive, I could get a divorce. So I did it, and that time we actually did split up for a while, but then we got back together and our battered marriage went on.

I finally succeeded after a trip I took to Switzerland in 1968. This time I was invited to speak at a conference in Zurich on new economic trends. I was the only woman speaker, which wasn't surprising in light of the fact that women in Switzerland didn't have the vote. In fact, some of the Swiss economists or businessmen, or whatever they were at the conference, would take me for walks after lunch and tell me proudly how they were protecting their women from the nastiness of the vote. I didn't find them or the conference in the least intimidating so that wasn't a test. So I said to myself: "All right, after the conference in Zurich, I will go to Paris for three days by myself. And if I can do that and not die, I will go home and get a divorce."

I had never been to Paris before and I stayed in the Relais Bisson, a lovely little hotel on the Quai des Grands Augustins. People in the theater used to stay there and I'd heard about it. The hotel overlooked Notre Dame. I had a bathroom as big as my dining room back home, with a bidet—I'd never used a bidet before—and a cozy bedroom overlooking the bookstalls on the Left Bank. There was a wonderful two-star restaurant, which I think is still there, and I remember ordering a platter of wild strawberries.

I loved walking in Paris and sitting down at a café on the Seine and ordering a café au lait or a dozen oysters. I remember walking by a restaurant at suppertime and going inside and ordering *"pigeon."* You couldn't have a bad meal in Paris. I had a lovely French publisher, who wined and dined me, and I met my French translator. They were quite wonderful to me. My translator, Yvette Roudy, was getting into politics and was a devoted follower of Mitterrand. She took me to meet him and said by way of introduction: "You are both my leaders." So I passed the test being alone in Paris and finally acted.

When I got home, I told Carl that it was over, that he had to get out. I loved symphonies, which Carl didn't, so I hadn't gone in years, and I said: "I'll go to the Philharmonic, and when I get back you have your clothes out of here." Going anywhere on your own was a big deal then—many women didn't—and I guess it was such a shock to him that he did it. In fact, he did it so readily that he must have known the marriage was over.

The first lawyer I had was Ephraim London, who had given me the language for the abortion rights legislation in New York. But Ephraim just sort of exacerbated things between us. Carl had a woman lawyer, quite an eminent one, I think her name was Julia Perle, but nothing was getting resolved. I suddenly realized that all the money I'd saved up was going to go to lawyer bills, so I switched from London to my friend Milton Carrow, the divorce lawyer who had seen Carl beating up on me years before in our car in Rockland County. "Just get the divorce," I told him.

Milton told me that the only way I was going to get a divorce from Carl was to buy him out. So I had to sell the apartment in the Dakota and split the proceeds with Carl. We also sold the house on Fire Island within the year. I wasn't asking for alimony, but even so it was a long and stormy period.

Carl was no longer living in the apartment, but somehow he'd get back in. I don't know whether I changed the locks or I didn't change the locks, but whatever, he managed to get back in. It scared me to death to come back home and know someone was in the apartment. On one such day Carl tried to kiss me and then to beat me up. I may have called the police, but I doubt it. They weren't interested in domestic disputes then. Later, the women's movement would make an issue of family violence, but in those days the police didn't want to be bothered.

I finally got a divorce in Mexico, which you could do then very quickly if it were uncontested. I remember combining the divorce trip to Mexico with a lecture in the Episcopal Cathedral of Jackson, Mississippi, of all things. I did not tell the church ladies who met my plane in Jackson why I was coming from that direction. I kept the divorce as quiet as possible to "protect" the movement. But at last it was done.

Looking back on it, I realize that Carl was so fearful that in my new independence I'd leave him that he made inevitable that I would. The way he'd handle it was either messing around with other women and making sure I'd find out, or this beating me up. In contrast, when I went to my analyst, my agenda always was— can this marriage be saved?

The shrink knew he had to give me kind of the nerve to break out of it. I was going to be permanently scarred, the doctors told me. The black eyes were getting serious. It was incredible, though, how I blocked the truth. When I saw a friend with a black eye like mine, I said to her, "Oh, how did it happen?" when obviously what had happened to her was the same thing that had happened to me. But nobody wanted to admit it or talk about it then. It was too humiliating.

The big problem was the discrepancy in our achievements. I was such an old-fashioned dame underneath that I didn't like making more money than Carl. When I was at the stage of making real money, I didn't capitalize on it but thought of ways to protect it from his deals. I couldn't shake the convention that the man should support the family. It was disgraceful to hold on to all that in my marriage, but I did. That's where I was.

At the same time, I loved the wider world I was entering. It was fun. It was exciting. To start a movement and be able to do something about the inequities that had held women down for so long became for me almost a mission. And the time was so right in that era of promise. I felt so privileged to be a part of it. It was marvelous, really.

I realize now that what I really wanted was to beat up on Carl for not letting me enjoy it, but instead, I'd taunt him to the point where he'd beat up on me. There was some kind of a weirdness there. The drinking obviously made it worse. One weekend we'd gone to Cape May, New Jersey, where we'd never been, on some sort of reconciliation weekend, and sure enough, we got drinking and I got beaten up. The irony is that he would get so upset when that happened that he would cry. He didn't want to be that way.

I still sometimes think, if I'd been stronger inside, I could have made him stop. And for years I'd feel guilty about the divorce because it did break up the family. Fortunately that was the era where mothers always got custody so there was no question of that. The kids were then twelve, sixteen and twenty, and certainly old enough to have their own lives, but we all lost something.

I look back and I wouldn't have missed any of the rich texture of family life, marriage and children—arguments and whatever notwithstanding. We had a big table which opened up to seat perhaps twenty people and Carl and I used to give wonderfully raucous dinners. We loved artichokes and I remember one dinner where we all got a little drunk and threw the artichoke leaves into, or at least toward, a big bowl in the middle of the table. I remember the clam chowder parties we'd have at the house on Fire Island when Emily went clamming, and the big white restaurant bowls I bought at the Bridge kitchenware shop. The liquor store always had a big sale at the end of the summer so they wouldn't leave any bottles on the island over the winter and I remember buying a bottle of Chartreuse. It was icky and sweet and after some dinner party later back on the mainland I heard this noise and there was Jonathan, sitting at the table drinking the Chartreuse—and oh, was he sick. Jonathan had taken up the drum around then and he had a band which rehearsed at our house. The police would come because the noise was so horrific. They were wonderful years and I feel blessed to have had them.

Soon after the divorce, I went out to California for a NOW board meeting—and ended up staying a month. Michael Murphy, the founder of Esalen where the human potential movement had recently been launched, had invited me to visit the center in Big Sur and I decided to take him up on it. I had real training in Gestalt psychology and I was very curious about the use of Gestalt and other forms of experiential psychology for groups. My plan was to go from the board meeting in San Francisco to Esalen for the weekend, then on to LA to do some television. My stopover at Esalen coincided with a training workshop for therapists being run by Virginia Satir, the famous family therapist. She invited me to sit in on the workshop. I was so wild about it, I asked if I could stay for the rest of the month.

A great debate ensued. Many in the workshop of shrinks protested that I was not a professional therapist and had no right to join them. Others argued that they hadn't been allowed to bring their wives so there was a lot of "why should this woman be allowed in?" I felt quite uncomfortable listening to the arguments, but Virginia was very persuasive. "It's true that she's not a therapist but she is a change agent and I think it's important to give her this kind of training." In the end they voted to let me stay.

I had to go down to LA and get rid of my obligations and evidently they didn't think I'd come back since they'd been so brutal in their discussion. But I did come back and I got a great deal out of that early group therapy. There were several natural hot mineral baths on a cliff ledge overlooking the Pacific and sometimes you could lie in the tubs and watch passing whales. People went into the tubs nude and I remember thinking "not me, not me," but I made myself do it. Then I encountered a doctor I knew from East Hampton in the nude on the massage table and we looked at each other and he simply said, "Hi, Betty." I was mortified. My background was very Peoria bourgeois and the idea of being nude, even taking off your clothes with a man you were going to sleep with, was a big deal for me then. But to take off your clothes otherwise—wow. But I think it was a good technique because it made people less defended.

I would return to the institute as often as I could, sometimes to lead groups. Virginia Satir became my teacher and mentor and I took Jonathan later to a family therapy retreat Virginia ran. She was very helpful to him—and to me. When I got back to New York, I started working with John Pierrakos, who was a shrink but not your conventional shrink because he, too, had been trained in the dynamics of Gestalt, Reich, whatever. I don't know if therapy is still that way, but at that time, everyone I knew was in some kind of group analysis, and it was good, at least for me. Though I can't pinpoint the exact effects and what technique produced what, the group therapy did help me to resolve things and go on in the tumultuous years after the divorce.

I made the decision to step down as president of NOW in 1970. I could have been reelected had I wanted to be. I was a good leader, and I had a lot of influence and a great deal of support. But first of all, I didn't think I wanted to be a lifelong organization leader and to have a lifelong presidency as they do in the NAACP. And second, the nominating committee had slated Aileen Hernandez to run for president. In those days women only ran for office if they were uncontested. In any event, I wouldn't have opposed a minority woman. So I stepped down.

There's no doubt that the decision to run someone against me stemmed from internal politics. There were people in NOW who wanted me to step down as president, the conservative side who saw me as too radical, the radical side who saw me as too conservative. And who knows what role was played by the CIA and FBI agents. In any event, Aileen was a good administrator and I knew she would make a good team with Wilma Scott Heide, who would replace Kay as chair. If the nominating committee hadn't nominated a woman of color, I wouldn't have stepped down. But they did. And I did.

I wrote my last speech as president of NOW in March 1970, on the airplane to Chicago for the fourth annual NOW convention to be held in Des Plaines, Illinois. I didn't usually write out my speeches. I just gave them. But this time I wrote what would turn out to be a two-hour speech. It took the volunteers from

Chicago NOW half the night to mimeograph it and the next day after I delivered it, Kay Clarenbach would teasingly compare me to Fidel Castro. But I'd had a great idea on the plane which I wanted to propose at the convention.

The germ of the idea had come from a woman in Florida, Betty Armistead, who had sent me a letter reminding me that August 26, 1970, would be the fiftieth anniversary of the vote for women and that the original suffragettes had proposed a general strike of women in the final stages of their battle half a century before. Shouldn't NOW have some sort of similar action to commemorate the anniversary? Yes, I decided, somewhere between La Guardia and O'Hare.

The women's movement was beginning to get a lot of trivializing media attention: big attention paid to the Miss America Beauty Contest and supposed bra-burning, a lot of talk about "women's libbers," an expression I never liked. It is true that we were in the midst of a "leave-off-your-bra-and-girdle" movement, but that came more from male designers like Rudi Gernreich. Maybe it was more than a coincidence that fashion designers picked up on the women's movement and designed clothes that symbolically liberated women from all that confining stuff. But the media naturally picked on any extremist stuff that was sexy, like the SCUM Manifesto, which had nothing to do with the women's movement.

There was an especially big hullabaloo in the press when Kate Millett's book, *Sexual Politics*, came out in 1969. Kate was a member of NY NOW, and while it would not have been politically correct for me or any woman to attack Kate in our "Sisterhood Is Powerful" era, I must say I was dismayed by that book. Though there was a lot of brilliance in it, I felt that there was also a lot of warped stuff. Her diatribe against men was tactically, strategically, ideologically misdirected, in my view. As mad as a woman might be at her husband or at her boss or at society in general for the way she'd been treated, the relationship between men and women was too human and complex to discard.

The media loved to write stories about the extremists who continued to make literal analogies of the women's movement with class warfare or race warfare. Down with men. Down with marriage. Down with motherhood. Down with anything women have ever done to attract men. The male chauvinist pigs, the bastards, brutes, the patriarchs. Down with everything men have ever done in history. There was no doubt that women's anger was real and justified. But the women's movement was about *changing* the conditions that made women rightfully angry, not getting stuck in a war of women against men.

I was always sort of bemused at Robin Morgan, the founder of WITCH, and with her manifesto that all men should be killed at birth. Well, what about her own son? It was ridiculous. It was always my mandate, my rule that we were creating an ideology for this revolution, and that we were improvising as we went along, but our revolution had to test against life. If it opened life for women and therefore for others, fine. If it didn't, forget it. And the anti-man manifestos which the media loved to write about were not real, did not express the feelings or the situations of most women.

We clearly needed a serious action to get the focus off sexual politics and back to women's move for equal opportunity in jobs, education, training, the right to control our own bodies and the issue of child care, which we were finally addressing. We needed to do something to make the nation realize how big this women's movement really was, and to demonstrate to ourselves the recognition of our political voice.

I knew, not only from the size of the audiences I was getting at my lectures but from the letters I was getting, people wanting a NOW chapter in Arizona, in Syracuse, whatever, that there was tremendous momentum out there. NOW was up to three thousand members when I stepped down as president, with ten chapters in thirty cities. But I knew there were hundreds, thousands, probably millions of women and men out there who supported our movement and I wanted to focus all that energy. Why not have a march in New York and in other cities like Chicago and Pittsburgh where we had enough people? Why not call for an action that women could do in their kitchens or their own backyards? So as I stepped down, I called for a massive demonstration and twenty-four-hour strike for equality on the fiftieth anniversary of the vote, August 26, 1970.

"I propose that the women who are doing menial chores in the offices cover their typewriters and close their notebooks, that the telephone operators unplug their switchboards, the waitresses stop waiting, cleaning women stop cleaning, and everyone who is doing a job for which a man would be paid more—stop—and every woman pegged forever as assistant, doing jobs for which men get the credit—stop," I told the cheering members at the NOW convention. ". . . And by the time those twenty-four hours are ended, our revolution will be a fact."

The members of NOW gave me a standing ovation when I finally finished, but the new NOW leadership was not as enthusiastic. It was made clear to me the next day by Karen DeCrow and others still on the board that I had to organize this action on my own because Aileen Hernandez was not interested. She and others in opposition evidently thought it was a wild scheme, not worthy of NOW's meager resources and a source of embarrassment were it to flop.

I understood the risk of calling for such a massive action and organizing it all in just four months with no money. I also knew that it had to be bigger than NOW to succeed and that it required getting together a coalition. But there's something in Jewish theology about your duty to use your life to make life better for those who come after. I felt that mission strongly. It wasn't enough just to start a movement for women's rights. You had to make it happen.

TEN

Triumph and Treachery Within the Sisterhood

How did I have the nerve? Those marches, I now know, cost millions of dollars to produce and we didn't have any money. How were we going to pay for leaflets and posters and renting loudspeakers? I was sharing a summer house with friends in the Hamptons on Long Island, and I had no idea until we started getting invitations to benefits. These days, of course, there are benefits every ten minutes it seems in the Hamptons, but the concept then was relatively new. So after we were invited to one "radical chic" benefit for Native Americans and then to another for Cesar Chavez and the grape pickers, I thought, "Well, why shouldn't the women out here have a benefit to raise money to support our march?"

Ethel Scull and her husband, Bob, a collector of Pop art and a taxi mogul with a fleet of cabs in New York called "Scull's Angels," had a very big place in East Hampton. I approached Ethel to host the benefit. She had burst on the social scene in New York and she always invited me to these great parties where you'd have a bus take you from the art opening to the restaurant or whatever. Tom Wolfe and I were high on her guest list, I guess, to lend a little intellectual *éclat*. She'd introduce us as "This is Betty Friedan, the author," or "This is Tom Wolfe, the writer," or something like that. Sometimes she'd get us mixed up and introduce me as "the novelist." Anyway, I went to see Ethel and she agreed to have a fund-raiser at her pool for the women's march. I suspect that her motive was not so much to support feminism as it was to climb the social ladder. She wanted her name on the invitation to read "Mrs. Robert Scull" until I told her in no uncertain terms that she had to host this benefit in her own right, not as her husband's wife.

While the benefit was getting organized in the Hamptons, I was in the scorching city trying to get the word out about the march. Someone lent the march organizers and me an office in a building in midtown as a headquarters, but it wasn't air-conditioned. I remember going to a publication party for my friend Al Toffler's book, *Future Shock,* after a strike meeting and arriving drenched. I don't recall ever having hot flashes, though I must have had a menopause somewhere around that time, so I don't know whether the sweat came from the heat or a hot flash. But it was graphic.

I asked Karen DeCrow to coordinate August 26 for NOW, while my job was to gather a broad coalition of women for the major march in New York. I remember going to see Bella Abzug and Amy Swerdlow, who had started Women Strike for Peace, one of the few women's things going at the time, and getting them involved. I also drummed up support among newly rebellious professional women who were just beginning to organize, as well as the young radical women in their blue jeans, no bras and afros. There was enormous tension at some of the early meetings. The young anti-establishment women refused to come uptown to the meetings while the establishment women refused to go downtown to lofts in the East Village.

We did manage to agree to drop the idea of a women's national strike. It seemed too radical and even counterproductive to ask women to walk off their jobs if they weren't organized in unions and the movement itself wasn't strong enough to protect them. Because we were so diverse, we also agreed that women should participate in whatever actions they chose to during the week leading up to the march on August 26. We didn't begin to have a large enough staff to coordinate it all, and besides, I wanted women to organize themselves. When people called us from NOW chapters in Boston, Chicago, Kansas City, Minneapolis and elsewhere and asked what actions they should take, we answered: "You organize whatever you want."

The benefit at Ethel Scull's on August 8 turned out to be a

riot. I wanted the pool party to be socially glamorous in the hopes of attracting the monied matrons in the Hamptons, so I'd asked Gloria Steinem, Gloria Vanderbilt Cooper and Edith de Rham, a socialite and author, to be co-hosts. Still, Ethel locked the doors to her house, evidently anticipating barbarians at her gate. At $25 a head, there were no barbarians, but there were busloads of press from New York, lured no doubt by a free party at a fancy pool rather than their interest in women.

The press got quite a story, however. While I was giving a poolside speech on our demand for *herstory*, not just *history*, Jill Johnston, a columnist for *The Village Voice* and the future author of *Lesbian Nation*, slipped into the pool, stripped to the waist and started swimming laps. I grew ever more impassioned to divert attention, not realizing that the elastic in the neck of my otherwise demure scoopneck dress had broken and my boob was hanging out. You can imagine the horrible pictures of me that ran in the press the next day. But the news stories would prove invaluable in getting out the word about the march on August 26 and the call for national actions.

We managed to raise $5,000 at the benefit, enough to rent sound trucks for the march in New York and to produce buttons and leaflets. The demand was so great for the flyers that we had volunteer crews in the office running the mimeograph machine day and night. (The radicals consented to come uptown as the pace became frantic.) God knows how we did it, but the word really seemed to be getting out to suburban housewives, lawyers, secretary pools. The phone in the office never stopped ringing. The last couple of days, I learned from people later, the networks kept trying to get ahold of us but they never could because our phones were always busy.

We had all sorts of outrageous actions going on in the lead-up to August 26. One NOW task force in New York smuggled a huge banner in sections by boat out to the Statue of Liberty and for three hours draped it over a railing around "lady liberty" with the call: "Women of the World Unite." Another group picketed the advertising agencies that had created sexist ads with signs reading: "This ad insults women," while women working at City Hall turned the grounds into a day care center, bringing their own children and inviting other women to bring theirs, to demonstrate working women's demands for child care.

Creative juices were flowing all over the country. Bulletins were coming in from Louisiana where women working at one newspaper substituted men's pictures for women's in the engagement and marriage pages; from Massachusetts where women persuaded the Protestant churches to turn their pulpits over to women as they had to the suffragettes fifty years before. On the Sunday before the march, I shared the pulpit at the famous Arlington Street Church in Boston with Mary Daly, a professor of theology who had written *The Church and the Second Sex*. The press coverage of these actions spread the word worldwide. In Holland, Dutch women marched on the U.S. Embassy in Amsterdam to demonstrate solidarity with their American sisters.

Washington, too, was caught up. It was no coincidence that on August 10, 1970, the same day that women in New York took over the Statue of Liberty, the House of Representatives passed the Equal Rights Amendment. After being bottled up in committee for forty-seven years, the ERA was passed by a resounding vote of 350 to 15. In New York, Governor Nelson Rockefeller proclaimed Wednesday, August 26, a holiday in an emotional ceremony at Seneca Falls, and a caravan of women who had been wending their way to the birthplace of the suffrage movement attended the celebration as the governor paid tribute to Susan B. Anthony, Elizabeth Cady Stanton—and me!

The mayor of New York City, John V. Lindsay, was not as enthusiastic. He refused our requests to close Fifth Avenue for a few hours for our march, citing problems with traffic and interference with business. I was totally insulted and made no bones about it to the press. Irish, Italians, ethnic minorities of every description were allowed to parade up and down Fifth Avenue in every month of every year. Why not women? Fifty years before, the suffragettes had marched abreast down Fifth Avenue. Was the mayor of New York saying that women deserved that privilege only once in a century? But Lindsay remained resolute, restricting our march permit to the sidewalk with a little spillover into the street.

On the morning of the 26th I had no idea how many women would show up for the march. The press covered my every move during the day so I spent some time purposefully getting my hair done at Vidal Sassoon before going on to women's actions around New York, and ending up near Wall Street for lunch. NOW had recently won the historic public accommodations case against McSorley's, so I joined a group of women protesting the absence of women from the Stock Exchange by eating at Whyte's, another male-only landmark on Fulton Street.

The men in the restaurant were buzzing with the news of the day. "My wife said she would mow the lawn and I would make dinner," I overheard one man say to another. "I started to tell my secretary to go out for coffee, and she just stared at me," came a remark from another table. I was quite pleased in the midst of this male consciousness-raising session when one man came over to our table and asked for my autograph.

The march was due to start at 5:00 p.m. to get the crowds on their way home from work, and to make it an appropriate time for women coming in from the suburbs who could then spend the evening in town with their husbands. One suburban housewife and mother of four who had addressed envelopes and made hors d'oeuvres for the benefit had already made the march. Madeline Collins had to meet her husband early for an important business-social event of his, but the march was so important to her that she had come to New York in the afternoon and marched the whole parade route on her own, wearing a handwritten sign: "Women Strike for Equality."

While Madeline was early for the march, I was almost late. I couldn't get a taxi in the rush-hour traffic, so I took a Madison Avenue bus uptown from headquarters. The bus was jammed, inching its way uptown. Where was everybody going? It wasn't until I got off the bus at 59th Street and joined the women waving at me and hurrying toward Central Park where we were to gather that I realized we might have a crowd. The reality dawned when I rounded the corner onto the park and saw not hundreds, but *thousands* of women and men and babies and grandmothers beginning to mass.

The press would later estimate that thirty thousand people marched in our strike for equality that day. I think it was many more. When the march spilled out of the park onto Fifth Avenue, I was in the front row between Judge Dorothy Kenyon, a suffragette veteran in her eighties (who refused to ride in the car we'd provided), and one of the young radicals in blue jeans. We kept jumping up to look back at the marchers behind us, but we could never see where the march ended. The mounted police were trying to make us march on the sidewalk, but I saw how many we were. There was no way we were about to walk down Fifth Avenue in a little, thin line. I waved my arms over my head and yelled, *"Take the street!"*

What a moment that was. Suddenly there we were, holding hands, marching in great long swinging lines from sidewalk to sidewalk, down Fifth Avenue. The police were incredulous seeing all these women marching and carrying big banners, like Bella's group—"Women Strike for Peace—and Equality"—and smaller homemade signs like "Uppity Women Unite" and "Don't Cook Dinner—Starve a Rat Tonight!" I loved the group of suburban housewives who marched with ironing boards and a sign reading: "Don't Iron While the Strike Is Hot," and another group who wore aprons with the legend: "For This I Went to College?" What were the police supposed to do? Mow us down? So we spread out and marched down Fifth Avenue from Central Park and 59th Street to Bryant Park in back of the New York Public Library on 42nd Street. The route was electric.

People leaned out of office windows and cheered. Passersby left the sidewalks to join us. There were a lot of spontaneous actions and shows of support, especially from my friends in the art world. Steve Weil, a friend who was then at the Museum of Modern Art, yelled: "Betty, Betty, look, we're here!" as we passed 53rd Street and what looked like the whole museum came outside with a very artistic-looking banner—"MOMA Supports Women's Equality."

The Whitney Museum was represented in a different way. I'd had a long talk with the museum's administrator about whether women were discriminated against in the art world. He'd insisted to me that they weren't until I asked him whether the museum had ever had an exhibit of women's paintings. They hadn't.

It was so obvious to me, but not to him, why women weren't better represented in any of the arts. You might have a few exceptional geniuses emerge, like Jane Austen. But what about Shakespeare's sister, for example. Or Mozart's? Girls for the most part were told to keep quiet and not interrupt their brothers who were busy writing or painting or practicing their scales. It takes a lot of nerve to be creative, to have the confidence to say a new yes and break into new territory as a musician or a writer or an artist. There simply couldn't be much expression of female genius when the general situation of women was denigrated, to say nothing of women's lack of training and professional experience and opportunity.

Museums were run by men and men selected the artists they would show. They didn't take women seriously any more than women took themselves seriously. I'm convinced that many more women might have been great artists if they had had enough self-confidence to do it and block out their own time without babies underfoot and get the training and have a studio. There were token successes that everyone could point to, like Georgia O'Keeffe, over and over again, or Marie Curie in the field of science over and over again. But for the vast majority, no way.

So I wasn't surprised by how oblivious my friend at the Whitney was as to why there were so few recognized women artists and why their work was often buried. On August 26, the women at the Whitney turned out in droves for the march—the ticket takers, the women in the gift shop, elevator and switchboard operators, assistant curators, even the administrator's own secretary, leaving instructions behind for the men to do their jobs.

The march ended at a rally behind the Public Library. I spoke, Gloria spoke, Bella spoke, as, among others, did Kate Millett and Eleanor Holmes Norton, the able lawyer who was then representing forty-six women on the editorial staff at *Newsweek* in a sex discrimination suit against the magazine. The crowd was still huge. No one wanted to leave.

Women who hadn't made it to the march in New York evidently felt much as we had. We found out later that women across the country had organized demonstrations and rallies in more than ninety cities and small towns in forty-two states. There were countless spontaneous demonstrations. As we marched in New York, women elsewhere were marching on the beach or in their own backyards, or up and down the halls of their offices. One told me she just marched around by herself. The press estimated that the number of women who'd organized for themselves on their own behalf was more than 100,000!

We ended that triumphant day at the Village Gate at a party

given for me by the owner, Art d'Lugoff. It was a great end to a great day.

The march is probably the high point of my political life. Everything happened just the way I had wanted it to. The turnout was so huge that all the networks and the wire services and the newspapers had to cover it. Pete Hamill wrote: "All women looked six feet tall that day." But then, all the stories were positive.

The journalists covering the movement wanted to be objective, but all the women reporters obviously identified strongly with the actions. When Judy Klemesrud, a *New York Times* reporter, died at a very young age, I said at her funeral, "We were hers and she was ours." Everyone said later I shouldn't have said that with all the *Times* people there, but it was true. The editors would finally resort to assigning men to the beat and they became just as supportive. I remember Sidney Hertzberg, then at *The New York Times*, following me around the day of the march and writing such a lovely story. But they all did.

The momentum would carry through the November elections. When Congress convened, thirteen members were women, including Bella Abzug newly elected from New York. While the numbers were encouraging, so was the pattern. For the first time ever, none of the women who won seats were widows who had run to succeed their late husbands. They were all elected in their own right.

The kids and I moved to an apartment at a semi-collective on West 93rd in 1970. From Didi Allen, a very good screenwriter and director, and her husband, Steve Flieschman, I had heard about the bunch of young families who had jointly bought nine brownstones on 93rd Street and converted them into apartments with a big, communal garden. We sublet an apartment at 9G, as it was called, and lived there for a while. At least Emily and I did. Jonathan was in his last year of high school when we moved and Danny was at Princeton.

Emily and I spent as much of the summer of 1970 as we could at a "commune" of friends I put together in the Hamptons. The house on Fire Island was being sold and I couldn't see renting a house or a cottage for the summer for just the two of us. Emily was thirteen. It was easier for me to organize a revolution than contemplate renting a house alone. What we needed, I decided, was a commune, a kibbutz, a chosen family. After twenty-two years of married life, I didn't want to start whatever my new life was going to be, all alone.

I had had a sort of affair right after I split from Carl with Tom Wolf, whom I'd had a crush on—and I think he on me—all during my Parkway Village life with the little kids. Tom, who became a vice president of NBC, had had me come and be the interviewee while he was trying out Harry Reasoner and others to be the host of *Calendar.* We never did anything about it then. When he got divorced, I was divorced, too. I remember going away with him for what turned out to be a disastrous weekend at his cabin in the Catskills. We were having a wonderful time, but out of habit, I had left my number.

I got a phone call in the cabin. It was an aide of the prime minister of India. Indira Gandhi was in America and wanted to see me. "Tell her I'm sorry, but I'm busy," I told the aide. "Well, she wants to talk to you," the aide said. What could I do? So I spent some time with her on the phone. And then Tom and I went for a hike, and halfway up a mountain coming toward us was a Girl Scout troop with a male leader. So there was a big fuss about, "Oh, here's Betty Friedan." That sort of thing is ruinous— *ruinous*—to a relationship with a man. Between Indira Gandhi and the Girl Scouts, the weekend didn't go so well, and you know where.

Had the roles been reversed, I wouldn't have felt diminished. I would have felt thrilled that I'd acquired a man with such great stuff. But as it was, it gave him a headache, as I recall. We remained very close but the relationship never really recovered.

Another affair, this one with Arthur Whitman, a fellow magazine writer, was sadly cut short. It began in Florida where I had a lecture and he had a magazine assignment and we rendezvoused afterwards. We spent a wonderful week on Sanibel Island, holed up in a shack on a bayou where we'd take off each day in a boat with a can of sardines, a loaf of bread and the makings for martinis. Soon afterwards Arthur went to Mexico and came back with hepatitis. He didn't respond to treatment and, in 1970, he died.

I proposed the idea of a commune to my old friend Arthur

Herzog whom I had demonstrated with against the Vietnam War at the Democratic Convention in Chicago in 1968. Arthur was in the process of a divorce, as was another old friend I approached, Si Goode, the newly elected president of the American Sociological Association. "We're obviously not that good as choosers in the marriage thing, and the danger is that out of loneliness, we'll choose badly again," I told them. Carl had rushed into a second marriage with a beautiful model which would only last two years. I didn't want to do that. "What we need is not so much sex," I said to my friends, "as being able to sit around in your bathrobe and not be alone." Arthur, who had a little adopted son Matthew, and was going around then with Betty Rollin, an editor at *Look,* signed on, as did Si, who was involved at the time with my friend Cynthia Epstein. The "commune," with an ever-revolving group of "chosen family," would stay intact for the next four years.

My God, we had fun. The first house we rented was in Sagaponack and belonged to the daughter-in-law of Diana Vreeland, the flamboyant editor of *Vogue.* Sagaponack was still a rural hamlet at the time, the Hamptons not having been discovered. We would sit on the patio, look out over the potato fields and fantasize about peeling the potatoes, distilling them and starting a bootleg vodka business.

I discovered deep friendships within the commune. The tension between Carl and me had not made it easy for friends. He'd been defensive in particular around my writer friends. But now I made a lot more friends. Friends are an extremely important part of my life, stemming probably from my miserable adolescence in Peoria when I had so few and from all the years of my marriage when I spent most of my time with Carl. So the commune was a deeply satisfying way for me to begin my new life.

The next year we rented Sheldrake Cove, a big lovely old house on Georgica Pond in Wainscott. Barney Rosset, the editor of Dial Press, gave me a kayak and we'd go out on the pond and commune with the swans. Shana Alexander, then an editor of *McCall's,* came to visit for a weekend with her Welsh lover. He was a big, bawdy, poetic man and read us a Yeats poem about swans while we were out on the water paddling among them. Swans are quite dangerous, of course, but we didn't know that then. We spent a lot of time watching them and the other people canoeing on the pond: "Look, a nuclear family!" the cry would go up when a Mommy/Daddy/and TwoKids canoe went by.

Other people joined the commune: Karl Fossum, a psychiatrist who was one of the leading figures in the abortion rights movement and now owns two abortion clinics, and his friend, Martina Leonard; Ashe Lang, an international lawyer, and his wife, Shirley Johnson Lang, who taught economics at Vassar; Martha Stuart, a wonderful woman and very much like the Martha Stewart of today, who had two great kids, Barclay and Sally, about Emily's age. Martha produced a talk show for Channel 13 in New York and was great at entertaining. She'd make centerpieces out of great big baskets of fruits and vegetables and give wonderful Thanksgiving dinners in her house on Bank Street. She was going around at the time with Dick Cornuelle, the executive director of the National Association of Manufacturers, which sounded a little conservative to us, but he was sort of a liberal conservative and would write interesting stuff about industry later on.

People came and went from the commune, like David Pearce, the eye doctor; Richard Laupot, who owned a lighting fixture factory in New Jersey; Harold Wit, an investment banker at Allen & Co. who became a great friend of our commune. Harold was interesting and odd, a rich banker who wrote poetry. He brought us Heidi Fiske, our lady of Wall Street, who made orderly charts of who owed what. That prompted huge fights about money. Someone would say, "Well, I was on a diet that week, so I shouldn't have to pay a full share for food," or, "I don't eat breakfast." It was a riot. We cooked communally on the weekends and Betty Rollin tried to organize the meals by assigning titles. She would be the Duchess of Dessert, somebody else would be the Countess of Casserole, someone else the Sultan of Table Setting or the Prince of Pots.

We drank a lot, which made some of the evenings pretty hazy. I remember the night Arthur and I worked out a brilliant law about the political process—something about the interrelationship between politicians and heat or politicians and light. Anyway, I wrote it all down so we wouldn't forget it and passed it across the table to Arthur, but our insights caught fire in the candle and the next morning we couldn't remember what we'd been so brilliant about. We had an uproarious time at those Saturday night dinners.

Several presidential candidates came to visit us at Sheldrake Cove in 1971, Fred Harris, senator from Iowa, Gene McCarthy. Some candidates were beginning to realize that the women's vote could be important. I remember telling our landlady that the slip-cover was torn on the couch in the living room and it really had to be replaced because we were expecting visits from two presidential candidates. She came into the living room which was kind of a mess and said, "What this place really needs is a good *wife!*" We didn't get a new slipcover, but she started clipping hedges like mad. Every time I looked around, there she was clipping and clipping. I suppose she wanted to see the candidates.

The last house we rented was in East Hampton on Drew Lane and belonged to the John Drew theatrical family. It was in the middle of real wealth, very near the ocean, with a private path leading to the beach. I wasn't completely comfortable among the multimillionaires in East Hampton. And it wasn't surprising, I guess, that the neighbors on Drew Lane rather raised their eyebrows at our little commune. I guess we were a little avant-garde for the neighborhood, but as one of the kids said: "Who's ever heard of a commune with three Mercedes in the driveway?" Still, we decided we needed a counselor for community relations and we turned to a gay friend of ours, Tommy Baer, who lived at the foot of Drew Lane in the carriage house that now belongs to Martha Stewart. Tommy advised us to have a block party.

One of the commune members, Allen Buchswald, bought up all the duck liver in the surrounding towns to make pâté for the party. Niels Diffrient, another member, and a great designer, bought a huge American flag from a gas station and hung it from the house. Our ingratiate-ourselves-with-the-neighbors party was all set to begin when it started to rain. We had to move the party inside and in the resulting crush, the floors of the house got so impregnated with duck pâté that we had to have them redone. The neighbors had a very good time, however, and we never felt shunned again.

The commune broke up in 1973 after our second year on Drew Lane. It probably would have survived longer if we hadn't had to keep moving from house to house and signing new leases, but, if I remember correctly, nobody seemed too eager to renew a lease with us. Perhaps it was because we were getting so much publicity. The women's movement was exploding in the wake of the 1970 march and there were a lot of interviews with me in those houses and articles being written.

There were changes within the commune as well. As couples broke up or remarried, the members started going off and buying their own houses. But the commune—I'm too snobbish to call it a group rental—served us well in those years of non-marriage and divorce. We were each other's family when we needed companionship and fun. And we forged strong bonds that remain to this day. Emily and Sally are still close friends, and when Betty Rollin calls me, she identifies herself as "Other Betty," the way little Matthew Herzog differentiated between the two "Bettys" so many years ago.

It was at our first commune house that I realized that the initial phase of the women's movement was over. The next thrust had to go beyond marches and consciousness-raising to organizing political power. If we didn't, I was afraid that the movement would peter out and turn against itself. In fact, I could see it beginning to happen.

Though I was no longer president of NOW, in my mind, NOW was going in the wrong direction. It was being taken over by the more radical elements who were preaching "out of the mainstream into the revolution," just as the mores of America were swinging in the opposite direction. This was no longer the hippie sixties. It was the beginning of the conformist seventies. I wanted to continue in the mainstream. The rhetoric of revolution didn't have much meaning in America of that era.

In NOW's original statement I had written a call for "action, not just talk, to break through the barriers that keep women from participating in the *mainstream* of American society." That's the way great numbers of women had come into it. The radical fringe and its revolutionary agenda did not speak for the mainstream women who were changing on their own terms. Women were no longer an inert mass, but America was not moving toward revolution. It was time for something new.

I knew from the huge audiences at my lectures that there was an identification with the movement that went beyond the confines of NOW and was larger than all the feminist organizations put together. I knew from the politicking I was doing on the side at the conventions and from the summer visits of the presidential candidates that there was a growing interest in women's issues and women's votes. And I knew that it was women who had sent Bella and others to Congress in 1970. Bella had called me and asked me to help mobilize women for her campaign and I had. Bella was notoriously hot-tempered, probably worse than me, and some women had warned me off: "Oh Betty, Bella's so mean," or "she's so bad-tempered," or "she hasn't got a very good disposition," and I had said, "You don't have to cuddle her, you don't have to hug or embrace her, but she's a fighter and she'll fight for women and we should use our power to elect her. It doesn't matter if you think she's hot-tempered and bitchy, since I am notoriously hot-tempered and bitchy. I don't think it's a requirement to be sweet to be an effective leader or activist." So I had rounded up women to help elect Bella.

But one election, two elections, were the tip of the iceberg. I could see that a vital area, where women had a potential for power but were not exercising it, was in electoral politics. It was clear from the exit polls I had gotten hold of after the '68 election that what we now call a "gender gap" was beginning. Yet the Women's Division of the Democratic Party was still running auctions, looking up zip codes and addressing envelopes. Even the progressive arm of the Democratic Party in New York—the New Democratic Coalition—was mired in chauvinism. Sarah Kovner and I had to take over the stage at a pre-presidential election year convention to point out that not one of the major speakers was a woman. So I convened the original meeting of what would become the National Women's Political Caucus (NWPC).

My vision for the NWPC was to bring together Republican women, Democratic women, old and young women, those not aligned with either party, to speak for themselves, finally, in the halls of government. The goal of the caucus would be to elect women to national office and to organize grassroots chapters to elect women to state and local office. It was time for women to "make policy, not coffee," soon to be our slogan.

Such a concept—women hadn't organized politically since the suffragette movement—would attract a broader segment of the population, I felt sure, than NOW or the other "women's lib" groups. There were a lot of women who came to my lectures who did not consider themselves feminists, who were turned off by gender politics. A political voice that advanced the issues of equal opportunity and equal pay and child care would appeal to them, I was sure, and it would not attract the female chauvinists and the political extremists who wanted nothing to do with mainstream politics.

I was, in fact, beside myself at the damage being done to the women's movement by extremists and the "radical chic." Sexual politics was once again overshadowing the mainstream issues of abortion and child care in the winter of 1970 and fomenting an image of the women's movement as just a bunch of lesbians. The furor centered on a *Time* magazine cover story on NOW member Kate Millett, which discredited her as a spokesperson for the movement because she had admitted to being bisexual. Personally, I didn't care if she was bisexual. That was her business. But I hated the tactics of the radical lesbians who had forced Kate publicly to state she was bisexual during a meeting at Columbia University. I didn't think Kate—or anybody—should have been forced to come out of the closet like that and again I suspected *agents provocateurs*. Kate, in fact, later had a nervous breakdown.

The furor about Kate coincided with a backlash to the legal gains we had made on abortion rights and child care in New York State. The legislature was trying to undo both by cutting the funds for child care and codifying restrictions into the new abortion law. I called for a protest march to give Governor Rockefeller the courage to veto the legislation. The August 26 march had been so successful just four months before that I resurrected the Women's Strike Coalition to organize this march. To my surprise, the action turned out to be as much about lesbianism as it was abortion rights and child care.

It was snowing, of course, the day of the action, and as we were marching from Governor Rockefeller's office to Gracie Mansion, the official residence of the mayor of New York, someone tried to get me to wear a lavender armband. I refused. "I called this march," I told whoever it was, "and I called it for child care and abortion rights. I'm not going to mislead the people who came out in this miserable weather to march for those issues and I'm not pushing lesbianism. If you want to do that, go right ahead, but not me." When we arrived at Gracie Mansion where we were going to speak from some makeshift platform, I saw that the other speakers—among them Gloria, Kate and Flo Kennedy, a radical feminist—were all wearing lavender armbands and that someone was distributing them to people in the crowd. I was furious during the speeches—I didn't mention anything other than the threat to abortion and child care—and even more furious afterwards when I had a drink with the president of NY NOW, Ivy Bottini, Kate and Gloria.

The Women's Strike Coalition was planning to hold a press conference, they told me, and declare we were *all* lesbians, in solidarity with Kate and other bisexuals and lesbians, struggling for liberation in a sexist society. I was vehemently opposed and told them so. I was certainly in solidarity with Kate and with the other friends of mine in the movement who happened to be lesbians. And I was and am against repression of any kind. But I didn't think it was a good strategic tactic in any way. To say, "We are all lesbians," was total bullshit, and I wasn't going to do it.

I had written *The Feminine Mystique* and helped start the women's movement, after all, on the basis that a woman should not be defined in terms of her sexual relation to a man, but as a person participating in this society in her own right. Well, I wasn't going to suddenly say women should be defined in terms of their sexual relations to other women! I didn't think then and still don't that the women's movement for equality was synonymous with lesbianism. I'm more relaxed about the whole issue now than I was then, but I knew, and I was right, that sexual politics was not the way to go for the movement. Sexual politics was bad business.

I didn't agree with *Ms.*, the "feminist" magazine Gloria created in 1971. The early issues were filled with all these anti-male dictums: women weren't supposed to shave their armpits or their legs, they weren't supposed to wear makeup, they weren't supposed to do anything that would make them attractive to men. It was so annoying to me that Gloria would preach this kind of doctrine in *Ms.*, and at the same time be dating some very glamorous men and having her hair streaked at Kenneth, a very fancy New York salon. I occasionally had my hair done at Kenneth and saw her there, under the dryer, holding *Vogue* up in front of her face so no one would recognize her. But then, I was never into radical chic.

Gloria and the others went ahead and had their we-are-all-lesbians press conference anyway. I was not there. In fact, I felt so deceived that they had planned the lavender armband caper at the pro-choice march behind my back and used me as a front for their agenda that I pulled out of the Women's Strike Coalition. I was so angry I even threatened to sue if my name was ever used again in conjunction with their activities. To some, of course, that merely confirmed that I was homophobic. But that was not true then, nor is it now.

The National Women's Political Caucus would be in keeping with the mainstream and I got an overwhelming enthusiastic response when I started contacting a broad range of politically active women: Midge Miller in Wisconsin; Martha McKay in North Carolina; Michigan's Elly Peterson, the former vice chair of the Republican Party; Fannie Lou Hamer, whom I would campaign for in Mississippi in her congressional race; Congresswoman Shirley Chisholm; Priscilla Buckley, the politically conservative editor of the *National Review* whom I had known at Smith and shared a house with in New York. They, and many other women I spoke to who had never shown much interest before in women's rights, were ready to start a political caucus of and for women.

Ironically, the only woman who resisted me was Bella Abzug, the congresswoman from New York I had worked to elect. "This is my turf," she screamed at me over the phone. She was even more furious when she heard about the other women I had already asked to be convenors of the National Women's Political Caucus. Bella evidently felt I should have come to her first, but she was a freshman in Congress and so out of protocol I had gone to more senior members like Martha Griffiths, who was leading the fight for women on Capitol Hill. In the end I got Bella and I got Shirley and I got Gloria.

Two thousand women, fewer than half of them NOW members, came to the organizing conference of the NWPC at the Statler Hilton in Washington in July 1971. We wanted to get the

ERA, national child care and abortion rights into both party plat-
forms, and we wanted to get women elected to office on national,
state and local slates. Research was coming out about this time
from the Eagleton Institute at Rutgers University that the addition of as many as two women to a state legislature would begin
to change the agenda, not just in terms of women's rights but in
terms of more priority for legislation affecting life—child care,
health care, senior citizens, even the environment. Life issues
would have much more priority on every level the minute you
had a few women.

I had already helped launch the first women's political caucus at the grassroots level by the time of the conference, and it
was a great success. The prevailing wisdom at the time was that
there were no "qualified" women to run or do much more politically than empty the ashtrays in the men's smoke-filled rooms.
But that was certainly not what I found at a meeting I was invited
to in the suburban Long Island town of Hempstead. A housewife
and a few of her neighbors, who were thought, of course, to have
no political skills, had contacted virtually every women's group
in a five-town area, from the women's auxiliary of the Veterans of
Foreign Wars to church and synagogue groups, the PTA, the
League of Women Voters, the AAUW, even students at local colleges. Their response to forming a women's caucus and wielding
real political power had been so enthusiastic that the meeting had
to be limited to two women from every organization. Within
three months, they got the first woman nominated for the 1971
elections by the Democratic Party, they were looking for candidates for judges, convention delegates, and so on, and beginning
a voter registration drive aimed at women and eighteen-year-
olds, who had recently won the right to vote.

With grassroots models like this one, I was convinced we
were well on our way to a larger, broader political force than the
constituency of the Old or New Left, one that spoke to the real
concerns of most contemporary Americans. But there were already trouble signs within the caucus leadership.

Gloria and Bella brought New York radicals like Brenda
Feigan Fastau, a young lawyer, and Flo Kennedy, the flamboyant
black lawyer who wore cowboy boots and tons of silver and
turquoise jewelry, to the organizing conference in Washington.

They were very East Coast and hardly mainstream. I objected to them, just as Gloria and Bella objected to Liz Carpenter, Lady Bird Johnson's former press secretary from Texas, whom Shana Alexander had brought in. Liz, who would devote years of her life to getting the Equal Rights Amendment ratified, was denounced for having been part of the Johnson administration and therefore associated with the Vietnam War.

I went out to help organize different chapters of the NWPC after the organizing meeting. I went to Arizona, combining lectures with organizing a chapter in Phoenix. I went on barnstorming trips to Iowa and Columbus, Ohio, and to Oregon, Missouri and Mississippi. At that point you always had to worry that there might be some major attempt at disruption on the abortion issue, people screaming "murderer" at you and waving around pictures of fetuses. But I always came back reinvigorated by the passion that was driving women to raise their political voices in the American mainstream.

The ideological differences among the NWPC leadership were growing. One of the four founding members, Shirley Chisholm, announced her intention to run for the Democratic nomination for the presidency of the United States in 1972, the first black woman to seek the nomination of a major political party. NOW endorsed Shirley's candidacy, as did I by running as a convention delegate for Shirley in the Democratic primary in New York. I had no idea at the time that I would have to mount my own little campaign. I had to raise something like $8,000 to run as a delegate, a daunting exercise which would keep me out of politics. I can't stand raising money for anything, much less myself.

Shirley expected the NWPC to endorse her candidacy, just as we who ran as her delegates all over the country expected help from the caucus. But there would be none. The decision was taken at a meeting I must have missed to write off Shirley's race as unwinnable and to concentrate instead on two other surefire primary races: Sissy Farenthold, who was running for governor in Texas, and Bella, who had lost her congressional seat when her district was redrawn and had chosen to challenge a Democratic incumbent.

I was outraged at the uses of the caucus for selected purposes. The decision about whom to support for what office should have been taken at the local levels. Empowering *all* women to find their own political voices was the point and the strength of the caucus. My outrage was shared by many others in the national caucus who'd received the call telling them to go to Texas to help Sissy and New York to help Bella. William Fitzryan, the Democratic congressman Bella was challenging, had a long and excellent voting record on peace and women's rights and there was no reason to turn him out of office. There were charges of "female chauvinism" from the liberal male journalists who had supported Bella and the women's movement in the past and "coldbloodedness" from almost everyone because the congressman had recently undergone surgery for throat cancer.

Many of us in New York wanted the NWPC to endorse Liz Holtzman, a quiet young lawyer from Brooklyn who was challenging a political Goliath and arch enemy of the Equal Rights Amendment, Emanuel Celler, for Congress. But the NWPC staff and Bella's cohorts said Liz had no chance of winning. With that dictum, it struck me, and others too, that we had merely traded in male political bosses for female political bosses.

And they would all prove to be wrong. Sissy lost in Texas, Bella lost in New York, and Liz won. Liz would go on to be a respected voice in Congress during the Watergate hearings on the impeachment of Richard Nixon. Bella would go to Congress too, but only because she was appointed to fill Fitzryan's seat when he died in office. Shirley Chisholm wouldn't go anywhere. When the NWPC refused to endorse her candidacy, she simply resigned.

The final rift between Gloria, Bella and me came after the 1972 presidential conventions, which were bitter enough in themselves. The National Women's Political Caucus was holding its first convention in Houston and one of the first orders of business was to elect officers. There is no question in my mind that if I'd run to be the head of the NWPC, I would have been elected. But for some reason, I didn't want to. I think I was right, in the end, not to get hopelessly entrapped in the organizational structures, and I had a very good candidate for the top spot—Martha McKay of North Carolina.

I didn't want the NWPC to be a radical chic, New York thing, and Martha believed, as I did, in the principle of a broad, independent, political mobilization of women. We didn't use the term "politically correct" then, but neither she nor I was interested in a party-line narrow radical feminism. Coming from the Midwest, I had a sense of how to speak to all women, not just a little radical chic group. I had lived my adult life in New York, but there was strength, I guess, in coming from Peoria, Ill. I knew when I was speaking to and for women—lots of women, not just the New York types who sometimes got carried away by narrow definitions. And that was what the battle was really about.

Martha did not win the top spot. The female party bosses had their way again and we ended up with Sissy Farenthold from Texas who was okay. But when other officers were elected from Texas, I worried that the entire leadership would be in one state and not representative of the country. I also worried that the officers might be too easily controlled by the NWPC political machine. So I decided to run as an independent for the national steering committee to keep my eye on things.

There was no way I wasn't going to get elected. I'd started the damn caucus, after all, and traveled all over the country getting it off the ground. I had massive support at the time. There had been loud cheers when my name was put in nomination and I'd buried the ax with Bella by seconding her nomination to the steering committee. So it was clear that I was going to get elected. I stayed to vote but I had to leave before the vote was counted to get back to New York.

No sooner had I gotten home than I started getting phone calls from some of my friends at the convention in Houston. "You shouldn't have left, Betty," they told me. "You were way ahead and now, somehow, you're not elected." Well, it was clear that some monkey business had gone on. I evidently had the most votes by far after the first count, but then there was some confusion, someone took the ballot boxes away, someone went to Sissy and asked for a recount—and half my votes disappeared. According to *The New York Times* the next morning, I had been elected. But according to Sissy, who called me and apologized for the "mistake," I hadn't.

I was really mad, so mad I hired a Washington lawyer, Sally Katzen, to look into it for me. Sally, who is now head of the Office of Management and Budget in Washington, found irregularities and improprieties in the tallying of the vote and at the next meeting of the national board, she recommended holding new elections. But the board refused.

We could have made a lot of trouble at that point. Sally and other members of her highly respected firm, Wilmer, Cutler & Pickering, were prepared to take the case to court if I wanted to. But I was prevailed upon by Gloria, Bella and Olga Madar from the UAW at the board meeting not to go public with the lawsuit and I chose to drop it. I didn't drop it because they told me to keep my mouth shut—which they did—but because it would have been so damaging to everybody.

In retrospect, I think Gloria and Bella wanted me just to disappear, though I've never really understood why. Perhaps it was because I had an idea of a broad mainstream and I organized the caucus to be both Republican and Democrat, and Bella and Gloria were more radical. I also think they wanted to run it and they didn't want me to run it. I don't think there were any great noble reasons. They were always trying to maneuver me out, which forced me, in turn, to try and fight back.

People liked to ascribe the rift between Gloria and me to jealousy on my part of Gloria's looks, charging that I resented her because she was prettier. It indeed had been a bane in my existence that I wasn't pretty, though in my old age now, I'm not as bad-looking as I thought I was in my young age. But I always saw Gloria's looks as an asset to the movement. She contributed a positive image of beauty and glamour which was invaluable in refuting the movement's negative image of man-haters and lesbians.

But it was really maddening to be forced out of the caucus I'd started. I was just never good enough at that infighting and maneuvering. My strengths lay in inspiring and leading the masses and fighting the external enemies. But I was easily outfoxed within the movement and I wasn't so good at fighting for power. And it just wasn't worth it.

I wouldn't let myself get completely maneuvered out, however. The press still assumed at the national board meeting that I had been elected to the steering committee, so when a photographer arrived to take a picture of the new leadership, I just went up and got in the picture. I wasn't going to let them force me out just like that.

On the other hand, I had a dream. In the dream, I had a new house and I was putting everybody in their right bedrooms, but I didn't have a room for my little boy and my little girl. I had to find rooms for them. I found two sweet little rooms in the attic where I was going to put them, but when I went up the attic stairs, I was blocked by a big bureau sitting in the middle of the stairs. So I pushed the bureau over and shoved it down the stairs so I could go on up and put my little boy and my little girl into their rooms.

I take dreams very seriously. They are letters to yourself when your subconscious perceives something that needs attention. The little boy and the little girl in my Jungian dream represented my creative aggressive side and my creative feminine side and were telling me that I couldn't get bogged down in all this bureaucracy, that it was in the way of my creativity. I see that clearly now, though I don't know how clearly I saw it then. But in retrospect I think it was probably good that I didn't spend my life continually fighting to control organizations.

The pattern was always the same. I would start one organization; it would be taken over. I'd start another organization; it would be taken over. It's amazing, really, how many organizations I started in the first five years of the movement that are still going strong—NOW, NARAL, the NWPC—and they'd all be taken over. And I'd get forced out. I either didn't know how to fight that or wasn't able to.

But it didn't matter much whether I had a title in these organizations. What would frustrate the hell out of my enemies was that they could screw around and outmaneuver me and keep me from being elected president of this or president of that, but it wouldn't stop me because people wanted to hear what I had to say. I was asked to lecture, the media reported what I had to say, and I had plenty of places to say it. Plus I wrote. So I sort of figured out that my contribution was going to be offering some vision.

Whatever the differences within the leadership, the organizations I helped to found were having a profound impact on the structure of American society. It was no longer business as usual. The mobilization of so many women at the march in 1970, and the politicizing of so many women over the next two years by the NWPC was translating into the action I had called for in NOW's Statement of Purpose. Because of our pressure for political reform, women made up 40 percent of the delegates to the 1972 National Democratic Convention in Miami, triple the number from 1968. Women made up 30 percent of the delegates to the Republican Convention that same year, almost double the number in 1968.

The power of the women's vote was being felt all over the country. The 1972 fall elections sent five more women to Congress—Marjorie Holt, Yvonne Braithwaite Burke, Barbara Jordan, Pat Schroeder and of course Liz Holtzman. And in the heat of the women's movement and the political momentum we all had contributed to, the Senate passed the ERA in 1972 by a resounding vote of 84 to 8.

It was all going very, very fast and very well. By the end of the year, the Equal Rights Amendment had been ratified by twenty-two states. Eight more states would follow in 1973, bringing the total to thirty. But I continued to be shaken by the "dirty tricks" of my sister leaders in the women's movement. From 1973 to 1976, I would stay away from any confrontation or even contact with Gloria Steinem or Bella Abzug.

I removed myself completely from the organizational turf battles. I bowed out of politics and gave up any thought of running for the Senate, which several people had approached me about. What I had to give, I decided, was mainly as a thinker, which may sound presumptuous, but I felt a certain responsibility for the women's movement. And I knew that I could continue to advance women's rights by teaching, lecturing and writing.

ELEVEN

Travels with Emily and the Women's Movement

The first years after my divorce were hardest on Jonathan, who was finishing high school and still living at home. Danny was at Princeton, Emily was barely a teenager, and I think in retrospect that I leaned on Jonathan too much. In spite of it all, he was doing brilliantly at Dalton. He was head of the student government, he played Puck in *A Midsummer Night's Dream,* he was on the baseball team. He was just your model everything to everyone.

Jonathan wanted to go to Harvard. He applied to Stanford and a couple of other colleges, but Harvard was his first choice. Nobody ever thought he would have any problem getting into a top college. He was a terrific leader, he had a strong academic record—he was your absolutely golden young man. But just before the time came to apply to college, Jonathan began to tangle with Dalton's headmaster, Donald Barr.

The drug culture of the sixties was spilling over into the seventies and the kids at Dalton began experimenting with drugs. Barr took a very hard line against even first-time offenders while Jonathan, as head of the student government, tried to get more humane treatment for the kids rather than just expulsion. He tangled with Barr on that. And he tangled with Barr over the Vietnam War, which was in full swing at the time. Nixon had recently expanded the war by sending U.S. troops into Cambodia and

Jonathan organized a protest among the students and teachers. They set up tables all over Manhattan and they collected about twenty thousand signatures protesting the invasion.

I was very proud of Jonathan for showing such leadership and moral courage. I supported his activism on behalf of the other students at Dalton and against U.S. involvement in the horrors going on in Southeast Asia, just as other parents at Dalton were supporting their kids. I actively encouraged him. When I was in Paris during the student uprisings in '68, I brought home all these wonderful, radical posters from the barricades for him.

Jonathan did not get into Harvard. He didn't get into Stanford, his second choice, or any of the other colleges he applied to. He was devastated. And, it turned out, it was all because of Barr. A friend of mine was on the board of overseers at Harvard and he thought it so strange that Jonathan didn't get in that he took me to some reception or other at the Harvard Club in New York where the director of admissions was speaking. During the question period, my friend introduced the hypothetical case of a boy who had a brilliant record and was also very activist. Would that activism eliminate him for consideration by Harvard? The Harvard dean said, "Well, I think we would think twice."

It was horrifying to me that Jonathan or any young person should be questioned by Harvard or any college for having the courage to express their moral and political beliefs, but the academic world was very uptight at the time. A student protest against the invasion of Cambodia at Kent State University in 1970 had left five students dead and ten wounded when the National Guard opened fire on them. Closer to home, students had taken over Columbia University and occupied the president's office. But it turned out that there was more to my friend's hypothesis.

"Is this a boy whose mother is famous?" the dean of admissions asked my friend after the reception. Some time later, he looked into Jonathan's record and found a letter from Dalton's headmaster implying all sorts of untrue things about Jonathan and referring to me disapprovingly as his rabble-rousing mother or something like that. But whatever it was he said, it was not a letter that Jonathan's own record would have warranted.

One of the trustees at Dalton became aware of this outrage at the very last minute, and somehow got Jonathan an offer from

Columbia which he accepted. But it really was a terrible experience for Jonathan. It was awful for me as well, visiting the sins of the mother on her son. The fact that all this took place at the time of the divorce just compounded it.

Jonathan went off to Columbia just as Danny was entering his last year at Princeton. Danny had gotten into Princeton at the age of fifteen, which I and a lot of other people thought was much too young. I had wanted him to take a year off and go to Europe or take a postgraduate year at a prep school. I'd felt the same way when Danny's school wanted to skip him not one grade but two. I didn't want him to get isolated by his brilliance, to be the only boy whose voice hadn't changed the way I'd been isolated among the girls who all had breasts when I was still in Mary Janes. Not good. But Danny insisted on going to college. He was a mathematical genius and had won a big scholarship, and at that point he was going to be a mathematician or a physicist. But he went through an interregnum at Princeton where he turned his back on mathematics and decided he was going to be a writer. He switched his major from physics to English, and, in fact, wrote a novel which nobody has ever seen.

Danny dropped out of Princeton for a year, which sent me into a panic (this was before it became so common for kids to drop in and out of college). I told him: "If you're going to leave college, you have to support yourself. There's no money around. You either go to school or you go to work." I thought that would do it, but within about two days he got a job. I don't know whether he went to friends of mine, but he got a job in the CBS newsroom. He went back to Princeton the next year, but somehow he managed to persuade them to let him live in New York and he and his girlfriend got some sort of loft. I don't know how he managed to do that as an undergraduate, but he did.

Danny ended up graduating with high honors in English, but math was in his genes and he got back to it. He worked with Thomas Kuhn for a while on the philosophy of science, introducing me to the concept of the paradigm shift, and then he went to get his Ph.D. in physics at Berkeley.

Just as Danny was entering graduate school at Berkeley, Jonathan, who had finished his sophomore year, dropped out of Columbia. He decided he was going to be a salmon fisherman, and he moved to Lummi Island, one of the San Juan Islands off the coast of Washington. Emily looked at a map and pointed out quite unkindly that it was the farthest away he could get from home in the continental United States.

I was very supportive of Jonathan's move and took Western lectures to get out to see him. I remember going out fishing with him on his boat in the middle of the night and telling him how proud I was of his self-sufficiency. "That's great you're earning enough money to have your own fishing boat," I told him, which kind of deflated him, I guess. He was living in a small cabin without running water or electricity and I guess he didn't really want me to support this nomadic, rebellious move.

Jonathan used the income he made in the summer fishing to go to Israel. He was getting very spiritual, first with the Indians in the Northwest, then deciding to channel his spirituality into his own religion. There was quite a famous guru/rabbi, Zalman Schechter, with whom Jonathan took some workshop out west and who became his mentor. I had a very close rapport with Jonathan and I remember having a dream while he was on Lummi Island and in the dream, Jonathan was crying. I got so upset that I called to see if somehow I could talk to him, but, of course, he was out in his cabin. "How is he?" I asked the woman who answered the phone. "I've had this disturbing dream. Is he all right?" "He's been very depressed lately," she told me.

It turned out that the rainy weather in the state of Washington was probably the cause of his depression. I had experienced that same rainy weather firsthand. When I first went to Seattle to lecture, I had been so impressed by the beauty of Washington and the sort of frontier feeling of it that I called up Carl and said, "You've got to come out. We've got to move here." But then it began to rain and rain and rain. I certainly get depressed by the weather and I guess Jonathan did too. And I sensed it all the way across the country. I just knew it.

After four or five years as a salmon fisherman, Jonathan came back to New York. Danny had been working on him to make the move, as had his grandfather, who went to see him on Lummi Island and suggested subtly that he would have to have some profession besides fishing if he migrated to Israel as he was then planning to do. His grandfather's visit and Danny's persuasion finally moved Jonathan to go back to college. Jonathan returned to Columbia and graduated with a degree in engineering.

Emily and I were more roommates really than mother and daughter after Jonathan went off to college. I tried to take Emily with me on lectures, arranging longer trips to coincide with her vacations because I didn't want to leave her at home alone for any period of time. We had a housekeeper but I just didn't want to leave her. One of our first trips together was to Brazil in 1971 for the publication there of *The Feminine Mystique*.

Brazil was just emerging from fascism and the regime was quite repressive during that period. But the Brazilian publisher putting out *The Feminine Mystique* could get away with publishing a left-wing book on women, even arranging big publicity for it, because no one took women seriously. It would be the same in Spain where I was invited to lecture at the end of the Franco days and in Iran during the time of the Shah. If I'd lectured on labor economics or human rights it would have been dangerous, but because no one took women seriously, you could have a big public meeting on women's issues and nobody in power would notice.

I was severely criticized by people in the women's movement for going to those countries. And it is true, of course, that I could have said, "I refuse to go and lecture in this repressive regime." But I was always invited, and used, perhaps, by the progressive forces who were trying to open up their societies democratically. I thought that was important, so I always accepted such invitations.

I've always found it interesting that whenever a Fascist or authoritarian regime takes over a country, one of the first things they do is take away the rights of women and persecute Jews. At about the same time the Nazi Germans started persecuting the Jews, they abolished all the feminist-type organizations. Women were supposed to confine themselves to "Children, Kitchen and Church." But I have found that women can be a good subversive influence. Before feminism swept the world, women were considered to be a conservative political force who, from timidness and fear, would buy a conservative, even reactionary regime. But after women began fighting for their rights, standing up for themselves and finding their own political voice—enjoying autonomy—they were no longer the conservative political force they had been presumed to be. They became if anything a progressive political force. I wonder if any larger historians, not just feminists, know that or have documented it. But it's true. And it was beginning to happen in Brazil.

Our trip did not get off to a good start. Emily and I were going to meet in Mexico, where I was attending an international conference of psychiatrists and psychologists on *Isla Mujeres*, the "Island of Women," before going on together to Brazil. Well, dammit, if I didn't leave my record of vaccinations behind in New York. I made frantic last-minute phone calls to Emily to find the shot record and bring it with her. I thought everything was all set, only to get a desperate call from Emily. She was stranded in Miami because Mexico wouldn't let in any kid without a "tourist card" signed by both parents because of all the kids who had run away to Mexico in the sixties. Luckily, we had relatives in Miami, and by the time I managed to get a call through to her there, my fifteen-year-old Emily had figured out that we could skip Mexico altogether and meet instead at the airport in Panama. The chaos was just beginning.

When my plane stopped in Panama, I dashed into the airport to find Emily, but of course I didn't have my health card. They stopped me at immigration and put me in quarantine where, over my protests, they were going to give me all the shots I'd just had in New York for yellow fever, typhoid, cholera and God knows what else. Suddenly I saw Emily through a glass door and rushed toward her, yelling, "Give me the card" as security guards chased me, blowing their whistles. It was a mad scene. Emily managed to hand over the shot card, but by then the Panamanian officials thought I was some sort of international criminal and hauled me off to an office where I was held for several hours. Again Emily came to the rescue, suddenly arriving in my detention room with a sympathetic, English-speaking Panamanian official. I was released and Emily and I proceeded to Brazil.

We stayed in Rio with Sari and Eric Seiff, a friend who was counsel to the Agency for International Development. There were quite a few teenagers around for Emily and she spent a lot of time with them on the beach while I met with a broad spectrum of women—from the homeless squatting in Rio's *favela* to Sari's more affluent neighbors.

One of Sari's friends, who along with so many other women in Brazil had dropped out of high school to marry and begin a large family, had gone back to high school. She was planning to go on to the Catholic University and become a psychologist. A group of impoverished women in the *favela* who were grandmothers in their early thirties said they wanted birth control and education to make their daughters' lives better. It was exactly those seeds of autonomy that repressive regimes needed to crush. Women are the key to the family, so if the women become a progressive force, it goes beyond the woman herself. It affects the whole family. Even the nun who took me around the *favela* was beginning to question why she did the work of a priest but couldn't celebrate mass. "I don't think that's fair," she told me.

Members of the Brazilian press started following me wherever I went. Their editors sent reporters out to ask Brazilian women if they wanted equality. But if they expected to find a docile community of women who had little aspiration beyond having their hair done and their fake eyelashes in place by 10:00 a.m., they didn't. The women—housewives, students, office workers—agreed with me. Evidently, it was all too much for this machismo society. One newspaper finally ran a front-page editorial which said in effect: "Yankee lady, go home! Stop stirring up our women."

I was very impressed with Emily on our trip to Brazil. We would never have gotten there, after all, if she hadn't been so determined to get me out of detention in Panama. But she was the youngest of the children and I still thought of her as my little girl.

I began to see her with new eyes the summer after we returned from Brazil and I went to visit her over Parents' Weekend at her Quaker camp in Vermont. The counselors kept saying: "Oh, you're Emily's mother. Your daughter is something." It turned out that Emily and a group of her friends had decided it was unnatural having all the boys' cabins on one side of the lake and all the girls' cabins on the other, so Emily had led an elaborate and successful movement to integrate the cabin areas.

I realized then that my Emily was becoming a leader. She had always seemed so different from me—sweet where I was sour, patient where I was impatient. She was such a lovely little girl and somehow I had never thought of her as having the strengths of leadership she was exhibiting at that camp. She was very much like me, whether she liked it or not. And whether I liked it or not, my little Emily was growing up.

My visit to Emily's camp produced another revelation. I had persuaded a friend to drive me to Vermont because I had given up driving when we moved to the city. His condition, which I eagerly agreed to, was that we stop en route for a Friday night concert at the music festival in Marlboro. I was looking forward to seeing my friend, the festival's coordinator, Sonya Kroyt, whose late husband, Boris, had founded the Budapest String Quartet. I was also looking forward to the intensity I feel when I listen to great music. But nothing prepared me for Pablo Casals.

Casals was going to be conducting a concert on Saturday night and we went to the rehearsal on Saturday morning. He was very old, around ninety-four, but he commanded such respect that when he entered the rehearsal hall, everyone in the orchestra and audience rose to their feet. I remember watching him conduct and having a sense of an incredible power coming from this frail, elderly man. He conducted with his whole body, his whole person. You knew, or at least I felt, that you were in the presence of ultimate human self-realization. It wasn't until the end of the rehearsal that I saw that my blouse was wet with tears. Later, when I asked them about it, the musicians confirmed that there was something Casals drew from them that they didn't know they had. There was something unknowable in the way this man was conducting that was as mysterious and as moving as anything on earth can be. And I'll never forget it.

After visiting Emily at camp, I returned to Marlboro where the women musicians wanted to talk to me. I hadn't planned that. I had wanted to spend the weekend just listening to beautiful music and seeing Emily. But I so admired the women's exceptional talent and shared their resentment of the discrimination they faced. The New York Philharmonic Orchestra had only recently allowed women to audition! Casals, too, had showed his bias during rehearsal when he instructed a female musician to stop playing the French horn "like a woman," whatever that meant. It would be years before musicians would be judged on their talent and not their gender. Nothing gives me greater pleasure now than counting the numbers of musicians wearing black skirts and dresses on a symphony stage. But in 1971, that was a long time coming.

Emily and I went to Italy together the next year, 1972, for what turned out to be a frenetic trip. I was the first woman to be asked to lecture by the Associazione Culturale Italiana, a lecture series sponsored by the Agnelli family to bring together Italy's "men of letters." True to form, the translator who accompanied us to my first lecture at the old Opera House in Turin assured me that no one in that city knew or cared about the women's movement. He was wrong. Several thousand women and some men came to hear me, and even greater numbers came to my lectures in Milan and Rome.

I had barely begun my remarks in Milan when the women in the audience complained that the male translator was not representing accurately what I was saying about women's need to demand political power. That was unsettling enough, but when he apparently refused to translate my comments about the Catholic hierarchy, birth control and abortion, they began to shout him down. It was too much for him I guess to translate my query as to why the church was making such a fuss over the fetus and women's eggs and no fuss about all the priests' sperm that didn't get translated into babies. His silence prompted angry women to move toward the stage to take over the translation. At least some semblance of order returned when one of the women turned out to be the calm and quiet translator of the Italian edition of my book, *La Mistica della Femminita*, and the lecture, now accurately translated, continued.

Milan was just a warm-up. We went through *three* translators in Rome, the audience there was so impassioned. I was used to hecklers but the heckling in Rome started before the translator, a woman this time, could even begin. There were competing hecklers—a furious man in the front waving his fist and shouting at me, a group of young women in leather jackets and jeans shouting "Down with men!", other protesters scattered noisily throughout the audience. They heckled one translator after another off the stage until a young blond American woman in a mini-skirt climbed up beside me and took over the translating. By extraordinary coincidence, the young woman, who was living in

Rome at the time, turned out to be the great-granddaughter of Lucretia Mott, one of the conveners of the first Women's Rights Convention in Seneca Falls in 1848.

The chaos was nothing compared to the abortion rally a group of Italian feminists asked me to speak at the next night in the Piazza Navona. Hundreds of women showed up despite the freezing rain, but so did a bunch of fascist thugs and police on motorcycles. By the time I got there, they had herded the women against a building wall and were surrounding them. I was furious, as was my friend Joan Cook, who was then living in Rome. She fended off some of the guys with her umbrella while I climbed up on a café table to speak. A hippie student took it upon himself to block the café manager who was pulling on my skirt to get me down and we held our little abortion rally in spite of them all. But all this violent opposition was a positive sign to me. Women were obviously emerging as enough of a political force to warrant such reactions.

Emily and I had calmer moments on that trip to Italy. We spent a wonderful Thanksgiving Day in Venice, walking over the bridges and along the canals, shopping, eating and floating around in gondolas. And in Turin we went to a dinner at Gianni Agnelli's *palazzo* which his wife, Marella Agnelli, gave for me. Needless to say, the home of Italy's richest industrialist—he owns Fiat—was quite a showcase, with its marbled floors, tapestried walls, butlers, footmen and women's faces straight out of *Vogue.* Emily was so fascinated by the *palazzo* that she kept leaving the dinner to go to the john so she could explore.

Emily was well on her way to becoming a lovely, warm young woman and I remember everyone was waiting for me to have a double standard about sex when it came to her. I had had to learn to come to terms with the mores of the young with Danny and Jonathan. When Danny first dropped out of Princeton and was living at home, he had a girlfriend and often he would not come home for the night. The next day I would say, "Couldn't you call me and let me know so I don't sit up worrying?" So he called a couple of times, but it seemed so constrained and awkward that I said, "Oh, forget it. The kid can take care of himself."

It was less jarring when I was invited to give a workshop at Tahoe and told I could bring my kids along to go skiing, and

Jonathan decided to bring his girlfriend, Judy. The kids skied while I did the workshop and I tried a little beginning skiing. I was doing okay until I had to use the ski lift. I got so terrified having to jump off that lift at just the right time with all that roaring machinery that after that, I went cross-country skiing.

For all my recent enlightenment, there were still moments. I kept stumbling over a suitcase in our apartment at "9W" when we got back from Tahoe. "Whose suitcase is this?" I asked Jonathan. "Judy's," he said. "Why is it here?" I asked. "She's living here," he informed me. "Does her mother know?" I asked. "Her parents are mad at her and they kicked us out," Jonathan said. I called up the mother to say that Judy was at our house.

So everyone was watching me about Emily. I had come to terms with the sexual behavior of my sons, but she, after all, was my little girl. Would that be a different story? I wasn't sure myself. One of the nice things about living in New York at the time was that kids didn't start dating early. They hung out in groups and gangs. It wasn't until after her junior year at Dalton that she began to go with one boy, though I was the last to know.

I found out when I ran into my friend Helen Kaplan at a party during the summer of '72 when I had my commune on Drew Lane. Helen was a psychiatrist and a famous sex therapist. I had interviewed her years before for the special issue I edited of the *Ladies' Home Journal.*

"Oh Betty, isn't it wonderful about Philip and Emily?" she said to me at that party. I was slightly taken aback. The last I knew, Emily had been seeing Philip Kaplan's best friend. I obviously hadn't caught up. "Just think of the children they would have with both of us as grandmothers," Helen said. "Helen, you can pay for the abortion," I said.

Sure enough, it turned out that Emily had, indeed, taken up with Philip. She was living at the commune that summer, recovering from mononucleosis, and I guess Philip was helping her feel better. Emily had planned to go hosteling in Europe that summer, but had had to cancel because of the mono. I hadn't known about Philip because I could only come out to the house on weekends. The other members of the commune who were there all week long with Emily and Philip couldn't wait to see my reaction. But I guess I disappointed them. I simply knocked on

Emily's door and said: "Emily, I know Philip is in there. Don't you think he should come out and say hello?"

I had thought, in fact, that sex might have come sooner for Emily. Carl had visited her the summer before at camp and informed me dourly that I had better "get her some pills." Well, I had no intention of doing that. She was only fifteen, and though I may have been naive, it seemed to me that too many mothers and fathers were force-feeding their children into a preoccupation with sex or into a kind of unreal sexual behavior like buying girls bras before they even had breasts or, in the extreme, exploiting them with suggestive costumes and makeup.

So, instead of sending birth control pills to Emily, I'd sent her a letter. "As you're probably discovering, sex is wonderfully exciting and mysterious and powerful. It should be treated with responsibility and respect and loving care. Not that you'll necessarily heed my advice, but advance on it slowly and *only in accord with your own real feelings.*" Emily told me later that she read the letter aloud to her cabin mates and they found it "hilarious," which meant either they thought me hopelessly old-fashioned— or I was ahead of their time. In any event, I did not impose a double standard on Emily but treated her relationship with Philip as natural and normal.

I would never deny the importance of sex in its mysterious reality. I wanted my daughter to have that part of her life freer of conflict, more integrated with her whole self than it was with me for too many years. I've never thought that human sex is morally wrong or, as some did then, that it was an enemy of women's liberation. To the contrary. I've always found sex liberating, an expression not only of intimacy, but confidence. I've always thought the most confident women enjoyed sex the most and made the best partners because they had the courage and self-esteem to embrace it.

There was all this talk at the time about sex and the liberated woman. The so-called sexual revolution was in full swing with the advent of the pill, but I always thought the sexual revolution had far greater implications than just sex. The availability of birth control allowed women not only to take control of their bodies but to define themselves by their contribution to society, not just in terms of their reproductive role. Isolating sex from the broader movement was a mistake. I remember being brought in to help write a speech for one of the Rockefellers, it was either Laurence or David, who was putting up the money for a program to control population growth in South America, and telling him, You can distribute all the IUDs you want, and you do need to do that, but you also have to make sure the women have equal opportunity in education and training and jobs so they can have some future and security in life beyond breeding sons.

The talk about sex in America seemed often frivolous, even ridiculous to me. I remember going to a conference on "The Female Orgasm," where most of the psychologists, psychiatrists and therapists in attendance were middle-aged men and the pressing issue was women's inability to have orgasms. Was the answer vibrators, or other sexual machines? I suggested that the answer lay less in machinery which further distanced women from their human condition and more in lifting the denigration many women felt in their day-to-day life. Those men looked at me as if I were crazy, the same way, probably, that I would look at Marabel Morgan, author of *The Total Woman*, who advised wives to keep their husbands from straying by welcoming them home in the evening wrapped in Saran Wrap and wearing nothing but black lace garter belts and ostrich feathers.

All the talk about bedroom politics seemed to me as diversionary to the real agenda of the women's movement as, often, it was absurd. At a women's conference in California, I listened in disbelief to a radical feminist debate about the superiority of the clitoral to the vaginal orgasm because it enabled women to do away with men altogether. The pseudo-radical instruction for the poor misguided women who still preferred sex with a male partner was to insist on being on top. The more usual, "missionary" position merely reinforced the woman as dominated and the man as dominator. As one who loves the missionary position herself and hardly feels "dominated," I didn't know whether to laugh or cry.

Emily applied to college that winter and mercifully did not run into Jonathan's problem. She got into Harvard as well as all her other top choices. A friend of mine at Harvard, Marty Peretz, knew about her admission ahead of time and called me with the news, but Emily was over at Philip's house. When I called her there, the housekeeper wouldn't let me speak to her. "They're asleep," she told me. "Well, knock on the door and wake her up," I told the housekeeper. "She just got into Harvard!"

Emily went off to Harvard in 1973 with Jonathan. Parents usually drive their kids to college and help settle them, but "I'm my own me" daughter was not about to be "Betty Friedan's daughter" at Harvard; she was going to be Emily Friedan in her own right. I was very sympathetic to that. I didn't want my mother anywhere *near* my college. That was going to be *my* territory.

Emily did invite me to come up for Parents' Weekend her freshman year, which caused me to immediately reshuffle my plans. This was the first time I'd been invited to get anywhere near the place and of course I was going to come, but I had a lecture commitment in California for the same weekend. I got Shana Alexander to give the lecture I was supposed to give, for four figures, and off I went to Cambridge. I toured the campus with Emily, looking at this and that, and she introduced me to some of her professors. But when it came to Saturday night, she casually told me she had a date that night, and good-bye. "You'll be fine in my room," she said. Fortunately I had friends in Cambridge, Mogie and Nancy Lazarus, so I went and had dinner with them.

I had been quite nervous when Emily was getting ready to leave home, but my terror of being alone turned out to be ill-founded. I had a lot of friends by then and I had moved into the same building as one of my oldest friends, Natalie Gittelson. Natalie was recently divorced and just as she had seen me through my divorce, I had seen her through hers.

Natalie had moved to 1 Lincoln Plaza, a triangular building right across from Lincoln Center, and she urged me to look at apartments there. 9W had been great and very convenient when Jonathan and Emily were still in high school because they could take the crosstown bus to Dalton. But I was subletting that apartment and that wasn't going to go on forever. So I looked at 1 Lincoln Plaza and found the only really suitable apartment was the one the building managers were using as a rental office. It had two big bedrooms, one on either side of the living room, so in effect Emily, who was then in her last year of high school, could have her own suite. They agreed to rent it to me.

I loved my new West Side neighborhood. The East Side is so waspy and antiseptic. I sometimes visited friends from college who had an apartment right off Madison Avenue in the 80's but, like so many East Side apartments, it was very dark. My apartment at 1 Lincoln Plaza was on the fortieth floor and filled with light, overlooking Lincoln Center on one side and Central Park on the other. The building also had a swimming pool on the roof and several levels of roof terraces, which was great for sunbathing. I started swimming religiously at one point, sixty laps every day, to stay in shape.

I cooked when I had someone to cook for. For lunch I kept some cottage cheese or sardines in the fridge, but if I didn't have a lunch date, I often didn't eat lunch at all because I was always trying to lose weight. I didn't cook dinner either. Except for an occasional scrambled egg, I would always meet someone and go out for dinner.

I was having a very satisfying affair at the time with David Manning White, a professor at Boston University. I'd met David, an expert on mass communications and the author of several books on popular culture, through my interest and training in Gestalt psychology. A friend of mine, Barry Oshri, was running sessions on the use of Gestalt in new group leadership training in 1970 for the National Training Laboratories and he'd invited me and David to be on the faculty. I'm not going to say sparks flew or the earth moved when we met, but there was immediate, mutual chemistry. David came to see me in New York shortly after the workshop ended. He spent the night in the guest room I'd made out of Danny's room at 9W, but the next morning, after Emily had gone off to school, he came into my bedroom. I held out my arms, he came into the bed, and thus began the wonderful, passionate relationship David and I would have for the next ten years.

David had great *joie de vivre* and was great in bed. I love sex, though I hardly know what it feels like anymore, and our affair satisfied enough my need for intimacy. I say "enough" because David was married and had been for twenty years or so to a very attractive biochemist named Catherine whom he had no intention of divorcing. She was quite wealthy and they had a lot of children, five sons, I think. He was devoted not only to the money and the children but to her, personally.

It was unfortunate that David was married, but I was over fifty then and virtually all the men I knew were married. That's just the way it is at a certain age. A shrink would say that I only went around with a married man because I didn't want to get married and there might be some truth to that. There's no doubt I was afraid of getting married because it had been so difficult for me to separate from Carl. But whatever the reason, I never had any wish, really, that David would leave his wife.

Our affair suited my life. I was all over the place lecturing, organizing, God knows what, and rarely home. David would come to New York when he could on weekends or college vacations and we would have wonderful sex, sometimes spending all day in bed. I remember once being in bed with him and Gloria calling me about something and David pawing me while I was trying to talk to her. He got a big kick out of that. His wife was very virtuous and I think that was one of the reasons he was crazy about me—I wasn't very virtuous, so he could be nice and dirty with me.

It was hardly a secret affair. I remember being invited to lecture in Vienna by the Austrian government and somehow finagling to bring him along. I took David with me on a lecture tour to Alaska and to Jimmy Carter's inauguration in Washington where we had great seats, thanks to Joan and Walter Mondale. Our affair was very intense wherever we got together, whether in New York or some area of the country where we both had lectures—we'd meet sometimes at the Hilton at O'Hare Airport in Chicago.

All my friends knew him, which presented a bit of a problem. I think he felt insecure with my friends, so he'd start namedropping and it would embarrass me. I don't think I was right to be embarrassed, but I won't deny that I was. More unsettling about our relationship was that David's wife came to know about it—and accept it—which I didn't like at all. She didn't seem to object at all that David was having this affair with me which, really, I thought was weird. In fact, I've always thought she would have loved a *ménage à trois*. She and David even wanted me to come stay at their house in Richmond, Virginia, where they'd moved after leaving Boston, but the whole thing made me very uneasy and I refused.

I had other male friends as well, like Richard Laupot, whom I had met at an art opening around the time I moved into 1 Lincoln

Plaza. He took me out to dinner and it turned out that, like me, he loved really wild travel, not resort travel but off-the-beaten track travel. So we went to Africa over the Christmas holidays in 1971. We found ourselves in Timbuktu on Christmas Eve and wouldn't you know there was no room at the inn, which, in this case, was a hostel, so they gave us mattresses and we slept on slabs in a cave. In one hotel we had to sleep on ironing boards. Mercifully, I had bought this wonderful outfit on sale, a jacket and pants in a sort of heavy non-wrinkly brown-and-white checked silk or rayon print which didn't show dirt. I wore that every day, everywhere, including a memorable New Year's Eve in Morocco. We were told we should go to a New Year's Eve celebration at the house of prostitution and it was an absolute hoot. The few women that were there were completely covered in their *chadors*, and at midnight, the men all embraced and kissed each other.

Emily had given a New Year's Eve party in the apartment while I was gone and to my horror, when I got back, my bust of Lincoln was gone. It turned out that some drunken boy had dropped it out of the fortieth-floor window. It's a good thing he didn't kill anybody, though it was only made out of plaster of Paris. But oh, I was so unhappy. I didn't mind them painting mustaches on things, but I had bought that bust of Lincoln at an auction years before and I loved it.

I was teaching through all of this, at the New School in New York, at the College of New Rochelle, at Northwestern University in Evanston, and at Temple University in Philadelphia. Temple had offered me the Dilworth chair in 1970, soon after I stepped down as president of NOW. It was named for Richardson Dilworth, a wonderful mayor of Philadelphia who was more of an intellectual Adlai Stevenson type than the usual cigar-smoking politician and was endowed to bring in a visiting professor to the social sciences who was actively practicing social sciences in the community. If I remember correctly, I was the first person invited to hold that chair. (I was also offered a similar kind of chair in the history department at Northwestern. That chair had just been installed to bring in someone who was actually making history, a live history maker. I think I was the first person in that program, too. It was a very good program and a lot of fun.)

I taught at Temple one day a week, and commuted at times by seaplane from the East River to downtown Philadelphia. I stayed at the hotel where legionnaire's disease first broke out and at one point I remember feeling very flu-like, so maybe I got this legionnaire's disease that was evidently transmitted by pigeons. I still had asthma and every once in a while I had to go to an emergency room, but it didn't stop me from doing anything.

As I began to lecture more and teach, I had to articulate more clearly what had been my seat-of-the-pants ideology for the women's movement. I remember holing up at the hotel in Philadelphia and formulating that the women's movement was only the first stage of a profound sexual revolution, not of women against men, but of women and men breaking out of obsolete unequal sex roles. The second stage would have to be a redefining of love, children, marriage, all the elements that used to define women inside the home, and the restructuring of institutions without. Changing the nature of both work and home would have to go further than the previous structures that were—and still are—based on the lives of the men of the past whose wives took care of the details of life; new, innovative institutions in society would have to take the place of the old extended family; the family and child rearing would have to be restructured to go beyond the completely mother-centered woman's role to a new partnership between men and women and the community. Otherwise, young women like my daughter who expected to have both career and family would end up feeling bitter and betrayed by the women's movement.

I never believed in feminism *or* the family or feminism *against* the family, though I could understand the disillusionment with family of earlier feminists. If your mother had eight children and died in childbirth, there could be a lot of negative stuff about being a mother. In researching prior feminist generations, I found, in fact, that there was a lot about mothers who had not had good lives which in turn caused their daughters to repudiate the role of women. The only image the daughters had of a free person was a man, so they wore pants to be like men.

The pendulum had swung in the opposite direction in reaction to that earlier kind of male-aping feminism during the fifties and into the early sixties, with the attempt once again to define women solely in the role of wife/mother/sex object. There was a dangerous dynamic there, I thought, as I mapped it out. If you continued that polarization of women either as pretend-men or women-solely-as-homemaker, you'd just keep going back and forth from one extreme to the other. You couldn't free women without somehow putting it all together.

Women had to move ahead in professions and careers and society and have their own voice politically *along* with the *choice* to marry and have children. The combination was critical. Historically and from my study of psychology, I knew that people drew from their own actions, their own achievements and accomplishments *as well as* their intimate relationships to define themselves as part of society. Everyone needs to love and be loved. Sitting in that hotel room in Philadelphia, I had to put the theory, the ideology, and the strategy of the second stage together. That was my main contribution, I suppose.

I taught The Second Stage first as a course at Temple and later published it as a book. I never wanted the course to be narrowed to women's studies. I was opposed to separatism and the focus on women alone. The revolution was larger than that. Later I would use the words "paradigm shift" to define the necessary restructuring of the workplace, family and gender roles and would try to push the women's movement in that direction for the rest of the century. I worked it out in the course I taught at Temple.

There was tremendous interest abroad about the women's movement in America. Women from many other countries had been coming to see me, even from Russia, wanting advice and help to organize their own movements. I was also getting invitations from foreign organizations.

With Emily at college, I was freer to accept foreign lecture tours and writing assignments. On more than one occasion, however, I often didn't find what I expected. I went to Israel in 1973, where I expected Prime Minister Golda Meir to support the women's movement—she didn't; I went to Rome where I hadn't expected the Pope to receive me—he did; and I went to Paris to interview Simone de Beauvoir who I thought would be a soulmate; she wasn't.

I had been looking forward to my trip to Israel, my first,

where I was to speak at an international conference of women journalists. In my mind, Israel symbolized many of the ideals I was working toward in America: men and women sharing equally in the responsibilities and details of daily life in the *kibbutz*, in religion, in the compulsory military service for both genders, in political leadership. But I was disillusioned.

At the Wailing Wall, holy symbol of the survival of my people down through the centuries, I was angered by the wooden barrier separating men and women. My pride over the alleged equality of Israeli women in the army and on the kibbutz quickly dissipated. The women soldiers were a kind of charade: they were trained in military skills, but not allowed in combat units. The young women were in fact being used as psychological bait for the young men. Watching women make a parachute jump, I was told that "seeing the girls do it, the boys wouldn't dare to be afraid."

Golda Meir was disappointing. Though I had admired her from afar, she turned out to be no different from the many male Jewish leaders in the United States who considered "women's lib" a threat to the Jewish family. She refused to even meet me.

It struck me as ironic that Pope Paul VI *did* want to meet with me, though I'm still not sure why. By any measure, we were at opposite ends of virtually every issue involving women and the church. Even though men were leaving the priesthood by the thousands, the Pope's new encyclicals drew the same hard line: no women priests, or even serving as altar girls, no sex or marriage for priests, no birth control for Catholics, and certainly no abortion. The directives coming from Pope Paul in Rome forbade nuns to relax their strict dress code and to move out of their convents into the daily lives of their communities. The American nuns I knew, who had come into the women's movement from the very beginning and were now staunch advocates of the ERA, had abandoned their habits years ago. I used to have to plead with them to wear them for press conferences or when we met with members of Congress.

To many feminists, the confrontation between the church and women's movement looked like war to the death. But for all the traditionalist statements from the Pope, there was also a quiet softening of attitudes. That same Pope had also set up a special commission in the spring of 1973 to look at the position of women in society and the church and a lot of militant nuns and priests were on the commission. Because of the enormous new foment over the status of women in the church and because so much was going on within the church on the role of women, I felt strongly that we should apply pressure sparingly.

The idea of me actually going to see the Pope came from my friend Murph—Father Francis X. Murphy of the Holy Redemption Order in Washington. Father Murphy, whose pen name was Xavier Rynne, had covered the Vatican Council II for *The New Yorker*, and we had had countless discussions about the church and women over Thanksgiving dinners at Martha Stuart's house on Bank Street. So when he suggested that this was a good moment for me to talk to the Pope, I was intrigued.

I was going to be in Rome for a few days in the early fall of '73 and Murph set up introductions for me with some Jesuits at their headquarters in the Borgo Santo Spirito. Elena Bartoli, director of the Jesuits' Visiting Bureau, sent me to meet with various Jesuit leaders up and down the dark, marble corridors. They were eager for me to meet with the Pope. "Fill out this form," Elena said to me, handing me a four-page application for a private audience with the Pope. I didn't really expect to be granted the audience after I spelled out every one of my concerns for women in the church, including birth control and abortion.

I had no sooner gotten back to New York when the request was granted in Rome. Everybody told me to go back and do it fast before the Pope discovered my position on abortion and women as priests and God knows what else and changed his mind. On reflection, he must have known my positions, but everybody was amazed that I got the audience.

I had less than a week to prepare and I remember frantically calling Harvey Cox, the eminent theologian who was teaching at Harvard Divinity School, and saying, "Harvey, I've got this audience with the Pope. You've got to brief me." He said: "Can't you find a rabbi to brief you?" and I said, "I don't even know any rabbis." So he helped me. And so did Murph and a whole lot of other people like Elizabeth Farians, a Catholic theologian in Ohio who sent me a collection of biblical and church pronouncements putting down women.

Then there was the whole question of a hat, because a woman has to cover her head in the presence of the Pope. I objected, as did my advisers in the women's movement, because the covering of a woman's hair is a symbol of submission and the acceptance of an inferior status. I was warned, however, that if I didn't wear something on my head, I wouldn't be let in. I knew this famous hatter, Mister John, through Shana, and I went to him and told him the problem. He saved the day by making me a little halo which didn't touch my hair or really cover it. The halo stuck up *over* my head with the help of bobby pins, but it could do the job of a hat. I think I donated it to the Smithsonian.

I was also supposed to kiss the Pope's ring, but I wasn't Catholic and I said I wasn't going to do that. So the idea was that I would give him a little present so that everybody's hands would be so busy nobody would notice. I decided to bring him the symbol of the women's movement, the biological sign of the female over an equal sign which looked very much like a cross. Many of us wore that symbol around our necks on fake gold chains, so I decided I'd wear one and bring another to give to the Pope.

I remember feeling quite intimidated as I walked through the Vatican courtyards and past the stone images of so many saints. Snippets from the biblical quotations Elizabeth Farians had sent me kept running through my head—"Sin began with a woman, and thanks to her, all must die," from Ecclesiasticus; "Every woman ought to be overcome with shame at the thought that she is a woman," from St. Clement. The Pope, however, was warm and welcoming.

I had been advised that our private audience would be very short and warned not to talk too much. But the Pope seemed as curious to meet me as I was to impart my message to him. The gift exchange worked. He gave me a jewel box bearing a medal with his likeness on it and I reciprocated by giving him the feminist chain. He seemed fascinated by the symbol of the women's movement and he didn't take notice that I hadn't kissed his ring. "I bring you this with the wishes of the women of America that the church which has at times been oppressive of women might now become a force for the liberation of women," I told him. "As you can see from this symbol, when women are completely equal to men, it becomes a different kind of cross." He accepted the equality cross and commended me in English for my work on behalf of women.

The Pope insisted to me that the church had always upheld the "dignity of women." I urged him to go further and embrace the full personhood of woman just as the church embraced the full personhood of man. He looked puzzled at the notion, but it turned out that the translator was having difficulty translating "personhood" into Italian. I kept waiting for a Vatican official to move me away from the Pope, but he wanted to talk about the study he had commissioned of women in the church and society and at work, about his personal anguish at a current news story about three women in Portugal who had been jailed for their attempts to organize women. He took my hands in his to convey his concern for women and I was as touched as I was heartened.

When I got back to New York, my friend Father Murphy, writing as Xavier Rynne, claimed in *The New York Times* that my meeting with the Pope or his meeting with me was one of the most significant events of his papacy. The National Assembly of Women Religious, the organized nuns in the United States, were equally enthusiastic. For a long time afterwards, when I crossed paths in airports with nuns in their habits, they would come over and give me a hug.

There was tremendous anticipation both inside and outside the church when Pope Paul VI died in 1978 and Pope John Paul I took his place that there would be a great liberalization as far as women were concerned. Unfortunately, Pope John Paul would die after thirty-three days in office and the subsequent—current—Polish Pope, John Paul II, was not in the advanced wing of the church. So the liberalization so many of us anticipated in the seventies has not really taken place. But it will. The only force still keeping the church alive is the Third World, and the nuns I know are increasingly acerbic about what's going on. Over and over I hear them say: "We're not going to let our lives be dictated by a bunch of old white men in skirts."

When I was getting ready to have that audience, I got interested in theology. There was a Catholic archbishop in Canada who was very liberal, as opposed to an archbishop in San Diego who threatened to excommunicate any Catholic member of NOW and other American archbishops who had banded together to fight the ERA and overturn the abortion laws. So after I got back, I made NOW convene a session on women in religion, and I got Protestant, Jewish and Catholic theologians together, including Rosemary Reuther, a feminist Catholic theologian.

The question then being asked was: Is God dead? Should it not also be asked: Is God male? To see divinity in our sense of the highest in female as well as male terms meant a spiritual transcendence, which I think is happening now. The session on theology was quite good, though nobody could understand why I wanted it.

My interview with Simone de Beauvoir in Paris was no less surprising. I was a great admirer of de Beauvoir, more for *The Mandarins* and her memoirs than for *The Second Sex*, to tell you the truth. I had read *The Second Sex* when I was a young housewife with kids, but it didn't influence me as much as it depressed me. *The Feminine Mystique*, which I started writing ten years or so later, would lead to action, whereas her book was just depressing. But she had recently embraced radical feminism and proclaimed it a superior paradigm for the liberation of society to the Communist or Socialist ideology she had previously embraced.

I had high expectations for my meeting with this intellectual and cultural heroine. I was writing a column then for *McCall's* and I hoped that Simone de Beauvoir and I could issue a joint statement about the women's movement which would take the focus away from the anti-man, anti-motherhood, anti-marriage of sexual politics that didn't speak to the position of most women. Together we would rally the women's movement to keep fighting for equal jobs and equal opportunity.

We met in her house, surrounded by memorabilia from her life with Jean-Paul Sartre, her longtime lover. She had an interpreter and I had an interpreter. She obviously knew English and I had gone to Berlitz to brush up on my middlewestern French, but it was better to have interpreters. It gave me time to think, at least. And I needed every minute I could get.

To my horror, I discovered that Simone de Beauvoir and I disagreed on virtually everything. When I said women need better jobs and to earn more to achieve equality and change society, she responded disparagingly that if we really wanted to change society, women "should not accept important posts" and become part of the "elite" of a society she rejected. "Women don't need leading jobs to eat," she said. She went on to classify the comforts of the family, the decoration of one's home, fashion, marriage, motherhood all as enemies to women. "As long as the family and the myth of the family and the myth of maternity and the maternal instinct are not destroyed, women will still be oppressed," she said. "Well, then, how would you suggest that we perpetuate the human race?" I asked her, to which, astonishingly, she replied: "There are enough people on earth"!

It was a lot of silly nonsense, right down to her utopian vision of housework—whole communities of men, women and children setting aside a day to collectively darn socks, another day to do the collective washing and so on. She wasn't addressing the real world and the realities of most women's lives. Marriage and motherhood could not be seen just as evil. To define women solely in these terms, yes. But the whole thrust of the women's movement in America, I thought, was to eliminate the either-or: political voice versus marriage, career versus motherhood.

The look on my face when I walked out amused the interpreters. "Look," they said. "You're an American pragmatist and she's a French mandarin. You're talking in different worlds." But I remember being so disappointed with our dialogue during what I realize now was her abstract, Mao period.

To me, women's financial parity and independence was critical, which is why, in 1973, I helped found the First Women's Bank and Trust Company and became one of its first directors. The First Women's Bank was the fourth women's organization I helped to found, highlighting the financial obstacles women faced in business and their everyday lives. Equality in credit had been a NOW issue for several years because it was very hard, if not impossible, for women to get their own credit, be it a credit card from a department store or a mortgage from a bank. If women were divorced, even if they'd been making more money than their husbands, somehow the credit was always considered his. Women's income or savings were not counted.

Still, I was a little ambivalent about helping to start the First Women's Bank, because I was always a little ambivalent about alternative organizations. I suppose it was good to give a model, but the separatist stuff wasn't the way. What you really had to do was change the mainstream, and that the bank start-up accomplished in very short order. Within two short months, we got legislation passed in Congress banning sex discrimination in credit. Under the Federal Equal Credit Opportunity Act, no individual could be denied credit on the basis of gender or marital status and women's and men's incomes had to be counted as equal in determining credit eligibility.

It was clear by the mid-seventies that the momentum of the women's movement was unstoppable. Feminism in all its forms was sweeping the globe, with America leading the charge. By 1973, my friend Pat Burnett and I had helped establish NOW chapters in over twenty countries, and had even gotten NGO (Non-Governmental Organization) status with the United Nations. I thought—I knew—it was time to have an international meeting of feminists, but it was clear that we needed a bigger venue than my apartment.

I raised a little seed money from the liberal philanthropist Stewart Mott, I believe it was, to get something international started and we got the woman president of Lesley College in Cambridge to host an international planning meeting. Quite a few women came to the first International Feminist Conference I convened in December 1973, but it was clear that we couldn't do further conferences privately. You'd only get the wealthiest of women who were able to pay their fares to come. We needed international government support. So after the meeting in Cambridge, we went to see Kurt Waldheim, then Secretary-General of the United Nations. The United Nations had sponsored the Year of the Ocean and the Year of the Child, we pointed out. Why shouldn't the United Nations designate 1975 as the Year of the Woman and have an international conference?

A preliminary meeting was held in Iran in 1974. Helvi Sipila, a friend of mine from Finland and a high-ranking official at the United Nations, organized it with the support of Princess Ashraf, the Shah of Iran's sister and her country's ambassador to the United Nations. I was invited to attend, as was the Australian writer Germaine Greer, author of *The Female Eunuch*.

I liked Germaine well enough. When she first came to America in 1970 to publicize her book, I had invited her out to the commune for a visit and to make her welcome. Her book was more problematic. *The Female Eunuch* was a combination of good stuff and a sort of naughty child exhibitionism, like having her picture taken nude in a bubble bath. That's just what I had objected to in Kate Millett's book: half of *Sexual Politics* was brilliant and the other half was an abstract sexual extremism that didn't apply to women's lives.

Germaine and I had had some interesting disagreements over the years. She had come to some NOW meeting where the focus at that point was enforcing Title VII. She couldn't understand why we were so interested in jobs. "Why are you bothering with jobs?" she kept saying. "That's not what it's all about." Her take on the movement was so weird that everyone was taken aback. So I finally said to someone: "It's because she's from the British upper class and she doesn't understand the importance of jobs to women." She's not, I know. But it was a really interesting blind spot. Germaine had written all about sexual politics in *The Female Eunuch*, but she had no interest in women's major concern—employment.

I don't know what set her off at the conference in Iran. She would claim later that at one point I purposefully kept everyone waiting when in fact I didn't think there was anything scheduled until evening so I had gone swimming. I didn't know that they were waiting for me to change my clothes. She also had a fit about my apparent commandeering of one of the few nebulizers in Teheran for my asthma when in fact I was having a rather bad asthma attack and simply asked if there was a nebulizer available. But goodness, she would later write the nastiest, bitchiest article about me in *Vanity Fair*. I still don't understand why. Perhaps it was because she thought I should talk about abortion all the time to the women in Iran, and I didn't think that was the thing to do. You have to talk where people are at. You can't go that far ahead.

I also caught a lot of heat from feminists for going to Iran. But while it was true that the Shah was repressive—the SAVAK, the secret police in Iran, was "disappearing" people left and right—part of the Shah's attempt to modernize Iran was his embrace of women's rights. The very fact that there was a women's organization in Iran headed by my friend, Mahnaz Afkhami, that the

Shah's sister, Princess Ashraf, was the honorary chair of the women's organization and was Iran's ambassador to the United Nations, that the Shah welcomed the international conference and granted me not only an interview with him but with his wife, Farah Diba, were signals to me of social change. Besides, we were organizing internationally and it was important to meet and network with as many women from other countries as possible. So I have never had any regrets about going to Iran. Besides, Princess Ashraf bankrolled our international conference.

What I did regret, besides Germaine Greer's attitude, was missing the 1974 NOW convention in Houston. The theme of the convention was "out of the mainstream into the revolution," which was out of tune with the direction America was moving in. The incoming president, Karen DeCrow, campaigned on that slogan if I remember correctly, which ignored the concerns and realities of middle-class women.

If I had been there, I think I might have been able to stop the turn toward extremism, but I went to Iran and I missed it. I later came to think that the CIA had deliberately gotten me out of the country so that NOW could get taken over by *agents provocateurs*. That may be paranoid. But the takeover wouldn't have happened if I hadn't been in Iran.

NOW was so wracked by divisiveness and internal power struggles by the 1975 convention in Philadelphia that it seemed on the brink of imploding. The election of officers and key actions and resolutions were so bitterly contested that it took three sessions of all-night voting to arrive at consensus, and even then, the American Arbitration Association had to be called in after charges of fraud were lodged. In the end, Karen DeCrow was reelected president and Ellie Smeal chair of the board. And they continued to espouse the rhetoric of "out of the mainstream into the revolution."

The new, radical leadership, which called itself the Majority Caucus, was more obsessed with that rhetorical sexual "revolution against the oppressors" than it was with moving on to stage two of the women's movement and reaching out to male labor leaders and farsighted public and corporate planners to incorporate the structural realities of women's lives into the mainstream of work and society. For NOW to preach revolution and continue to see women only as the downtrodden and oppressed did not speak to the thousands of women who had graduated by then from law school and medical school and business school and were moving on. "But I want to be in the mainstream," said a woman waiting on line with me at 3:00 a.m. to vote at the convention in Philadelphia. "That's what I've been out of as a woman."

In retrospect, I realize now that we were guilty, all of us, for the divisiveness in NOW. We should have risked articulating our differences and throwing the agenda wide open for all women to discuss and decide. I'd felt the same way about the National Women's Political Caucus, but the other founding leaders wanted so badly to control the outcome that they didn't let grass-roots women decide anything for themselves. The impetus for "unity, unity" in the so-called sisterhood had so overwhelmed the airing of the very real ideological and cultural differences within the movement that it was turning on itself.

The real wars we needed to wage were against the well-financed forces in corporate America, in the government itself, which was threatening to undo the affirmative action mechanisms required of federal contractors. America was in a recession in the mid-1970s and equal opportunity was considered by many to be a "luxury." Women were facing layoffs in unprecedented numbers—last hired, first fired—which is why I convened an Economic Think Tank in New York in 1974 with the help of Mary Jean Tully. Chair of the NOW Legal Defense and Education Fund, of which I was a board member, Mary Jean was the first person to think big enough about fund-raising for the movement. Whenever I had a project of a feminist nature I wanted to do, I always got together with Mary Jean to help organize it and raise the money. We had to begin to think about the new problems ahead, and new solutions, like job splitting and the restructuring of roles and responsibilities so that women could secure their place in the workforce. Yet the "revolutionary" new leadership of NOW was calling for a "general strike against the system" dubbed "Alice Doesn't." Taking its title from the film *Alice Doesn't Live Here Anymore*, on October 29, 1975, the tenth anniversary of the founding of NOW, "Alices" everywhere were instructed not to go to work, not to shop for groceries or cook or to sleep with their "oppressors." Not surprisingly, only a few women went along with the idea and the strike was a failure.

There was too much at stake for many of us in NOW to turn our backs on the organization we had helped to found. After the early momentum, the ERA was stalled. Only one state, North Dakota, ratified the Equal Rights Amendment in 1975 and moves to rescind were beginning in the thirty-four states that had already passed it. In New York and New Jersey, two of the most progressive states which had ratified the federal constitutional amendment, the passage of state ERAs failed by large margins. We couldn't afford to ignore the hollow movement NOW had become and send out the wrong message. Shortly after the negative votes in New York and New Jersey, a Louis Harris Poll found that a vast majority of women (65%) supported efforts to strengthen women's status in society, but few (17%) thought that women's organizations were helping. Contrary to the self-styled "revolutionary" new NOW leadership, the majority of women polled did not think of themselves as an "oppressed group." "It is clear that if women's organizations campaign for women's right in the name of 'liberating women from oppression,' they are going to ride into a storm of disbelief," Lou Harris reported.

Thirteen "independents" on the NOW board and former NOW leaders asked me to meet with them in a hotel room in New Orleans in November 1975 to come to grips with the crises in the women's movement. We laid everything on the table—the movement's preoccupation with lesbian rights, the disconnect from the majority of women who supported equality but not "women's lib," the overemphasis on racism, poverty and rape, everything and anything but the problems of white and black middle-class American women. We agreed that NOW had to recapture the mainstream and turn its attentions outward from infighting and power struggles if it was to remain the viable movement so vital to our daughters' futures.

The press was full of death notices of the women's movement after we left New Orleans. To our amazement, our little meeting in a motel room appeared in the *Washington Post* as "NOW Faces Major Crisis," in *Time* magazine as "Womanswar" and on the front page of *The New York Times* under the headline: "Thirteen NOW Leaders Form 'Dissident' Network." Even Emily, now nineteen, my decidedly non-radical-feminist daughter at Harvard, took notice. "What went wrong?" she asked. "Is it serious?"

Well, of course it was serious. But then, so was the women's movement. The media coverage which so amazed us was testimony to the true strength of the movement. By the end of 1975, there were NOW chapters in seven hundred cities and more wives were working outside the home than any time in the history of the country—up 205 percent since the end of World War II. West Point and the other venerable military academies were opening their doors to women by order of President Ford; Title IX of the Education Amendments of 1972 barring sex discrimination in college athletics was finally coming into effect, paving the way for young women to be eligible for the athletic scholarships traditionally available only to young men; and the Little League was avoiding the fifty-seven discrimination suits brought against the organization by "voluntarily" inviting girls to play baseball.

Women in the church were making remarkable progress. Eleven women, including a member of NOW who founded a feminist parish in upstate New York, were ordained as the first female priests in the Episcopal Church by four progressive bishops, challenging the denomination's male rules and practices. (The Episcopal Church would officially recognize their ordination two years later.) Catholic nuns were coalescing as well. At the National Leadership Conference of Women Religious in 1974, around six hundred nuns approved a resolution calling on the church to ordain women as priests.

Value was finally being given to women's work, with the muscle of Title VII. In an unprecedented first, the steel companies were forced to pay $56 million in back pay and wage adjustments to women and minorities industrywide; AT&T settled with the EEOC for the second time, agreeing to pay $30 million in back pay and wage adjustments to women in management who had been discriminated against; and the Bank of America agreed to pay $10 million in compensatory pay increases to its women employees.

That's why there was big money opposition to women's equality, to say nothing of the fact that maybe the powers that be—or rather, were—sensed that they were losing women as an inert, passive, scared and docile mass. Whether the corporate, economic, political, religious or other elements of power that fought the women's movement or subversively organized a backlash knew this or not or sensed it or not, they had reason to try to stop the women's movement. Despite the bickering and infighting in NOW, women had become a new force in society and a threat to the status quo and its power brokers.

It seems to me now that we had more power than we were using, that we have never really used our full power. Had we known, none of us, including me, would have been so stunned at our strength or at the forces lined up against us, both in America and increasingly abroad. The women's movement, we were about to discover, had stirred up a global hornet's nest.

TWELVE

Rules of Engagement

The threats began before I even left for Mexico City in June 1975 for the first UN-sponsored World Conference of International Women's Year. Anonymous letters arrived warning me not to speak where I wasn't wanted or I would be denounced "first as an American and then as a Jew." On the plane to Mexico I sat next to an attractive man who then mysteriously turned up as a fellow guest at a remote weekend retreat I'd been invited to and wanted to take me hiking in the mountains. Then, though I hadn't told anybody where I was going to be for the weekend, a strange woman suddenly materialized at the house in the middle of a thunderstorm to warn me not to say anything about a recently released report from a radical feminist group claiming that Gloria Steinem was a CIA agent.

Coincidence or not, it was unnerving, so much so that I locked myself in my bedroom that night and called Pat Burnett at her hotel in Mexico City to get me out of there. The trouble was, I wasn't sure *where* I was, so she couldn't. After a sleepless night, I left early to return to Mexico City, where we'd already been warned by the NOW representatives working at the United Nations that American feminists would not be welcome.

The anti-American sentiments were so high in Mexico City you would have thought the American feminists, both official members of the delegation and unofficial attendees—including

Carole De Saram, president of New York NOW; Dorothy Height of the National Council of Negro Women; Dorothy Haener of UAW; and me—were the real enemies, not global discrimination and bias. One unfamiliar group of women who would identify themselves only as "citizens of the world" disrupted virtually every one of our meetings or caucuses as soon as the subject turned seriously to women. No one knew where they had come from or who was paying for their expensive hotel suite and their seemingly inexhaustible supply of liquor. Among them was a woman who claimed she was American and broke into several television interviews I was doing with foreign journalists to insist that I did not speak for "American feminists."

Six thousand women came to Mexico City from non-governmental organizations in eighty different countries, the vast majority to talk about the issues of job training, family planning and work. But they hardly got a chance. The official delegations, many headed by wives of heads of state and dominated by men, were there to further their own political ends, not women's rights. It was outrageous. When Leah Rabin of Israel rose to speak at the official conference, the Arab and Communist bloc delegations walked out. Mexico's president, Luis Echeverria, announced to thunderous applause that women's liberation required the "transformation of the world economic order," while the Soviet and Chinese bloc held firm that any World Plan of Action for women's equality was essentially nonsense until colonialism, neocolonialism, racism and foreign domination were eliminated.

It was so frustrating for me and for all the women who had come to Mexico City, many at our own expense, to have our voices lost in agendas that had little or nothing to do with women. Why should "Zionism is racism" be a major order of business for the women's movement? It had nothing to do with the women's movement one way or the other. We were resentful that the women's conference was being used for others' nefarious purposes. Even the Mexican government sidelined us. What we wanted, and had insisted on before we got there, was a place big enough for all the women from NGOs and women's groups to get together and really hash things out. Instead, we were given small rooms in a medical center an hour away from the official UN conference.

There was nothing to do but to call for a march. And God, everybody got so nervous. I was summoned by the Attorney General of Mexico, Pedro Ojeda Paullada, who was also president of the conference and head of the police. He proceeded to interrogate me about the purpose of the march, convinced that it was a plot to demand his resignation as conference president. The American ambassador sent for me next, telling me he'd had a call from Mexico's minister of internal security to shut me up. Our ambassador was grateful, I think, to have a reason to explain how the rights of a private citizen in our democratic system of government prevented him from shutting me up. In fact, whenever I was asked to lecture in foreign countries, the American embassies were always supportive and often asked me to lecture at the embassy as well. Someone attached to the State Department once told me that feminism was becoming the best American cultural export.

I was grateful, too, for the furor over the march. With Mexico's Attorney General, I bartered the possibility of the march he was so frightened of for a big enough hall for all the women to meet in.

We achieved a beautiful unity in that great hall that overcame cultural differences and phony barriers and concentrated on our concerns as women. While the Arab, Communist and Third World blocs among the official UN delegates across town continued their week-long filibuster, women from six continents in the great hall approved a ten-year World Plan of Action to ban sex discrimination in education, employment and political decision making as well as other violations of women's rights. But that unity we achieved in Mexico and the power of an emerging international network of women proved to be too threatening to those who profited from women's subservience.

Agitators began disrupting our meetings in the great hall, staging fights for the media. A group of planted Mexican "feminists" tried to silence us by telling us to move out of our hotel to a remote spot for our own "safety." I began to be followed by men wearing guns, though I still don't know whether the gunmen were protecting or threatening me. What I do know is that the disruptions intensified at our global speak-outs in the great hall and climaxed when a group of men barged into the room and led the disrupters up the aisle. In the chaos I was pinned against the wall and caught in the glare of television lights, while a Mexican journalist insisted that the women had fallen to fighting and demanded that I admit defeat. Well, I wasn't about to do that. Quite the opposite. It was the power of women's *unity* in Mexico City that had prompted this violent disruption.

My friends were worried. I saw three of them appear at the edge of the television lights and motion for me to come with them. One of them, a city councilwoman from Detroit, told me to take her arm, and together, the women walked me into one of those cubicle offices and made me sit down and keep my head below the glass partition. It was not until later that they told me that the men leading the disruption were armed.

The American ambassador sent for me and advised me to get out of town because he said he could no longer protect me. I left the next morning, and I took with me some useful lessons. Though we were beginning to have a sense of our own international power, we had somehow allowed the conference for women to be used—quite successfully—as a political pawn. The World Plan of Action became a hollow document when it was passed by the official delegations without any means to implement it. And the Mexicans managed to get in language linking it to the overthrow of imperialism and Zionism, etc., forcing the U.S. delegation to abstain or to vote against it.

The difficulty of doing anything concrete for women through the United Nations would become even more apparent at the Mid-Decade World Conference on Women in Copenhagen in 1980. America was once again the focus as the "imperialist aggressor" and Israel the scapegoat. Some Third World women hung a portrait of Ayatollah Khomeini in the conference hall and anointed Layla Khalid, a PLO terrorist who had helped hijack a plane, the conference "heroine." With the PLO disrupting every meeting, we finally set ourselves up in an old Danish church to discuss feminism.

It was becoming clear that feminism was not going to be allowed into the councils of world power. Though many more of the official delegates in Copenhagen were women who had risen to some political power since the Mexico conference, most were being manipulated by their regimes and governments back home. Women were too valuable as cheap or unpaid labor in many countries, and kept politically passive through lack of education and training, to risk a move toward equality. To make sure their women delegates hadn't been co-opted by feminism, many countries would fly in male diplomats in the last few days of the conference to replace the women delegates and ensure the approved votes would be cast.

America had taken a much more productive note of International Women's Year, thanks to Bella Abzug, who introduced legislation into Congress to establish a national commission to commemorate IWY and who, finally, after two years, got it passed and funded. Among other activities, a National Women's Conference was called with delegates from every state to be held in Houston. I was somewhat critical of the conference at first because it wasn't really organized to do anything.

The National Women's Conference convened in November 1977, presided over by Bella. The agenda was far-reaching—the ERA, employment discrimination, child care, the plight of women after divorce—all the issues that were important for women. Twenty thousand women came to the conference, including two thousand voting delegates. Rosalynn Carter was there, and Betty Ford and Lady Bird Johnson, and Coretta Scott King. I was a delegate at large. The twenty-four planks the convention would vote on for a national plan for action echoed NOW's Bill of Rights for Women, which we'd written ten years before and which was adopted at our second annual NOW convention. But this was no NOW convention. We had to suppose that feminists were in the majority, though we really didn't know because some of the delegates came from states where there were no feminist organizations. And we knew there would be some dissenters. A huge crowd of Mormons had taken over the IWY state conference in Salt Lake City and voted down all the proposals for the plan of action, including the ERA and world peace, while the contingent from Hawaii was stacked with other anti-ERA Mormons who had taken over the conference there.

I was worried about any divisiveness at the national conference because of the ERA, which was stalled three states short of ratification in 1977. We were at a crucial stage in my home state of Illinois and I had been working hard to get the ERA ratified before the March 1979 deadline. I knew that one of the favorite tactics of the anti-ERA protagonists was to enflame the lesbian issue to undermine support for the constitutional amendment and I was worried—and correctly so, it turned out—that the Houston conference with all its media coverage would give them a perfect opportunity.

There was a huge lesbian presence at the conference, though I don't think any lesbian group organized it. They came with lavender balloons printed with the words: "We are everywhere." The balloons provided just the fodder I'd feared for the national press. My brother, a progressive Republican businessman in Peoria who had given money to support the campaign for the Equal Rights Amendment in Illinois, was really upset about the images coming out of Houston. He got in touch with me, as did Carl, who called to say, "Why don't you get rid of those balloons?" I remember one big banner had something like "Dyke Power" printed on it.

It cannot have been an accident that the lesbian issue arose stridently just as we needed maximum unity. And in Houston it was being pushed far beyond its logical proportions. I did not think at all that this came from the responsible women leaders who happened to be lesbians. They were as appalled by it as I was. It was coming from whoever was funding the enemies of the women's movement, those who wanted to discredit the women's movement, who wanted to prevent the passage of the ERA.

In order to preempt any debate, I decided to quickly second the resolution affirming lesbian rights which everyone thought I would oppose. The enemies of the women's movement wanted nothing more than to have us mucking around on national television, fighting over the lesbian issue. And given the enormous diversity of the women at Houston—from the South, from the Midwest—we could have had a debate going on for days on the lesbian question. I gave a little speech about supporting the rights of all people, and not letting this issue be used by our enemies to divide and divert us from our main purpose, which is equal opportunity. The resolution passed and the "lesbian issue" *got off the airwaves.*

To this day I think some of the demonstrators in Houston were planted to weaken the authority and the effectiveness of this exploding massive force to transform society. "Stop ERA," an organization founded by Phyllis Schlafly shortly after Congress sent the amendment to the states for ratification, even tried to prove in court that the federal funding of the National Commission to Commemorate the Year of the Woman was illegal. It failed.

In the end, the delegates in Houston voted overwhelmingly—80 percent in favor—for the national plan of action, including support for the ERA. The "anti" delegates could deliver only 19 percent of the vote, the exact same percentage of the general public that a Roper Poll had identified before the conference as supporting the anti-ERA views of Phyllis Schlafly and her ilk. What had been the "radical" goals put forward by NOW in 1967 were now, ten short years later, clearly the national objectives of the vast majority of American women.

A misleading image was being presented on television, however, by the "fairness doctrine," which was going into effect about this time and required the networks to give equal time to both sides of an issue. Phyllis Schlafly and her ladies in the Eagle Forum, an offshoot of "Stop ERA" they founded in 1975, were minuscule in numbers compared to NOW and the NWPC and other burgeoning feminist organizations, but if a network had me on, they also had to have Phyllis Schlafly. It may have looked balanced, but it wasn't. Even if you added up all the little reactionary groups like hers, you still didn't have any great massive memberships, whereas as the huge traditional women's organizations became feminist, I truly spoke for millions of women. I was working personally with the Junior League, for instance. I was on the national board of the Girl Scouts and I tried to get them to sell ERA with their cookies. The YWCA, the AAUW—they all came out for the ERA. So, early on, did the League of Women Voters, which is not supposed to come out for anything.

But there I was paired up with Phyllis Schlafly again and again. It always just killed me that she would go on and on about feminism and the ERA being against the family, condemning all these awful career women, when she was being paid to travel the country. She was no sweet little housewife rushing home to make dinner. We didn't know where all the anti-ERA money was coming from, but we knew it was there. There were big economic issues. Women still earned only 59 cents for every dollar earned by men and their cheap labor was a staple of the American economy.

Though we'd gotten the Equal Pay Act extended to cover women and men in professional, executive and administrative jobs, the premise of equal pay for equal work wasn't doing the trick because more women were in jobs that were not equal. The law did apply to the women who were working in the same jobs as men, so I didn't disparage the law as an advance, but we quickly realized that you had to go beyond Equal Pay for Equal Work to Equal Pay for Work of Equal Value or Comparable Worth. We began to have a lot of thinking and writing about the pay equity issue at the same time Phyllis Schlafly was going around the country denouncing "careerists" and extolling the superior virtues of marriage and family life.

Though the term "family values" had not crept into the language, her big pitch was to paint feminism as opposed to the family, as the destruction of family. But as a mother of three treasured children, I wouldn't let her get away with it. Ironically, her son and Danny were graduate students in physics at Berkeley, so every time she'd try to paint me as a rabble-rousing enemy of the family, I'd say: "Now Phyllis, you know that's not true. Your son and my son are getting their Ph.D.'s together in California. You know I'm a good mother."

It was really quite amusing that the two boys were studying together at Berkeley and even shared the same mentor, Izzy Singer, a famous mathematician at MIT. Izzy obviously found it amusing, too. "Both of your mothers should sit next to each other the way you do," he would tease the boys. "I want them both to come out here when you get your degrees and sit next to each other."

But I was not about to let the right wing, the opposition to women's rights, take ownership of family values. I really resented the mislabeling of feminists as careerists when the vast majority of working women *had* to work to make ends meet. But I also resented the tactics of the women in the group La Leche, who made a fetish of breast-feeding and would push a baby in my face in the middle of a lecture, as much as I did the right-to-life fanatics who called me "Baby Killer." Feminism had to project a positive image of family and fight for policies supporting the kind of family in which women are not the servant of the family but equal participants. It is a different kind of family, with different issues: If women share the breadwinning, for instance, then men should share the housework. There had to be new thinking about that and the other new realities of family life that were evolving on their own.

I loved a headline I saw one day in the paper—"American Men Not Doing 50% of the Housework"—and I quoted it all over the place. The idea that it should be assumed that American men might do 50 percent of the housework was a marvelous advance. After all, these were the sons of the feminine mystique whose mothers picked up their pajamas off the floor and buttered their sandwiches and drove them to Little League games. The idea that men were beginning to share the household responsibilities, that a man wasn't a wimp if he really wanted to share and take part in child care and the household, was in the air. It didn't mean just that he flipped the hamburgers on the outside grill with his favorite barbecue sauce and a chef's cap on while she cleaned out the toilet bowl. Sharing had to be sharing. I didn't assume that all men were going to do the ironing, but then, neither would all women.

There had to be new thinking, too, about divorce. The Schlafly school was issuing dire warnings about the traditional protections women might lose if the ERA went through and Congress, not states, legislated divorce, alimony and child support. Well, that was a hollow warning. The real tradition was that too many ex-husbands paid no attention to any divorce laws and weren't supporting their ex-wives and children at all! In 1974, I had helped convince New York State to hold a conference on marriage and the crisis of divorce, and so many women came, the big hotel in New York we held it in wasn't nearly large enough. And it was no wonder because the reality was so shameful. The statistics at the time showed that divorce could drop a woman's income by as much as 70 percent and that over half of the single mothers who were legally due child support, myself among them, received none at all.

I had never asked Carl for any alimony, though he would tell the newspapers I had. All I ever asked him for was to share in child support, which he never really provided, including his obligation to pay Emily's tuition at Harvard. He even sent her a telegram when she was accepted at Harvard, saying, "You stay home and go to Hunter College." Emily had called me in tears and I said, "Honey, you know you don't have to do that. You know you can go to Harvard. I'll pay, if need be."

I finally realized I was going to have to take Carl to Family Court to collect any child support, which was horribly embarrassing. At least they let me go down the back stairs to evade reporters at those court hearings. When he still didn't contribute his share, I sued him again in a higher court. I won again in 1975 and got a court order for the money. But it was no use. Carl still refused to pay. By that time I was spending so much money on lawyers trying to collect the child support (while the boys were telling me that Carl was spending all his time avoiding making any money so he wouldn't have to pay anything) that I finally thought, "Okay, forget it. Just get him to pay the legal fees and that will be it." There was just no point. So I paid the children's expenses and Emily's college tuition.

I was more fortunate than many women because at least I had the capacity to earn a good living. Many of the women getting divorced as those fifties marriages dissolved had been housewives most of their lives, and they weren't earning equal to men. Some came into divorce completely like displaced persons. It really was a crisis that demanded new thinking and new, enforceable laws. Women were getting the short end of the stick in divorce cases.

As feminists, of course, we didn't believe women should ask for alimony. We wanted the equal disposition of property to be law in New York, as it was in California. Most of women's energies then had gone into building up their husbands' careers and, therefore, their mutual fortune; so we felt strongly that women should be awarded half or equal shares. But in retrospect, I don't think we were right to settle merely for equal disposition of property. There should have been some sort of severance pay—a severance package—for women who in those days, in great numbers, were housewives and had no job training. In the end, we didn't succeed in getting severance pay or even equal distribution in New York. Instead, divorce settlements became based on the "equitable" distribution of assets, which left it up to the judges, who then were all men, to decide the monetary value of the wife's contribution to the marriage and her husband's career. Most judges did not give equal shares to the wife.

The new divorce laws seemed an improvement nonetheless. And so did the new custody guidelines beginning to be used by the courts in the late seventies which put the best interests of the child first. It was progress to me that the woman should not automatically get sole custody of the children in a divorce just because she was the mother. There were a lot of fathers who were passionately involved with their children, as depicted in the 1979 film *Kramer vs. Kramer.* Though I was very thankful I had been awarded custody of my children in the mindless "mother" bias of 1969, I thought it was all right for both parents to be evaluated in a custody suit and for the judge's decision to be based on what would be best for the child.

For all the social change and the new perceptions of sex roles, however, the ratification of the ERA remained elusive. Illinois became a great battleground in the countdown toward the 1979 deadline. I went to Chicago for a great ERA march on Mother's Day and I lobbied in Springfield. I even went back to Peoria where some of my Republican friends were all for the ERA. My friend Harriet Vance Parkhurst, whose husband, Parky, was then a state senator, helped organize the women for ERA and we had a torchlight parade. I was also scheduled to debate Phyllis Schlafly in Illinois, but on the way out in the plane I lost my voice. I called my friend Bob Easton, who was practicing as a pediatrician in Peoria then, and croaked over the phone to him. He prescribed something that didn't work so we tried tea and honey, but that didn't work either. He finally told me: "Betty, you've just lost your voice because you're within miles of Peoria!" I went ahead with the debate anyway and I think I won out of sympathy.

But we just couldn't win Illinois, whose House of Representatives required a three-to-five majority vote. There was a lot of money pouring into the anti-ERA organizations in 1978 and the images of the lesbian presence at Houston which had so troubled my brother were still fresh in people's minds. Twice that year the ERA came to a vote in Illinois, winning by a vote of 101 to 64 the first time, but ultimately failing by six votes to achieve the necessary majority. The second round failed by only two votes.

I remember when Liz Holtzman came to me with the idea of getting Congress to extend the deadline for the ratification of the ERA. I was skeptical but I agreed to help. I got Joan Mondale to invite all the Senate wives to breakfast with me. And I got them to agree to lobby some of the recalcitrant senators with me. Peachy Hollins from South Carolina was one of them, and while we were on our way to see Senator Robert Byrd, her husband found out and called to tell her to get out of there. But Peachy held firm. Many other women from various organizations lobbied Congress as well and our efforts proved successful. The House and the Senate voted to extend the deadline for ratification to June 30, 1982.

While Joan Mondale was supportive of the ERA, Nancy Reagan wasn't. We had been at Smith together though I knew her only vaguely, she an actress and I the editor of the newspaper and the literary magazine. We also both came from Illinois and if I remember correctly, we had taken the train home together on several occasions. I had followed her career as a professional actress after graduation with great interest because virtually no one but she and I were working. That was the era when Smith "girls" got married right out of college and did good volunteer work in the community.

So I was surprised, I guess, when she exhibited no interest in supporting the ERA. The first time I tried to get her involved was on a bus at the 1976 Republican Convention in Kansas City. I sat down next to her and said: "Nancy, from one Smith girl to another, you have to be for the ERA, you know." But I didn't get anywhere.

I tried again at the Gridiron dinner in Washington after Ronald Reagan was elected in 1980. The head correspondents of the Washington news bureaus are members and can invite non-journalists to the Gridiron and I was there along with the historian Barbara Tuchman as the guest of my friend Richard Dudman, the Washington bureau chief for the *St. Louis Post-Dispatch*. (He and I had met on the press bus for some presidential election and had become great friends. I used to stay with him and his wife, Helen, a wonderful woman who had been the women's page editor of the *Washington Post* before moving into public broadcasting.) Somewhere in the course of the evening's events I went up to Nancy Reagan at the head table. Once again I evoked our Smith legacy and implored her to use her influence to help us with the ERA. And she said, "Oh Betty, Ronnie and I are for equality and Ronnie and I are for women's rights, we're just not for amendments." I'm afraid that Nancy Reagan, Smith girl or not, did not really do very much for women.

I really wanted that ERA. There would be enormous implications if it got ratified and established a woman's right to equality under the law. A whole new territory would present itself—pensions, insurance, property laws—for which there were no legal precedents. As more and more women went to law school, whole bodies of new thinking were evolving as they started tackling these questions. It was thrilling. The only ERA issue I had a hard struggle with was the draft, which, of course, was raised during the debates about the ERA. "Well, do you want women to be drafted?" I would be asked time and again. Now I could not see marching with a banner saying I wanted women to be drafted. I had been very opposed to the Vietnam War, after all. But I worked out that while I was not for anybody being drafted, if there were again such a thing as a just and necessary war like World War II, then there would be no reason for women not to be drafted. This didn't mean that a pregnant woman or a mother of young children was going to be drafted. Men weren't either. And it didn't mean that a woman who was five feet tall was going to have to carry a 200-pound machine gun or whatever. But women couldn't ask for equal opportunity without sharing equal responsibility.

Even with the extension for the ERA, however, I knew it would take a miracle for the amendment to be ratified, what with the anti-family, man-hating rhetoric coming from the very vocal opposition. We had to recapture the mainstream message. The White House was planning to have a conference on the family in 1980 to which I would be a delegate, and everyone was a little leery about what was going to come out of that, given all these attempts to pitch feminism against the family. So I got the idea that we should have our own feminist conference on the future of the family, which we did in 1979 under the auspices of the NOW Legal Defense and Education Fund.

I also put aside a new book on aging I was researching in order to write a series of articles for *Redbook* magazine on men, women, work and the family. Those articles, which expanded on the concepts I'd started developing as visiting professor of sociology at Temple, looked at the generation who had inherited the women's movement and were trying to live the new equality we had fought for. I did a lot of interviews, and then, with some degree of dread, decided to expand them into my third book, *The Second Stage*.

Lecturing has never been work for me, but writing is. If I'm *not* writing, however, I feel guilty because that means I'm not working. This counterproductive dynamic of dread and guilt has been, and is to this day, compounded by the extraordinary success of *The Feminine Mystique*. It was a hard act to follow. When you've written a book that's had the impact that book had, you end up competing with yourself.

My second book, *"It Changed My Life,"* had been published in 1976. It consisted mostly of magazine pieces and speeches I'd already written about the early years of the women's movement with new interstitial tissue linking them. So I didn't consider that a real book. I eased my way into *The Second Stage* the same way. Because I knew I had to get back on the horse and ride again, I did the series for *Redbook*. When the collection of articles seemed enough, I turned them into a book. I knew *The Second Stage* wasn't going to be a big book, so at least I didn't have that trauma to deal with. But I also knew it was an important book.

I wrote *The Second Stage* fast, which is very unlike me, so that it would be published before 1982, the extended ratification deadline for the ERA. On the one hand, I hoped the new thinking in the book, which held up family—not jobs—as the new feminist frontier, might provide the catalyst to get the ERA ratified. On the other hand, if the ERA failed, the personal truths and social observations about life after the first stage would serve as guidelines in the second stage to keep the movement alive.

Yes, there had been a quantum leap in consciousness in just one generation, changing expectations and releasing both men and women from obsolete sex roles. But the first stage of the revolution did not provide the answers or even ask the questions as to how this generation and subsequent generations were going to incorporate that new consciousness into their everyday lives. We were either at the beginning of the end or the end of the beginning.

The young women who had benefited from the first stage and were succeeding in the professional world were raising uneasy questions. "How can I have the career I want and the kind of marriage I want and be a good mother?" or, "Will the jobs open to me now still be there if I stop to have children?" or, "Do I always have to be superwoman?" The men who were living with them were asking new questions as well. "Being a father has become very important to me. Why doesn't *she* support the family and let *me* find myself?"

I was especially interested in interviewing the men who were beginning to change. Their movement was quieter. They didn't have to march with banners. The few men who tried to write books about the so-called men's movement were either on some thinly disguised move to escape from alimony or trying for their own glory to latch onto the women's movement, which was simply not applicable to the situation of men. Nonetheless, a change in the role of men had to happen and was happening.

The necessity for women to break through the feminine mystique was more glaring, but there was also a comparable necessity in stage two for men to break through the masculine mystique. The whole outmoded definition of masculinity was no longer workable and livable, optimal or doable for the age we were living in. I spent a fascinating week observing institutional changes as a consultant at the U.S. Military Academy in 1979, from which I wrote a chapter, "Reality Test at West Point," in *The Second Stage.* The first class of women was about to graduate and I wanted to see what changes there had been, if any, in that most macho of cultures. There were many.

West Point was having an identity crisis of sorts in the late seventies, and not just because of women. There'd been a cheating scandal among the male cadets the year before women were admitted, which had brought into question what leadership should be in the modern, all-volunteer army. The macho John Wayne command-and-control model, they'd decided, was not viable anymore for a volunteer army in a society becoming more and more conscious of the values of equality and diversity. Everything militated against a John Wayne model not only in American society but in a world that was increasingly democratic, where racism was suspect, and Third World countries could no longer be treated like lackeys.

What fascinated me was that the entrance of women into West Point coincided with the implementation of this new style of leadership. They'd brought some very sophisticated officers onto the faculty who'd been sent off to Harvard to get their masters in the social sciences in order to study what effect West Point was having on the women, what effect the women were having on West Point, and what new questions all this raised.

The women were certainly as good as the men academically, so that wasn't an issue. They were *better* than the men in the essential officer skills necessary to form a solid sense of cohesion in their units, inspire a commitment to a common task and work together as a group. Only in physical tests did the men outdo the women; on average, the men could run faster and longer and lift more weight. That one advantage for men was being trumpeted as a total negative for women, especially among the young male cadets to whom physical prowess was synonymous with manhood. I've never heard so much about upper body strength in my life as I did that week at West Point. But it turned out to be blown out of all proportion. I interviewed one much-decorated Vietnam veteran who said: "All this upper body strength complaint against women is ridiculous. We've just been through a war in Vietnam and upper body strength did not give us an advantage. We were nearly defeated by four-foot-five North Vietnamese, including women."

The young female cadets were tough. They had to be as they were outnumbered ten to one by sometimes hostile young men. But they were well along in their own evolutionary thinking. The women had been issued regulation uniforms including skirts, which they didn't wear. They wore pants to fit in with the men. But they were getting tired of it. I was talking to them one day and the women said: "We're sick of wearing pants. Why don't we all wear our skirts for the next dress parade." They were saying, "All right, we don't have to be like men. We can be women."

That story really moved me, as did the interviews I had with the women lawyers for *The Second Stage*. They too had gone through the same period as the cadet women, first trying to imitate the men and their jugular-biting style and then getting confident enough to try out their own style. Some of the women lawyers I talked to noted that everyone in their law firms worked late, so they would leave the lights on in their offices, rush home to have dinner with their kids and then return to the office.

I loved stories like that and looked for them. Though no one has done definitive research on it, the questions would be: When you get a critical mass of women in a field, be it law or the military, how do they change the culture, the policy, the practice, to say nothing of the theory? And what should institutions do to incorporate new patterns of professional training and advance that go beyond the male model, not only for women but for men whose wives were now also working?

In *The Second Stage* I laid out what I saw as the necessary changes to keep the momentum of the movement going and to help both men and women reconcile their new freedom with their needs for love, children, family and home: parental leave, flextime, job sharing, part-time and split-shift work, company-sponsored day care and new home designs to permit communal housekeeping and cooking. Without some or all of these adjustments to the new realities, I felt strongly that the very freedoms we had fought for in stage one could end up being the sources of frustration and even bitterness for our daughters.

The Second Stage was published in 1981 and was immediately attacked by some feminists who didn't like what I had written about the movement's self-defeating infighting, male-bashing and preoccupation with sexual politics. I guess the fact that I didn't see men as the enemy but rather as participants in remaking the institutions that were keeping both women and men from living full lives was too heretical for the radicals. But it was exactly those attitudes that were alienating the movement from the mainstream, fueling the rhetoric of our opponents and jeopardizing the ratification of the ERA.

And dammit, we would lose the ERA in 1982. Though every poll showed that a majority of Americans supported the amendment, a handful of legislators in four key states kept blocking it. At one point during the extension, some of the pro-ERA women had a conference, but they didn't invite me to it because I'm so straight. I don't believe in telling lies. And they said at that meeting, "We are not going to get the ERA, but it's such a good organizing issue, let's not admit it." I wouldn't have gone along, I suppose, though in retrospect I'm sure there are some good purposes that one should lie for. Nevertheless, I would fight to the end to get the ERA, which would fall victim ultimately to ideology and the gender gap. Whereas 75 percent of the women legislators in the four key states voted to ratify the ERA, only 46 percent of the male legislators did. And while a majority of Democrats voted for it, 75 percent of Republicans voted against it.

I felt genuine sorrow when the ERA failed. For me, it was not just an organizing issue. Having laws against sex discrimination in employment and education—Titles VII and IX of the Civil Rights Act of 1964—had made a real difference, opening many jobs and even national basketball to women. But laws can be changed. We need equal rights for women written into the Constitution.

In the midst of the battle for the ERA, I bought a house in the old whaling village of Sag Harbor. I had been renting one house after another since the commune broke up—a house in East Hampton which was so unsummery that my friend Susan Wood, a photographer, brought over armsful of colorful sheets she was shooting for a manufacturer's brochure and we covered all the chairs and couches with them and hung them as curtains. That house was known as the House of Sheets. Then I rented another house with a friend, but that didn't work out very well because she had a nervous breakdown. The last house I rented before I started looking for a home of my own was a little guest house in Wainscott next door to my friends the Roses.

I found the house I live in now on the first day I looked. I saw three houses that day (one, a huge corner house down the street that my friends Richard and Kathy Reeves bought a few weeks later) and chose a modest saltbox that had been built by a ship's carpenter in the *Moby-Dick* era. It was bigger than it seemed from the street and sat on one-third of an acre ending in Sag Harbor Cove. Over the years, I would enlarge the kitchen, turn what had been a side stoop into a long dining area and merge a shed to make a writing and sitting area. I also broke through into the attic to make a sleeping loft and created another loft over the kitchen.

Buying the house was one of the smartest things I've ever done. I started going out to Sag Harbor every weekend unless I had something big to do in New York. It became home for me and a favorite hangout for my kids, especially when they started having kids of their own. I can sleep fourteen in the house, with the seven grandkids in the lofts.

Shortly after I bought the house, I got a call from *Newsday*, the Long Island newspaper. "We're doing a feature on Sag Harbor," the reporter said. "How did you know Sag Harbor was going to be 'in'?" "In?" The thought hadn't crossed my mind and frankly, I didn't care. But I was always good at choosing houses and places to live. Sag Harbor had—and still has—a strong sense of community, which I've always thought is very important. Some of my first magazine articles were about houses and community and communal living, as was a portion of *The Second Stage* which I wrote in that house in Sag Harbor.

I also agreed early on to speak at a fund-raising lunch in Sag Harbor in support of the Jermain Library. It was not something I particularly wanted to do—I would rather have accepted a brunch invitation for that Sunday morning in August—but I was new to the community and wanted to become a part of it and I believe in libraries anyway. I hadn't expected to be attacked, however. After the lecture there was a question-and-answer period, and this dame, who was publishing a now defunct newspaper in Sag Harbor and was quite reactionary, waved something in the air and said: "You signed the Humanist Manifesto. How dare you come into this community and preach your ideas of godlessness. Answer yes or no: do you believe in God?" It was absolutely outrageous. Of course I had signed the Humanist Manifesto which Bertrand Russell and his group had issued some years before, calling for peace, social progress and everything any reasonable person would be for. In fact, I had insisted on signing it. They had all these great men signing it and no women, so I'd called them up and said: "How come you don't have any women signing this thing?" No one would dare do that now, of course, but they were totally flustered and said: "Oh dear, oh dear. Well, would you sign it?" and I said yes.

But here was this woman waving it around, saying, "We have a woman here, influencing our children, who doesn't believe in God." I was completely taken aback. But instead of standing on my constitutional right to freedom of religion and my privacy of conscience, I found myself answering: "How dare you question my religion and my belief in God! I am proudly a Jew, and according to my religion, I have lived my whole life in religious terms. In my religion, the Jewish religion, it is your duty to *use* your life to make life better for those who come after us, and I have done that by helping make life better for future generations of women and men as well."

It was an indignant but good response, I think, but this horrible woman didn't let up; not only did she continue to rant and rave about my "godlessness" in her newspaper but to write letters about my dangerous influence on the community to the other, more substantial, local weeklies. I began to get concerned after garbage was thrown on my lawn and downright nervous when I was attacked by a dog. I used to jog around Otter Pond, and one day a woman's dog started chasing me, growling and snapping at my legs. I saw the dog's owner standing on the porch and called out: "Get your dog back. Get your dog on a leash." And she said: "Why don't you go back where you came from?"

That rotten newspaper publisher was inflaming the community against me and I finally called the head of the library. "Look, I was trying to be helpful to you and raise money for the library, and I don't deserve to be treated like this," I told her. "You've got to make her stop." I guess they put some pressure on her and she did finally shut up.

Emily was feeling pressure of a different sort at Harvard, mostly from Carl. She was about to be junior Phi Beta but Carl's hostility remained so intense after the divorce that she couldn't study. When it became clear that she did have an awful lot of intelligence, Carl did nothing but harass her. "What do you want to be? Another Betty?" he'd say to her. It was like he was punishing her for reminding him of me. It was terrible.

Thank God I found a very good woman shrink for Emily in Cambridge. Not only was Carl refusing to pay her tuition but he was telling her things like: "I love you, but you're getting to be a junior Betty and I hate her worse." No good. He'd also started going around with girls Emily's age, which didn't help the situation. The shrink was very helpful in getting Emily through this and back on track. She didn't make junior Phi Beta but she did go on to graduate from Harvard with honors.

While she was still at Harvard, I took Emily to a symposium in Israel where I'd been invited to speak along with David Bazelon, the judge who was married to my cousin, and their granddaughter. Their granddaughter was also named Emily and was about ten years younger than my Emily. So the two Emilys went off together when we were doing our symposium stuff. I also took Emily on a graduation trip to England before she entered Harvard Medical School. We sailed on the *QE2*, where I paid our way by giving a couple of lectures. It was a painless way to sing for your supper and we had a ball. We were sitting at the captain's table and every morning the dining-room steward would ask us if there was something special we wanted for dinner, and of course we always thought of something—baked alaska, caviar, whatever. After dinner we would gamble, but I set a $25 limit so we would never lose too much. There were some students Emily's age on board going over for Fulbrights, so she found some young people to hang out with.

It was not easy to get into Harvard Medical School. Everybody congratulated her and said, "Oh, you're going to do great things for women, like your mother." "Not me," she replied. "I'm not a feminist." After her first year at medical school she was with me in Sag Harbor and she said, "Mom, I have news." "What," I said. "I'm a feminist," she replied. I said, "Really? What happened?" and she said: "One year of Harvard Medical School." The next year she invited me up to Harvard to talk to the medical students.

Emily took a year off in the middle of medical school to do some sort of extern program in New Mexico. The summer before she had worked as a waitress at Bobby Van's, a restaurant in Bridgehampton, and she started having a fling with the Irish chef, which I was not too ecstatic about. Then she went out to New Mexico and he went out to help her drive home and that, to my relief, was the end of it.

We ended up at Harvard together in 1981. I was invited to be a fellow at the Institute of Politics at the John F. Kennedy School of Government for a year and I taught a course I named "Transcending Sexual Politics." Emily was in her last year of medical school and Harvard was her territory, so I had to be very careful not to invade it too much. By then Emily was going around with Eli Farhi, to whom she is now married, who was also at Harvard Medical School and doing a joint program at MIT. I remember distinctly when she started telling me about him, that their initials, EF, are the same, that he had invited her to go to Walden Pond.

There was one very moving moment with Emily I'll never forget. She and I were having dinner at one of the little restaurants around Harvard and we were talking about her plans with Eli and she told me she was worried about leaving me alone. She and I had been in the same boat: neither of us had a steady guy and now here was Eli. "Honey, nothing makes me happier than to see you have some nice guy that you like, and he's even Jewish," I told her. "Having you worry about leaving me alone would be the last thing I would want." I was touched but appalled almost, that she would feel that way.

I took Emily to St. Barts in 1982 during her last vacation from medical school. I figured it was the last vacation she was ever going to take with me. The roads in St. Barts were so perilous I would never have dared to drive myself, but Emily was so competent. For years we had been more pals with each other than mother and daughter and we had a wonderful time. But there is no doubt about it, after she started seeing Eli, I was much more alone in a way.

I had recently broken up with David Manning White, though neither of us wanted to. But it just made me so uncomfortable knowing that his wife knew all about our relationship and even supported it. And reasonably I knew that if I didn't break up with him, I would end up alone anyway. Catherine had cautioned me about that once when we were somewhere together and I'd gone into the ladies' room and she came in after me. "He's never going to leave me," she told me in effect, "and I don't want you to end up alone." It was really quite nice of her to say that. She wasn't saying, "Take your hands off my husband." She liked me. She identified with me. And she was right: I knew that while I was involved with him, I wasn't really looking that hard for somebody else.

I did meet a marvelous man in Ireland, though I only saw him once. I had given a lecture in Dublin to the newly formed Women's Political Association and I met him the next day through Liz Shannon, the wife of the American ambassador to Ireland, Bill Shannon, with whom I was staying. I was immediately taken with David Green, the director of Celtic Studies at Dublin's Institute of Advanced Studies, and he, evidently, with me. David, whose wife had died recently, was a huge man with a huge laugh, a huge intellect and a flowing beard. We bought each other bottles of wine over lunch with Liz and another friend, then had Cognac at his beautiful house overlooking the sea. Liz had to drag me away to pack up and leave Dublin that evening, but David and I made great plans to meet again. As fate would have it, he dropped dead of a heart attack several months later while getting into his car at Dublin Airport.

I had a great crush for a while on Jeremiah Kaplan, an eminent publisher (he was the head of Macmillan) and a friend of David Manning White's. I had met Jeremiah at some publishing do and I'm sure David had told him all about me (that I was a good lay—who knows?). When I told him I'd heard a lot about him, he, with a big twinkle in his eye, said: "Well, I've heard a lot about you." I didn't take up with Jeremiah until after David, of course. I was always very monogamous.

Jeremiah was married too, but his wife had Alzheimer's. It was very sad. He would take her along when we went out to dinner and she would sit at the table and just smile. Finally he had to put her in some kind of a nursing home. Jeremiah and I continued to have this quite wonderful flirtation but we didn't do anything about it for a long time. We just enjoyed each other's company. I remember having some tickets to an opening in New Haven and we drove up and we went somewhere great for lunch and just had a lovely day. I was crazy about him.

I remember one hilarious rendezvous with Jeremiah in California where I lived part-time, teaching at USC, in the late eighties. He was coming out for some sort of board meeting and we made plans to meet at my house and then drive up to Yosemite for the weekend. But we never got there. We went to bed the night before and we were messing around and we'd had too much to drink and he fell out of the bed. I didn't think much about it until he called me up the next day to say the trip to Yosemite was off because he'd broken his toe. "How did you do that?" I asked him. "Do you really want to know?" he said.

I adored Jeremiah, but it never really became an affair because he was on so many beta-blockers. When you go to bed with someone you're crazy about and it doesn't really work, that's pretty devastating to the man. He didn't want to talk about it, so then you don't have this lovely flirtation anymore. In later life, I have not been too eager to have that test with men friends my age or older because if it didn't work, the guy would be so mortified that it would effectively end the relationship. So I learned it was better to have a little edge of a flirtation, but not to test it. I've had this experience several times, but the guys just won't discuss it. I'd tell them it doesn't matter, but of course it does. It's too bad. And it's unfair.

Despite all this stuff about feminism and the ongoing complaint that men have all the power, in some ways we're better off as women. We don't have to get it up. It would be terrible to have that pressure all the time. And it only gets worse with age when sex can become a very iffy proposition.

My involvement with the women's movement was also not exactly good in a sense for my life with men, which continued to interest me a lot. I never felt as alive if I didn't have a man. And I love sex. Still, my high profile could be pretty threatening to men. Only one man, though I can't remember who, ever told me he was tickled by it, that he got a big kick out of it, that he felt proud.

I remember some shrink I was going to when I was younger saying, "Why don't you wear a wig?" That, for some reason, offended me. I wouldn't have disguised myself just to salve a guy's ego, though maybe I should have. Much later, when there were a lot of women in careers and becoming successes, men would take the new sex roles more in stride. But I understood the problems men in my generation had in adjusting. For centuries, women were supposed to reflect the brilliance of their partners, not the other way around. It was a rare man who didn't feel intimidated by the public side of my life.

Jonathan was the first of the children to get married, though I was the last to know about it. My kids had begun to get very annoyed that they kept showing up in magazine articles and newspaper stories and it got so that any time one of them had a family announcement they'd tell me, "and no national media." So if somebody was going to get married or somebody was going to have a baby, I'd be the last to know.

I found out that Jonathan was engaged when I told Emily that Sag Harbor would be a wonderful place for her to get married and she said: "Well, you're going to have a wedding to deal with before that." It turned out that Jonathan and his girlfriend, Helen Nakdimen, had decided to get married. I was delighted.

I tried to figure out how I could have a kosher wedding feast for Helen and Jonathan in Sag Harbor, which wasn't easy. But it was important to Jonathan. A lot of his friends were into Judaism in a big way and Jonathan himself had gotten into Jewish mysticism and gone to Israel with every intention of moving there, though in the end he didn't. He and his friends were part of a whole new wave among the young who were embracing Judaism or Catholicism or whatever religion they were in, a wave that had begun in the sixties after the black movement told the white civil rights activists they weren't needed anymore and to get involved in their own organizations.

I finally worked out a solution with Baron's Cove, a local inn. There was a kitchen in one of the buildings that they would hand over to me and whomever I got to make it kosher after Saturday dinner. The wedding was going to be on Sunday and someone came out from New York to do whatever you do—wands, fire, prayers, whatever—to get it all koshered.

The Reeveses gave me their house down the street for all the in-laws, including Helen, who slept there the night before the wedding, even though she and Jonathan had been living together for ages. But she chose to sleep alone the night before her wedding out of respect for her parents and propriety. She paid an unexpected price: The Reeves didn't know it, but their attic bedroom was full of fleas, and poor old Helen got all bitten up.

I had engaged the little synagogue in Sag Harbor as a precaution if the weather wasn't good, but it turned out to be a beautiful day. Jonathan and Helen got married in our yard in 1981 under the wedding *huppa* we'd built down by the water and then we went to Baron's Cove in a procession for the lunch. It was wild. Their friends carried Jonathan and Helen on their shoulders the half mile or so to the inn and everybody in the wedding party was singing and dancing around them. The neighbors along the route all came out on their porches to gawk, prompting Harold Wit to quip: "I think the pogrom will begin any minute." But they were all smiling and waving.

Three years later, Emily and Eli also got married at the house in Sag Harbor. My daughter, the doctor, was doing her residency in pediatrics at Boston City Hospital by then, and Eli was a cardiologist. Harold Wit had a whole field of wildflowers at his house and the boys went over to collect great armsful of them to build the *huppa* down by the water. It was a very very hot day in June and there wasn't much shade in the yard, but people took refuge where they could find it.

My grandson Rafi, Jonathan and Helen's three-year-old, started off the service. We had kept him with us in the house while the guests and family waited at the *huppa* and when we were ready, we told him: "Go on, Rafi. Run, run, run. Mom and Dad are waiting to give you a kiss down by the flowers." And off he ran to begin the ceremony. Then Martha Stuart's daughter, Sally, played the flute and Carl and I escorted Emily down the lawn. It was a lovely wedding, despite the heat. Afterwards we all went to lunch at a restaurant on the Sag Harbor dock right on the water. Though some of Eli's relatives came from Israel, Emily's wedding didn't have to be strictly kosher.

Danny was too busy being a physicist, I guess, to get married. After getting his Ph.D. in physics at Berkeley, he was a professor at the University of Chicago for a couple of years where he worked on super-string theory. I stopped off to see him whenever I was on my way to give a lecture somewhere in the Midwest and one day, over lunch, I said: "You have to explain super-string theory to me. I'm not dumb. People are asking me what you're working on and I need an answer." Well, he explained it to me, but it didn't do any good. Super-string theory is beyond Einstein. I may be quite intelligent but I simply couldn't keep in my mind whatever it was he told me.

I tried again at Princeton, where Danny went next to do postgraduate work at the Institute for Advanced Study. Also there visiting Danny was Ragnheidur (Agga) Gudmundsdottir, the only woman physicist in Iceland, whom he had met at a physics conference in Sweden. Agga was going to sit in on a seminar he was teaching that afternoon and I told Danny I wanted to go too and hear him in action. "Oh, you won't understand anything and it's embarrassing having my mother come to class," and blah, blah, blah, he told me. "Never mind," I said. "Agga's coming and I'm coming too."

Well, these physicists communicate in mathematical symbols, not English. Danny would write something on the blackboard in mathematese and they'd talk in what seemed like dots and dashes and they all seemed to be communicating, but I couldn't figure it out. You have to be able to think in mathematical terms and I just couldn't. The others could, however, all of them world-class physicists from all over the globe.

You can imagine how proud I was in 1987 when Danny won a MacArthur Award "genius" grant, though I still don't understand the nature of what he won it for. But I know how it felt when a Nobel laureate in physics told me that "in physics circles, you're known as Daniel Friedan's mother." "Lovely," I said. And I was just as happy when Danny and Agga got married in Iceland in 1989 and I inherited Birgitta and Lara, her two lovely daughters from a previous marriage, as my granddaughters. I had my artist friend Sid Solomon paint a welcome sign for them the first time they came to Sag Harbor and I invited all my friends to meet them.

Sag Harbor was also the setting for a weekend seminar on political, economic and social issues I helped convene in the summer of 1987. We were in the torpor of the Reagan years and to my mind, nobody was doing any creative thinking at all. I was particularly bothered by racial inertia. There was, and is, a large population of black middle-class professionals in Sag Harbor—doctors, lawyers, writers, educators—but they kept to themselves and we kept to ourselves and there was no dialogue between us at all.

I'd run into Bill Demby at the post office the summer before and wondered aloud to him why this was so. Bill, an old friend, a writer, professor of English at CUNY and black, said he thought the silence between blacks and whites in the community came from a paralysis of will in the wake of the civil rights movement. So he and I set out to undo that paralysis. The vehicle, which we called the Sag Harbor Initiative, involved intellectuals and thinkers from both communities getting together on the common ground of ideas.

It was a smash success. Here were all these great minds in the community, who would otherwise have spent the weekend playing tennis or going to the beach, gathered in the local high school. Among the panelists on "The Retreat from Equality" were Eleanor Holmes Norton, then a law professor at Georgetown

University; Dr. Kenneth B. Clark, author, professor emeritus of psychology at CCNY and one of the foremost scholars in race relations; and Angier Biddle Duke, a former U.S. ambassador to Spain and Denmark. Other panels—"The Political Process" and "The Intellectual Wasteland"—drew Bob Hirschfield, a professor at CUNY and a former member of our commune; Basil Paterson, a lawyer and former New York secretary of state; Pete Peterson, the former secretary of commerce in the Nixon administration; and the writers E. L. Doctorow, Gail Sheehy, Judith Rossner and Robert Caro, among others.

We got enormous media coverage in *Newsday*, the Long Island newspaper, *The New York Times* and the fledgling cable business. News 12 Long Island televised the sessions, which were then rebroadcast on C-SPAN. Pete Peterson said later that more people told him they'd seen him on television at the Sag Harbor Initiative than during his entire tenure as a member of Nixon's cabinet.

It is disappointing that the Initiative didn't really lead to anything and all those great ideas and panel discussions didn't translate into action, but valuable bonds were forged. I have real friends and neighbors now in the black community, like Bill and Pat Pickens, Doug and Clementine Pugh and, of course, Bill Demby. We get together to support our common causes—and each others' causes. Before the Initiative in 1987, there had been no interaction at all. So on that level alone, the Sag Harbor Initiative did lead to something.

By then I was commuting between Sag Harbor and California, where I had moved part-time to teach in 1986. The next quite turbulent chapter in my life would revolve around the University of Southern California and my book, *The Fountain of Age*, which I finished writing there. I never expected either my work there or the book to be as controversial as they turned out to be.

THIRTEEN

Shattering the Age Mystique

The lunch with gerontologist Bob Butler at the Cosmos Club in Washington had not begun well. It was 1978 and the club, of which I am now a member, did not take women. I had to come in through a side entrance which always annoyed the life out of me. At the Harvard Club and other male emporiums, I would often just march across the forbidden territory and watch them all shudder.

Bob was then head of the National Institute on Aging and had won a Pulitzer Prize for *Why Survive?*, a book about the terrible treatment of older people in this country. He wanted to get me interested in the subject of women and age.

Well, I sure as hell wasn't interested in age. I was fifty-seven then and going strong and still wondering what I wanted to be when I grew up. I used to fret that I didn't have a real career because I really didn't. Well, I was a writer, but I'd do anything not to write, especially about something so depressing. Why was he coming to me? I certainly had no feeling then about getting old or being old. I don't now and I'm seventy-eight. I feel as full of beans now as I did then.

But I got interested in spite of myself when he pointed out that all the theory and policy about age was about men, even though women live eight years longer than men in the United States and make up most of the over-sixty-five population. Bob thought the women's movement should be taking on Social Security and Medicare. I was more interested in asking why he thought women lived so much longer than men. He didn't know. "Our research doesn't really address that question very well," he said. So I told him I'd look into it.

I had always been curious, in fact, as to why women lived so much longer than men in America, because it didn't use to be the case. But even after women stopped dying in childbirth, the gap between the life expectancy of men and women continued to widen. What was the reason for it? And why wasn't anybody studying it? If I were a man, I would want to know what their secret was.

I did some preliminary research at Columbia with a grant from the Ford Foundation and followed up on Bob's list of the few places that were doing research that might shed light on the puzzle, but I was purposefully approaching the subject in a very abstract way. I was getting too close to age myself. When people said: "What is this I hear, that you're doing a book about age?" I'd say, "No, no. I have this hypothesis about changing sex roles and the aging process."

So it was with relief that I put the aging project aside to write *The Second Stage*. I had signed a book contract to do the book on age, however, and when I was offered the fellowship at the Harvard Institute of Politics in 1981, I felt I had to return to the subject. Though I had been offered the fellowship because of my work on women, I was told I could also use all the resources of the university for my own purpose. Great, I thought. I have to master the field and find out what's been done on age before I can really pursue why women live longer than men.

Well, to my amazement, in all this great university Harvard, there was absolutely *nothing* on age. I audited wonderful courses in evolution taught by Stephen Jay Gould and Edward O. Wilson. But only at the medical school did I find something on age, and at that a depressing seminar on the policies and practices of nursing homes. So I tried the theological school, where I thought there might be something on spiritual development in the later years, but the only such seminars were titled "Funeral Services" and "Concepts of the Afterlife." I said to my theologian friend Harvey Cox: "Well, come on. I thought you'd have a cross-cultural course on the value of older people in society or in the church or *some-thing.*" But nothing. I was struck by a sense of *déjà vu* from the early days before the women's movement, when male "experts" on women used to talk authoritatively about "women's problems"—and missed most of what was relevant.

I wanted to look at this new period of life on its own terms. Not many people were doing that. My thought was that this extra one-third of life that so many were now enjoying was or could be a period of continuing growth and contribution to society, but there was no theory, practice or policy. How could there be when the "experts" thought of older people as "them," sick, helpless, senile, incontinent, childlike, dependents? I'll never forget attending a meeting of young whitecoats in the age field, talking about "them," figuratively holding their noses, and discussing the ethics of who turns off the machine and when. There was only one other person there besides me with white hair. That tended to be the case in the field then. "Do you really think it's necessary that 'they' give consent before we turn off the machine?" asked one. It was utterly horrifying to me.

The interviews I was doing with older people—in a retirement hotel and a trailer community in Florida as well as a retirement community in Laguna Hills, California, where my own mother was living—showed a vitality and a new dimension of personhood in age which contradicted the preoccupation of the gerontology profession with gloom. Everything for them was deterioration, decline, Alzheimer's, though I discovered to my surprise at Harvard that only 5 percent of the population over sixty-five suffers from that dread disease. Who was studying the 95 percent who didn't? I'd go to conferences—standing room only—to listen to a lecturer on incontinence. Then way down in the basement there would be a little workshop on creativity in age.

My mother, Miriam, was the perfect example of undiminished zest. She was a real card shark and tootled all over Southern California throughout her eighties running duplicate bridge tournaments. I'm not a bridge player myself, but I know that duplicate bridge requires prodigious feats of memory. One of her friends, a banker, had gone to nursing school in his sixties. "How did other people react to this?" I asked him. "I think there were probably eyebrows raised among my peers," he replied, "but my family was very supportive."

The first time I spoke on the discrepancy in life spans—I gave it some provocative title like "Why Shouldn't Men Live as Long as Women?"—it was at a convention in 1983 in Albuquerque, New Mexico, of what was then called the Western Gerontological Association, and the audience response was very interesting. I'm a good lecturer and I can usually feel a very good feedback and I did get that from those gerontologists in Albuquerque, but there was also something else. Later, in talking to some of the women, they told me that I had made a lot of the men very uncomfortable. "Why?" I asked. "I wasn't carrying any feminist flag in the speech. I was just addressing the question of why shouldn't men live as long as women." And they said: "We just think the way you talk and the feeling you put into it is too real and human. You don't just read a dry, abstract speech, and it makes the men uncomfortable."

As time went on, I began to get to know a few of the key people in the age field who were irreverent and rebellious and they became my underground at these gloomy gerontology conferences. David Guttman at Northwestern told me at one point: "Oh Betty—death is the big thing this year." He charted one conference for me and 90 percent was about nursing homes, debility, decline, dying, senility and maybe about 10 percent about anything at all vital and creative. It was insane, given the longer-length life spans women had already been enjoying for decades.

I was determined to break through the view of age only as deny-at-all-cost deterioration and decline-from-youth-as-peak-of-life to the new years of life that so many Americans were in fact living so well. One of them, a wealthy retired builder in Chicago who had taken to writing a lot of poetry in his later years, gave me the title for the book. I was telling him about the number of older people I'd interviewed who were active and content in their "third age" and not looking for the fountain of youth. Could it be, he mused, that they had found the fountain of age?

I started going through one month of magazines to analyze how the image of women and age was portrayed in the mass media, a variation of what I had done for *The Feminine Mystique*, but I didn't find any images of older women at all! First I listed numbers of women who might be over sixty-five—well, forget it. There'd be one old granny in a rocking chair. Even the ads that were selling rheumatic remedies and showed all the nerves and muscles in a woman's back and shoulders used a model who was no more than thirty. It was such a revelation, the absence of imagery. I kept having to scale back. First I said over sixty-five, then over sixty and then finally over fifty. All you had was Jackie Onassis and Mother Teresa.

The lack of any imagery of women over thirty or forty was my takeoff point for denial of age. In our youth-obsessed culture, corporations were making an incredible amount of money off women on unguents and anti-aging masks, face-lifts, wrinkle lotions—"How to Look Young," "How to Stay Young." At the same time, men with white hair were—and are—seen as powerful. I remember a vivid ad of a man with white hair, very handsome, and he was putting a mink coat over the naked shoulders of a bimbo. At least the image of a wrinkled Clint Eastwood playing an aging Secret Service agent in *In the Line of Fire* was more realistic as he ran, huffing and puffing, alongside the presidential car; his reward, however, at the end of the movie was a twenty-eight-year-old woman FBI agent.

It was no wonder American women were obsessed with denying age and going to such lengths not to look older. Power comes from authenticity, so why shouldn't a woman look her age? I liked it when my hair began to go white around my face. It softened my features. When it went all white, I thought maybe I'd do something daring, like dying it purple or more subtly, the sort of flattering tan color my cousin had turned her hair. But my hair grows so fast the roots would need to be touched up all the time. I think it's perfectly human to wish to look good, so I'm not going to dig myself into a hole on this by swearing I won't ever try coloring my hair. But wanting a new look is one thing. Desperately seeking false youth is another.

Still, the research on aging was so depressing that I dreaded writing the book. Maybe I was secretly afraid of getting older. "I'm not interested in age," I kept saying to myself at the endless conference sessions on "The Problems of Older Women" or "Loneliness." "Why am I doing this?" Then I would go out in the field to interview healthy, vital older people or to a spa like Rancho La Puerta in Tecate, Mexico, and come back energized.

The importance of diet and exercise to health at any age was just beginning to seep into the national consciousness in the early eighties and I became a true believer. It was Shana Alexander, I think, who introduced me to Deborah Szekely, the founding light behind Rancho La Puerta and the Golden Door. Deborah told me she would keep me healthy and fit for years to come if I came to Rancho twice a year, which was easier said than done. It required flying to San Diego and I wasn't going to do that every two minutes.

There was a time, however, when I had a very, very hectic lecture schedule out west so I decided to go to Rancho for a few days, and it was great. There was a different exercise class every hour, wonderful hikes, and fabulous, organic food. The combination of the vegetable diet and the exercise was quite revivifying, which was not only great source material for the book, but for me after I passed the sixty-year mark in 1981. When I got home I joined a gym, started working out on the treadmill and changed my eating habits. The thick, juicy steaks I was raised on in Peoria passed into memory and now I can't remember the last time I ate red meat.

I went to Rancho as often as I could, once with my friend Natalie, another time in 1983 over Christmas with Arthur Dubow. Arthur had just gotten divorced and I urged him to come with me because I knew how hard the holidays are the first time you're alone. He was also too fat and I was worried he was going to have a heart attack if he didn't lose weight. We had a great time, though I'm not sure Arthur lost any weight. I got up early every morning to do the 6:00 a.m. climb up Mount Kuchumaa—even though I was always last, I did it—and I'd get back and there would be Arthur in one of the hot tubs, surrounded by ladies. "Arthur, you're supposed to be exercising," I'd dress him down, but of course he wouldn't budge.

Arthur was also going to use the time at Rancho to give up smoking, but I don't think he managed that either. He was too busy planning the margarita party we decided to throw in our villa on New Year's Eve. We went into town to get the tequila and the guacamole and the chips and laid a fire in the fireplace. The only thing we neglected to do was to check the flue and when we lit the fire, all our guests were smoked out.

One of them was a zesty woman whom I had thought to be

around thirty-three until she'd arrived at Christmas dinner with her children, grandchildren and the "younger man" she was living with. She mentioned an experimental wilderness survival program for people over fifty-five that Outward Bound was going to be trying out for the first time in September. I was immediately interested.

I had always been envious of the people who went on Outward Bound. It was just the sort of wilderness hiking thing I would have loved to do when I was younger, but Carl wasn't that interested. It was so stupid that I never went and did things by myself; we're so socialized to this two-by-two. So when I got the material about the Outward Bound program in the North Carolina mountains, called "Going Beyond—Intensive for Adults 55+," I signed up. I wanted to do it for myself, of course, but I also wanted to be professional about it. I figured that such programs would attract a cross section of the adventurous older people I wanted for my book, not just from the East Coast or the West Coast, but from a wide geographical range. Too many of my interviews were West Coast and East Coast.

I made it fine through the first two days of whitewater rafting, shooting rapids with drops of twelve feet or more. In fact, seven of us in our 55-plus group pulled together so well that our river guides said that we did it better and with fewer casualties than younger groups; they hadn't been called on nearly as much for rescue as they were for the younger people who often fell overboard. Later, when I wrote about Outward Bound, I wondered whether age contributed to an ability to work together or whether it was a lack of competitiveness that made the more mature group different from the macho college kids.

The beginning of the backpacking phase in the mountains, however, was almost the end of the survival course for me. I always overpack in civilian life, though I'm getting a little better, but I could hardly stand up under the weight of my backpack let alone hike up the mountain. I got rid of excess clothing, but I still couldn't carry the pack. I finally had to crawl up the trail on all fours. "Oh well, that's really age," I thought. "I'm not even going to be able to do this. I'll have to quit." The expedition leader came back to check on me and it turned out that the backpack I had didn't fit me. It was hitting me in the wrong places. So he switched me to a backpack that did fit me and I could carry it. It wasn't age at all, which was very important to me.

We did it all, rappelling off cliffs, the twenty-four-hour "solitary" in an unexpected thunderstorm, staving off hypothermia the next night by zipping our wet sleeping bags together to pool our body heat. It was marvelous fun. We knew each other only by our first names, though some of the women recognized me, it turned out later, but I don't think they told anybody while we were out there.

Somewhere climbing up ridges and over the rocks, I became really good friends with this one guy, Earl, a big insurance mucky muck from Charlotte, North Carolina, who had gone to Dartmouth in the late 1930s. Earl was a burly guy who usually led the expeditions for our group and liked to help me through the rough spots. To my surprise, when we revealed our last names and our ages at our last campfire, it was Earl at seventy-two who turned out to be the oldest. So much for decline and deterioration.

Earl and I would remain friends long after Outward Bound. He would come up to New York every year and take me dancing at the Rainbow Room. He was a really good dancer and I love to dance. I had been much too self-conscious in my younger years to be a good dancer, but when I finally grew up, I loved it. Bel Kaufman, who wrote *Up the Down Staircase*, used to give dance parties in New York with her partner Sydney and they were great because one is self-conscious cavorting around in one's later years in a roomful of young people.

But as much as the Outward Bound expedition was exhilarating and reinforced the thesis for my book, it also made me further doubt my ability to write it. We had been camping on top of a mountain on a beautiful moonlit night. Looking at the sky, I suddenly realized I was seeing four moons. I'd gone to the eye doctor before I left and he had told me I might have a cataract and there I was, seeing four moons. I was panicked.

Who was I fooling, extolling the zest and vitality in older people when I was losing my eyesight? Cataract meant old. Cataract meant deterioration. And I wasn't even sixty-five. I dropped the age project when I got back to Sag Harbor, and didn't tell anyone I was having trouble seeing. Driving at night got so hairy, however, that I finally went to the doctor. I would need surgery, he said, for the now confirmed cataract. I was scared. I only have one good eye. The other eye I evidently never use. If I were a child today with that kind of eye condition, they would have found a way to correct it, but they didn't then. So the surgery on my one good eye was a little nerve-wracking.

The first operation was on election day, 1984. I remember standing outside Bloomingdale's in New York with a bullhorn and a bandage over my eye, exhorting people to vote for Mondale for president. Well, that wasn't very successful, nor was the operation. The second one was, however. After a successful lens implant, I saw more clearly than I had in years. It seemed to me that medical advances like that which prolonged and enhanced human functioning were surely part of the fountain of age, and so I returned to my research with new energy and even militancy.

I had come to understand, through my own experience, the panic that trapped those of us who are growing older into clutching at the illusion of physical youth. It took so much effort to hold on to that illusion, to keep the fear of age at bay, to pretend that we are something we are not. The realization came for me when a woman about my age with dyed red hair came up to me in California and said: "I hear you're doing a book about those poor old people. Isn't that nice of you to be doing a book about them." And I said to her: "I'm not doing a book about *them*. I'm doing a book about *us*."

I really got into the book after that, but there were so many distractions in my life that in the end, it would take me more than ten years from that first lunch with Bob Butler to produce *The Fountain of Age*. I was lecturing, teaching, traveling, researching, over-researching for the book, an unfortunate and lifelong habit, in any case doing everything I could to avoid it. That included accepting an invitation in 1983 from the Cambridge Union Society to debate.

I was really looking forward to the trip to England. I had never seen Cambridge or its venerable rival, Oxford, where one of my favorite mystery writers, Dorothy Sayers, set so many of her Lord Peter Wimsey stories. What I had not anticipated was the arrogance and rudeness of Britain's most privileged young men.

The proposition that my debating team and I were asked to

advance was "This house believes that feminism is good for men," but the negatives who preceded me didn't take it seriously at all. It was all just a big joke to them. I can't take feminism as a joke. I can make some jokes about it, but feminism is the serious project of my adult years and it was serious business. So to listen to these fops declaring all feminists to be man-haters who saw men as "nothing more than a set of marauding genitals," or to be told that I was one of the "sad women running away from their radicalism of the sixties" and not worth listening to, made me furious.

I gave them hell. "I accepted your invitation to speak at this male bastion and confront this serious social issue," I said to them. "I can't tell you how more than irritated I am to hear it treated as a joke. It is not a joke." Back and forth we went, me deriding their "foppish humor," they defending their right to be fops. "Madam, you will find that when I'm at my most foppish, I'm expressing my true feelings," said one of the foppiest ones.

Mercifully, I had a strong and good response from the audience, almost half of whom were women. But a debate is judged on win/lose and I was told at the end my side lost. I was slightly chagrined but it wasn't the end of the world. Then suddenly, later that evening, the master of one of the colleges came rushing up to me to tell me there had been an error in tallying the vote and that my team had won. Personally I think some wiser head in the Cambridge hierarchy decided it wasn't good for the university to have the debate on feminism being good for men won by the naysayers. So it all got changed.

The next day I went punting on the river along the "backs" of the colleges and it was beautiful, beautiful, beautiful. But I was really horrified at some of the stories the student women were telling me, such as the boys bringing them their laundry to wash.

Perhaps it was naive of me, but I was amazed by how many people still didn't get it. On another trip of journalists to Nicaragua in 1984—another distraction—Marxist Sandinistas told us proudly that they were providing women with child care, nutrition programs and sewing machines when what the women really needed were literacy programs and job training and computers. Liberation theology and the priests who were practicing it in Nicaragua and other Central American countries really excited me intellectually, but the gray, drab bureaucratic realities of communism in action turned me off, as always. I would have lasted three hours in a Communist regime, with the commissars' condescending and ignorant attitudes toward women.

American politicians were starting to catch on by the 1984 presidential campaign. The gender gap had been confirmed four years before in the Carter-Reagan presidential election when, for the first time in history, women had voted differently from men: 46 percent of women for Reagan compared to 54 percent of men. The midterm elections in 1982 had shown more or less the same gap and the impact of women's political power in state, congressional and gubernatorial races; senators and governors were toppled by women voters.

Walter Mondale was challenging Reagan in 1984 and there was a lot of talk about Mondale selecting a woman as a running mate. I didn't pay that much attention at first. I wasn't interested in a token, symbolic gesture. It was only after I studied the numbers and realized that women were registering in greater numbers than men, voting in greater numbers than men, and far more apt to vote Democratic than men (53% to 47%) that I became convinced that the Democrats' only hope of victory was to run a woman for vice president. So I got involved. Another distraction.

I didn't know Geraldine Ferraro, but on paper, she sounded right. The candidate had to be someone who had held elective office and she was the congresswoman from Queens; she came from a Catholic, working-class background but she was courageous enough to be for choice. I don't think her actions in Congress had been exceptional but they'd been good on pensions for women and she'd voted right on other issues. She was also attractive, married and the mother of three children.

Walter Mondale invited me and a group of twenty-two other women leaders to St. Paul, Minnesota, on the Fourth of July 1984. Ann Richards, the popular treasurer of Texas and a top vote-getter, told Mondale that the women's vote had been decisive in the midterm elections in her state, as did Marlene Johnson, the lieutenant governor of Minnesota, for hers. Women gave secretly to the women Democratic candidates, Marlene said, out of sight of their Republican husbands.

I had great faith in Mondale. He had been an early supporter of the ERA in the Senate and had written the best piece of child care legislation ever seen in this country, only to have it vetoed by Nixon. The Mondales were also personal friends. My friend Harold Wit had helped with Mondale's financial backing from the beginning, and had taken me to their house for dinner. At this Fourth of July meeting in Minnesota, I told him that the women's vote was going to be crucial for him and that the medium was the message. If he had a woman as his vice president, that would really say it, beyond just saying that he was for women's rights and for the ERA, etc. Naming a woman vice president would signal the "new idea" that millions of voters, men as well as women, were yearning for in American politics.

A week later Mondale announced that Geraldine Ferraro was going to be his running mate. My phone never stopped ringing until I left for the Democratic Convention in San Francisco in mid-July where, for the first time, I was no longer a reporter scrambling for press credentials, but a Mondale delegate. I remember being struck by how quickly our revolution had transformed society. Instead of fighting for stronger language on women's rights in the platform as I had for twenty years, I was fighting in the women's caucus to moderate the plank on affirmative action by taking out the divisive word "quotas." And, for the first time, a woman had been nominated by a major political party to run for the second highest position in America.

Mondale would lose, of course. But he was a very good guy and I've never been sorry I supported him. Ferraro's breakthrough candidacy would pave the way for other women in high office. Would Madeleine Albright be secretary of state today without Ferraro's pioneering role? Would Elizabeth Dole have made a serious run for the presidency in 2000 or Hillary Rodham Clinton for the Senate in New York? I doubt it. Ferraro was a vital part of the evolutionary role of women as leaders in the nation's consciousness, who would be judged not on their gender but on their merits.

That was not the case in Israel in that same summer. I was one of the keynote speakers at a dialogue on women's rights. I had no interest at first in going to yet another meeting on women's status. I had moved on to other issues and interests, but this was yet another welcome distraction from my book. The

American Jewish Congress asked me to co-chair its Commission on the Status of Women in 1984 and wanted me to go to Israel. I agreed on the condition that the sessions would not be restricted to legalistic women's rights matters, but would include a dialogue about feminism and Jewish "survival." I gave them the title "Woman as Jew, Jew as Woman."

I had never considered myself religious. I am the daughter of a secular city, of the generation that witnessed the Holocaust to ask: "Is God dead?" For me as for other Jewish feminists, religion perpetuated the patriarchal tradition that denied women access to Judaism's most sacred rituals and enshrined them within the strict confines of their biological role. The Judeo-Christian religion kept alive that feminine mystique which was at the heart of the problem.

It took the confidence born of the women's movement for me and other Jewish feminists to embrace our Jewishness, but in a new way. We took on the task of making Judaism accept that women are equal to men in the sight of our God. It was a daunting task in light of the familiar men's prayer, *"Blessed are you God, our Lord, King of the universe, who has not made me a woman,"* and the woman's prayer, *"Blessed is the Lord, King of the universe, who made me according to your will."* Advancing women's equality turned out to be as daunting in Israel.

The religious right was steadily gaining political power in Israel and in direct proportion came an erosion of women's rights. With no separation of church and state to protect women from the determined, anti-feminist attacks of the Orthodox religious leaders, young women were being excluded from a state-supported system of religious high schools, and the fundamentalists were pushing to establish separate schools for boys and girls at all levels.

The Orthodox rabbinate was exerting control of women's lives through Israel's all-male religious courts, which dictate the terms of marriage, divorce and many other aspects of a woman's personal life. Under religious law, men cannot be divorced against their will while women can. And the Halakic laws, supposedly God-ordained, could only be interpreted by the rabbis. Women could not even appear as witnesses before these religious courts, nor serve as lawyers or judges.

I listened carefully at the conference to the women's frustration over the monolithic religious tradition, backed by the state, which decreed the rigidly separate, unequal male and female roles in the family—the women stayed home and had babies and the men prayed, studied and fought wars. Few women had careers. Most worked part-time in low-paying, low-status jobs and were excluded, according to Yael Dayan, a writer and the daughter of the Israeli general Moshe Dayan, "from all positions of power in the society, the military, the political parties, the university, the Government."

And it stood to get worse. As we were meeting, a new coalition government was being formed by Shimon Peres, the Labor Party leader, and Yitzhak Shamir of Likud. Who knew what women's rights were being bargained away to gain the support of the religious political parties? Yet the women, who unanimously passed a resolution decrying the potential losses, were timid about mounting a public protest. So I suggested they march to deliver the resolution.

The women moved through the streets of Jerusalem to the King David Hotel, where the negotiations were going on, and with mounting confidence insisted on meeting with the closeted leaders. Their aides said no, of course, but as the television cameras whirred, both Peres and Shamir did come out to talk with them. What a sense of empowerment the Israeli feminists must have felt, that same sense of collective confidence we had felt during the march in New York in 1970.

There would be no further giveaway of women's rights in the coalition government that was formed under Shimon Peres, and for the first time, the Knesset would take up the issue of women's equality. The American Jewish Congress would set a goal of full equality for women and set up a permanent network of Jewish women across political, religious and national lines, uniting American Jewish women with their sisters in Israel.

Egypt was another matter—and another distraction. Jehan Sadat had invited me to visit her on my way home from Israel and I spent a few days with her at her summer home in Alexandria. We spent a lot of time eating mangoes and walking around the grounds of her government villa, talking about our grandchildren. But we also talked about the religious backlash against women in Egypt. Women had made great progress during the presidency of Anwar Sadat, Jehan's late husband, but the same forces of fundamentalism, Muslim this time, were trying to undo it. Where Jehan had insisted on her photograph being shown in the media to support her causes—she took her oral examination for her Ph.D. on live television to promote education for women—Hosni Mubarak, the current president, had ordered newspapers not to carry any pictures of his wife or report on her activities.

The "fanatics," as Jehan and her friends called the fundamentalists, were trying to overturn the divorce laws Jehan had fought for as first lady which merely required a husband to tell his wife if he were divorcing her or taking another wife and gave her a claim to the family home if she had small children. As I flew back to New York, I thought about the similarities between Israel's religious courts and the fundamentalist forces in Egypt. Thank God, I thought, for the sense of our founding fathers who made a clear separation between church and state in our Constitution.

But the religious right was playing a noisy and organized role in the Mondale-Ferraro campaign, using abortion as a rallying cry. Hecklers carrying identical "Abortion Is Murder" signs followed Ferraro everywhere while Catholic priests and archbishops denounced her from their pulpits. Even the supposedly secular president of the United States, Ronald Reagan, and his supposedly secular Republican Party, were calling for prayer in public schools and insisting that all future judicial appointees oppose abortion. No country, no society, was immune to the threat women posed to the patriarchal tradition and power embodied in organized religion, be it centered in the White House, synagogue, mosque or cathedral.

Yet there was a curious passivity to the backlash among women who should have known better. Instead of mobilizing protests at the steady erosion of women's rights in Reagan's America—the Attorney General's announcement that he would seek to reverse the twelve-year-old *Roe v. Wade* decision legalizing a woman's right to abortion; the elimination of federal aid to poor women seeking abortions and to Third World family planning clinics which offered abortion counseling; the move by administration officials to nullify the executive order we'd won twenty years before banning government contracts to companies or institutions guilty of sex discrimination; the administration's move to legally undo equal pay for work of comparable value—the women's movement was imploding in internal power struggles and sexual diversions. Instead of tackling the issues that affected most women's lives, the movement was obsessed with banning pornography. The failure to mobilize the next generation to confront new threats and problems with new thinking was extremely frustrating to me. I had been too passionately involved in the movement to watch it go quietly into the night. So, despite my desire to move on to other things, I kept getting drawn back into it.

I went to Nairobi in 1985 for the UN-sponsored Third World Conference on International Women with more of a sense of duty than anticipation. Bella went too, both of us sent by the American Jewish Congress. The movement was so dispirited at home that there were very few other card-carrying American feminists in Kenya. NOW had even scheduled its own convention in New Orleans for the same time, as if the United Nations was irrelevant to women.

We expected a lot of trouble in Nairobi, after the earlier UN conferences in Mexico City and Copenhagen. A lot of countries did not want their women infected with power feminism and would do anything to get us off the track, anything to keep us from getting together and talking about women's rights. Having been through this for a while, we knew who was behind it. There were powerful elements in the Catholic Church that did not want women to get together on their right to control their own bodies and their reproductive systems. There were economic issues. In many parts of the world, women were either cheap or virtually slave labor.

Nearly 17,000 women from 159 nations came to Nairobi for the ten-day conference, the vast majority, like us, to attend the unofficial forum, "Forum 85," the rest as official delegates. Bella and I were determined this time to keep people from messing up the conference and using the burgeoning international women's movement for other political agendas. The Reagan administration had instructed the official U.S. delegation, led by Maureen Reagan, to walk out if the question of Zionism was included in the conclusions reached at Nairobi and we certainly didn't want that. Bella and I saw eye to eye on all this. She was a stormy person as am I, but we made a terrific team when we fought together as we did on issues like this. We went around warning key women leaders that irrelevant issues like Zionism would be used to divert us and not to let that happen.

A wonderful woman from Jamaica was going to preside over the conference and we talked about how I could be useful and we got the idea that like the elder of a tribe, I'd sit under a tree at noon every day and women who wanted to could come and discuss the issues of importance to them in their respective cultures. It was also a way of keeping tabs on what the temperature was at the conference and, if the focus was getting all wrong or disruptive, to get it back on track. We were determined to have a dialogue on the real problems and concerns of women which, at the prior conference, all the missions with male delegates or floozies or flunkies of the male politicians were not in the least interested in.

The circle under the tree worked beautifully. The word got around and a lot of people came to my baobab tree—Third World revolutionaries, Arab and Israeli women, Japanese, Greek, Latin and wonderful African women, many of whom had traveled to Nairobi by bus from their villages. It wasn't me lecturing or anything like that. I would just lead the discussion on "Future Directions of Feminism" and go where the women there wanted.

The "party line" had always been to respect the traditions of other cultures about women and not to force Western ideas of equality on them. I bought respecting cultures. And I bought that the conditions of women's various societies would dictate what issues were important for them. For some, literacy was important, not abortion. But in discussions with women under the tree, I began to wrestle very hard theoretically and personally with the idea that you should respect the cultural traditions that keep women shrouded and invisible in *chadors* or mutilate women sexually, like the clitoridectomy, so they would never have sexual enjoyment in their lives. No. I thought there were certain absolute things that under no culture would you respect. Would you respect slavery? Certain things in women's lives have to be absolute and under no culture should you respect the mutilation of young girls.

There were big arguments about the *chador* as well. I was always amused when I was in Iran or other ultra-conservative Muslim countries to see sophisticated women wearing *chadors* and underneath designer jeans, painted toenails inside their sandals. I suppose the *chador* was a good organizing tool to mask their radicalism. But the shrouding of women is a denial of the personhood of the women. I was not going to say I respected the culture and the custom that denies a woman's existence by not allowing her to be seen in public or walk openly in the street. There are certain rights of women that do have to be absolute and I didn't hesitate to say so. No one can condone any practice of any society that mutilates women or denies their personhood. It seemed hypocritical and condescending for educated women who really believed in the rights of women to wear the *chador*. It went against my grain.

We shared many more concrete concerns under the tree: How to move ahead and earn a living in a man's world without losing one's best values and strengths as women; how to advance women's rights when our governments were preoccupied with conflicts like that between the Arabs and Israelis or, among the superpowers, the nuclear arms race that was draining their resources; how to progress, even underground, in the midst of the spread of fundamentalism.

Our tree itself became the point of a skirmish with the forces of fundamentalism. When we arrived for our noon dialogue one day, we found the baobab occupied by veiled and shrouded Muslim extremists and their armed male guards. We moved to another tree. When we returned the next day, we found the extremists had occupied *both* trees. So we had our dialogue in the sun. The global lesson learned was not to waste our energies but to regroup and press on.

To my amazement, the women's movement emerged in Nairobi with sufficient strength to impose its own agenda of women's concerns over the male political agenda that had divided the world conference twice before. The delegates at the official UN conference reached consensus on a forward-looking program with global strategies to advance women to equality, and this time, managed to squelch the attempts by the Arab and Communist countries to include their "anti-imperialism" and "anti-Zionism" rhetoric. It was a stunning victory for the women of the world.

Kathy Hendricks was in Nairobi covering the conference for the *Los Angeles Times* and both our tickets back were for a few days after the conference ended, so we went on a safari. We saw a lion defecate or maybe it was copulate, probably both. But we got to the point that after you've seen one wild animal you've seen them all. It didn't thrill me all that much. I had been thrilled much more at the UN conference to see women on the move all over the world in their different ways, with their different strengths.

I came home strengthened myself by the progress and resolve of the women from so many different countries and cultures in Nairobi, but sobered by the stalemate and even setbacks to the women's movement in America. It was truly humiliating to realize that we were no longer the cutting edge of modern feminism or world progress toward equality. Even Kenya had an equal rights clause in its constitution.

I wrote a long article about the paralysis of the American women's movement for *The New York Times* a few months later, titled "How to Get the Women's Movement Moving Again." It had been five years since I'd warned that if the women's movement didn't move into a second stage and take on the problems of restructuring work and home, a new generation would be disillusioned and vulnerable to backlash. And that's exactly what was happening.

The "post-feminist generation," as young women were being called, was struggling with new problems and pressures. Many women I talked to were having second thoughts about their time-intensive professional careers, trying to have babies before it was too late, with or without husbands, fighting exhaustion being "superwomen" and "supermoms." But because the movement had not moved into that vital second stage, the women struggling with these new problems viewed them as purely personal, not political, and no longer looked to the movement for solutions.

No wonder the movement had stalled. "Feminism" was becoming a dirty word because so many of this supposedly "post-feminist" generation felt they had been sold a bill of goods by the women's movement and then abandoned. Instead of mobilizing young women to press for child care and flexible work hours, equal pay for work of comparable value, and equal Social Security and pensions for the women who chose to take care of their children and homes themselves, and to confront the growing feminization of poverty following divorce, the movement's energies were being diluted by fighting sexual issues like pornography.

I had my own battles to fight in Southern California, where I moved part-time in 1986 partially to continue my work on aging as a visiting scholar for the Andrus Gerontology Center at the University of Southern California, but primarily to get out of New York. My asthma had got much worse in the winter in New York and my doctor advised me to spend the winter in a warmer climate. So I sublet my apartment and went west. Though I was never crazy about California, I would spend the next seven, often stormy, winters there, with more distractions than ever.

As soon as I arrived, I was approached by women at USC's Institute for the Study of Women and Men in Society to help raise money. I liked the name of the institute because it included men, but it turned out they had used "men" in the title as a concession to get women's studies into USC. The women at the institute wanted to use me to lure rich Los Angeles women to give money to their women's studies program, but I made it clear that I wasn't going to raise money for something I wasn't going to be involved in. "You can't just use me as a beauty contest to raise money," I told them. "If I'm going to do something for you, then I want to be seriously involved. There are a lot of high-powered women in a lot of fields now in California. Why don't we get them together, not just to raise money for your program but for some serious discussion."

The truth was I wasn't much interested in women's studies per se, which in my mind ghettoized and marginalized women. I wanted to do a study of sex roles and get men involved. I've always felt that the roles that traditionally defined men and women restricted the evolution and growth of both sexes and were injurious to personal development, marriages, family—all of it. I've changed my mind in the sense that I now think women's studies made a very valuable contribution, and was and is important, but I was more interested then in seeing studies of both sex roles.

The series of seminars I proposed would be yet another distraction from my project on aging, but I was really interested in starting the kind of program where you bring together the academics who were teaching women's studies and supposedly feminist theory with women who were actually living the new role of empowerment in the political, professional and business worlds in Hollywood and Los Angeles. Together, we would discuss what new questions to ask about the new equality and how it was playing out among women, men, family, work and public policy, a dynamic I'm still working on today. My mission was to make feminist thought keep *evolving*. Any "ism" can get stuck in orthodoxy and I saw that happening. The last thing you wanted was feminism hardening into dogma.

Thirty-five to forty people came to the first meeting of the Betty Friedan Think Tank, as it became known—professors, students, community leaders, entertainers, political people. Over the seven years of its existence, all kinds of high-powered people would get involved with the think tank—my friend Marilyn Bergman, an eminent movie and TV director who did a lot of Barbra Streisand stuff and would be the first woman president of ASCAP (the American Society of Composers, Authors and Publishers); Laura Geller, who is now the rabbi of the biggest synagogue in Beverly Hills; and Judy Resnik, a brilliant law professor who is now at Yale.

The key person in the think tank was Diana Meehan, the director of the Institute for the Study of Women and Men in Society, who funded the monthly seminars. Diana, who had gotten her Ph.D. and done work on the image of women in television, was married to Gary David Goldberg, the director who had launched Michael J. Fox in the television series *Family Ties.*

Our first discussion in the think tank involved a lawsuit in California against the state for its law requiring employers to grant a new mother up to four months unpaid disability leave as well as job security. The case involved a woman who'd worked as a cashier at California Federal Savings & Loan, had a baby and wanted her job back. But the forces who wanted to prevent maternal leave and job security for women sued the state of California, claiming discrimination against men. The case was heading toward the U.S. Supreme Court and I told the think tank that we had to explore and do the conceptual work necessary to arrive at a theory of equality that accepts and affirms differences between the sexes.

We took up this case and we formulated a very important doctrine: that you couldn't have a model of equality or law that is based solely on the male body. Pregnancy is a temporary disability even though men don't get pregnant just as a prostate operation is a disability even though women don't have prostates. This wasn't a special protection for pregnancy. This was merely a fact of life for women. Ramona Ripsten, head of the ACLU, wrote an amicus brief for the court expounding the proposition that equality for women had to affirm the differences between men and women, and we signed it. It was very important to start raising these questions and thinking about public policy.

I remember standing next to Chief Justice Burger after Marie Ritter's Gridiron lunch while we were waiting for our cars and saying, "Mr. Justice, I suppose this isn't the time to discuss it, but pregnancy *is* a disability, a creative disability," and he had laughed. But women are the people that give birth to children, and if pregnancy leave was seen as discrimination against men, then there could be no such thing as equal opportunity. What I was trying to develop in the think tank was a real awareness that laws and policies couldn't be based solely in terms of the male model. You had to go beyond it. It couldn't just be equal pay for equal work if women didn't have equal jobs. There had to be structural changes and models of employment that were not just based on the lives of men. And that's how my think tank began in the state of California.

I went to the Supreme Court for the hearing of *California Federal Savings and Loan v. Guerra* in 1987. It was the first time I'd been there since the Court heard *Roe v. Wade* in 1973 and this time marked another significant victory for women's rights. Using our reasoning in its ruling, the Court wrote that maternal leave and job security for women were not sex discrimination against men and affirmed the right of women to have a child and come back to work at the same job. When we got back to Los Angeles, a flood of television cameras heralded our triumph.

The think tank took up other legal cases, like one about pornography in firehouses, and other issues that made it uncomfortable for women in the workplace as well as more personal issues like surrogate motherhood. Women having surrogates carry their babies for them was, in fact, the biggest fight we had in the think tank. Some women felt absolutely that it meant a two-tiered society, that women who were rich could afford to pay someone so they wouldn't have to get fat; others felt just as strongly that liberated women should have the right to do whatever they wanted with their bodies. That was a very lively session. Frankly, I did see the issue as cutting edge. I could visualize my granddaughter marching for the right to carry her own baby in her belly.

I would choose one general theme for the think tank to focus on each year and send out reading material before the meetings so people would be informed about the subject at hand. One of the articles in one advance packet when we were discussing relationships was something ridiculous by Andrea Dworkin from the *New York Times Magazine*. Andrea believed that any sexual penetration was rape.

Barbra Streisand came to one of those sessions on relationships. I remember her saying in her little voice: "I'm Barbra Streisand and I'm interested in what happens to relationships when women have power." No one was as powerful as Barbra, but a lot of the women in the room, including me, could relate to her to some degree. When a woman is perceived as a powerful person—and *is* a powerful person in her orbit—she sometimes becomes threatening to men and women. Barbra is a fine person and a feminist, and I was always trying to get her to issue a statement or speak out on some big battle, but she is very shy. The idea that she would talk and not just read a written statement must have scared the life out of her. Marilyn Bergman, who was also founder of the Hollywood Women's Political Committee, always said that Barbra would lend her name to a cause but she was just very nervous about speaking. I found that hard to believe, but there it was.

When *Yentl* was released in 1983, there was a study group about Jewish lore and the Talmud at Barbra's house. The study group continued for a bit and I joined it. It was great fun. The think tank also did something once at Barbra's house—one of her houses I should say—and it was amazing. My God, she had so many styles, like every room was decorated in a different period.

I was getting increasingly annoyed with the women's studies people. I never could bear politically correct feminist party lines and some of these people were not only completely P.C., but got to approve each new subject for the think tank. One year I wanted to focus on love and call it "Love, Marriage and Other Forms of Intimate Bonding," and they said, "Love? With whom? Intimate bonding? With whom?" You know, like, *men?*

I got so fed up at this ridiculousness that I swore that if the overall atmosphere at the women's studies institute didn't improve, I was going to quit. It was outrageous to question the value of heterosexual relationships. Even if marriage had been oversold and even if motherhood had a mystique to it, they were and are values that go beyond the feminine mystique. It amused but also annoyed me when women I knew in perfectly good, happy heterosexual relationships would parrot that anti-male, anti-sex line.

I understood the depth of anger in women, which they had every reason to feel and had suppressed for generations, at being put down in society and even on the pedestal at home. But that anger was now out and it seemed to me that the more we moved to change the situation, the less angry at men we would be. I certainly experienced that in myself.

So we went ahead and had our think tank sessions on "Love, Marriage and Other Forms of Intimate Bonding," which turned out to be fascinating. We had women who were straight and involved in heterosexual relationships and women who were gay and involved in homosexual relationships and we all discussed the basic principles of relationships and how they evolve and what the new questions were when women were really moving into positions of equality. It really interested and amused me, I guess, when people who were straight and people who were gay compared notes and found that lesbian relationships often took the same patterns as obsolete, traditional male/female ones.

But I really began to take a mounting aversion to women's studies at USC.

Diana Meehan was so enthusiastic about the think tank that she wanted to give a lot of money to endow a professorship for me and make the think tank permanent, but the women's studies people would have none of it. Not only were they so P.C., they were also negative and quite insulting both to me and to Diana, who had given a lot of money to them and would have given much more. In retrospect, I think they just wanted me to go away because my course was evolving and diverging from party-line feminism.

When it became clear to me—or the women's studies people made clear to me—that my think tank wasn't exactly welcome in their department, Warren Bennis invited me to have it under the auspices of the Harvard Business School.

Warren ran the Leadership Institute and he was sympathetic to the troubles I was having with the politically correct. He was extremely generous. He told me I could just work on my book and run the think tank, but I told him I wasn't going to take the money from the business school—I had to teach a course. So I dreamed up a course—"Women, Men and Management"—and joined forces with a hot-shot beautiful woman on the school faculty, the only woman at that time.

I was always very careful to work with other women academics. There were so few women on these faculties, especially business school faculties, and I was not going to be used to disguise that fact or get in the way of any woman who was there.

I liked teaching at the business school, which I would do again in the fall at NYU in New York, because I felt that business and the corporate world was where the new equality was happening and had to happen. It wasn't just academic theory but was actually taking place. In fact, the corporate world was a very good laboratory for me. I loved it when I was asked to come in and talk or be a consultant at corporations like J. Walter Thompson or Xerox or the telephone company or 3M in Minnesota. I loved dealing with the real. I was never interested in just abstract theory.

I dealt with the real as well in a course I taught at USC's journalism school. The course had been called "Women in Newspapers" when Jack Langguth, my great friend and a professor of journalism, first brought me into the school, but I changed it to "Women, Men and Media." I brought in women from the *Los Angeles Times*, magazine editors, women directors, producers and screenwriters from movies and television and we would all analyze the representation of women in the media, both the image and the reality of who was making the image. It was a really good course.

Jack kept encouraging me to call a national conference on Women, Men and Media. The journalism school had had a very successful conference on the coverage of the Vietnam War. He took me to Felix Gutierrez in the journalism department and the two of them took me to see the guys at the Gannett Foundation who agreed to underwrite the national conference. (Felix is now one of the top people at the Freedom Forum, which had been the Gannett Foundation.)

I did some inquiring around to see which publisher had been best on women and it turned out to be Al Neuharth, a wonderful, flamboyant guy at *USA Today* who had a terrific record of hiring and promoting women. Al couldn't work on the conference with me because he was going on a round-the-world retirement trip, but he promised he would send me someone. I thought he'd send me some token woman, but he sent me Nancy Woodhull, and no token woman she. Nancy, a founding editor of *USA Today*, and I became natural partners and a very good team.

We put together a three-day seminar in 1988 on women as they were projected in the news media and the actual participation of women in the news-gathering process. It was so successful—and so revealing—that Nancy and I simultaneously got the idea to continue "Women, Men and Media" as an ongoing, monitoring enterprise called "Betty Friedan's Media Watch" to keep tabs on what was happening. The representation of women in the mass media has always been a very important Rorschach test that both reflects and influences the situation of women in America.

Every year we published a study which started out very crudely: we took one month and just counted the number of times women had bylines or were mentioned, quoted or pictured on the front page of ten major papers around the country. Well, you couldn't believe how low it was. Though women formed 51 or 52 percent of the population, they represented something like 10 percent of the people quoted on the front page, and were pictured in fewer than a quarter of front-page photographs and at that, usually as the wife of. Our first study in 1989 found that *The New*

York Times was the worst newspaper of all. Women were amazingly absent from any depiction on the front page.

We would release these studies every year to various organizations and the press, and Nancy got the idea that we should send advance copies to the newspaper publishers for their comments just before the annual convention of ANPA, the American Newspaper Publishers Association. Max Frankel was then editor of *The New York Times* and he not only disparaged the study methods as "bizarre and unworthy" and our findings as "bean counting" but remarked: "Well, if we had front page coverage of tea parties, then women would be on the front page." This so outraged the women who worked at the *Times* that the next day they wore tea bags to work on their lapels. Max really did have a bit of a blind spot about women. Can you imagine him saying, "If *The New York Times* ran a story about watermelons, then there would be blacks on the front page"?

The New York Times was not alone in relegating women to invisibility and symbolic annihilation. We looked at television network newscasts in 1989 and found that women were the subjects or focus of interviews fewer than 15 percent of the time—NBC was the worst at 8.9 percent. Stereotypes would persist. Our February 1991 report during the Gulf War found that the vast majority of stories were about military men—their jobs, their weaponry and their opinions—while the few stories about military women centered on their heartache at leaving their families. There was not one article or editorial during the entire month on the impact on a father of leaving his children to go to war.

There's no doubt, however, that our annual media reports not only raised consciousness but had an effect. I remember people at Knight-Ridder telling me that after a few years of our watchdogging enterprise they began to be very conscious as they made up the front page. All kinds of people asked for our studies and began to do their own versions of them, which I thought was wonderful. When we went to Beijing in 1995 for another UN conference on the status of women, our studies would precede us and be applied to the Chinese newspapers.

For all that I was involved in interesting work in California as well as endlessly researching the book, I missed home. I was never crazy about Los Angeles, mostly because I won't drive on the terrifying freeways. I'd sublet an apartment in Santa Monica or Venice where I could walk to a lot of things, but I didn't feel my life was under my own control. I never felt permanent enough about LA, so I lived each year in a different place.

I remember one sublet where you went down a cliff in a glass elevator overlooking the beach; it was owned by a friend who sold it for big bucks to some Japanese. Another year I lived in Santa Monica near the old mall. But I didn't like it that much. There was no sense of community in Los Angeles, no "there" there such as in Sag Harbor or even in New York City. I like being part of a community and I don't like a culture based on the automobile where everybody has to drive miles. I like a little dense community like Cambridge or Sag Harbor, or even New York where you live on the West Side or you live in the Village or you live in SoHo. They are all concentrated communities and that's what I like.

Of course I had friends in Los Angeles and I made new ones, like Jack Langguth at the journalism school. I also had Norman Lear. Norman would show movies at his house on Sunday nights, and a lot of us would go for the pre-dinner movie followed by the after-dinner movie. So California certainly wasn't all bad. It just wasn't home.

I commuted back and forth from Los Angeles to Sag Harbor or New York, if my apartment wasn't sublet. I'd been working on the age project for eight years by the late eighties and every year I'd send the mounting boxes of research back and forth. There were not only all the distractions delaying the book, but I'm a compulsive researcher.

I went to the Pritikin Longevity Center in Miami Beach in 1988 because it fit in with the book and I wanted to do it personally. Pritikin had one of the few programs that wasn't just cosmetic but really assumed there could be vitality in age. That had a real effect on me, personally. My cholesterol and blood pressure were borderline and in those years, I was always needing to lose weight. In just two weeks at Pritikin I lost ten pounds and dramatically lowered my cholesterol and blood pressure by following the center's combination of a no-fat diet and exercise. I looked really good and I felt good and it got me started. I would jog for forty-five minutes or do the treadmill.

Again, I thought I'd find an interesting cross section of people at Pritikin who were tuned in, who wanted to be vital in age. Which I did. I interviewed guys at Pritikin who had been at death's door and had really been given up and were being brought back to life. And I interviewed women whose health and well-being were also improving rapidly. In the process, I found a pattern that was consistent with all the research I'd been doing. Whereas most of the men at Pritikin had already suffered heart attacks or other life-threatening conditions before coming to the center, the women were there to prevent such conditions. The women, many of whom had seen their husbands' health deteriorate, were, like me, taking new charge of their own aging.

While I never would find out definitively why women live longer than men, it was exactly that hypothesis that was guiding and instructing my research. One of my theories was that women aren't brought up to be men and therefore are not instructed or expected to "tough out" aches and pains, let alone illnesses, to be "manly." Another theory of mine was that women are more sensitive to the things going on in their own bodies because they are more sensitive to reproduction and survival. Women may go to doctors more and seem to be sick more, but often it is that sensitivity and lack of macho that contributes to their appreciably longer life span.

It was after I began to do interviewing on that path and began to be asked to do lectures on that path that I posited these questions of mine on the heretofore unspoken assumption that age didn't have to be just a period of deterioration and decline, that there could even be new growth and development. To my amazement, I discovered that such an assumption was very threatening, even to the experts on age. I became aware of what I called an "age mystique" that was as powerful as the feminine mystique and was almost harder to pin down and break through—this definition of age only in terms of a programmed deterioration from youth as the peak.

All my research was showing that in age as in youth the important things are work and love. Not surprisingly, the longest-lived people were in professions in which there was no forced retirement, among them symphony conductors, Supreme Court justices, artists and rabbis. It was clear why symphony conductors tend to live so long—their work involves physical activity as well as continual mental activity; Supreme Court justices, while not physically challenged, are continually challenged mentally by new cases which reflect an ever-changing society, plus the fact that they have an ongoing social structure and remain a meaningful part of the community; rabbis the same, though I don't really know why rabbis should live longer than other men of the cloth. As for love, all these long-lived groups have the support of family or people that take the place of family along with the continued challenge of their work.

I'm sure that's why my mother lived as long and as vitally as she did. Though there are no studies on longevity and contract bridge players, at eighty-seven she was still running all these duplicate bridge games. In fact, all the duplicate bridge people I interviewed for *The Fountain of Age* were so active that I figured that duplicate bridge, just like the Supreme Court, gave structure to their lives and new things to continually master in terms of memory. The constant mental stimulation kept them—and my mother—going in a very active way.

I would go visit my mother at Leisure World, the senior community she was living in in Southern California, and the first thing she'd always ask me was, "How's your love life?" She would have liked to go on a cruise, to meet some men, or whatever, instead of being at Leisure World, but she'd lived there for almost twenty years and had friends and activities there. She ran the duplicate bridge tournaments, walked every day and tootled around in her car. She was a very dynamic woman and always doing something new; her grandchildren got her interested in ecological vegetarianism and she knew a lot about it.

When all that activity was taken away from her, my mother died. She'd had a couple of accidents in her late eighties—a broken leg, a broken hip—but she'd made a remarkable recovery and got around quite well with a cane. It all began to go downhill when a young doctor said she had too much stress—I think she was having back pains or something—and that she should quit running the duplicate bridge games. That, to me, was a great mistake. When he told her that she should resign, he took away an enormous part of the framework that sustained her life, that gave her a viable structure.

Things started going wrong after that at Leisure World. She had her wits about her, but she let the bathtub overflow a few times and she began to skip meals and the consensus was that she couldn't stay on living there alone. There was no one in the family who could have lived with her there, so we really had no alternative but to move her. One of her granddaughters, my brother Harry's daughter, Nancy, was a social worker and was quite close to her. She found a good nursing home in Milwaukee. So we moved her there.

I had an absolute aversion to nursing homes. I really thought they were terrible places and so did my mother. Later, when I finished writing *The Fountain of Age,* I thought I might have found some alternatives, some living setup where she might have been able to stay in California with her friends. But there was nothing that I knew to do about it then. I took a lecture in the Midwest so I could go see her at this place and it utterly depressed me as it must have her. "Mother, have you found someone to play bridge with?" I asked her. But my mother was a real snob: "Oh darling, please, with these people?" she said. There were no bridge players in that nursing home. She was reduced to playing Bingo.

I was at USC in 1988 when I got the call that my mother had died. She didn't have a heart attack or a stroke. My mother died, I think, because she just was not going to live in that setting any longer. I think she simply decided to hell with it. I really do. On the other hand, she was ninety when she died, and she'd lived a good life, given her possibilities.

I had come to some sort of peace with my mother in our later years. I greatly admired her courage and her determined energy to live well right up to the moment that the structure was taken away from her. Even her doctor admitted to me later after reading *The Fountain of Age* that it had been a mistake to tell her to quit running the duplicate bridge games. But you can't undo the past.

I ran into my friend Rabbi Laura Geller soon after my mother died. Laura asked, "What are you doing about her death? You have to do something." We were going to have a memorial service back in Peoria, but Laura summoned all my friends and colleagues in Los Angeles and we had a kind of wake. Everybody sat in a circle. A few had known my mother and they talked about her while the others talked about their own mothers. And I realized that Laura was perfectly right—you *must* celebrate, memorialize, whatever, acknowledge in some significant way what happens when the people die who are important in your life.

Laura and other people began working on other ceremonies for women's lives after that, like the *bas mitzvah* for Jewish girls when they reach thirteen. They also started working on dealing with things that happen in women's lives—menstruation, menopause, the last job, leaving home, marriage, widowhood, divorce. Each marked an important transition experienced by most women, and in their philosophy, called for ceremonies women could relate to.

It would take me four years to write *The Fountain of Age*, actually four summers. I lectured and taught in the winters and I wrote books in the summer: "*It Changed My Life*" in the commune on Drew Lane, *The Second Stage* and *The Fountain of Age* in Sag Harbor. As usual, I had too much research and too many piles of notes. It made me nostalgic for newspaper writing, where you write the story and it is done, and even for magazine writing, though the process drags on longer. But writing books, you're never done. It's always on your back.

I'd make rules about work—six hours a day during the week and not on weekends. Then the six would melt down to four, then to three, but at least I'd get it done. I'd do errands in the morning, then work 11–4, then go to the beach or something. I don't use a computer or a typewriter. I haven't set finger to typewriter since the second chapter of *The Feminine Mystique* when I started writing on a yellow pad sitting on the couch after the kids went to bed and reached another level of writing. I haven't turned back since. Margaret Peet, a minister's wife who originally came to work for me in the seventies as a manuscript typist, continues to type my handwritten pages.

When I finally finished the book during the summer of 1992, I was positively euphoric. The burden was lifted, I had no more guilt and I was planning to enjoy the first book I'd produced in eleven years. I was looking forward to promoting *The Fountain of Age* in 1993 and beginning a national dialogue about what were really revolutionary new ideas on attitudes toward age in America. What I hadn't counted on was nearly dying.

FOURTEEN
New Beginnings

Six months before the publication date, I had what I thought was an asthma attack. Well, that was certainly nothing new to me. I was going through a very hectic time finishing up my term at USC and addressing a panel at a national conference on "Women, Men and Media." I took my asthma medicine, gave the presentation and went on with my plans. Jeremiah Kaplan was in California staying with some friends and we were to meet and go on up to Yosemite. I was really looking forward to seeing Jeremiah, on whom I still had a big crush, and to going hiking with him and our friends in that beautiful national park.

Well, dammit, I couldn't catch my breath when we got to Yosemite. I still thought I was having an asthma attack, and I called my doctor in New York about stepping up my asthma medicine. "I'm not going to do that over the phone," she said to me. "You've got to go to a doctor there and find out if it's asthma or if something else is wrong and what it is." I told her I didn't know a doctor there. "Go to a clinic," she said. "I'm sure there's a clinic at Yosemite." She was right, of course. So I went to the clinic and the doctor there didn't think it was asthma, but my heart. Evidently there was fluid around it or something. He gave me some pills to reduce the fluid and told me to see a cardiologist.

My friends took me back to LA and I called Emily. She was practicing pediatric medicine in Buffalo, New York, and is such a wonderful and respected doctor in all areas that all my friends call her to double-check their own doctors' diagnoses and recommended treatments. No one does anything without Emily, including me—and also her husband, Eli, is a cardiologist.

I was already feeling better, but there was a funny pressure in my chest I hadn't felt before. I told Emily about that and asked her to ask Eli to find me a heart doctor in New York. What I was planning to do was to spend the weekend with my brother, Harry, in Palm Springs, then return to LA to teach my last class of the term before flying east. But Emily would have none of it. "I don't think you ought to fly with these symptoms," she said. "You can't just get on a plane now." She and Eli arranged for me to see a doctor Eli had been in training with and made me promise to get right over there.

My shortness of breath turned out definitely not to be asthma. I had somehow gotten an infection in my aortic valve and was in heart failure. The doctor wanted me to spend the night in the hospital but my friends had to leave and I didn't want to stay there alone. I called Emily from the gurney in the doctor's office to say I was going home, but she said: "No, you're not. I'm calling an ambulance right now and you're going directly to Good Samaritan Hospital. I'll meet you there."

So suddenly I found myself being shipped by ambulance across Los Angeles, which I certainly hadn't had in mind when I set out to go hiking. Besides, I felt fine after the fluid was drained and I really thought that everybody was kind of overreacting. Even when the doctor told me I'd need open heart surgery to replace the infected valve with a new valve, I still didn't let myself realize how serious it was. When I talked to Emily and she told me she would call the boys and be in Los Angeles that night, I said: "What do you want to do that for? You've got your own lives to deal with." And she said, "*Motherrr*, if you're going to have open heart surgery, of course we'll be there." So they all came. Even Carl came.

I guess I've always lived in some sort of denial, but on the other hand, I took care of my affairs. I got hold of Judy Resnik, a lawyer and one of my two closest buddies in LA. I needed Judith because I was worried about my will. I just had the crudest will at the time and I wanted to make sure it was airtight and left everything to the kids. "Don't worry about the will," Judy told me. "There's no time to do anything about it. Just concentrate on surviving, that's all." I asked Judith to get hold of Laura Geller, my other close buddy in Los Angeles. She told Laura about our conversation and said: "You'd better get over to the hospital and make sure Betty gets through the surgery." So Laura came over. "You should meditate," she told me, which was easy for her to say, but hard for me to do. I've never been good at meditating, I don't know what meditate means, I can't do it. "So give me a mantra," I asked her. Laura said, "Why don't you just use the *Shema,* the great prayer in Judaism: *'Hear, oh Israel, the Lord our God, the Lord is one.'* " There's some thought that the prayer must have originated during the transition from the different tribes worshipping all those different gods to a single principle governing the universe and it has always been meaningful to me. So that was the mantra I used when I went into the open heart surgery.

The operation was successful, but only briefly. The new valve they replaced my infected valve with came from a *pig,* so naturally, my body rejected it. What good Jewish heart wouldn't reject pork? So now I had to get a new aortic valve from a human being, from some corpse, from someone who had just died who had the right blood type or whatever.

Well, that wasn't easy. Everybody was looking for the right human aortic valve and there I was, my desperate heart ticking away in the hospital. Finally it was Thursday and I remembered what Emily or someone had said at some point that no one should have a serious procedure done in a hospital on the weekend because there's not enough staff there. So I said to the doctors, "I have some resources, can I try finding a valve?" They didn't think it would work, but I called my pal Sarah Kovner who was Donna Shalala's top aide at Health and Human Services. I told Sarah the problem, she got Donna out of a meeting at the United Nations, and about two minutes later I got a phone call from the head of heart transplants or organs or God knows what. It was never clear whether the valve replacement came from regular channels or from connections, but he got in touch with my doctor and within about three hours we had not one but two human heart valves to choose from: a middle-aged man and a thirty-five-year-old woman.

I chose the woman, of course, figuring my heart would not be likely to reject her heart, and back I went under the knife, to have open heart surgery for the second time in two weeks. The odds on my making it were probably fifty-fifty, but I didn't let myself know that at the time. And I didn't need to. I came through the surgery fine and there was no rejection this time, even though the thirty-five-year-old woman turned out not to be a thirty-five-year-old woman at all but a teenage boy! Everybody thought that was hilarious, especially Norman Lear, who showed up at the hospital with balloons reading: "It's a boy!"

My heart surgery hit the newspapers, of course, and was even a news item on television, so for months I couldn't go anywhere without somebody, even a cab driver, saying, "Oh, how *are* you?" to which I learned to reply: "I'm all right. Why do you ask?" I wasn't dead or even sick. I had to recuperate, of course, which I did at Dick and Kathy Reeves's house in Los Angeles with the kids watching over me like a hawk.

I was determined to promote my book no matter what shape I was in, and I did. Though Emily was furious at me, I made it to the American Booksellers Association convention in Miami just ten days after the second operation and addressed the convention. I had to go in a wheelchair because I was still weak and in some pain because the infection had traveled to my back. But as mad as she was at me, Emily never left my side and we got through it.

The Fountain of Age did surprisingly well, considering the timing. The postwar baby boomers who weren't supposed to trust anyone over thirty were now heading toward sixty themselves and the denial of age and the obsession with youth was at its peak. Just to have the word "age" in the title may have been too threatening at that stage. The book was mildly threatening to the gerontological establishment as well because it refuted so many of their gloomy preoccupations. Some of the best in the field, however, were very affirmative of it because after all, it led to a popular discussion of age where before there had been such denial.

The book got good reviews for the most part. One reviewer went so far as to call it "even more liberating than *The Feminine Mystique*." People who read it had the same "it changed my life" attitude, but it was a quieter book than *The Feminine Mystique. The Fountain of Age* didn't lead to marching in the streets.

The Fountain of Age was on *The New York Times* best-seller list for six weeks, though I don't think it was ever very high on the list. The book is probably still selling if the publishers have it available, which they almost never do. *The Fountain of Age* did well in England and very well in Australia, where it was a real best-seller. I spent two weeks promoting the book in Australia where I think it even hit number one. I'd never been there before and it was great fun. I loved Australia.

The Fountain of Age allowed me to add a master bedroom and my own bathroom off the kitchen of my house in Sag Harbor. The family had grown to eight grandchildren by 1993, most of whom spent at least some time there in the summer with their respective parents. Jonathan and Helen visited with their three children, Rafi, Caleb and Taya; Emily and Eli with their two, David and Isabel; and, less often, Danny and Agga with her two daughters, Lara and Birgitta, and their son, Benjamin. Danny and Agga spent most of the summers in Iceland in their apartment in Reykjavik and were looking at some acreage way up north. "What for?" I asked them. "What are you going to do with all that wilderness?" "Plant trees," they said. So I said it would be a good refuge for the family if there is nuclear war. Or more global warming.

I had all my children meet me when I finished the book tour, and we went to Virgin Gorda in the British Virgin Islands for Thanksgiving. Milton Carrow gave me his house but it wasn't big enough for everybody, so we also rented some rooms in the little resort right down the hill. Evidently Agga was not as acclimated to American bugs as we were and she got so bitten and swollen that she and Danny left about the second night. The bugs didn't seem to bother anyone else, but poor Agga was miserable. Still, we had a fun trip. We rented a boat and poked around and we rented a jeep with a fringed awning. There was a normal resort-type restaurant down the hill, but it was dull, so we'd go over the mountain and down to native restaurants on the other side.

I had a complete recovery from my heart surgery and felt very lucky. My dear friend David Manning White was not so lucky. He had the same heart valve replacement operation I had, but his new valve deteriorated later and he died in 1993. I didn't know until I got one of those Christmas cards people send with the news of all the members of their family on it. The card from his family said at the bottom: "our David passed away." I called Catherine, his wife, and she told me what had happened. "I loved him very much," I told her and she said, "He loved you and if you'd just been willing to share we could have all lived together." But as much as I truly loved David, I couldn't have done that.

I had a couple of other flings after David died—I took a professor of political science at Rutgers with me on the Australian book tour in 1994—but it was never really the same. I never replaced David or, later, Jeremiah when he died. A lot of men seem to have disappeared from my life.

Carl was still around and we did quite a lot of family stuff together with the children and grandchildren. When Danny became a father at nearly forty, I had invited Carl to come in from New Jersey where he was living to be on the phone to Iceland to celebrate the baby's *bris* (circumcision). We were both surprised when Danny told us the baby's name was going to be Benjamin Danielson. Friedan, we added? But no. Danielson. That was it. Period. So what's the big idea? I asked Danny. It was like he was turning his back on both his father and me. But Danny wouldn't budge.

Danny wrote us each a long letter with a tortured intellectual explanation about how the baby was a part of two tribes, the Iceland tribe and the Jewish tribe, but it didn't quite fly with me. Where was the American side? It was weird. But Danny had a big rationalization for all our objections and the baby remained Benjamin Danielson.

Benjamin's *bris* had to take place within the first eight days of life, but there probably wasn't another Jew in Iceland. I suggested importing someone from Denmark or flying over the *mohel* who had done Jonathan's boys, but he couldn't go because he was busy or it was a holiday or something. So they lined up a doctor in Iceland to do it.

I really wanted to be there, but I was just starting teaching at the business school at NYU and I didn't think I could miss the first week of class. "Daniel, since the baby isn't that kosher anyway, why can't you have it a few days later?" I asked him. But Danny wanted to stick to Jewish tradition. Emily and Jonathan went to represent the family, Emily providing the medical oversight and Jonathan the spiritual. They regaled us later with the tale of taking the baby to the doctor with Danny and Agga and being so horrified when they were told the baby was going to be given a general anesthetic that they snatched him away and went home. Emily picked up the phone and called the NATO base and found an American pediatrician who said he would be happy to do the *bris* because Danny was an American citizen. So off they went to the NATO base with the baby in a beautiful embroidered shawl and a *yarmulke* that Agga had gotten for the occasion and candles and they had the baby circumcised.

I continued to feel better and better after my heart surgery and suddenly realized that my asthma seemed to have gone away. When month after month passed with no attacks, I realized I didn't have to spend the winters in California any longer. I wasn't really thinking about what I'd rather do until I went to Washington for something and had dinner with my friends Marty and Sidney Lipset and Senator Pat Moynihan and his wife, Liz. Marty, a professor at George Mason University, was also a senior fellow at the Smithsonian's Woodrow Wilson Center for International Scholars and he asked if I'd be interested in being a fellow. Without hesitation, I said: "Sure."

The director of the Wilson Center, Charles Blitzer, called me that same night and asked if I would come to the center as a guest scholar and I readily accepted. I don't think they'd had many women, so when the idea of inviting me was proposed to him, he probably decided it would be good for the center. When he asked when I would like to come, I said for the fall, but I should have said for a year because the moment I got there in the summer of 1994, I knew I wanted to stay.

I've always loved Washington and, over the years, looked forward to going there if I had a writing assignment or a political mission. Not only did I find Washington a beautiful city with a lot of interesting people living there, but if you're interested in public policy as I am, that's where it's happening. And Washington didn't disappoint.

I loved working at the Wilson Center. There were about twenty different scholars appointed at the same time I was, a lot of them from other countries and from different fields. Dr. Ernestine Schlant, a German scholar and Senator Bill Bradley's wife, was writing about the Holocaust and how there had been a kind of blankout among some postwar German authors in their failure to examine the genocide. They didn't do anything bad, they just didn't do anything. She was very interesting and nice, but then, so were all the fellows and guest scholars. We had the option of having lunch together every day in the library. It wasn't exactly gourmet cuisine, but it was very nice, very convivial.

I conducted symposia at the center on women, men, work, family and public policy with my co-chair, Heidi Hartmann, a brilliant economist and founder of the Institute for Women's Policy Research, who had just won a MacArthur Award for her economic work on women's lives. Every four weeks we brought together leading people on women's issues with people from labor and corporate and Congress and public policy and we would discuss what I called the "paradigm shift" necessary to incorporate new realities into the workplace and people's everyday lives.

There were new questions to ask about the stresses of the nineties which required new solutions—the upsurge of "angry white men" in the epidemic of corporate downsizing and dropping incomes; the bitter scapegoating of women and minorities which was forming a new backlash; the overload of work on the smaller workforce and the stress caused by loss of family time; the generational polarization between an aging population and the projected tax burden of Social Security on the younger one. In a way you could say the seminars were just a continuation of what I'd been doing in the think tank at USC, but you had more people in Washington who were really involved in public policy. The symposia were very good and somehow I managed to finagle a second year at the Wilson Center as an adjunct scholar.

The New Yorker wanted me to do a piece based on the seminars. We'd recorded them and I started putting together all the tapes with Brigid O'Farrell, a visiting fellow at Mount Vernon College in Washington. It didn't pan out for *The New Yorker*. I'm not a *New Yorker*-type writer, but I had done all this work, so we decided to turn it into a book and call it *Beyond Gender: The New Politics of Work and Family*. It was not a big book deal; it was more academic, but I was quite pleased with it. Published by the Woodrow Wilson Center Press in 1997 and distributed by Johns Hopkins University Press, *Beyond Gender* was at least a fair record of the new paradigm seminars, and for the center, the biggest book they'd ever had. It was also a very pleasant publishing experience. Johns Hopkins sent over their director of marketing and their director of publicity and chief editor to meet with me. They asked a lot of good questions about contacts and markets for the book and were generally attentive. I was extremely impressed with the university press publishing experience compared to the norm.

Fellows at the Wilson Center get paid enough of a stipend to pay the rent in Washington and for two years I rented a *pied à terre* not far from Capitol Hill. When I was also offered a teaching job at George Mason University, I gladly accepted. George Mason turned out to be a very nice place to teach, but it was forty miles outside of Washington in Fairfax, Virginia, and transportation was a pain in the ass. It was too far and too expensive to go by taxi and I didn't have a car in Washington, so I had to arrange to drive back and forth with students who lived in town.

I taught a writing course at George Mason I had developed at USC called "Writing from Personal Truth and Social Observation," which is, of course, the way I write. Whatever a person's thoughts and passions, there has to be a personal involvement, grounded in experience, for good writing whether non-fiction or fiction. I told the journalism students then—and would continue to over the years—how I had written from that equation from my early years as a reporter to *The Feminine Mystique* and beyond. I would then ask them to do a piece of work along those parameters and we would spend the rest of the course reading their stuff and critiquing it. I liked teaching writing much more than women's studies. Not only was writing an easy course to teach, but I think it was also very illuminating and the students got something out of it.

It was such a hassle getting back and forth to George Mason, however, that when Lucyann Geiselman, the dynamic president of Mount Vernon College, wooed me away with lots of money in 1995, I accepted. I didn't realize until I got there that Mount Vernon, a women's college, was practically broke. You'd open a classroom door and the lights wouldn't be on or the heat wouldn't be on or both. It was weird. If I'd been a parent of a kid there, I would have sued. The college was really in pitiful shape and they never should have paid me that much money. I guess they thought that having me on the faculty as a Visiting Distinguished Professor might turn the tide.

It was, however, a way for me to stay in Washington and get paid, just as there were other good people on the faculty who like me wanted to stay in Washington. There was nothing wrong with that. You took the job because you got paid to stay in Washington.

As time passed, I found I didn't miss New York at all. I'd lived there at least part-time for almost thirty years and I felt I'd been there, done that. I never did go to the theater that much in New York, and there was and is plenty of cultural stuff in Washington, lots of good music, dance, art. Among my many friends in Washington were the directors of the Hirshhorn Museum and the Corcoran Museum of Art, the largest non-federal museum in Washington and one of the first fine art museums in the country.

It dawned on me quite suddenly one day that I should move permanently to Washington. I had been subletting my apartment in New York off and on for years, which was a headache, while I was subletting other people's apartments and living with their furniture instead of my own. I had this wonderful collection of furniture that I had acquired over the years and I missed it.

Getting the tenant out of my apartment at 1 Lincoln Plaza, however, turned out to be a terrible experience. She absolutely refused to leave and I had to come in in the middle of the night and tell her to get out. It must have scared the life out of her because she finally left. She really kind of trashed the place in the process and it took a week to get the apartment cleaned up and back in enough shape to go back on the market.

I was tired of the hassle of renting so I started hunting for a place to buy in Washington. Quite a few of my friends had little town houses in Georgetown, and I would have loved that, but I thought I should be in an apartment building. I get so much FedEx and mail that I needed a concierge, and besides, I didn't feel secure enough about Washington to have a house by myself. I had sprained my ankle on my book tour in Australia so I was very conscious of having to climb steps and I didn't have a car in

Washington and wouldn't have driven it anyway, so I had to be able to get a cab.

My friend Barbara Raskin pointed me in the right direction. She was divorced from her husband, Mark, and was living by herself in a big old house. "If I could get rid of this house, which I probably never can," she told me, "the only place I'd live is in the Wyoming." "What is the Wyoming?" I asked her and she told me it was this wonderful big old building where a lot of writers live. So I asked a real estate agent about the Wyoming and indeed, there was one apartment available. It was one or two rooms bigger than I needed because technically it was a three-bedroom apartment, but I bought it anyway, and happily.

I never would have been able to afford to buy such a big, really elegant apartment in New York. It has an atrium library completely lined with bookcases, with a black-and-white marble floor between the living room and dining room. I use one of the extra bedrooms as a guest room, another as an office for my assistant, Hilde Carney, and the third as my workroom. I have several desks and an extra dining table with leaves in the workroom. But as is my usual custom I do all my writing at the big, round table in the dining room.

I didn't have to do a thing with that apartment except replace the grungy hall carpeting. It came to me in the middle of the night that what the hall floor needed was Plaza Hotel red carpeting, but that was the only thing I had to do because everything else was in great shape. And my furniture, which had never looked all that great at 1 Lincoln Plaza, fit beautifully. I added two red loveseats which I bought at some wonderful little furniture store in Washington, to go in the living room. The living room is so large that it needed to be broken up into two seating areas, so I used the loveseats to make a separate, cozy nook. I'd always loved the idea of having two facing loveseats and now I do.

I was in my early seventies when I made this life move to Washington and that so impressed Barbara that she put her big old house on the market and sold it within one week and then she found an apartment in the Wyoming, too. She lived there in the other wing until, tragically, she died last summer. Frank Mankiewicz, whom I had barely known when he was Bobby Kennedy's press secretary, and later, head of National Public

Radio, and his wife, Pat O'Brien, who writes mystery books, turned out to be my neighbors. The Wyoming is a great place and I think it was very good for me, moving to Washington.

Everything about the city appealed to me—the beauty of it, the history, the ease of getting around. Washington was made for me. I love ceremonies and pageantry and Washington has more than its share. I've been to a lot of presidential inaugurations, including both of Clinton's, which were a lot of fun. But mostly I loved—and continue to enjoy—being at the epicenter of politics and public policy.

Newt Gingrich and his Contract With America were in full cry in 1995, posing an enormous threat to women. Conservative Republicans in Congress were calling for an end to welfare, knowing full well that the vast majority of welfare recipients were women and children. I was outraged at the demonization of welfare mothers, making poor women and their kids scapegoats of the culture of greed and its dirty underbelly of racism and growing middle-class economic frustration. Contrary to popular opinion, statistics showed that most people on welfare were not black teenagers turning out babies to collect welfare checks, but women who had lost jobs or been left by their husbands who were temporarily receiving assistance until they could get new jobs, get through school, or other job training. Many of my own students, especially the older ones raising their children alone, had had to go on welfare while they were trying to go to school. Cutting such support was so outrageous and counterproductive that without hesitation, I agreed to speak at a vigil of nationwide students and professors in front of the White House to urge Clinton to stand firm on the proposed slashing of Medicare, Medicaid, loans for education, child care and aid to families with dependent children.

Affirmative action was also under attack, not only as a rallying cry among the new Republican majority in Congress but in court challenges to college admissions and municipal contracts. Again, the backlash was fueled mostly by "white male anger" and discussed almost exclusively in terms of race, but women were being scapegoated as well. The reality was that white men still held a huge advantage in the job market, earning 49 percent more than minorities, including women. A government study of barriers to promotion confirmed what was termed the "glass ceiling" for women and minorities but was really a cement wall: white males held ninety-five of one hundred senior management positions defined as vice president and above in Fortune 500 companies.

The larger economic dynamics behind the backlash were being ignored by both the mainstream and the feminist media. While the working middle class scapegoated minorities and women for their financial insecurities, the real cause was corporate greed. As Heidi Hartmann pointed out at one of our symposia, it was the aggressive strategy of big business to pursue profits at any cost by eliminating jobs or keeping wages down. To divert white male anger, the companies encouraged the workers to blame affirmative action for the lower wages and diminishing number of jobs rather than the companies themselves. The strategy disguised what was really the increasing proportion of the wealth of the country going into the hands of the top 10 percent of the population.

We discussed these and many other economic and political dangers at the symposia I ran at the Wilson Center and continued to run for a while after I left the Wilson Center, at the American Enterprise Institute (AEI) for Public Policy Research. The AEI was and is a conservative think tank, but Doug Besharov, then an AEI director, and I worked well together. He let me use space at AEI to run my programs and to send out our mailings, which I thought was kind of amazing. We were given access to AEI's mailing list and we sent out to all those conservatives like Judge Robert Bork and Jeane Kirkpatrick, Reagan's former chief delegate to the United Nations.

I didn't know Jeane well, so you can imagine how startled I was when I took a plane from Washington to somewhere and she ignored the virtually empty plane to come sit next to me. We talked on the plane ride, and had a great time together. At one point I told her, "I hate your politics but I admire your guts." And she replied, "I feel the same way about you."

During the flight, Jeane told me about her problems as a woman with her fellow reactionaries, even when she was head of the U.S. mission to the United Nations. It was the same conversation I'd had over the course of the years with a lot of the powerful women I'd met, like the president of Norway. They'd let their hair down and tell me their troubles getting the men to listen to them, even if they were the heads of government or prime ministers or whatever their titles were. The only one who wasn't like that was Golda Meir. After one of the UN conferences on women, she had sent for me and Bella and several other Jewish women leaders and given us hell because she didn't think we were standing up enough for the Jews over the Palestinians and the right-wing Arab resolution "Zionism is racism." "I would not have permitted any anti-Semitic nonsense," she told us, which got my dander up. Bella and I had gotten that phrase eliminated at Nairobi so she had no business getting mad at us about that. But then, I knew from my first trip to Israel that she and many other women Israeli leaders had always been quite suspicious of feminism.

So, it would turn out, were the Chinese. The UN's Fourth World Conference on Women was held in Beijing in 1995, and reluctantly, I went. I wasn't very interested in going to Beijing. Who needed another world meeting of women? What was it going to accomplish? It didn't seem to have much point to it. But I went anyway, as did Bella, who had heart disease by then and was in a wheelchair.

Usually I like the countries I visit. I'd just done two terrific weeks in Japan where Walter Mondale was the U.S. ambassador and where women were really getting organized. I'd also recently done the great two-week lecture tour in Australia to promote *The Fountain of Age.* I've always loved going to foreign countries when I'm going with or at the invitation of some group or women who had achieved power, or even with the U.S. State Department, who always brought me together with the leading women and some of the men who support feminist policies.

But the Chinese disgusted me. Forty thousand women of all colors came to Beijing either as members of non-governmental organizations or official delegates, but the totalitarian Chinese authorities tried to keep us all in some sort of Muslim purdah. They penned us up in the isolated suburb of Hairou, an hour at least from the center of Beijing, presumably to keep us from infecting the Chinese people with our democratic, liberating ideas.

I ran several workshops at the conference, as well as covering it for the U.S. Information Agency and the Voice of America, despite the hassles the Chinese foisted on all of us. Promised shuttle buses never showed up, we were followed and harassed by the secret police, and speakers at the conference often went untranslated. The heavy-handed tactics of the Chinese outraged me and I really protested. The women from the NGOs had to march to get a space big enough to meet in, just as we had threatened to do twenty years before in Mexico. The Chinese authorities were incredibly patronizing, like "Let the ladies play, but don't take them seriously."

I did not like the whole scene. There was an incredibly stupid disinformation campaign, that all the taxi drivers should carry white sheets in their cars because there were going to be naked lesbians cavorting around. They were even told to carry disinfectants to protect themselves from AIDS from all these naked lesbians. It was as ridiculous as it was insulting to the women who'd gathered to discuss real issues and share information across national boundaries.

The Chinese attempts to trivialize and marginalize women's issues were not successful, however. CNN broadcast our protests around the world, which didn't make the Chinese look too good, and Hillary Clinton more than held her ground. "Women's rights are human rights and human rights are women's rights," she said to the cheers of delegates and the world watching on television. Madeleine Albright didn't mince words either, berating the Chinese for their inhuman one-child policy and gender bias, which was forcing parents to abandon girl babies in the streets or on the doorsteps of orphanages and to undergo forced sterilization or abortions.

Despite the authoritarian power in China and the scare tactics of the police, the delegates and the representatives from NGOs and movements from all over the world displayed awesome power in Beijing. There were the usual attempts by delegates from the Vatican and the Muslim countries to defeat the resolution on women's right to control their own reproductive systems, as well as a last-minute battle over the right of Muslim women to walk openly on the streets of their respective countries, but the reactionaries were outmaneuvered by the enormous political and tactical skills of the other women delegates.

The plan of action that emerged in the end asserted the basic right of women everywhere to control their own sexuality and reproductive process and to make a crime of genital mutilation and the abuse of women in the home or on the street. The plan demanded that women be educated equally with men and be extended bank credit to start their own businesses. There was even the suggestion that the gross national product of all nations include the unpaid work done by women in their homes and their communities. It was marvelous.

I returned to Washington revitalized as ever by the energy and esprit of the world's women. I was seeing that same energy and sense of entitlement to equality in my students and the daughters of my friends as they strode out into life with wonderful confidence and autonomy, embracing the great sense of possibility that now knew no gender.

I found I was getting tired of teaching, however. After Mount Vernon College finally went belly-up in 1996, I accepted what would be my last professorship, a four-month term at Florida International University in Miami. I accepted their job offer because (a) it paid well, and (b) it would get me out of the winter. But sunshine is not enough and four months was too much in Miami. I missed my friends, I missed Washington, and the winter didn't turn out to be that bad for the rest of the country anyway.

The people at Florida International wanted me to come back the next year but I didn't want to do it. Teaching did not seem to be the best use of my energy, so I decided not to accept another teaching job. Perhaps it had something to do with yet another heart valve replacement I had to have in September 1997.

I'd gotten another infection during the summer; the human valve had disintegrated and I had to have emergency open heart surgery in Washington. I quickly gave each of the kids about $10,000 to start with, just in case. "If I kick off, this will keep you going until they figure out my estate, and if I don't, you can just celebrate with it," I told them. This time the surgeons replaced the infected human aortic valve with a mechanical one and obviously, I survived. The new valve won't get infections and will probably outlive me, but during my recuperation I decided I should no longer live the hand-to-mouth, improvised existence I always had and that I should get myself organized and better supported. So I went to see Susan Berresford, the president of the Ford Foundation.

For a woman to be made head of the Ford Foundation was quite a marvelous feat, of course, and Susan deserved it. I didn't know her that well, but in my work over the years I had certainly encountered her and she had always been very good. I was sure she'd be full of good advice.

In our meeting, I told Susan what I was working on and what I wanted to do in terms of redefining the feminist focus on women and expanding it to larger societal terms. What we needed now was not more yammering about discrimination against women, but to move beyond a kind of strict feminist thought to the larger focus on women, men, work, family and public policy. The new challenge was to define the issues beyond the focus on women alone or women against men because the next set of issues and challenges for women was broader than that. Defining the new paradigm had been my imperative in the seminars and symposia at the Wilson Center and indeed the nub of my work since my first teaching job at Temple University in 1970.

To my surprise and delight, Susan indicated that the Ford Foundation would support such a program and that I should find the right institution to sponsor it and handle the money; the Ford Foundation couldn't just give it to me as an individual. So I thought of the institutions that I'd been involved with. It would be too small potatoes for Harvard, I decided, but NYU was a possibility. I'd worked for NYU and the School of Business and had a very good experience, but I also had a very good history with Cornell.

Cornell had been the first university in the country to offer an accredited women's studies course and I had worked with Sheila Tobias on designing what was then considered a revolutionary work. I remember giving a lecture at Cornell on "Tokenism and the Pseudo-Radical Cop-Out" in the early years, 1969 I think it was, which drew so many people that they had to move the talk out of the dining room of one of the dorms to the big auditorium.

More recently, Cornell had sponsored a very good program in New York City based on women and work, with a lot of labor people involved. I had lectured for them and gotten to know Francine Moccio, who ran that program for Cornell's School of Industrial and Labor Relations. So I decided to apply for the Ford Foundation support through Cornell, through the program on

women and work. Cornell loved the idea and gave me a distinguished professorship. Francine helped put the grant application
together, which was a huge amount of work, and in 1998 I got a
million-dollar grant from the Ford Foundation to support my
work on the new paradigm for the next four years.

I was pretty pleased with that—and still am. First of all, it
was a great affirmation of my continued work—and of me. They
didn't give me that grant lightly; I now know that they checked
with a lot of people. That they had confidence that I would still be
functioning in four years—I'm going to be in my eighties when
the term of the grant is up—was so heartening to me. I really liked
that little mark of confidence. On the other hand, I think it's deserved.

The program I'm running in Washington is not for undergraduates, but a program to bring policy makers together with
women leaders and thinkers as well as labor and civil rights leaders, advanced corporate people and economists. We're redefining
women's issues as societal priorities for life—children, older people, sickness and health, the environment even—and how the
new realities relate to evolving needs. The issues today are not the
same as the issues twenty years ago.

With women now half the labor force, and the majority of
women working most of their lives outside the home, the structure of work in terms of the male model has got to change. We've
got to restructure work and career lines to take into account childbearing and child rearing. It's important to have flexible work
structures so that one parent can be home until the children get
off to school and be at home when the children return from
school. Or have on-site corporate child care. In the new paradigm, we have to apply not just a little Band-Aid, but bold new
thinking.

Women are now providing 50 percent or more of the income
in at least 50 percent of American families, Heidi Hartmann
pointed out at a Wilson Center seminar. I may not be remembering that percentage completely accurately, but it's pretty close.
Yet there still isn't any real thinking about new kinds of sharing of
household services. Recent surveys of how much time who was
spending on housework found that women were spending much
less and the men were doing it just a little bit more, so the conclu-

sion had to be that *no one* is doing much housework, and that you get 25-watt lightbulbs to hide the dirt!

I think we should have the option of a much longer family leave for childbirth or any health emergency. What is it now, nine weeks, twelve weeks? In many countries, Australia, Sweden, women can take up to a year, two years, even three years of parental leave, and are guaranteed their original job or some kind of comparable work. I also think that family leave should be paid, so that people could afford to take it.

I was worried recently when research came out about the importance of brain stimulation during a child's first few years of life to increase the brain's capacity. I saw the possibility of the research being used by the naysayers in an attempt to push women home again, especially if there's an economic downturn. But it is also a strong argument not only for longer periods of parental leave but also for a really good national program to provide the sort of stimulating child care that other countries have, like Sweden and France, countries that are not as rich as we are.

I also think there should be a movement to shorten the work week in this big, rich country of ours to give people more time to spend with their families. We haven't had serious discussion about such a move in sixty years. That's the real unfinished business. Some other countries like France and Germany have already moved to a 35-hour work week. There's no reason we can't do that, either moving toward a four- or four-and-a-half-day week, or just shortening the work day. Innovative companies are also into flextime for their employees and job sharing. Critics of these innovations say that they are fine for those who can afford to earn less, but I think the option of working part-time is great for people with family obligations or who just want more time for themselves. Get a life, for God's sake.

It always strikes me as nice in France or Italy the institution of the lunch—not just the expense account lunch but the familial, good long leisurely lunch. That would be a good institution for Americans to emulate, or it could be a long, leisurely dinner in a restaurant or even breakfast on the way to work. I'd have breakfast out every day if there was a Starbucks near me; I can't make as good coffee as Starbucks.

The most critical issue, of course, remains child care. We are *still* the only advanced nation besides South Africa without a real national child care program. Clinton and Gore have come out for such a national program, but I don't see anything being done. In this period of economic boom and wealth in our society, we could afford to have a really good national child care program. It's a disgrace, almost an obscenity, that we don't.

If women realized how much more political power they have than they are using, we could very well have the beginnings of such a national program in place by now. Women elected Bill Clinton twice by more than a 20-point gender gap and could just have easily un-elected him during the Monica Lewinsky mess by calling for his resignation. But we didn't. My line was always that his public programs and policies have been basically good for women and his private life was his business and Hillary's. And that *is* what I believe, although he often came across on television as arrogant and even a little sleazy.

But what has he done with all this power we gave him? He could use that power to push for a national child care program and go beyond *saying* he's for national child care by using an executive order to *launch* it for any company or institution that has a government contract. That's exactly how we began to crack sex discrimination in the sixties. I think that should be done.

And while he's at it, he could issue an executive order eliminating all gender wage inequities in the federal government or under federal contracts. That would be a good thing to do. He's got to understand that he really owes women. While there's no doubt he's done some good things, like holding firm on a woman's right to legal abortion, he's also done harm. I think the destruction of the welfare system is really outrageous. What has happened to all these women who were on welfare? If they've got jobs, they are evidently very low-paying jobs and they don't have child care.

I'd like to propose to the president that we get a year of dialogue started in every community as we begin the new millennium on what should be the purposes and social values of this powerful nation. I think there has got to be a big values revolution to break through the defining and confining culture of greed that we're all locked into. It's awful that the main value in America at the beginning of a new century is material greed. The emphasis is acquiring more for more's sake, more individual success, more status, more things, but as a nation—what? How are we using our power? Those are the questions that interest me now.

I want to try to redefine the bottom line. We should have not just BLS and GDP and GNP but we should have QOL, an index of Quality of Life for women, for men, for children, for old, young, whatever. That should be an important measure of a community's progress, of the country's progress, of a company's status. I want to do that. These are issues that are important to address.

I'd love to see more research on the real effect hands-on fathers have on their children's growth and development. I suspect it is substantial. I love to see my sons and my son-in-law interact with their children. All three are hands-on parents. I think they're just as good at diapering, at feeding, at any of the domestic functions as their wives. They're just as concerned with their children's welfare as my daughter and daughters-in-law, which I think is really wonderful and, it turns out, healthy for the whole family.

Research is suddenly showing that men who do hands-on parenting live longer on average than their more distanced male counterparts. My guess is that the sensitivity they learn about what's going on in their children's bodies applies to what's going on in their own bodies, a self-awareness which I've always suspected is one of the reasons women have longer life spans than men. Or maybe it's something else. Maybe it's that men who get strength and satisfaction from hands-on parenting are relieved somewhat of the burden of machismo and are beginning to have a different model of male identity and male strengths. Machismo must be a tremendously stressful thing to maintain because underneath the bluster is always panic and terror.

I'm also seeing a healthy sense of shared domestic responsibility in my own family. Danny has taken over all of the cooking and is a very good cook. His culinary career began when he was on sabbatical a few years ago. He liked the role of family chef and now when I'm talking to him on the phone he often says: "I have to hang up now, my timer's going off." I don't know anyone else who uses a timer for their cooking, but being a scientist, of course he uses one.

Agga's very good for him, though it must be a little tough for her. Danny is a world-class theoretical physicist and has a cutting-edge institute for string theory at Rutgers University, while Agga took a time-out from studying physics and had a lot of wife and mother years when she was married before in Sweden. She's made up for it since, making it through four years of full-time school while raising three children. Still, I think it's too bad in a way that she's in the same field as he is.

It's important for her, as it is for any woman or man, for that matter, to have her own thing from which she gains self-esteem and satisfaction and not be identified just as Danny's wife. I told him he could and he did always negotiate that Agga had to have a job in physics where he was going to teach before he ended up at Rutgers. But I don't think that's enough. She has to have a job doing something of her own.

I think she got a little angry, annoyed, whatever, when she felt she was given jobs just because she's Danny's wife, but I feel that she's finding her own direction. Agga has a job now where she is developing ways to get minority kids and girls past their block against excelling in math and physics. I think that's very interesting and important work that she's doing.

Emily and Eli have a strong and equal marriage and there doesn't seem to be any power struggle in their relationship. She's the mother and she probably takes the main responsibility in planning their domestic life, but Eli certainly doesn't just "help." He's a very hands-on parent and whichever one of them gets home first determines who cooks the dinner.

They are both very, very busy. Eli is going into private cardiology practice in Buffalo, where they live, and Emily is not only practicing pediatrics but getting more and more interested in how you mitigate and prevent violence. The trouble between Carl and me in our marriage, I'm sure, is a big element in her interest. She's been working in a clinic that serves economically challenged families, but it looks like with all the funding cutbacks for public health and welfare all over the country her clinic will be forced to close down. It's a terrible testament to the greed of the few at the expense of the many poor in this rich, powerful country. Pregnant now with her third child, Emily is going into private practice with an African American doctor in the inner city.

Jonathan and Helen have more of the traditional marriage of

my generation. Jonathan was just made a partner and director of engineering in a big architectural firm in Philadelphia, so that's good. Helen, however, didn't have that set a career when they married, which is a shame, I think. She's taken off ten years or more with three kids and she's not having an easy time getting back into the working world. She went and got herself a rabbinical degree, but it doesn't seem to lead to a job. I doubt any parish is going to come up in Philadelphia. She's very talented artistically. She makes quilts that sell for $1,000 and are really works of art and she's now taking up sculpture, so she'll find her way sooner or later, I'm sure.

I wish that Jonathan would go into politics because he really does have wonderful leadership ability and is quite charismatic. But I guess going into politics today is not something that appeals to principled, educated men like that. It's a shame that it's not something that they think of doing. Not good. Not good.

I see my kids now and their generation bringing up very good kids, but there's no other cause that they are giving their energies and their lives to. There aren't the causes and movements today that were so much a part of me and my generation and the generation after me in the sixties and early seventies. You were aware you were doing your own career and your own personal life—marriage, love, children—but you were also aware in that era of a better world and a better society, of your duty to make it happen. It was like you were driven by some larger morality, which sounds almost presumptuous, but it was also quite wonderful to be a part of the movement to make society better, whether it was the civil rights movement or the student movement or the women's movement. That larger morality, that feeling of being part of something larger than yourself, is what carries social evolution and human evolution forward. It's very important and I don't think my kids' generation has that. It's a loss for them and for the betterment of society.

I have wonderful grandchildren, I must say, each intelligent and unique. They call me Betty, which I guess is all right, though I don't know why I didn't think of some name like Nana. The trouble is my association with that word "Granny." My mother had been Granny and she had not been a good act to follow and Carl's mother had been Grandma, and she was a pill. My own children started calling me Betty when they got grown up, so I guess it was inevitable that their children would, too.

I decided when they were born that I wanted to take each of my grandchildren on a trip just with me and I've begun. I took Rafi, Jonathan and Helen's oldest son, to Cuba when he was fourteen. Barbara Raskin had suggested Cuba when I told her about the grandmother trip. "Lying on a beach in the Caribbean is not going to be interesting for a fourteen-year-old kid," she'd told me. "Go to Cuba." The Caribbean beach sounded pretty good to me, but it's much better when you're traveling with kids to have something to explore. Barbara had a friend who could arrange the trip to Cuba, which can be difficult for American citizens, so we went. I don't remember that Rafi delved very much into the history or the politics of Cuba, but we had a lot of fun. The restaurants were not great but there were these *paradors* or whatever you call them, where you eat in people's homes. That was very interesting and fun.

Twelve-year-old Caleb, Jonathan's second son, got the next grandmother trip, in 1999. We considered going to the Galapagos—I'm fascinated with evolution and Darwin—or maybe to Venice. Caleb loves antiques and I could walk forever in Venice. We ended up going to the Loire Valley in France on an organized grandparent/grandchild trip called "Châteaux, Bateaux et Ballons." Caleb was the only boy and very popular. *Grandmère* even went up in the *ballon*! We had a great time together.

As I write this now near the end of the millennium, it's one hundred and fifty years since the first declaration of women's rights in America, and if you look at what we have accomplished in this century, it is stunning. I went to a play last winter in which Einstein and Picasso are talking in a café, and they tell each other that "*we* are going to define this century." It was all I could do to keep from standing up in the audience and saying, "Hey! *Wait* a minute! What about women? *Women* define this century." And it's true.

I don't know whether the history books are ever going to acknowledge it or not, but the major transformative force, at least for American society in this century, has been the modern women's movement. The official organizations I helped found thirty years ago, NOW, the NWPC, and NARAL, have been institutionalized and are still going strong. They spend far too much time, in my opinion, on turf matters and direct mail fund-raising, and are not as creative as they should be on issues and keeping up with changes in society, but they have become forces in our society and are not going to go away.

There's a lot of silly talk that the women's movement is dead. Well, it's not dead; it's alive in society! What used to be the feminist agenda is now an everyday reality. The way women look at themselves, the way other people look at women, is completely different, *completely different* than it was thirty years ago. The personhood of women, which is what it was all about as far as I'm concerned, never was women against men. The personhood of women is here today. Our daughters grow up with the same possibilities as our sons: The question, "What do you want to be, little girl, when you grow up?" is a real one. The inference is no longer "You're a pretty little girl; you'll be a mommy like your mommy."

She'll be a mommy if she chooses to be a mommy. Most do. She'll be pretty or she'll be not pretty. She can look the way she wants to look now. It's much better. There's no longer that cookie-cutter definition of what pretty is. I always thought I was ugly growing up because that model of beauty was blond Betty Grable—and blue-eyed Betty Boop—and I felt like an alien. Emily was looking at some old pictures she found the other day and she said, "But Mom, you said you were so ugly. You weren't ugly." And I looked at the pictures, and realized, no, I was not ugly, I was quite good-looking. But I grew up before Barbra Streisand. You couldn't think of someone who looked like me then as good-looking.

With the changing of women's position come new issues and new questions and a certain obsolescence about old rhetoric. While polls indicate that women completely affirm the whole agenda of the women's movement for parity, those same women often say, "I'm not a feminist." What you hear is, "I'm not a feminist *but* . . . I'm going to law school and I don't know if I'm going to end up a judge or a senator and I'll get around to having my one two or three children when I get around to it." Or, "I'm not a feminist, *but* . . . I just got a mortgage for a new house I'm buying and my newspaper is entering my stories for a Pulitzer Prize and I'm taking six months maternity leave when the baby is born next month." For a while there I'd give a lecture and I'd tell these young women: "Shut up with that 'I'm not a feminist *but.*' By the time I'm finished we're going to say, 'I *am* a feminist *and . . .*' because our revolution is not finished."

But then again, maybe it is. I've been thinking recently that we've come as far as we can or need to go in terms of women alone or women versus men. The women's movement for equality has reached a point in this country where women earn the majority of bachelor's and master's degrees and 40 percent of the doctorates. And it has all happened in less than thirty years. Whereas women earned only 4 percent of law degrees in 1970, the percentage was 43 percent in 1996. Roughly the same percentage holds for medical students: in 1999, women accounted for 44 percent of the freshman class at Yale Medical School. Fewer women opt for business school, but the rise in master's degrees in business disciplines is just as informing. Whereas women earned only 4 percent of MBAs in 1970, the percentage rose to 37 percent in 1996.

The most stunning success story has been in women-owned businesses. Even I have difficulty with getting my mind around the fact that there are currently more than 8 million women-owned businesses in America which employ 24 million people and generate $3.1 *trillion* in revenue. I am awed but not surprised that so many women have chosen to set their own goals and hours and business philosophies and gratified that they get the financial support and credit we worked so hard for. The rise in women entrepreneurs is in fact a revolution within a revolution. The number of women-owned businesses more than doubled between 1987 and 1997 and continues to rise; women are currently starting businesses at twice the rate of men.

We do have some unfinished business. Women still earn less than men—74 cents for every male dollar. But an analysis of the wage discrepancy in a book published in 1999 by the American Enterprise Institute showed that the discrepancy coincided with the years of child rearing when women choose more flexible jobs with lower salaries. So what's needed is a national child care program; what's needed is paid family leave; what's needed is more encouragement of men and women sharing housework and child care. Which is happening, but it should be more conscious. If the generation to come takes that sharing for granted, I promise you, that wage gap will begin to close.

NOW and the other women's organizations seem to me to be stuck a little in the time warp and rhetoric of earlier years. To my mind, there is far too much focus on abortion. I was among the first to establish the right of a woman to control her body and her reproductive system and it's very important that women have safe, legal, medical access to birth control and abortion if necessary. But in recent years I've gotten a little uneasy about the movement's narrow focus on abortion as if it were the single, all-important issue for women when it's not.

To me, all the emphasis on criminalizing pornography and sexual harassment and even rape is way out of proportion. I was incensed when they had all those marches to "take back the night." It's the *day* we have to work on. Once we get real equality and equal pay and economic control of our lives, we can take care of the night.

When the polling question is asked "What are the main concerns of women today?" the top answers are always jobs and family; issues like abortion and pornography are way down on the list. The far bigger concern for women is how to put jobs and family together, because jobs are still structured in terms of the men of the past whose wives took care of the children and the details of life. The women of today who make up half the workforce don't have such wives, but neither do the men anymore. The proof is in the number of Americans who are now eating out several nights a week, the boom in take-home food business, the thriving all-night grocery stores. Helping women and men combine work and family is the issue feminist organizations should be concentrating on.

I helped to start the women's movement, I feel responsible for it and I want its direction to widen. I don't like it when the movement gets stuck in a rhetoric that may have been necessary at one time but not anymore. And so my own work now is to help the thinking evolve, which I've been doing ever since I stepped down from active leadership in the 1970s through my teaching and my lecturing and the work that I'm doing now on public policy.

I say I'm no longer interested in just women, or women versus men. But I can't stop being. I've given my adult life to this, and anyway, when you have that focus, it opens up the whole world. There's no such thing anymore as women's issues. Women's issues are the world's issues.

The last thing I want to do now is start any more organizations. In retrospect, I think I did the right thing in starting all those organizations but not trying to hold on to personal power in them. I was very good at inspiring and starting but I could barely tolerate Robert's Rules of Order. I didn't have much patience with administering anything. But it is very gratifying to see how far we've come.

I did it for my father in a way, so that men would not have the burden of their wives' frustration at having to live through them. I did it for my mother, so that women would no longer have the discontent of dependency on their husbands, with no careers of their own. And I did it for my children, so that children would not have the burden of the mothers having to live through them. I came up with a catchy phrase for it all when some reporter asked me once what I wanted on my gravestone. It went something like "She helped make a world where women feel good about being women and free to really love men."

I've always thought the so-called war between the sexes would be transcended by the women's movement for equality. Women would finally be able to love men for who they really are and not so much because the man is rich or powerful or whatever. I remember talking about it with a conservative sociologist and he said: "Well, you'll still want men to be taller." (He was quite short, himself.) But not necessarily.

I always got such a kick that Henry Kissinger's wife is so much taller than he is. It was so interesting to me. When men have power, they don't necessarily have to be tall. So it stands to reason that when women have power equal to men, power issues may not be so virulent within marriage or relationships. Powerful women won't need men to be that much taller, and strong women won't need men who can kill lions. What a relief that would be for men, it seems to me. But then I've always thought of women's liberation as men's liberation as well.

• • •

Writing about my so-called life is making me think of life as a whole. The pluses. The not-so pluses. What I would have done differently.

One of my regrets is that I didn't have a real career. I would have loved to have gone to law school. Who knows, I might have ended up on the Supreme Court. I would have loved to have been an anthropologist or an archeologist or an architect, a planner. I love the question of what to do with space. There are a lot of things. I would have loved being the editor of the women's page of *The New York Times*. Or starting my own magazine. That's one of my greatest regrets.

I love the work I'm doing now with the Ford Foundation in Washington, but it's along the same avenue I've been on for years. What can I do that's really new? I could try writing a novel or a mystery, but I don't know how good I'd be at that. Someone just found in my papers a short story I'd written when I was at Smith, the last time I wrote any fiction. But I don't like, don't even read short stories. Maybe I should take a novel-writing course, or painting, or archeology or linguistics or who knows. It's like "What do you want to be, little girl, when you grow up?"

The personal truth of my aging is that I'm not in denial of it. I don't dye my hair, I haven't had my face lifted, I don't pretend that I'm not my age, although when I think that I'm seventy-eight, I think—how could that be? I just don't feel like whatever I would have thought seventy-eight would feel like. I just feel like myself.

When I was interviewing older people for *The Fountain of Age*, I'd ask, "How do you feel now compared to when you were forty or fifty or whatever?" I don't feel that different, although I don't feel the same either. I think that I am wiser, that I somehow let myself get less polarized, that I can hold contradictions and conflicts in hand even if they're not resolved. I can also get annoyed with a daughter-in-law and then the next day get over it.

The truth is that I've always been a bad-tempered bitch. Some people say that I have mellowed some. I don't know. But it feels like I am not quite such a bad-tempered bitch, though maybe I am. I'm trying to remember the last time I lost my temper and I can't, but that might just be a failure of memory. Since my last heart valve operation, I sometimes have a short-term memory glitch.

I'm not ready to die nor am I about to. My mother lived to ninety, after all. Probably I'm belatedly addressing what theoretically people should address earlier for their last third of life. Dylan Thomas's widow, Caitlin, wrote a book called *Leftover Life to Kill* because that's how she felt after her husband died. But that's not true anymore. There are a lot of women in my generation and the several generations which followed who really began to blossom and move and come into their own after forty-five, after the children went off to college. So if my mother lived to ninety, I probably have another dozen years. I'm not about to sit in a rocking chair. I'm very game for new adventures. When I got back from France last summer, I went off to Italy, where I rented a villa in Tuscany with a friend, and then to Alaska on a cruise sponsored by the magazine *The Nation*.

Getting divorced was the hardest thing I ever did. I was so terrified of being alone. That doesn't bother me anymore. But then, I'm almost never alone. I have so many friends. Wherever I go, I always have people I know. The children and grandchildren are constant sources of pleasure and Carl and I are good friends now. He visits me in Sag Harbor or I visit him in Florida almost every winter.

In retrospect, I think how lucky I am that my life should have converged on history the way it did. The adventure of being able to use my life to transform society in a way none of us then would have ever dreamed possible is gratifying beyond measure. Whatever experiences I've had in my life—my education that I never thought I used in a real career, my mother's frustration which I finally understood, my learning experiences as a journalist in the labor movement, getting fired for pregnancy, freelancing for women's magazines in the "happy housewife" era, doing early voter research, plumbing the economic as well as the psychological underbelly of American life, the lasting joys as well as the regrets of my marriage, my aging—all of this I've used finally. I've used it all. Who knows how I'll use it next?

Index

PICTURE CREDITS

*Courtesy of the Friedan Family 1, 2, 10, 16, 17,
  18, 19, 22, 29, 41, 42, 43*
Courtesy of the Goldstein Family 3, 5, 7, 9, 12
Courtesy of Shirley Shapiro Pugh 4
*Schlesinger Library, Radcliffe Institute,
  Harvard University 6, 8, 11, 13,14, 15, 24,
  31, 34, 38*

Corbis/Bettmann-UPI 25, 32, 33
AP/Wide World Photos 27, 35
*Leonard McCombe, Life Magazine © Time
  Inc. 28*
© *Steve Schapiro 20, 21, 23*
© *Peter Gould 30*
© *Henry Grossman 20, 26*